Nuclear Proliferation Problems

Nuclear Proliferation Problems

SIPRI

Stockholm International Peace Research Institute

The MIT Press
Cambridge, Massachusetts and
London, England

Almqvist & Wiksell
Stockholm

First published by Almqvist & Wiksell
26 Gamla Brogatan, S-111 20 Stockholm

in collaboration with

The MIT Press
28 Carleton Street
Cambridge, Mass. 02142

and

126 Buckingham Palace Road
London SM1W 9SD

ISBN 0 262 10015 0

Library of Congress Catalog
Card Number: 74-8307

Printed in Sweden by
Almqvist & Wiksell, Uppsala 1974

PREFACE

Article VIII.3 of the Treaty on the Non-Proliferation of Nuclear Weapons (NPT) states that: "Five years after the entry into force of this Treaty, a conference of Parties to the Treaty shall be held in Geneva, Switzerland in order to review the operation of this Treaty with a view to assuring that the purposes of the Preamble and the provisions of the Treaty are being realized". This Review Conference should take place in March 1975.

The economic and technical restraints on the production of nuclear weapons, once severe, have steadily decreased. And a number of states have, through peaceful nuclear programmes, now accumulated the technical expertise and knowledge, and the fissile material necessary to produce nuclear weapons. As time passes the number of such states will grow. Whether or not these states will take up their nuclear weapon option in the future will depend mainly on political considerations. For many states the main political barrier to proliferation is the NPT. And the future success of the NPT will depend to a large extent on the outcome of the 1975 Review Conference. This conference will, therefore, be a crucial event in the field of arms control and disarmament.

For this reason, SIPRI decided to assemble a group of leading experts from a variety of countries to discuss the problems likely to be raised at the Review Conference and to make proposals for consideration at the conference. The meeting took place in June 1973. The proceedings of this meeting and an analysis of some of the major military and security consequences of the worldwide spread of peaceful nuclear technology will be presented in a two-volume publication. The present volume contains the papers presented at the SIPRI meeting. The second volume will take up some additional specific problems of relevance to the NPT Review Conference.

This volume was edited by Dr Bhupendra Jasani, a member of the SIPRI research staff.

November 1973

Frank Barnaby
Director

5

Errata

Page 158. Under *Abstract,* line 10, delete: and plutonium in the same manner as uranium.

Page 162. Under *Physical security,* line 11, sentence should read:
1. Two stipulations frequently prescribed are an option for buying back plutonium produced with supplied fuel, if it is not needed by the consumer, and a provision that plutonium not being utilized in reactors be located in storage facilities designated by the supplier.

Page 165. Under *VIII. A maximum proposal,* line 16, to page 166, line 2, sentences should read: The prohibition of that relationship is not the most urgent matter but if Western Europe were to reach a point of political integration where it could inherit both the nuclear power status of France and Britain and the special relationship between Britain and the USA, it would constitute an opportunity for rapid proliferation. Moreover, that country would become the greatest single new nuclear power that could be envisaged.

CONTENTS

TABLES AND FIGURES

14

PART II. THE NPT SAFEGUARDS

3. NPT safeguards

TABLE

LIST OF PARTICIPANTS

Prof. Hannes Alfvén
Royal Institute of Technology
Department of Plasma Physics
S-100 44 Stockholm
Sweden

Dr Frank Barnaby
Director
SIPRI
Sveavägen 166
S-113 46 Stockholm
Sweden

Dr Peter Boskma
Polemological Institute
Rijksuniversiteit
Ubbo Emmiussingel 19
Groningen
The Netherlands

Prof. Francesco Calogero
Institute of Physics
University of Rome
Piazzale delle Scienze 5
00185 Roma
Italy

Prof. Hilding Eek
Stockholm University
Faculty of Law
Tegnérgatan 57
S-111 61 Stockholm
Sweden

Prof. Vassili Emelyanov
Academy of Sciences of the USSR
Leninsky Prospekt 14
Moscow B-71
USSR

Mr Simha Flapan
New Outlook
8, Karl Netter Street
Tel Aviv
Israel

Ambassador Alfonso Garcia-Robles
Permanent Representative of Mexico
to the UN
Permanent Mission of Mexico
to the UN
8 East 41st Street
New York, N.Y. 10017
USA

Mr Jozef Goldblat
SIPRI
Sveavägen 166
S-113 46 Stockholm
Sweden

Prof. Bertrand Goldschmidt
Commissariat à l'Energie
Atomique
29 rue de la Fédération
B.P. 510
Paris XV
France

Dr John Hopkins
J-Do, Los Alamos Scientific
Laboratory
P.O. Box 1663
Los Alamos, N.M. 87544
USA

Prof. Dr Wolf Häfele
Institute for Applied Systems
Analysis and Reactor Physics
D-75 Karlsruhe
Postfach 3640
FR Germany

Prof. Ryukichi Imai
Japan Atomic Power Co.
1-6-1 Ohtemachi
Chiyoda-Ku
Tokyo
Japan

Dr Bhupendra Jasani
SIPRI
Sveavägen 166
S-113 46 Stockholm
Sweden

Dr Alexander Kaliadin
Institute of World Economics
and International Relations
2, Yaraslavskaya St., 3K8
Moscow
USSR

Dr David Krieger
Center for the Study of
Democratic Institutions
Box 4068
Santa Barbara, Calif. 93103
USA

Dr Vitali Kuleshov
Academy of Sciences of the USSR
Leninsky Prospekt 14
Moscow B-71
USSR

Mr Arend Meerburg
Foreign Ministry
Plein 23
Den Haag
The Netherlands

Prof. Jorma Miettinen
Department of Radiochemistry
University of Helsinki
Unioninkatu 35
SF-00170 Helsinki 17
Finland

Prof. Gunnar Myrdal
Institute for International
Economic Studies
Stockholm University
Sveavägen 166, 19th floor
S-113 46 Stockholm
Sweden

Dr Jan Prawitz
Ministry of Defence
Fack
S-103 20 Stockholm 16
Sweden

Mr Reinhard Rainer
IAEA
Kärntnerring 11
A-1011 Vienna
Austria

Prof. Bert Röling
Polemological Institute
Rijksuniversiteit
Ubbo Emmiussingel 19
Groningen
The Netherlands

Mr Ben Sanders
IAEA
Kärntnerring 11
A-1011 Vienna
Austria

Prof. John Sanness
The Norwegian Institute of
International Affairs
Parkveien 19
Oslo 3
Norway

Prof. Bernard Spinrad
Oregon State University
Department of Nuclear Engineering
Corvallis, Oregon 97331
USA

Mr K. Subrahmanyam
Director, Institute for
Defence Studies and Analyses
Sapru House
Barakhamba Road
New Delhi 1
India

Prof. Mason Willrich
Consultant
Law Department
Pacific Gas and Electric Co.
77 Beale Street
San Francisco, Calif. 94106
USA

18

Part I
Nuclear technology

1. Introduction

In March 1975, a Review Conference of the Treaty on the Non-Proliferation of Nuclear Weapons (NPT) may be convened to examine the success of the NPT as a means of controlling the proliferation of nuclear weapons. This monograph will discuss some of the issues that affect the proliferation of nuclear weapons and are likely to be taken up at that review conference.

Part I will deal with nuclear technology, its growth and military consequences; Part II, safeguards; Part III, the peaceful uses of nuclear energy; and Part IV, the security of non-nuclear-weapon countries. It will be seen that concern over the shortage or expense of various fossil fuels has in recent years led to a greater interest in nuclear fuel as a source of energy. The implementation of safeguards is a method of preventing non-nuclear-weapon countries, parties to the NPT, from using that nuclear energy for nonpeaceful purposes, while methods of restraining nuclear-weapon countries include a halt in the vertical arms race and better security guarantees regarding the non-use of nuclear weapons against non-nuclear-weapon countries.

The first question to be dealt with is how the world's future energy demands can be satisfied. Considerable concern has recently been expressed over the availability of fuels to satisfy this growing demand. In some countries this has even created an air of crisis. It is important, therefore, to understand the nature of this crisis since it is estimated that total energy requirements for the world will multiply by a factor of about five by the year 2000.

There are several possible sources of energy: (1) fossil fuels: coal and lignite (solid fossil fuels), petroleum, tar sand and oil shale (liquid fossil fuels) and natural gas, (2) hydroelectric energy, (3) tidal power, (4) geothermal energy, (5) solar energy and (6) nuclear energy. Of these, the first and the last are likely to provide most of the world's energy for the foreseeable future. Some of the other sources have potential advantages of abundance, accessibility or cheapness but the technology is much less developed than that for fossil fuels and nuclear energy.

There is no doubt that, theoretically, there are sufficient world reserves of some fossil fuels to fulfil energy needs for at least the next few centuries. For example, it is estimated that by the year 2000, only about 2 per cent of the world's total coal and lignite reserves will have been consumed but the share of these fuels in total energy production is diminishing as it becomes increasingly difficult and expensive to recover them. However, this decline need not be permanent if improved technology can provide better and more economical methods of obtaining these materials. Ultimately recoverable reserves have been variously estimated to be between 45×10^{14} to 75×10^{14} kg of coal. Unfortunately, the recovery of most of these reserves will be very costly.

As for the liquid fossil fuels, petroleum is the most accessible and convenient. It is estimated that world petroleum reserves are almost 350×10^{12} kg coal equivalent; this includes proved reserves, probable reserves and possible reserves. Cumulative consumption of petroleum by the year 2000 is estimated to be 305×10^{12} kg coal equivalent, which would leave only about 13 per cent of the total reserves. [1] However, a substantial amount of oil can be extracted from tar sands and oil shale. Although the extraction of oil from tar sands and oil-impregnated rocks has been slow, recent rises in the price of crude oil and some recent advances in technology may result in increased extraction and utilization of this source. The amount of oil reserves obtainable from tar sands is not accurately known but it is estimated to be about 163×10^{12} kg coal equivalent. Recent advances in technology have made it possible to use oil shale directly as fuel in thermal power plants. It is estimated that, by the year 2000, about 178×10^6 kg/day coal equivalent of oil shale will be produced in the United States. [1–2]

The other form of fossil fuel which is being rapidly depleted is natural gas. It is estimated that world natural gas reserves once amounted to about 233×10^{12} kg coal equivalent, 8 per cent of which had already been consumed by 1970. By the year 2000, the reserves will be reduced to 74×10^{12} kg coal equivalent or only about 30 per cent of the initial reserves. Although these figures are incomplete they show the trend.

It is evident that there is no immediate energy crisis from the point of view of the availability of solid fossil fuel although there is, in fact, a serious crisis in regard to costs. In societies which consume large amounts of energy, small differences in cost can become enormously significant. Moreover, sources of cheap energy are important to accelerate the development of underdeveloped countries.

The question then is what other sources of energy can be developed after fossil fuels are exhausted, bearing in mind that if time is used efficiently in investigating these sources, a major crisis might still be averted. Of the possibilities mentioned above, considerable research and development has been devoted to nuclear energy due to its economic advantages and military attractions. Nuclear energy can be divided into two types, one in which the fission process is used to produce energy and the other in which the fusion process is used. Research and development has been concentrated mainly on fission because it is technologically simpler.

Since in many countries, nuclear energy is more economical than other established sources of energy, it will probably be used extensively in the immediate future. However, the feeling among nuclear engineers is that economics may not necessarily be the only important parameter in develop-

22

ing nuclear energy; safety and reliability are also factors. For example, there is a certain amount of scepticism with regard to the safety and reliability of light water reactors (LWRs) as systems for producing electricity on a large scale. Nevertheless, the nuclear industry is growing and this growth brings with it the danger of nuclear weapon proliferation, a danger which will increase when fast breeder reactors (FBRs) are developed.

About 2.5 per cent of the total world electrical generating capacity is at present produced by nuclear power and it is estimated that by the year 2020 this will increase to about 40 per cent. Some projections suggest that this could even reach 75 per cent. The vast nuclear energy industry will then be based on both thermal[1] and fast breeder reactors.[2] However, the growth of the use of breeder reactors is uncertain because of their environmental hazards and their lack of clear economic advantages. Also, thermal reactors are proving to be more durable than many had believed, but this does not meant that FRBs will not be built. Eventually, high temperature gas-cooled reactors (HTGRs) will also be built to produce hydrogen gas and other secondary fuels such as gasified coal, and it is thought that FBRs, while generating electricity, will have enough breeding gain to sustain the HTGRs.

In Western Europe, however, where two FBRs are in operation, one under construction and four others planned, a somewhat different philosophy prevails. It is felt that breeder reactors will be commercially significant by 1990 at the latest, and probably earlier in some countries. Moreover, Western European countries are beginning to collaborate on developing their nuclear potential. Electricité de France (EdF) in France, Rheinisch-Westfälisches Elektrizitätwerk (RWE) in the Federal Republic of Germany and Ente Nazionale per l'Energia Elattrica (ENEL) in Italy have recently grouped together to build the first commercial breeder reactor of about 1 000 megawatts of electricity (MW (e)). [3]

Another factor which affects the development of FBRs is the availability of low-cost uranium. It is argued that as a result of the greater use of uranium in thermal reactors, all of the presently known lost-cost uranium will be exhausted by the end of this century. Such arguments have been used to stimulate breeder reactor technology, for which the preferred fuel is weapon-grade plutonium-239. Although it is true that FBRs utilize uranium more efficiently, there is some doubt as to whether a shortage of low-cost uranium will actually occur in this century. At present there is a world surplus of uranium and, except in countries such as Britain and France, uranium prospecting has practically stopped. Britain has recently discovered enough uranium ore to satisfy its energy needs for about 50 years at the current electricity demand [4] and France has found a considerable quantity in

[1] A reactor in which the fission chain reaction is sustained mainly by thermal neutrons. Most reactors are thermal reactors.
[2] A reactor that operates with fast neutrons and which produces more fissionable material than it consumes.

Niger and is now searching for further deposits in that area in partnership with Japan. France is also continuing a collaborative uranium prospecting effort with Germany, Italy and the United States.

It is clear that a considerable amount of fissile material will be generated by nuclear reactors and all of it will become available at nuclear fuel reprocessing plants. For example, plutonium-239, which is suitable for use in nuclear weapons, is produced in similar quantities in both thermal and fast breeder reactors. One hundred and fifty kilogrammes of plutonium could be produced per year in a 1 000 MW(e) light water reactor while 230 kg of plutonium could be produced in a breeder reactor of the same power output. An examination of the nuclear fuel cycle indicates that weapon-grade plutonium-239 first appears at the output of a chemical reprocessing plant. The other fissionable material suitable for nuclear weapons is enriched uranium-235 which first appears at the output of a uranium enrichment plant. There are two main types of enrichment plants: the gaseous diffusion plant which is the most common and the gas ultracentrifuge which is now the focus of considerable interest.

It is often argued that the danger of the proliferation of nuclear weapons based on enriched uranium will be greatly enhanced if the present trend towards developing several types of centrifuge continues in various countries. As to plutonium-based weapons, the danger of their proliferation will increase with the greater use of fast breeder reactors. It was to reduce these dangers that the Treaty on the Non-Proliferation of Nuclear Weapons was negotiated.

References

1. "World Energy Requirements and Resources in the Year 2000", United Nations Report in *Peaceful Uses of Atomic Energy* [Proceedings of the Fourth International Conference, Geneva, 6–16 September 1971] Vol. 1 (New York, Vienna, UN and IAEA, 1971) pp. 303–23.
2. King, H. M., "The Energy Resources of the Earth", *Scientific American*, Vol. 225, No. 3, September 1971. pp. 60–70.
3. Rippon, S., "Euro-Utility Scheming", *Nuclear Engineering International*, Vol. 17, No. 189, February 1972, p. 67.
4. "Uranium Found in Britain", *Nature*, Vol. 243, No. 5408, 22 June 1973.

2. A projection of nuclear power and its associated industry

B. I. SPINRAD

Abstract

A new projection is presented of the extent to which nuclear power will be installed in the various regions of the world. The projection takes into account recent energy problems of advanced countries and forecasts appreciably less nuclear power in the immediate future than would be indicated from national nuclear projections. However, even this very conservative projection yields the result that nuclear power will become a mighty industry.

Similarly, it is demonstrated that converter reactors of the types now developed have the capability of remaining economically viable for an appreciable period. The near-term significance of the breeder reactor is thereby muted. Since the underdeveloped countries will be installing major nuclear grids at a later date, they will be the ones most affected by the breeder and by competing technologies further from realization.

I. *Introduction*

In 1970, a projection of world nuclear power growth up to the year 2010 was prepared. [1] At that time a world total electrical generating capacity of about 12 500 GW[1] was expected. (The actual figure was somewhat under 11 000 GW, but the People's Republic of China was not included in that total.) Of that, it was expected that three-fourths would originate from nuclear fission.

The 1970 projection was intended to be conservative in regard to growth of electrical generating capability and realistic as concerned the penetration of nuclear power into the electrical generating industry. By and large, the projections are not much changed in three years, primarily because the rates of increase in electrical demand in advanced countries seem to be decreasing and because costs of nuclear and fossil-fuel options have, for different reasons, stayed in a relatively constant ratio.

In this chapter a new projection is presented. The results are somewhat changed because of new assumptions concerning population growth and

---

[1] A GW (Gigawatt) is 10^9 watts, and is approximately the output of a single large nuclear power plant.

25

energy costs. In recent years, population increase has slowed in many parts of the world, whereas, energy costs in constant value money have stopped going down and appear to be close to a minimum now.

Another new factor which is incorporated here is the use of more conservative estimators for the asymptotic penetration of nuclear power into the world electrical energy market, and for the introduction of new types of power plant, particularly the liquid metal fast breeder reactor (LMFBR), as standard equipment. The 1970 projection was appreciably influenced by the official programme statements of the major countries developing LMFBRs; the current one is a more personal estimate of the situation in which a degree of conservatism has been added to the commercial introduction date of LMFBRs.

II. *Energy*

The scenario for energy demand may be considered optimistic with regard to the future needs of advanced populations. That is to say, a variety of forces; social, demographic, economic and technological, are converging to slow down the rate of increase in per capita demand in advanced countries. It certainly seems that in the USA, which is the world's largest energy user, the signs of a 10 kW/capita electrical demand asymptote are visible; in countries with a lesser history of energy profligacy, such as Western Europe, Japan, or the Soviet Union, there are clear indications that the US experience will be taken as an example or a warning.

However, the asymptotic world will be very highly energy-intensive (as the 10 kW/capita figure indicates). The avoidance of resource shortages requires making do with materials won from limitless resources—stone from the earth and plastic from the materials of the air—and recycling more limited materials such as metals. All of these local decreases in entropy require thermodynamic work. The avoidance of pollution similarly requires increased segregation and purification of the constituents of our effluents—which also takes work. Thus, we can expect that the major resource which will distinguish richer from poorer (even though no one need be very poor) will be the availability of manufactured work.

To supply the needed energy, a variety of technologies are assumed to be available:

1. Natural energy sources of the types now available: hydroelectric (from rivers, tides and impoundments); atmospheric, primarily wind-power; and geothermal. On the scale of need, these are significant, but not large resources. Perhaps 10 per cent of ultimate need can be supplied from them. There is little prospect of development improving their availability, but what can be made available will always be available at low cost.

2. Power from fossil fuels: coal, oil and gas. On a long-range basis, their

resource availabilities differ by almost an order of magnitude, there being abundant coal on the earth, marginal oil, and scarce gas. We may expect that over the next 50 years, our supply of fluid fuels for transport use will switch to fluids manufactured from coal at some small cost penalty.

3. Power from converter reactors of the types now commercially available. The uranium to fuel such reactors is in no greater supply at near current costs than petroleum is. However, the industry is not yet a large volume one, and it has unrealized economies available to it which will balance the predictable increases in raw material costs for about 40 years.

4. Power from breeder reactors. The penetration of breeder reactors into the nuclear power market will quite probably be slower than the national programmes of advanced countries predict. The major question mark is that we cannot predict how rapidly the price of power from breeder reactors will come down from its present status of about twice the cost of converter reactor power.

5. Solar energy and fusion. The magnitude of the research, development and work-scale required to bring them into commercial competition with present sources of energy is enormous. This makes it highly unlikely that man-made fusion or its natural counterpart, solar energy, will contribute significantly to energy supplies, beyond photosynthesis, for the next 50 years.

The qualitative prognosis:

1. The most immediate current trend is an increase in the price of oil as demand for petroleum products increases.

2. The only immediate response available to the consumer is to substitute coal-fuel plants and converter reactors for oil within the available price margin. As demands for oil transport increase, the price will continue to rise until coal and nuclear power take over all of the central-station market, and the central-station share of the energy picture will continue to rise.

3. Fission power from converter reactors is cleaner and cheaper than coal now. In a few years, coal fluidization will recover some share of the power plant business for that resource; at some later time, gasified and/or liquiefied coal will furnish the marginal market for easily transported fuels.

4. The breeder reactor will become a conventional power source only when it furnishes power at prices comparable with current systems. The durability of the economy of converter reactors and the development of economy in coal fluidization make it likely that crossover costs will be less than 50 per cent above current generating costs—a tougher market to crack than generally expected by breeder advocates.

III. *Nuclear power estimates*

As in reference [1], detailed projections of nuclear power are obtained from a projection of:

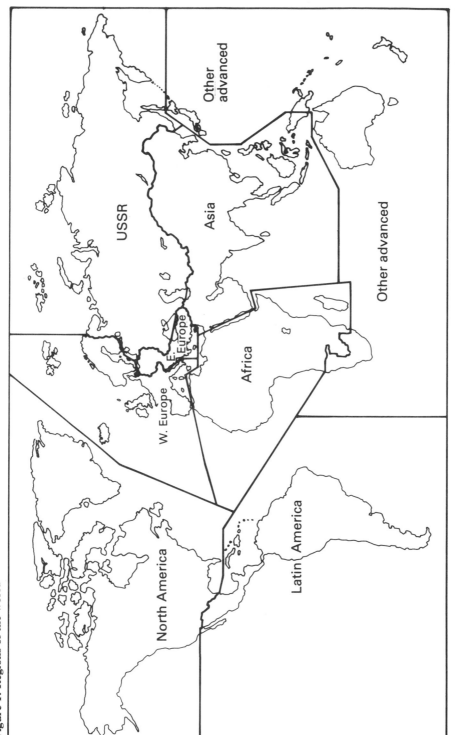

Figure 1. Regions of the world

28

Figure 2. Annual rate of growth of electrical power demand in the regions of the world

Per cent

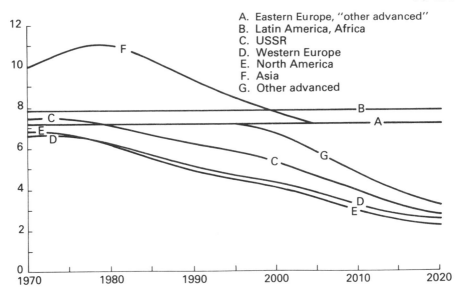

A. Eastern Europe, "other advanced"
B. Latin America, Africa
C. USSR
D. Western Europe
E. North America
F. Asia
G. Other advanced

1. An estimate of the growth curve in electrical power demand for each region of the world.

2. An estimate of the rate of penetration of nuclear power into the market for new generating capacity.

These two projections and their consequences, are presented here. Most of the data are given only in graphic form, since the precision implied by tabulated data would be misleading.

Electrical power demand

The curves presented here are based on a division of the map of the world adopted in reference [1] and presented here as figure 1.

Figure 2 presents a projection of the rates of growth in electrical power demand for these regions. This figure incorporates the following changes from the estimate of three years ago:

1. The projections for North American growth rate are slightly re-duced in the 1970–80 decade, based on three years' experience in the 1970s; the projections past 1980, which were considered very conservative three years ago, are now consensus opinion, and are retained. Decreases in population growth and increases in energy costs due to environmentalist pressure are now apparent, and both are depressing the rate of growth of energy demand previously expected.

2. The projections for Asia, which now can incorporate figures for the People's Republic of China, are revised upward. It now appears that

Figure 3. Projected annual electrical generating capacity

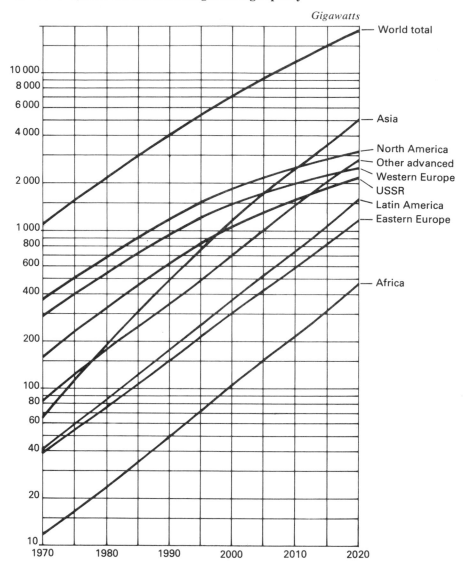

enough internal capital can be generated in Asia to finance a high rate of electrification at least until the 1940 per-capita consumption of the United States is achieved.

3. The projections for the Soviet Union, which had been prepared on the basis of a 10-year lag behind the USA in rate-of-growth-falloff pattern, have been adjusted to retain this pattern compared with the new US projection.

4. The projection for Latin America has been adjusted upward to match that previously assumed for Africa. The population growth rate in

Table 1. Nuclear penetration of the electrical generating market

Period	Nuclear per cent of total capacity added
1970–75	20
1975–80	40
1980–85	60
1985–90	70
After 1990	80

Latin America is the highest in the world, and allowance must be made for this fact.

5. Projections for Western Europe, Eastern Europe, and Africa remain the same.

6. Projections for a group of countries (Japan, Australia, New Zealand, Oceania and South Africa) which have been lumped together as Other Advanced, have been altered so as to illustrate their approach to the typical advanced country asymptote as their population stabilizes.

Figure 3 integrates these figures to provide a running curve of the world generating capacity, by regions.

Nuclear penetration of the market

Whereas in reference [1] separate curves for nuclear penetration of the market for generating capacity were presented for the various regions of the world, a current appraisal permits us to simplify the picture considerably. Only two regions of the world, Africa and the USSR, are lagging behind at the moment. Market penetration for the remainder of the world (nuclear commissioning/total commissioning) is over 20 per cent; it will reach 50 per cent by 1980, and level off at an upper asymtote by 1995. The African picture is arbitrary, but will remain a small part of the world electrical scene for the next half century. Statements of Soviet officials repeatedly have indicated that over the long rum, nuclear energy will play essentially the same role in the USSR as in Western Europe or North America.

One further change in the world scene is due to the probable success of large-scale fluidization of coal, its role in stabilizing the price of petroleum, and the consequent retention of a reasonable share of the power plant market by fossil-fuelled plants. For this reason, the asymptotic penetration of nuclear power has been lowered to 80 per cent, from the 90 per cent value of reference [1]. (The penetration of the market referred to here is, of course, the market for new capacity installed; the penetration of nuclear power into installed capacity will lag behind by 10–15 years.) Standard market penetration for five-year intervals is thereby presented above in table 1.

31

Figure 4. Projected annual nuclear electrical generating capacity

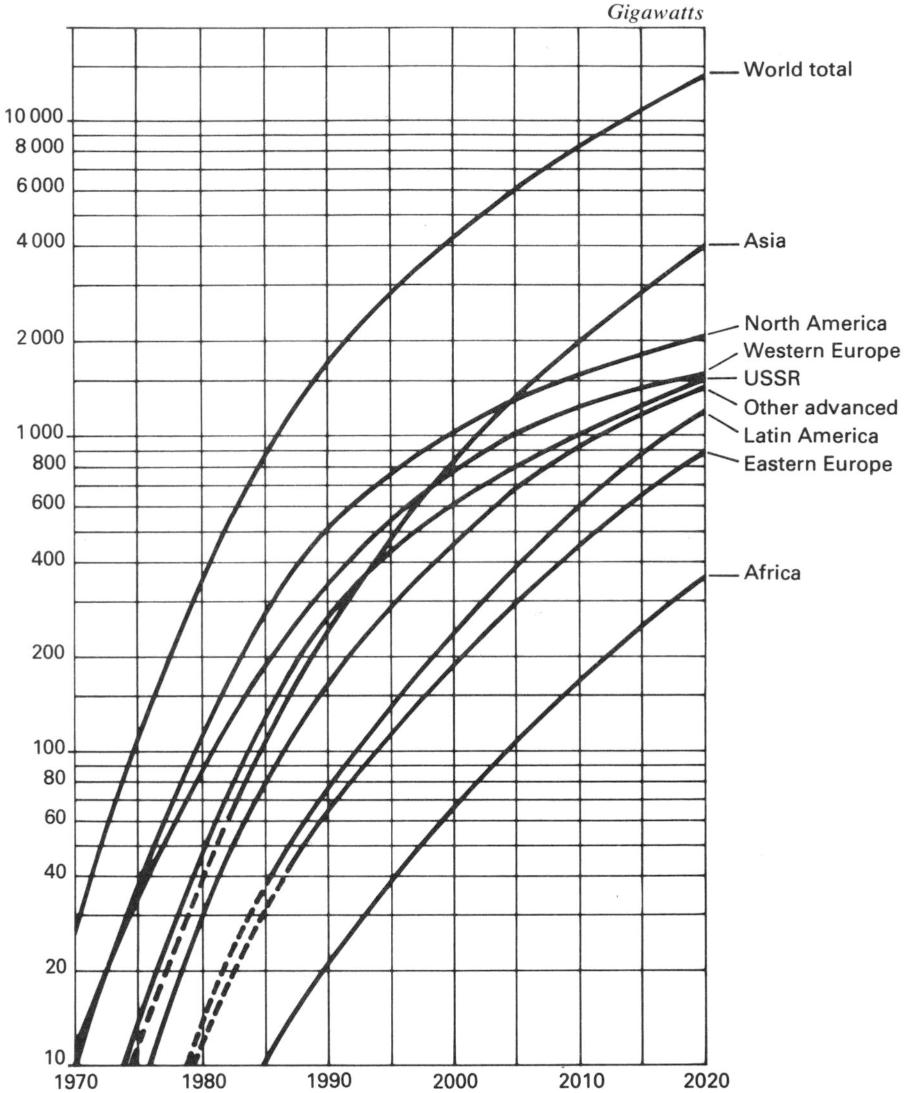

Gigawatts

Nuclear capacity

The data of table 1 may now be combined with that of figure 3 and with the known 1970 base of nuclear generating capacity to yield figure 4, which represents the updated version of the nuclear power projection.

Figure 4 may be compared with the recent forecast of the US AEC, [2] which is divided into "US", "Communist", and "Foreign Non-Communist" forecasts. To compare with the one presented here, I have taken US in my projection to be 90 per cent of North America; Communist to be USSR, Eastern Europe and 40 per cent of Asia; and Foreign Non-Communist to be the remainder. The comparison is given below in table 2.

32

Table 2. Comparison of BIS forecast with US AEC forecast

| | Projected nuclear capacity in gigawatts | | | | | |
| | USA | | "Communist countries" | | Other countries | |
Year	BIS	AEC	BIS	AEC	BIS	AEC
1975	38	54	20	8	57	39
1980	104	132	84	20	182	141
1985	235	280	272	56	363	303
1990	455	508	420	146	815	578
1995	695	811	720	318	1 335	968
2000	945	1 200	1 280	600	1 975	1 450

The AEC's figures for 1975 and 1980 are undoubtedly more authoritative than mine, since most of the nuclear power to be commissioned by 1980 is now on order. On the other hand, the US AEC forecast is, for the USA, biased upward in terms of nuclear capacity deliverable in this decade and not yet ordered. For the USA past 1980, this bias continues as a result òf my selection of a diminishing power demand growth rate to be supplied by the nuclear market; standard US electrical capacity projectio᠎ are consistently higher than my North America curve in figure 2 woul indicate, and the BIS (B. I. Spinrad) projection follows the same basic trends as the AEC low curve (which is not listed in table 2).

For the rest of the world, the AEC projection lags about six years behind the BIS projection of nuclear capacity. The figures for both "Communist" and "Other countries" assume that much of Asia is now beginning to enter an industrial era that will be characterized by a high and durable rate of growth in energy demand, particularly electrical energy demand.

The projection for the years 2000 to 2020 must fall virtually into the realm of imaginative fiction. However, certain qualitative features of the projection are worth noting.

1. I have probably overdone the rate of growth of the countries labelled Other Advanced; the asymptotic curves for this group may be evidenced even sooner than I have projected.

2. The year 2000 represents a "knee" in the growth curve for most advanced regions, and also the point at which the total growth of electrical and nuclear capability (GW installed/year) in the underdeveloped world (Africa, Asia, Latin America, Eastern Europe) overtakes and surpasses the growth in the advanced world. This point is significant, and its ramifications will be discussed later in this chapter.

Burners and breeders

The breeder era is probalbly not as close as enthusiasts have hoped or as opponents have feared. The primary reason is the probability that burner reactors will prove to be economically durable even as their primary fuel, natural uranium, is becoming more expensive. This is supported by the following arguments.

1. Nuclear fuel fabrication and reprocessing are currently very small-scale industries. As early as 1985, the volume of business in these industries will multiply tenfold. Even a very conservative, low-exponent scaling law will predict very great economies in these fuel cycle costs with time, not even considering technological process improvements. A fourth-root scaling law (that is, a rule by which unit costs decrease as the fourth root of industrial volume) would lead to a factor of more than three reductions in unit costs when the nuclear industry is a hundredfold larger than it is now. This condition will be reached around the year 2000. Such a factor of three is consistent with costs in other industries fabricating ceramic materials and recovering chemicals from contaminated mixtures.

2. As nuclear fuel becomes more expensive as a material and less expensive to work with, re-optimization of the fuel cycle occurs. Directions of re-optimization under these conditions are: lower enrichment tails assay; lower reactor burnup; lower reactor feed enrichment; and higher conversion lattices.

The last of the items listed above is, at least in part, automatically assured by the previous two items, since lower feed enrichment and a lower burnup design imply the loss of fewer neutrons to fission products and control materials.

As a further consequence of this trend, we can expect that through the use of plutonium recycle, burner reactors will, on the average over the next 30 years, consume in the fission process around 2 per cent of the natural uranium mined—roughly twice as much as present methods of operation, even with recycle in present lattices.

3. The major item differentiating uranium sources as more or less expensive is the magnitude of chemical work which must be expended in the milling process. As low-concentration uranium ores become attractive, the amount of research effort devoted to improving the milling process can be expected to increase, and payoffs in the form of 10–20 per cent reductions in milling costs can be confidently assumed. Since milling cost is almost the whole cost, these reductions will accrue to the nuclear fuel cycle directly. A summary of these arguments is presented in table 3.

The numbers in table 3 indicate a 0.22 mil/kWhr (17 per cent) increase in the cost of the nuclear fuel cycle (as it contributes to electrical power cost) resulting from adjustments and economies in the industry to a period in which virgin U_3O_8 cost is assumed to increase by a factor of 4.5.

The basic argument for the breeder is its potential for elimination of fuel cycle costs. Present demonstration units are very far from this goal; however, assuming this may be achieved, the total margin is 1.5 mills/kWhr. It is estimated that the typical capital costs for a light water reactor contribute 4–6 mills/kWhr to the price of electricity, and that an LMFBR would, after lengthy development, have capital costs about 25 per cent higher. Thus, the economic competitiveness of LMFBRs requires simultaneous achievement of two development targets: essential elimination of fuel cycle costs and reduction of plant capital costs to less than 125 per cent of LWR plant costs. These simultaneous goals must also be realized in competition with CANDU-type reactors, for which the capital cost factor is going to be easier to overcome, but the fuel cycle margin would be even less. There are few predictions, even by breeder enthusiasts, of achieving this goal before the year 2000.

The result of this analysis is that the rest of this century will remain the era of the burner, although we may expect that advanced converters of high conversion ratio will play a significant role. From 2000 on, the breeder will probably be able to satisfy our power requirements, at reasonable cost, forever, unless or until superseded by a more economical, abundant source such as solar energy or fusion.

A corollary of this analysis is that the more technologically advanced societies of the world will account for most of the nuclear power installed up to the year 2000, while the underdeveloped countries will have most of what is installed thereafter; thus, the breeder should be of far more interest to the latter group.

It appears that we have here one more case of a new technology whose exploitation by advanced societies will deplete a world resource, making it necessary for later-developing parts of the world to utilize still more advanced technology.

IV. Related industries

In this section we examine the industrial sectors related to nuclear power. These are: uranium mining and milling; enrichment; fuel fabrication, including fuel-material preparation; chemical reprocessing and waste disposal.

Uranium mining and milling

The following assumptions are made in estimating the volume of the uranium mining industry at the end of the century.

(a) The nuclear electrical capacity is represented by a simple exponential curve:

Capacity (GW)$=4\,000\,e^{0.0921\,(t-2000)}$

where t is time in years. This fits the World Total curve of figure 6 reasonably well between 1985 and 2000, a period when most of the world's uranium consumption is expected.

Table 3. Burner reactor fuel cycle costs in mills per kilowatt hour

	1970	2000	Comment
Fuel fabrication changes	.20	.06	Scaling law
Chemical steps (conversion, reprocessing)	.17	.05	»
Enrichment	.41	.41	Increased unit costs, but less enrichment needed
Pu credit	(.22)	[.35]	More Pu made
Net enrichment charges	.19	.16	Full Pu recycle
U_3O_8 purchase	.36 ($8/lb)	.81	Half rate at $36/lb in 2000
Working capital	.37	.43	*40 per cent*
Total (excluding Enrichment and Pu credit)	**1.29**	**1.51**	

(*b*) The load factor of nuclear plants is taken as 0.75.

(*c*) Two per cent of the natural uranium mined undergoes fission.

(*d*) Electrical conversion efficiency is one-third.

Under these conditions, the cumulative uranium used (of which 98 per cent remains as depleted stock) is

$$U \text{ (kg)} = 1.79 \times 10^9 \, e^{0.0921 \, (t-2000)}$$

The cumulative uranium requirements for future years are listed in table 4.

These numbers are about a factor of two lower than US AEC estimates [2], primarily because the latter assumed only 1 per cent utilization efficiency for uranium mined. As explained already, my estimates assume significant improvements in conversion ratio of reactors installed during the later years of this century.

The plants in existence by the year 2000 should be able to be fuelled for the nominal plant lifetime which in the electrical industry is over 30 years. In 2000, the annual demand would be 165×10^6 kg; thus, an additional $4\,900 \times 10^6$ kg of natural uranium will be required by these plants during the 21st century.

A tentative availability-price curve for natural uranium has been published by Pigford. [3] According to this curve, the $7\,000 \times 10^6$ kg needed

Table 4. Cumulative virgin uranium requirements (world)

Year	Amounts of uranium (10^9 kg)
1985	450 (overestimate)
1990	710
1995	1 120
2000	1 780

Table 5. Annual requirements of separate work (millions of units)

	1980	1985	1990	2000
USA	15.3	22	32	39
"Communist"	12.0	20	32	53
Other	13.8	25	44	81

by the next generation of burner reactors is judged to be available at about $40/lb, a price which compares well with the "development assumed" £35/lb figure used to estimate the durability of burners.

Enrichment

The AEC forecast [2] is the primary reference for this estimate. In this area, requirements of the "communist" countries are not available, and it is simply estimated that the requirements will be met from enrichment plants located in these countries. Estimates for them may be arrived at by scaling power demands, which has been done in table 5.

The numbers listed above are adjusted from those of the AEC reference in two ways:

(a) For the years 1990 and 2000, they have been multiplied by the ratio of the BIS power estimate to that of the AEC (table 2). A further factor of two-thirds has been taken to account for the generally higher efficiency of uranium use expected.

(b) For 1985, the geometric mean of the AEC 1980 value and the adjusted 1990 value is used (see table 5).

At the moment, the USA is committed to building new plants to satisfy domestic requirements (including, however, some requirements for fueling plants exported from the USA) as estimated. However, it is likely that current estimates of the US domestic need are high. We may, therefore, expect the USA to overbuild domestic diffusion plant capacity up to about 1985, by which time prudence will have dictated construction of about 36 million units of capacity (the US high estimate at this time). By this time, Western Europe will probably also have about 10 million units, so that these centers will, together, be able to meet world demand.

Between 1985 and 2000, the USA will be able to satisfy local needs for enrichment with nominal additions to their own plant. Western Europe may be expected to add enough capacity to meet its own needs as the ability to purchase US capacity declines. However, very substantial enrichment capabilities will need to be added to meet the expected needs of non-communist Asia, particularly Japan and India; and starting in 1985, we may expect these countries to install considerable capacity of their own (or, as an alternative, to buy into a combined ore-enrichment industry located in an ore-producing country such as Australia or Canada).

In summary, the scenario of world enrichment capacities is that the four current enrichment centres—USA, USSR, China and Western Europe—will take care of their own needs with some schedule adjustments if over-building in one country or another occurs. In addition, a new enrichment capacity is needed for Japan and India, either in the form of separate regional plants or through commercial cooperation with a third symbiotic country.

The appearances are that the profileration of enrichment capacity will have to be considered within the context of the NPT by about 1985.

Fuel fabrication

The same curve as was used to estimate uranium requirements may also be used to explore the fuel fabrication industry. With a plant efficiency of one-third and a load factor of 0.75, and an assumed average uranium burn-up of 20 000 MWD/1 000 kg of fuel loaded, the annual loading rate becomes:

Annual load of U (kg) $= 165 \times 10^6 \, e^{0.0921 \, (t-2000)}$

Thus, in 2000, the annual fabrication tonnage will be 165×10^6 kg, and working backward we get 104×10^6 kg in 1995, 66×10^6 kg in 1990 and 41×10^6 kg as an overestimate for 1985.

The comparable 1970 figure is more nearly 2×10^6 kg, with most of this effort expended on cores for reactors to be commissioned in years to follow.

The typical light water fuel is UO_2 (uranium density 10 g/cc) in rods of about 3 mm radius. The rods are of the order of 3 m in height. One thousand kilogrammes is about 120 such rods, or about 350 m of rod. The estimate for the year 2000 is that about 55 000 km of rod will be fabricated —more than enough to encircle the earth! A complete fuel element is about 80 rods, so the number of fuel elements to be made is over 200 000.

The volume of business by 1990 seems adequate to justify an automated mass production industry, and to justify the significant economies of scale which have already been described.

Fabrication tonnage will, of course, continue to increase as new fast breeders enter the market, but the rate of fabrication per unit plant capacity (electric) will only be about 1 : 4 in terms of tonnage. (Thermal and fast reactors require about the same length of rod but fast reactor fuels require roughly half the diameter.)

Chemical reprocessing

The amounts of material to be chemically reprocessed are the same as those fabricated about four years earlier. Thus, by adding another year to the cycle, reprocessing amounts will be about 170×10^6 kg in 2005, 110×10^6 kg in 2000, 70×10^6 kg in 1995 and 45×10^6 kg in 1990. Reprocessing rates from power reactors in 1970 were well under 1×10^6 kg. Again, the mass market effect needs no further illustration.

Chemical reprocessing differs from fabrication, however, in the type of problems which are involved in scaleup:

1. The presence of enriched uranium, and of plutonium, imposes criticality-safety limits on the unit size of equipment. A chemical plant built to handle, for example 3×10^6 kg/year, will require a large set of parallel process lines rather than a few large lines. Thus, only economies of scale arising from commonality of systems are available. For large throughputs, the advantages of dry head-end processes such as pyrochemistry and fluoride volatility may be very attractive, as criticality-safety is easily assured for low enrichment fuels in the absence of water.

2. As plant scale increases, so does the throughput of plutonium. A plant handling 3×10^6 kg/year with 1 per cent plutonium concentration is throughputting 30×10^3 kg of Pu/year. A 1 per cent loss of Pu, a number which is now conventional, is 300 kg per year, a quantity which is intolerable for nuclear safeguards and which is worth \$3 million. Even a 100 parts per million (ppm) loss of Pu is significant to safeguards, and the 10 kg which would presumably be discarded with fission products is probably the biggest obstacle to acceptable disposal of them.

I therefore see no way out of a development requirement that future reprocessing plants limit plutonium losses to some extraordinarily low level —perhaps one-thousandth of 1 per cent. The plutonium loss problem is aggravated in a fast reactor which passes at least twice as much plutonium through the reprocessing plant per unit electrical capacity.

Waste disposal

Each thermal megawatt day of fission power produces about one gramme of fission products. These are isolated at the reprocessing plant where the question of what to do with them arises.

Table 6. Long-lived solid fission products

Isotope	Half-life (years)	Yield (U-235 fission) (per cent)	Ci produced per GW-Yr reactor thermal energy
Se^{79}	6×10^4	0.056	6.5
Rb^{87}	6×10^{10}	2.5	2.9×10^{-4}
Zr^{93}	1.1×10^6	6.45	41.0
Tc^{99}	2.1×10^5	6.1	200.0
Pd^{107}	7×10^6	0.19	.19
I^{129}	1.7×10^7	0.9	.37
Cs^{135}	2.6×10^6	6.4	17.0

There are some obvious expedients available for part of this problem. For a large reprocessing plant, the power available from fission product radioactivity is significant and may be recoverable for use in the plant itself. Averaged from one to five years after reactor shutdown, the shutdown heat from fission products is about one-millionth of the reactor power. A 10 million kg/year plant thus has available about a megawatt of process heat to be piped from tank storage of nuclear waste. After five years of storage, the heat is no longer useful, and the fission waste is to be chemically immobilized and put away. The combination of chemical immobilization and deep disposal (for example, in a cavity created by a Plowshare explosion in a dry stratum 5 000 m below ground level) seems on the face of things sufficient to assure against re-entry into the environment before the fission products have decayed away. (The assumption is that such buried materials would have a time scale of millenia as a minimum for re-entry to the environment.)

As nearly as I can tell, there are only a few really serious concerns in applying this method. These concerns are Kr^{85}, Pu and long-lived solid fission products. These last are listed in table 6. They have high specific activities by virtue of their long lives, but require detailed attention. The activities of the items in table 6 do not, however, appear to warrant concern.

Plutonium isotopes have just the wrong half-lives for either permanent disposal or feeble activity. As already mentioned, I believe that the quantitative recovery of plutonium, to a degree which would be otherwise economically ridiculous, is a very important research and development problem.

As to Kr^{85}, there is excellent ground for hope that the current processes for its entrapment, such as solution in Co_2 liquid, adsorption and chelating, can achieve a Kr retention of about 99 per cent, an acceptable degree of contamination since krypton from current nuclear power plants is not a significant radiological hazard, and this krypton is in fact about 1 per cent of what will be produced around the year 2000.

References

1. Spinrad, B. I., "The Role of Nuclear Power in Meeting World Energy Needs", *Environmental Aspects of Nuclear Power Stations* (Vienna, IAEA, 1971) pp. 57–82.
2. *Nuclear Power, 1973–2000*, Document WASH-1139 (Washington, US Government Printing Office, 1972).
3. Pigford, T., *Fission Reactors*, Report M 72-50 (The MITRE Corporation, 1972).

3. Fast breeder reactors

B. M. JASANI

Abstract

Of the several methods of energy production available, nuclear fission has received the most attention and of the several types of nuclear reactor developed, fast breeder reactors, particularly the liquid-metal-cooled fast breeder reactor (LMFBR), are now attracting the maximum resources.

Different types of breeder reactor are described briefly and the LMFBRs are considered in detail. The predicted economic advantage of these reactors needs re-examination. The recycling of plutonium in light water reactors (LWRs) in various countries is also examined. If plutonium is recycled the energy cost for LWRs is about the same as that for LMFBRs. It is shown that several countries have ambitious breeder reactor programmes despite many technical and economical difficulties and uncertainties. The possible availability of large quantities of weapon-grade plutonium adds to these difficulties. It is, therefore, concluded that serious thought should be given to what the development of breeder reactors entails.

I. *Introduction*

Of all the available methods for energy production, the one based on nuclear fission has received the greatest attention. In the United States, for example, there are 29 power reactors in operation with a generating capacity of 14 683 000 kilowatts and 131 more plants are either being built or planned. [1] Most of these reactors are of the light water type. These, however, have low thermal efficiency (about 32 per cent) compared to a fossil-fuelled plant (over 40 per cent). A further disadvantage of a light water reactor (LWR) is that it utilizes effectively only the scarce radionuclide uranium-235 present in natural uranium. It is estimated that this incomplete use of natural uranium would exhaust all of our presently known resources of low-cost uranium in less than 30 years and as the demand for uranium increases, the price of uranium may also increase from about $8/lb in 1970 to over $15/lb by the year 2000. [2] Therefore, unless substantial quantities of low-cost uranium are found or a reactor which uses uranium more efficiently is developed, nuclear power will not be able to compete with fossil fuels.

Considerable resources have, therefore, been devoted to the development of the second generation of reactor—the breeder reactors. In table 1, for example, funds allocated for various types of energy research and development in the United States are shown. It can be seen that about 42 per cent of the funds for energy research and development in 1972 were utilized for the development of the fast breeder reactors. The breeder reactors use about 70 per cent of the energy in the uranium, but the types of reactor which are now under extensive investigation make available plutonium which could be used in nuclear weapons, thus encouraging proliferation of such weapons. It is, therefore, necessary to examine the development of this technology in detail.

II. *Breeder reactors*

There are basically two types of breeder reactor: thermal reactors and fast reactors. These can be further subdivided by the type of coolant used to transfer the heat produced by the fission reaction in the core of the reactor to a power-generating system. Water or molten salts are generally used for thermal breeder reactors and steam, inert gas or liquid metal are employed for fast breeder reactors.

An important advantage of a molten-salt breeder reactor (MSBR) is the absence of fuel fabrication problems since the fuel is mixed with a molten salt which acts as a coolant. Also the design of an MSBR is such that the fission products are removed by an on-line processing plant thus avoiding the problems of transporting highly radioactive fuel to a reprocessing plant. However, these advantages are somewhat nullified by the presence of large quantitites of highly radioactive fission products circulating through the entire primary system. The development of such reactors has proceeded slowly [3–4]; therefore, the following discussions will be confined to the fast breeder reactors.

Fast reactors can be fuelled with highly enriched uranium or a mixture of plutonium-239 and uranium-238 but the most efficient fuel is plutonium-239. Fission of a plutonium atom is produced by a fast neutron generating about 2.5 new neutrons for every neutron consumed. One of these neutrons is used to maintain the fission chain reaction and the rest of the 1.5 neutrons are absorbed by uranium-238 to produce 1.5 atoms of new plutonium. One of these atoms is used as the new plutonium fuel atom leaving a net gain of about half an atom of plutonium for every 1.5 atoms of uranium-238 used up. Much of the breeding takes place in the so-called blanket which surrounds the core of a breeder reactor. The blanket consists of uranium-238 which can be depleted uranium-238 remaining after the enrichment process.

Of the three types of fast breeder reactor—the steam-cooled, the gas-cooled and the liquid-metal-cooled—serious work on the first kind has been largely discontinued and, until recently, the second type has not received much attention; however, it is useful to consider it briefly here since a considerable amount of interest is now being shown in it. The third type is discussed below in greater detail.

Gas-cooled fast breeder reactors

In a gas-cooled fast breeder reactor (GCFBR) an inert gas, such as helium is used to transfer the heat from the reactor core to the steam generator. Helium has several advantages: it is chemically inert; it does not become radioactive (therefore, no intermediate heat exchange is required) and it is transparent so that maintenance of such reactors is relatively easy. In determining whether a breeder reactor is economical, one of the factors to be considered is the neutron efficiency which is measured by the reactor's doubling time—the period required for the reactor to produce about twice as much fissionable material as was originally present. Since helium is a poor absorber of neutrons, doubling time of less than 10 years is expected for GCFBRs.

A disadvantage of a gas-cooled system is that the heat capacity of a gas is very low so that it has to be used at high pressures (between 70 and 100 atmospheres). This means that the reactor must be enclosed in a pressure vessel. However, the problems associated with the use of gas at high pressures are reduced by the development of prestressed concrete vessels and, since gas-cooled thermal reactors are already in operation, substantial experience with gas-coolant technology is already available.

Although the GCFBRs have many advantages over other types of reactor, the liquid-metal fast breeder reactors (LMFBRs) have been the prime subject of development efforts. From table 1 it can be seen that in 1972 in the United States, slightly under 60 per cent of the total amount of money spent on nuclear energy went for the development of the LMFBRs. In the United Kingdom a similar proportion of the total R&D on nuclear energy is being spent on the development of LMFBRs. [5]

Liquid-metal fast breeder reactors

A number of LMFBRs using sodium as a coolant have already been built. In such a reactor, fast neutrons (0.1 to 1.0 Mev) are used to maintain the chain reaction and, therefore, no moderator is used so that the core of the reactor is smaller than that used for a thermal reactor with the same power output. The absence of a moderator has the advantage that fewer neutrons are absorbed unproductively; thus, the rate at which new fuel is created is greater. The more efficient a reactor's use of neutrons, the lower the potential cost of the power produced. The lack of a moderating material means that there is a higher power density[1] in the core of a fast reactor that requires

[1] The rate of production of heat per unit volume for an LMFBR is about twice that for a light water reactor.

Table 1. Funds allocated for various types of energy research and development in the United States

US $ mn

Programme	1972	1973
Fossil fuel energy		
Production and utilization of coal	76.8	94.4
Production of other fossil fuels	23.8	26.1
Nuclear energy		
Liquid-metal fast breeder reactor	237.4	261.5
Nuclear fusion	47.2	65.1
Nuclear fuels process development	35.0	42.0
Other civilian nuclear power	90.7	94.8
Solar energy and fundamental energy policy studies	9.8	13.4
Geothermal resources	0.7	2.5
Other energy related programmes	38.3	61.0

Sources: "Liquid Metal Fast Breeder Reactor Demonstration Plant", *Hearings Before the Joint Committee on Atomic Energy, Congress of the United States,* 92nd Congress, 7, 8 and 12 September, 1972. Gilette, R., "Energy", *Science,* Vol. 179, 9 February 1973, pp. 549–50.

the use of an efficient coolant like sodium. The breeding process depends upon maintaining high-energy neutrons so that the use of a coolant like sodium minimizes their capture in the system. Sodium has high thermal conductivity and low vapour pressure at temperatures of interest for LMFBR applications so that the system can be used at low pressure which results in more efficient thermal energy conversion. The thermal efficiency of such a reactor is over 40 per cent.

Sodium has several disadvantages, however. It is opaque so that refueling and other operations in the reactor core have to be carried out blind. It becomes intensively radioactive when exposed to neutrons so that radiation shields must be used to protect workers near sodium which has been through the core and the blanket. Two radionuclides of sodium, sodium-24 and sodium-22, are produced as a result of the interaction between the neutrons and the sodium coolant. Sodium-24 has a half-life of 15 hours and it decays to stable magnesium. Because of this short half-life it is less of a problem than the second radionuclide, sodium-22, which has an appreciably longer half-life—2.6 years. It is, therefore, much more serious from the point of view of the potential radiological consequences of a sodium spill or fire. The problem is minimized, to some extent, by the use of a secondary sodium loop which is heated by the primary one after sodium has passed through the reactor core and the blanket. It is the secondary sodium loop which produces the steam. The design is further complicated by the fact that sodium is chemically highly reactive, particularly when it is in contact with air or water.

The higher neutron fluxes within the LMFBR cause radiation damage to some of the structural materials of the reactor and this has not been entirely resolved. [6] Moreover, LMFBR operates very close to the limits of an uncontrolled chain reaction so that if a major loss of coolant occurs, the radioactive heating would be sufficient to melt the reactor fuel and release large quantities of fission products.

Economics of the fast breeder reactor

The fact that a breeder reactor can produce its own fuel by converting isotopes of uranium into fissionable plutonium has been one argument given in favour of breeder reactor techonology. The other argument is an economic one. In determining whether a breeder reactor is economical, factors such as neutron efficiency, the cost of fuel fabrication and reprocessing and the cost of construction are perhaps most important.

For neutron efficiency, 6 to 20 years have been theoretically predicted as the doubling times for various breeder reactor designs. However, doubling times of more than about 10 years are not considered economical; for LMFBRs the doubling times may not be much less than this, whereas shorter doubling times for GCFBRs could be achieved due to the fact that a lesser number of neutrons are absorbed by helium.

Owing to the high toxicity of plutonium, new fuel fabrication and reprocessing techniques are being developed. The fuel for an FBR consists of plutonium oxide or a mixture of plutonium and uranium oxides. Plutonium carbide and other advanced fuels are being investigated and may ultimately be preferable to oxide fuels since, for example, the use of monocarbide would reduce the doubling time of a fast reactor to six to eight years. [7] In the United Kingdom, fuel cycle costs have been studied for different types of reactor and the fuel fabrication and reprocessing costs have been compared. It has emerged that, for a fast breeder reactor, costs are about £140/kg uranium in the core of the reactor and about £40/kg uranium in the blanket, compared to about £40/kg uranium for a gas-cooled thermal reactor (GCR) on a uranium feed. The penalty to the fast reactor is about £7/kW(e). A fast reactor would save about £11/kW(e) on uranium ore imports and about £8/kW(e) on separative work if used in conjunction with a steam-generating heavy water reactor (SGHWR). The fuel fabrication and reprocessing costs for the latter on a uranium feed are taken to be about £30/kg uranium (a larger number of plants is required to support the all-thermal-reactor programme leading to a lower figure). Thus, the penalty to the fast reactor is about £8/kW(e). This analysis assumes that GCRs will be installed until about 1980 when they will be superseded either by SGHWRs or by the advanced GCRs. The fast reactor programme will have a lead station in 1979 with a gradual increase in power up to 11 GW(e) by 1985. [8]

A similar study of the fuel fabrication and reprocessing costs for various types of reactor was recently made by the United States Atomic Energy Commission (US AEC) and the results are shown in table 2.

The cost of construction of a nuclear power plant varies from country to country. The French have estimated the cost of their 250 MW(e) Phénix

45

Table 2. Representative fuel fabrication and reprocessing costs

US $/kg

Reactor	Fabrication cost including fuel preparation		Reprocessing cost including conversion	
	Initial	Year 2020	Initial	Year 2020
LWR (w/o Pu recycle)	83	42	34	22
LWR (Pu recycle)	147	48	53	22
HTGR (with LMFBR)	243	89	69	34
LMFBR (introduction in 1986) includes core and blanket fuel	303	115	38	30

Source: "Cost-Benefit Analysis of the U.S. Breeder Reactor Program", US Atomic Energy Commission, WASH-1184, January 1972.

reactor at about 2 000F/kW installed, and the cost for the UK prototype fast breeder (PFR) is about £150/kW. [9] An analysis of the total plant capital cost has been made in the United States and a summary of the results for various types of plant is given in table 3. It is interesting to note that the difference in cost between the coal-fired and the nuclear power plants is relatively small.

In 1968, the US AEC made a cost-benefit analysis for their breeder reactor programme. [10] This study concluded that the direct financial benefits of such a programme would be $9.1 billion if the commercial LMFBRs were introduced from 1984. A more recent updated cost-benefit analysis has increased this figure to $21.5 billion if the introduction of the breeder reactors is delayed from 1984 to 1986 and assuming a discount rate (cost of money) of 7 per cent. [11] The increased benefits of $12.4 billion are made up of $6.7 billion due to the higher energy demand, $1.2 billion due to the higher separative work cost ($27.16/kg for 1970/71 and $32/kg thereafter) and $7.1 billion due to the higher fossil fuel costs and higher capital costs. These increases are partially offset by a $2.6 billion decrease due to the two-year delay in the introduction of the LMFBR. Delays in the breeder programme will reduce these benefits by $2 billion per year.

Further benefits are due to substantial savings in uranium resources and the separative work capacity. It is estimated that, with the introduction of

Table 3. Capital cost ($/kW(e)) of 1 000 MW(e) power plant (mid-1970)

Type of power plant	Run-of-river cooling	Cooling towers	Cooling towers and SO$_2$ remover
Coal-fired	191	205	239
Oil-fired	154	168	202
PWR	231	252	–
HTGR	223	238	–
LMFBR	257	272	–

Source: Bowers, H. J. and Myers, M. L., "Estimated Capital Costs of Nuclear and Fossil Power Plants", Oak Ridge National Laboratory, ORNL-TM-3243, 5 March 1971.

the breeder reactors, the requirement of U_3O_8 by 1986 will decrease by over 50 per cent. The separative work capacity without these reactors will increase to 27×10^7 kg per year by 2020; with the FBRs, it will increase to only 81×10^6 kg per year by 1992 and undergo no further increase beyond 1992. [11] Finally, the constructional cost for a light water reactor is between \$300 and \$400/kWhr of generating capacity and the cost for an LMFBR will be about \$20/kWhr more. [12]

A recent study, however, throws considerable doubt on these predictions. In fact, it concludes that LMFBRs may cost more to build and operate than the US AEC predicts. [12] The discount rate of 7 per cent, for example, used in the AEC cost-benefit analysis, is unrealistic; a 10 per cent rate is generally accepted as a realistic figure which would reduce the US AEC's projected net benefits on the LMFBR considerably. Furthermore, the AEC cost-benefit study depends on the assumptions that there will be a rapid rise in electric power demand, that uranium prices will increase rapidly, and that only LMFBRs are built in large numbers. If any one of these assumptions is substantially modified, the LMFBRs may not be able to compete economically with any of the more conventional electric power generators. For example, if the electric power demand is 20 per cent lower than that assumed in the US AEC projection, the discounted benefits decrease by \$6.7 billion. A 10 per cent increase in the capital cost of an LMFBR would decrease the benefit of \$21.5 billion to \$10.5 billion, indicating the sensitivity of the benefits to the capital cost. [13]

It is difficult to determine accurately the energy cost for the LMFBRs because of the sensitivity of cost analysis to the ground rules but it is generally accepted that the energy cost for these reactors is less than that for fossil-fuelled plants and certain thermal reactors. Estimates of the energy costs for a period between 1980 and 2020 have been made for various types of power plant; these are shown in figure 1. [14] By about 2020, the energy cost for an LMFBR will be about 4.5 mills/kWhr(e). It is interesting to note that if the LWRs are fuelled with plutonium, the energy cost for these reactors will be about the same as that for the LMFBRs.

Plutonium utilization

In thermal reactors the breeding process occurs to the extent that a considerable rate of production of plutonium will be achieved by the end of this century. By 1975, for example, the annual production of plutonium in the non-communist parts of the world will rise to 6 300 kg from its present rate of 1 400 kg per year; by 1985 the rate will be 100 000 kg per year. [15] The plutonium production rates for different types of reactor are shown in figure 2. These rates are very much in excess of the demands for fast reactor development programmes and the prototype and demonstration plants. The plutonium demand for these may level off at about 6 000 kg/year

Figure 1. Energy costs for various types of power plant

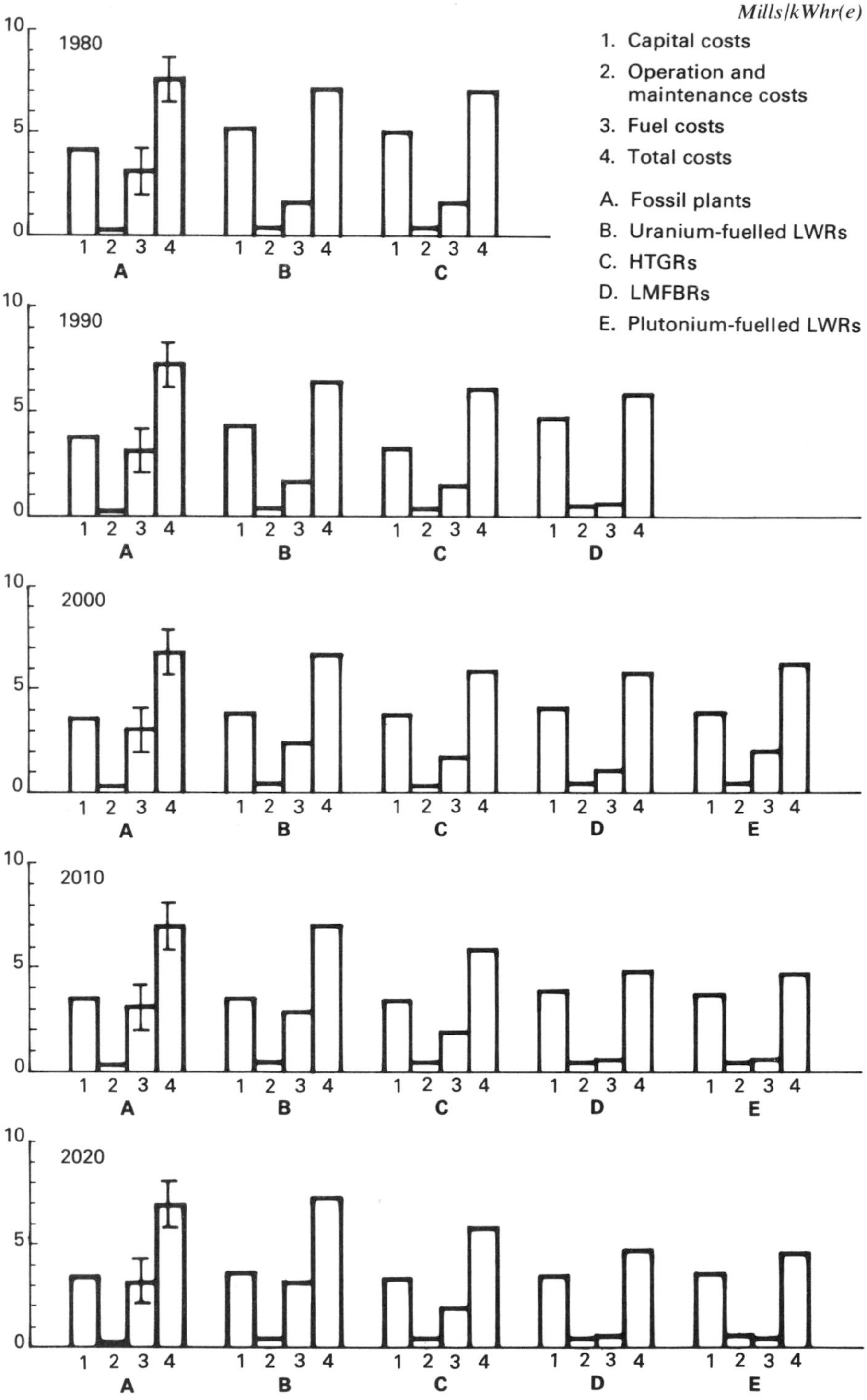
Mills/kWhr(e)
1. Capital costs
2. Operation and maintenance costs
3. Fuel costs
4. Total costs
A. Fossil plants
B. Uranium-fuelled LWRs
C. HTGRs
D. LMFBRs
E. Plutonium-fuelled LWRs
1980
1990
2000
2010
2020
0
5
10
1 2 3 4
A
B
C
D
E

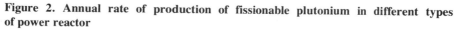

Figure 2. Annual rate of production of fissionable plutonium in different types of power reactor

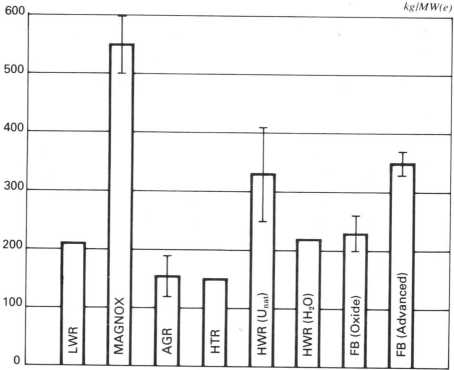

after 1975. [16] A substantial requirement for commercial FBRs is not likely to take place before the mid-1980s.

It is not certain how this surplus of plutonium is going to be utilized; the plans for plutonium utilization vary from country to country. The Magnox reactors in the United Kingdom, which have the largest plutonium production rate, may predominate up to 1975.[2] At that time the United Kingdom's accumulation of commercial plutonium will have amounted to about 15 000 kg. [16] The excess plutonium could either be recycled in the LWRs or stockpiled. A fuel cycle with plutonium replacing uranium-235 has been studied for various types of reactor in the United Kingdom and, on the basis of economics and the experience accumulated in handling plutonium, it is concluded that plutonium storage for its use later in fast reactors is preferable. [8]

Quite the opposite view is often expressed in the United States. Storage and inventory costs of plutonium have been computed and as the first commercial FBRs are not likely to be in operation until about the middle of the 1980s, it is concluded that storage of plutonium over this period is

[2] See figure 2.

uneconomical. From table 2 it can be seen that both the fuel fabrication and reprocessing costs increase when plutonium is recycled in LWRs but the fuel value added by the plutonium would be almost 40 per cent, assuming a plutonium value of $7/g. This means that there is about a $1 million per year incentive for plutonium recycle in a 1 000 MW(e) reactor. [15] It is considered better in the United States to recycle the plutonium in LWRs; programmes are already underway to resolve many problems concerning plutonium recycling in such reactors. [17]

In France the emphasis has been on the development and production of FBR fuel. Although studies of plutonium recycle in thermal reactors have been made, no plans for a large-scale thermal recycle have been declared. In the Federal Republic of Germany, a plutonium fuel development programme for FBRs has been underway but recently the German nuclear facilities have expressed interest in plutonium recycle. In Belgium, since 1959 Belgonucleaire and the Centre d'Etude de l'Energie Nucléaire (CEN), supported partly by Euratom, have been working on all aspects of plutonium recycle in LWRs; the present programme is designed to produce plutonium fuel initially for thermal recycle demands and later for fast breeder fuel. Most other countries with an active nuclear power programme are not yet at a stage where they can consider production of plutonium fuel on any large scale but they may have laboratories where plutonium fuel can be produced on an experimental basis.

Despite many technical and economic difficulties and uncertainties, the United States, the Soviet Union and many other countries have extensive plans for building LMFBRs in the very near future. In the following section of this chapter, plans of various countries for the construction of LMFBRs are outlined.

III. *Breeder reactor programmes*

The concept of breeder reactors dates back to before the time of the Manhattan Project. Since 1945 the US AEC and atomic energy authorities in other countries have been working continuously on sodium-cooled fast breeder reactor ideas. One of the earliest reactors, an experimental one called Clementine, at Los Alamos National Laboratory was used to explore the possibility of operating a reactor with fast neutrons, plutonium fuel and a liquid-metal coolant. The breeding principle was established in the experimental Breeder Reactor I (EBR-1) which produced the world's first nuclear-generated electric power.

Most major industrial countries are developing breeder reactors, particularly liquid-metal-cooled fast breeder reactors, on a national priority basis since they foresee significant economic and fuel supply advantages in this form of energy production. Large-scale breeder power generation implies the possibility of nuclear independence for countries without their own uranium reserves and/or separation plants. India, for example, with vast thorium reserves, hopes to become self-sufficient in nuclear power via the thorium-uranium-233 breeding cycle. [18] Each of these countries has committed significant resources to test facilities and demonstration plants. The Soviet Union is well on the way to constructing the world's largest LMFBR with a 600 MW(e) capacity. At the end of 1972, its 350 MW(e) LMFBR, BN-350, the world's first commercial breeder reactor, became critical. The UK is scheduled to begin operation of a 250 MW(e) demostration plant in the very near future and in France a 250 MW(e) reactor recently became critical.

Japan has announced plans to construct a commercial-sized demonstration plant for operation in this decade. French, Italian and West German utilities stated in May 1971 their joint plans to purchase two 1 000 MW(e) LMFBRs, the first to be located in France and the second in West Germany. More recent information indicates that West Germany, Belgium and the Netherlands have organized to assume a key role in the building and the operation of the SNR-300 and the large SNR-2 000; the capacity of the latter is expected to be 2 000 MW(e). The programmes of these and other countries are summarized in table 4.

IV. *Conclusions*

Assuming that nuclear fission is going to become the only economic means of generating electrical power, then breeder reactors will eventually be needed since uranium fuel for the LWRs is limited. However, from the above discussion, it can be seen that the economics of such reactors are in question. The fact that some fossil fuels are also limited is undeniable but, at present, there is a considerable wasteful use of energy. Moreover, it is surprising that relatively little effort is made to investigate other sources of energy.[3] Although ideal in many respects, nuclear energy still has many unsolved problems, for example the problem of reactor wastes. These wastes may amount to as much as 27 billion curies by the year 2000 and will have to be stored for a considerable period of time. [19]

Perhaps the most important problem is the fuel itself—plutonium-239. Not only is it a considerable health hazard owing to its high radiological toxicity but, as used in an LMFBR, it is in a suitable form for making nuclear explosives. Plutonium is ideal as a source of energy since one kilogramme of it can produce as much energy as about 3×10^6 kg of coal. About 1 000 kg of plutonium will be needed as fuel in a large LMFBR.

[3] See table 1.

Table 4 a. Fast breeder research reactors

Country/ reactor name	Type of reactor, fuel and fuel inventory	Power MW(e) (gross)	Date of regular power
Research reactors—in operation			
France Rapsodie	Loop [a]; Na cooled; highly enriched UO_2 (*85* per cent) and PuO_2 94 kg U and 40 kg Pu	–	Aug 1967
USA Sefor	Loop; Na cooled; enriched UO_2 (*18.7* per cent) and PuO_2	–	1969
USSR BR-5	Loop; Na cooled; plutonium (between 1959–64 the reactor operated with plutonium oxide fuel and in 1965 it was loaded with uranium monocarbide)	5	June 1959
Research reactors—under construction			
Japan Joyo	Loop; Na cooled; UO_2 (*23* per cent) and PuO_2 (*17.7* per cent) 162.6 kg UO_2 and 751.9 kg PuO_2	–	1974
USA FFTF	Loop; Na cooled; UO_2 (*22* per cent) and PuO_2 (*26* per cent) 2 530 kg UO_2	–	1975
Research reactors—planned			
Italy PEC	Pot [b]; Na cooled; UO_2 (*33* per cent) and PuO_2	–	1975

Notes and sources for tables 4 a and 4 b:

[a] In a loop-type reactor design, only the reactor vessel is filled with sodium. The liquid metal is circulated by pumps through heat-exchange loops mounted outside the reactor container.

[b] In a pot-type reactor design, a large tank filled with sodium encloses the reactor core and blanket and all the primary heat-transfer equipment.

"Power Reactors '73", *Nuclear Engineering International*, Vol. 18, No. 203, 1973.
Leipunskii, A. I. *et al.*, "Experience in Fast Reactor Operation and Design in the USSR", *Peaceful Uses of Atomic Energy* [Proceedings of the Fourth International Conference, Geneva, 6–16 September 1971] Vol. 5 (New York, Vienna, UN and IAEA, 1972) pp. 37–51.
Power and Research Reactors in Member States (Vienna, IAEA, 1972).
"India's Nuclear Power Programme", *Nuclear Engineering International*, Vol. 16, No. 184, 1971, pp. 755–57.
"Power Reactors", *Directory of Nuclear Reactors*, Vol. 4 (Vienna, IAEA, 1962).
Culler, Jr., F. L. and Harms, W. O., "Energy from Breeder Reactors", *Physics Today*, Vol. 25, No. 5, May 1972, pp. 28–39.

If these reactors are developed and commercial plants are built, then according to the US AEC's projections, commercial plutonium production will amount to about 30 000 kg annually by 1980 and more than 100 000 kg annually by the year 2000. Handling such quantities of plutonium will present an enormous problem since only microgramme quantities of plutonium are needed to cause lung cancer in animals. Health standards limit human exposure to a total body burden of 0.6 microgramme. Moreover, in the event of a major accident, it would be possible to contaminate an area permanently owing to the 24 000 year half-life of plutonium-239.

Table 4 b. Fast breeder power reactors

Country/reactor name	Type of reactor, fuel and fuel inventory	Power (MW(e)) (gross)	Date of regular power
Power reactors—experimental—in operation			
UK DFR	Loop; Na-K cooled; highly enriched uranium (*75* per cent); natural uranium blanket; 340.4 kg U	15	July 1963
USA EBR-2	Pot; Na cooled; highly enriched uranium (*52* per cent); plutonium in future; depleted uranium blanket; 599.5 kg U	18.5	May 1965
USSR BOR-60	Loop; Na cooled; UO_2 (*90* per cent); 0.176 tons U-235	12	Dec 1968
Power reactors—experimental—planned			
India FBTR (similar to Rapsodie)	Loop; probably Na cooled	30	1976
Power reactors—in operation			
France Phénix	Pot; Na cooled; UO_2 (*19.2* per cent) and PuO_2 (*27.1* per cent) 4 369 kg	250	1973
USA Enrico Fermi	Loop; Na cooled; highly enriched uranium+*10* per cent Mo (*25.6* per cent); depleted uranium (*0.36* per cent) blanket	61 (net)	Dec 1965
USSR BN-350 (first commercial breeder reactor)	Loop; Na cooled; PuO_2 (*23.19* per cent Pu) or UO_2; 1 158.5 kg U-235	350	Dec 1972
Power reactors—under construction			
UK PFR	Pot; Na cooled; PuO_2 (*24* per cent) and UO_2 (*30* per cent); 4 165.8 kg	250	1973
USSR BN-600	Pot; Na cooled; UO_2 and PuO_2 mixture	600	Dec 1972
Power reactors—planned			
France Super Phénix	Pot; UO_2 and PuO_2	1 200	1979
FR Germany KNK 2	Loop; UO_2 (*6.8* per cent); 1 828.9 kg	21	1972
Kalkar SNR	Loop; Na cooled; UO_2 (*20* per cent) and PuO_2 (*30* per cent); 4 673.8 kg	312	1980
–	–	1 000	1982
Japan Monju	Loop; Na cooled; UO_2 (*16.3* per cent) and PuO_2 (*22.3* per cent)	300	1977
UK CFR	Pot; Na cooled	1 300	1979
USA Demo No. 1	Loop; Na cooled	300–500	1978–80
Demo No. 2	–; Na cooled	300–500	–

Even if some of these technological problems could be solved, there still remains the question of whether the weapon-grade plutonium produced by the fast breeder reactors could be used by individuals or groups of individuals to construct crude nuclear weapons. Already the basic information necessary for the construction of a nuclear device is easily available; there only remains the uncertainty as to whether the individuals could have the necessary resources and weapon technology. Also, since the amount necessary for an explosive device is only a few kilogrammes, the safeguard technology has to be sensitive enough to detect any illegal diversions of small quantities of plutonium.

This enormous rush to build breeder reactors seems to be unnecessary particularly when the economic advantages of such reactors are in doubt and when there are still so many unresolved problems. Such programmes could well be delayed, and the LMFBR resources could be diverted to research and development on some other less hazardous energy-source projects.

References

1. *AEC News Releases*, Vol. 4, No. 5, 31 January 1973.
2. Benedict, M., "Electric Power from Nuclear Fission", in Lewis, R. S. and Spinrad, B. I., eds., *The Energy Crisis, 1972.*
3. Rosenthal, M. W., Robertson, R. C. and Bettis, E. S., "Molten Salt Breeder Reactors", *Nuclear Engineering International,* Vol. 14, May 1969, pp. 420–25.
4. Rosenthal, M. W. *et al.*, "Advances in the Development of Molten-Salt Breeder Reactors", *Peaceful Uses of Atomic Energy* [Proceedings of the Fourth International Conference, Geneva, 6–16 September 1971] Vol. 5 (New York, Vienna, UN and IAEA, 1972) pp. 225–37.
5. *Annual Report of the United Kingdom Atomic Energy Authority,* 1 April 1971, to 31 August 1972.
6. Nelson, Stuart, R., "Filling the Voids in Fast Reactor Technology", *New Scientist and Science Journal,* 25 March 1971, pp. 664–67.
7. Leipunskii, A. I. *et al.*, "Efficient Utilization of Fuel in Nuclear Fast Power Reactor", *Peaceful Uses of Atomic Energy* [Proceedings of the Fourth International Conference, Geneva, 6–16 September 1971] Vol. 9 (New York, Vienna, UN and IAEA, 1972) pp. 87–103.
8. Marsham, T. N. *et al.,* "The Technical Problems and Economic Prospects Arising from the Alternative Methods of Using Plutonium in Thermal and Fast Breeder Reactor Programs", *Peaceful Uses of Atomic Energy* [Proceedings of the Fourth International Conference, Geneva, 6–16 September 1971] Vol. 9 (New York, Vienna, UN and IAEA, 1972) pp. 119–30.
9. "Fast Reactors", International Conference at Aix-en-Provance, 2–4 September 1971 (Report), *Nuclear Engineering International,* Vol. 16 No. 186, November 1971, p. 940.
10. "Cost-Benefit Analysis of the U.S. Breeder Reactor Program", US Atomic Energy Commission, WASH-1126, April 1969.
11. "Cost-Benefit Analysis of the U.S. Breeder Reactor Program", US Atomic Energy Commission, WASH-1184, January 1972.

12. Hammond, Allen L., "The Fast Breeder Reactor: Signs of a Critical Reaction", *Science,* Vol. 176, 28 April 1972, pp. 391–93.
13. Whitman, M. J. *et al.,* "United States Civilian Nuclear Power Cost-Benefit Analysis", *Peaceful Uses of Atomic Energy* [Proceedings of the Fourth International Conference, Geneva, 6–16 September 1971] Vol. 2 (New York, Vienna, UN and IAEA, 1972) pp. 475–89.
14. Culler, Floyd L. (Jr.), and Harms, William, O., "Energy from Breeder Reactors", *Physics Today,* Vol. 25, No. 5, May 1972, pp. 28–39.
15. Larson, Clarence, E., "International Economic Implications of the Nuclear Fuel Cycle", *AEC News Releases,* Vol. 3, No. 32, 9 August 1972.
16. Rippon, J. E., "Plutonium—Problems and Possibilities", *Nuclear Engineering International,* Vol. 17, No. 189, February 1972, pp. 85–92.
17. Astley, Wayne D., Walke, Gerald, J. and Ladesich, John, "Plutonium Recycle Developments", *Nuclear News,* Vol. 14, No. 8, August 1971, pp. 29–32.
18. *Nuclear India,* October 1971, pp. 6–8.
19. Hammond, Allen, "Fission: the Pro's and Con's of Nuclear Power", *Science,* Vol. 178, 13 October 1972, pp. 147–49.

4. Uranium enrichment technologies and the demand for enriched uranium

P. BOSKMA

Abstract

Uranium enrichment plants have so far been limited to the territories of the nuclear-weapon states. This technology is still the only secret part of the nuclear energy business. Enrichment facilities give the physical capability for a country to produce uranium-based nuclear fission weapons and so far are the preferred way of producing thermonuclear weapons.

This situation will almost certainly change during the next decade. New enrichment technologies like the centrifuge and the jet nozzle process are already being used in pilot plants and techniques using rotating plasmas and lasers could possibly provide second generation enrichment methods. Many non-nuclear countries are developing these technologies which have some favourable characteristics in comparison to the gaseous diffusion process. The US monopoly position on the free market for uranium will certainly be challenged and enrichment plants will probably be built on the territories of non-nuclear-weapon states. Estimates of the future demand for enriched uranium indicate that decisions for new plants will be made during the next two to four years.

I. *Introduction*

This paper discusses the present situation in the field of uranium enrichment technologies and the future need for enriched uranium. Uranium enrichment plants on an industrial scale have, until now, been limited to the territories of the five nuclear-weapon states. Changes are to be expected in the coming decade, however. Several pilot plants using new technologies are in operation already. Enrichment facilities needed to supply the fuel for the rapidly growing number of nuclear power reactors all over the world will almost certainly spread to many countries active in the fields of nuclear technology or fuel production. An enrichment plant represents the physical capability for a country to produce weapon-grade uranium within a short period of time. It thus lowers the technological barrier for acquiring nuclear weapons.

The question can be raised about uranium-235's attractiveness for a country starting a nuclear weapon programme. The abundant availability of plutonium-239 in a country active in the nuclear energy sector will probably provide a cheaper and easier alternative as far as fission weapons are concerned. However, highly enriched uranium-235 is very probably still necessary, and in any case preferable, for thermonuclear weapons. Although in the future, fusion weapons could possibly be exploded by laser techniques (making fission technology no longer a necessary condition for a country to go nuclear), for many countries uranium-235 would still be an important ingredient for a medium-advanced nuclear weapon programme. An enrichment facility could then be of great importance.

Large-scale nuclear technology activities have been legitimized in many countries by the promised benefits of an important new energy source. This would provide a solution to the problem created by the diminishing resources of fossil fuels and the continued growth of energy consumption. During recent years it has become clear, however, that nuclear fission energy will have several serious social implications, notably safety problems and probably long-term health problems when used as a mass technology on a worldwide scale. By far the greatest energy consumption takes place in the highly developed countries, where energy is wasted on an enormous scale. One could have serious doubts about the benefits of such a development in which potential nuclear weapon capability is distributed around the world while no solution is offered for the world's energy problem.

However, the development of nuclear fission energy already has impressive technological momentum with strong economic incentives. The market for nuclear reactors and nuclear technology, including the fuel cycle, promises high profits and has started an enormous competition among the big industrial companies, many of them multinational in structure and difficult for national governments to influence.

II. *Uranium enrichment technologies*

Natural uranium has three isotopes—uranium-234, -235 and -238 in relative abundances of 0.006, 0.720 and 99.274 per cent respectively. Enrichment technologies are methods to raise the percentage of uranium-235. Nuclear power reactors generally use concentrations of 3–5 per cent; fuel for nuclear submarine reactors needs enrichment to roughly 30 per cent and weapon-grade uranium should be more than 80 per cent pure in uranium-235. [1]

Isotope separation is a rather difficult technological problem because of the similar chemical characteristics of the components. Most methods differentiate on the basis of mass. This section gives a survey of several tech-

Figure 1. A separation element

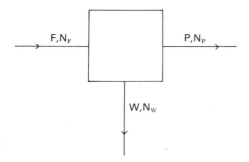

niques for uranium isotope separation. Some of them are used on an industrial scale while others are in the stage of pilot plants or still in the laboratory. The field is open, however, to new developments and several new techniques could possibly be attractive for use on an industrial scale in the future.

Some basic concepts

In a separation element an incoming stream of feed material F with concentration N_F is separated into an enriched stream of material P with concentration N_P and a so-called waste stream of material W with concentration
N_W (see figure 1). The separation factor α of an element is defined as

$$\alpha_P = \frac{N_P}{N_F} \qquad \text{(I)}$$

However α_P does not indicate the amount of uranium enriched. A better
characteristic figure for the performance of an element can be given by
introducing the concept of separative work (SW). It is based on the principle of defining a potential value to a stream of material depending upon
the concentration of the enriched material. Separating a stream of material
F with concentration N_F into its components needs an amount of separation
work:

$$\Delta U = PV_P + WV_W - FW_F \qquad \text{(II)}$$

In this equation V is the value function, which can be calculated to be

$$V = (2N-1)\ \ln \frac{N}{1-N} \qquad \text{(III)}$$

for the different streams of material.

For most methods α_P is much too small to produce the desired enrichment. This problem is solved by building cascades of elementary separation
elements with several units in series and parallel and feeding the next stage

with the enriched product of the former. The waste stream of a stage can be used as part of the input for a lower stage in the network. In the optimum condition $\alpha_P = \alpha_W = \alpha$.

For industrial production, an optimum network of elements can be calculated. The part of the cascade between the feedpoint and the output of the enriched product is called the enricher; the part between feedpoint and waste point is called the stripper. For such a cascade the separative work is approximately

$$U = P\left[(2N_P - 1)\ln\frac{N_P}{N_F} + \frac{N_P - N_F}{N_F - N_W}(2N_W - 1)\ln\frac{N_W}{N_F}\right] \qquad \text{(IV)}$$

The term between brackets is the value function for the cascade.

An example may clarify the formula given. Consider a centrifuge plant with a separative work capacity of 25 ton SW/year.
Table 1 lists the value function V for the production of reactor-fuel and weapon-grade material from natural uranium for a given waste concentration. For weapon production, such a facility would produce

$$\frac{U}{V} = \frac{25\,000}{200} = 125 \quad \text{kg}$$

of 90 per cent U-235 per year, sufficient for about 10 nuclear weapons. Although the arrangement of the cascade would be different for both settings, a small plant of this capacity could have military significance. It would probably need about 3 000 centrifuges. [2]

Table 1. The value function V

Product	N_F	N_W	N_P	V
Reactor fuel	0.72 per cent	0.12 per cent	3 per cent	3.6
Weapon-grade material	0.72 per cent	0.12 per cent	90 per cent	200

Technologies in use on an industrial scale or in pilot plants

Quite a number of technologies were explored in the USA during World War II. The present industrial production, however, is solely based on the gaseous diffusion technology although, during the war, the electromagnetic method and thermal diffusion were also in use. The electromagnetic method, [3] based on the principle that ions with differences in mass describe circles with different curvatures in a magnetic field, is the only method of producing highly enriched uranium in one stage. The economics of the process make it unsuitable as a mass production process.

A thermal diffusion column consists of two concentric tubes at different temperatures. In this radial temperature gradient, molecules with different masses diffuse to different radial concentrations. Convection currents transform the radial separation into an axial separation. In the Oak Ridge wartime thermal diffusion plant, using UF_6 under high pressure, a separation factor as high as 1.3 was reached. [4] Drawbacks of the method for large-scale use are the long equilibrium time needed and the high energy consumption.

The technologies to be reviewed here are the gaseous diffusion method, the ultracentrifuge method and the jet nozzle process. All three processes use as a source material, UF_6, which is a crystalline solid at room temperature but is easily vaporized. An important advantage of the use of UF_6 is that fluor has only a single isotope. A disadvantage is its corrosive character; special materials have to be used for vessels, pipes and pumps. [5]

The gaseous diffusion method

Uranium hexafluoride (UF_6) gas diffuses through porous barriers with holes smaller than the average free path of the molecules. Diffusion velocities are proportional to the average velocity of the molecules, which is inversely proportional to the square root of the mass of the molecules at a certain temperature. This defines the theoretical maximum separation factor to be 1.0043, which is rather small.

The feed material, UF_6, is compressed, passed through coolers to dissipate the heat of compression, diffused through the barriers and carried to the next stage. The porous barriers consist of sintered nickel powder, electrolytically oxidated aluminium sheet or saturated fluorcarbon plastics. [6]

The present empirical value of α is about 1.0016. This results in a large number of stages in the cascades, about 1 200 for an enrichment to 3 per cent.

The energy consumption of this method is very high, mainly because of the compressing and cooling of the UF_6. An example is the Paducah diffusion plant in Kentucky (USA). It has a capacity of 7 340 ton SW/year and contains 1 812 stages in two parallel arrangements for a 5 per cent enriched product. The investment costs have been $755 million; the installed power is 2 550 MW, and 4×10^8 gallons of water are required for cooling every day. [6]

The ultracentrifuge method

This technology is based on the difference in centrifugal forces experienced by molecules of different masses when rotating at high velocities in a cylinder. Introducing a longitudinal temperature gradient, a countercurrent stream of the material can be realized which enhances the separation factor substantially. [7]

A crucial parameter is the angular velocity of the cylinder, mainly limited by material properties and resonance phenomena. Materials with rotational velocities up to 700 m/sec have been realized. [8] The energy consumption is relatively small due to the operation of the centrifuges in a vacuum and low friction losses in the bearings.

The optimalization of the centrifuge is still in development. A sixfold increase in separative work capacity has already been reached for the German centrifuge [9] over the last decade and there are optimistic expectations about even better performances. Effective values of α for present centrifuges are estimated at about 1.2. Large R&D budgets are spent, especially in the Federal Republic of Germany, the Netherlands and the United Kingdom, to get the centrifuge technology to an industrial phase. This research is partly government financed. Pilot plants with capacities of 25 ton SW/year are being built at Almelo (Netherlands) and Capenhurst. An important problem is the length of life of the centrifuge. Test cascades have been running at Jülich for a period of 14 months without major problems. [9]

In the USA substantial amounts are also spent on R&D for centrifuge technology.

The jet nozzle procedure

This process, developed by Becker and coworkers in FR Germany, is based on pressure diffusion in a gaseous mixture of UF_6 and an additional light gas (He or H_2) flowing at high speed through a nozzle along curved walls. [10] The heavier molecules are less deflected and enriched in the stream with the largest curvature. The addition of He increases the velocity of the UF_6 molecules and thus improves the separation effect. A separation factor of 1.015 has been reached in experiments. [9] A small 10-stage pilot plant was built at Karlsruhe (FR Germany) and has been operating at full-scale capacity since 1967.

Research is continuing and several improvements still seem possible. An evaluation of the potentialities of the method, made in March 1971 in FR Germany by specialists in the field of uranium enrichment concluded that the project was promising. [9]

Possible methods relevant for future developments

Several developments in the field of uranium enrichment might possibly lead to new technologies. In this section we will mention some isotope separation experiments which are still in a pure laboratory research phase. It is, however, possible that some of them could be applicable for large-scale use.

The experiments are mentioned mainly to demonstrate that quite a number of alternative technologies are possible and could change the present evaluation of the situation in this field. This would result in a greater range of alternatives for companies or industries entering the uranium enrichment

61

business and enhance the probability of a proliferation of enrichment plants to non-nuclear countries.

Rotating plasmas

Instead of the mechanical method of the centrifuge, electromagnetic fields could be used to produce rotating plasmas where the ions also experience centrifugal forces. The velocities that can be reached are of the order of 100 000 m/sec, a value much higher than can be reached by mechanical means. Using these velocities, a very high separation factor can be reached. [11]

Laser techniques

Isotopes have slightly different spectral lines due to differences in mass of the nuclei. If the frequency of an incident intense laser beam corresponds to the resonance frequency of an atom, the light will be absorbed and the absorbing atom will carry the momentum of the incident photon. The de-excitation of the atom will, however, be spatially isotropic. Thus a net acceleration of the absorbing atoms in the direction of the incident photons will result. When lasers are available that can be tuned to exact resonance frequencies, they will provide an interesting enrichment technology. [12]

Another method of using lasers for enrichment is based upon the induction of isotope-characteristic chemical reactions. [13]

Although little information about the technologies used is available, there are several research projects in this field. A US firm in the laser field (AVCO Corporation) claims that lasers give a new approach to the enrichment problem. [14–15] Research on laser enrichment techniques is also going on in Australia. [16] FR Germany's office for science and education has allocated 100 000 DM for research on laser enrichment called "second generation enrichment". [17]

Ion exchange columns

The isotopes to be separated are mixed with an organic polymer or resin and inserted on top of a column containing fresh resin. This column is eluted with a solution forming complex ions with the isotopes. Adsorption co-efficients to the resin differ for the isotopes and different flow velocities give a separation effect.

The method has been claimed to be convenient for the production of macro-quantities of low enriched uranium. [18] Research on this method is going on in Japan. The separation factors, however, are low. [19]

A comparison of the major technologies

A comparison can be made among the three major current technologies on the basis of technological and economic data. Table 2 lists characteristic

Table 2. A comparison of the uranium enrichment technologies

	US gaseous diffusion	Centrifuge	Jet nozzle	References
Separation factor	~1.0018	~1.2	~1.015	[8]
Number of stages in the cascade	~1400	~13	~450	[8]
Minimal capacity for optimum economy (annual tons)	8750	1000	2500[a]	[9]
Connected power load (megawatts)	2050	30	950[a]	[9]
Specific energy consumption (kWh/kg SW)	2100	175–260	4350–6500	[8]
Construction time (years)	5–6	3	3	[9]
Specific investment costs $ per kg SW/year	120	120–170	76.5	[8–9, 20]
Costs ($ per kg SW)				
Capital	8.50	17.00	7.70	
Power[b]	12.50	2.30	29.50	
Manpower, operation maintenance	3.30	8.50	2.40	
Overhead, marketing	4.00	4.00	4.00	
Total costs	**28.30**	**31.80**	**43.60**[a]	[9]
Percentage of energy in the enrichment price	*40–50* per cent	*~5* per cent	*60–70* per cent	[8]

[a] Figures based on $\alpha = 1.020$.
[b] US power 0.6 cent/kWhr; European power 0.9 cent/kWhr.

data for the gaseous diffusion process, the ultracentrifuge technology and the jet nozzle process.

Diffusion technology has high energy consumption and needs large-scale cooling facilities. If an economically attractive price of enriched uranium is to be achieved, large factories would be required. For a medium-sized country this would be a rather expensive undertaking when no military arguments are involved but a cooperative venture among several countries might be an attractive undertaking.

Centrifuge plants can be built in relatively small units of about 1000 ton SW/year and they have a relatively low energy consumption. For most industrialized countries where energy prices can be expected to rise in the future and problems of thermal environmental pollution are serious, the centrifuge seems to be an attractive proposal. Moreover, the price of the enriched uranium is rather insensitive to the energy price. A further advantage of the centrifuge is the possibility of expanding the factory according to the market demands for enriched uranium.

For example a plant of 10 000 ton SW/year can be built progressively over a period of, say, 10 years, giving an annual investment of £50 million without materially affecting the plant's efficiency and hence the costs of separative work. [21]

Jet nozzle technology requires low specific investment costs to become economically attractive for medium-sized plants, but it has a very high power consumption. It could be an attractive alternative for a medium-sized country with cheap electricity, for example from a hydroelectric power station, and no serious problems of cooling capacity. One could think of underdeveloped countries with rich fields of uranium ore.

Another important factor is the number of years needed to bring a new plant into full operation. Centrifuge and jet nozzle plants need about two years' less construction time than a gaseous diffusion plant. This means that decisions can be better adjusted to the market demands.

The reliability of the technique is another important aspect. In this respect the diffusion technology has proven to be very good although no long-term data are available as yet for the other technologies. The reliability of the centrifuge seems to be no problem in the pilot plants so far but the production of centrifuges has been considered a limitation to the growth of this technology. For example, to meet an installation programme of 1 500 ton SW/year would require the production of 250 000 to 750 000 centrifuges a year. Nevertheless, it has been claimed that this could be realized by the 1980s. [21]

III. *The present situation and future demand for enriched uranium*

The future demand for enriched uranium can be estimated on the basis of the expected growth of nuclear energy consumption. Spinrad (chapter 2, p. 32) shows a long-term projection of the expected electrical capacity of nuclear power stations for various regions in the world. It also indicates the relative importance of nuclear energy production. If this projection becomes reality, nuclear reactors will produce about 60 per cent of the required capacity in the year 2000.

The data for the next decade are rather reliably anchored in existing plans for power stations. As to the long-term development, several sources of uncertainty should be mentioned. One is the problem of the extrapolation of existing trends including the economic and technological problems resulting from the fast growth of the nuclear industry. Apart from that, a discussion is starting in several highly industrialized countries of the feasibility of the continuing exponential growth of energy consumption because of environmental and ecological problems. This holds, in particular, for the extensive use of nuclear fission reactors. Apart from thermal pollution, the use of these reactors would give high quantities of radioisotopes, several of them with half-lives of centuries or more. A safe deposit for this radioactive waste over such long periods has not yet been found. Moreover the long-term effects of an increase in the level of radioactivity for large groups of people (delayed somatic and genetic effects) are still insufficiently known. Other critics emphasize the dangers of accidents with nuclear power stations in densely populated areas and the possibilities for national and international sabotage and blackmail.

Comparing the benefits to the rich countries of an exponential growth in energy consumption with the dangers and uncertainties inherent in the rapid installation of numerous nuclear power reactors, these critics feel the balance is on the negative side. This plea for a substantial deceleration of the installment of nuclear capacity could possibly gain momentum and influence future developments.

Nevertheless, a very rapid growth of nuclear power stations during the next 10–15 years seems very probable. This would result in substantial requirements for enriched uranium which cannot be provided by the present facilities.

Present facilities and the estimated demand
for enriched uranium

Table 3 shows the capacities and location of the existing enrichment plants producing on an industrial scale. They are all located in the nuclear-weapon countries and were originally built for military purposes. The production method is diffusion technology, although there is some uncertainty about the method used by China.

The US plants, operated for the US Atomic Energy Commission by private contractors, are probably by far the largest producers. They are currently operated at about 50 per cent of their capability (8 500 ton SW/ year in fiscal year 1971/72). [22] This capability gives the USA a kind of monopoly position for the non-socialist part of the world. It is US AEC policy to provide enriched uranium for nuclear reactors in the USA and abroad on long-term contracts. Since January 1969 a toll enrichment service

Table 3. Gaseous diffusion plants now in use

	Number	Place	Ton SW/year capability	References
USA	3	Oak Ridge Portsmouth Paducah	17 100	[22]
USSR	1	–	–	–
People's Republic of China	1	Lanchow	about 80	[23]
United Kingdom	1	Capenhurst	400	[18]
France	1	Pierrelatte	300	[18]

Table 4. Pilot plants

	Number	Place	Capability ton SW/year	Method	References
United Kingdom	1	Capenhurst	25	gas centrifuge	[2] [9]
Netherlands/ FR Germany	2	Almelo	2×25	gas centrifuge	[2] [9]
FR Germany	1	Karlsruhe	2	jet nozzle	[26]
South Africa	1	Pelindaba	–	secret	[19]

has been established. Customers can provide natural uranium and pay for the enrichment services. Until now gaseous diffusion technology has been classified and research on other techniques, such as the ultracentrifuge, has been kept under AEC control.

The USSR until recently did not provide enrichment services for countries outside the socialist bloc. However, several reactors have been built and fuelled in the socialist Eastern European countries. In 1971 the USSR announced long-term enrichment services for other countries. A contract has already been made with France for 250 tons SW. Negotiations with Sweden will probably lead to a long-term agreement on enrichment services.

The plants in the United Kingdom and France are too small for substantial export of enriched uranium and prices are not competitive with the US terms.

Apart from the plants for industrial production several pilot plants are in operation already (table 4).

Three pilot plants have been built by the companies of the tripartite cooperation for the development of centrifuge technology: FR Germany, the UK and the Netherlands. The German and Dutch plants, based on their own types of centrifuges, are located on Dutch territory. The technology of the South African plant is kept secret.

The future demand for enriched uranium can be estimated on projections for the installation of power reactors. As a rule of thumb each 1 000 MW(e) nuclear power station using enriched uranium has to be supported by a 100 ton/year enrichment capacity. [20] More detailed forecasts for the separative work requirements depend upon quite a number of assumptions, however. The complexity of the problem led US AEC member Johnson to make the statement: "Our computers reach a point in this kind of exercise where human judgement is more useful in getting an answer than further computerized problem elaboration". [24] Nevertheless, several estimates have been made for the world, not including the USSR, Eastern Europe and the People's Republic of China (see table 5).

The results are of the same order of magnitude. They demonstrate that the existing enrichment facilities will become too small and a serious shortage of enriched uranium will be met with at the end of the 1970s, unless

Table 5. The need for uranium enrichment capacity in tons SW/year

	1975	1980	1982	1985	References
World[a]	18000	38000	50000	70000	[8]
	19000	42000		80000	[25]
	19000	43000			[26]
	16000	38000		70000	[27]
USA	11000	21000	26000	35000	[8]
	11500	23000			[26]
	8000–12000	13000–22000			[28]
		15300		22000	Spinrad [c]
Europe[b]	3500–6500	7500–15000			[28]
	4400–7400	9000–15800		12300–24000	[29]
		13000			[26]
	6500	13000–14000		23000–26000	[30]

[a] Excluding USSR, Eastern Europe, People's Republic of China.
[b] Excluding USSR, Eastern Europe.
[c] See chapter 2.

new facilities are built. Keeping in mind that the time needed for getting a diffusion plant in operation is around five to six years (see table 2), many important decisions can be expected in the coming years. It should also be remembered that the building time for a centrifuge plant is about three years (table 2) and that such a plant can be built in stages of about 1 000 ton SW/year without materially affecting its economics. Given the uncertainties in the market demands, this could be an important consideration for several countries and industries in their choice of an enrichment technology.

Very little is known about the demands for enriched uranium in the USSR and the socialist Eastern European countries. It could be hypothesized that the USSR will continue to provide the enrichement services for Eastern Europe. Using the rule of thumb described above and taking the projected data for their nuclear power capability, while assuming that 80 per cent of the power reactors will be fuelled with enriched uranium, the enrichment capacities needed in the USSR can be estimated at 10 000–14 000 ton SW/year by about 1985. Spinrad's present projections (chapter 2) are even higher (20 000 ton SW/year). Data about China's future nuclear energy programme are difficult to obtain.

IV. *Conclusions*

From the point of view of the proliferation of uranium enrichment capabilities to non-nuclear countries, some conclusions can be drawn as to the technological and economic aspects of these programmes.

1. Several new technologies, not in the hands of the nuclear powers, are in development or could be developed for uranium enrichment plants. The ultracentrifuge technology, developed cooperatively by FR Germany, the

Netherlands and the United Kingdom, seems very attractive for medium-sized industrialized countries active in the field of nuclear energy.

2. The US monopoly position on the free market for enriched uranium will certainly be challenged because of the technological and economic characteristics of the centrifuge technology. An enrichment facility of their own would give industries in several countries a more independent and probably more competitive position. Economic arguments will be of great importance for the proliferation of enrichment plants.

3. The field of enrichment technologies is still very attractive. New technologies, apart from gaseous diffusion and centrifuge methods, will probably come up. The jet nozzle process might be a good candidate.

4. The future demand for enriched uranium is growing rapidly. Existing facilities will become too small by the end of the 1970s. Because of the time needed to get a large-scale plant into operation, decisions about new facilities can be expected during the next two to three years. A spread to the territories of non-nuclear-weapon states is very probable and would give near-nuclear-weapon countries the physical capability for a uranium-based nuclear-weapon programme.

References

1. Feld, B. T. *et al.*, *Impact of New Technologies on the Arms Race*, Proceedings of the 10th Pugwash Symposium held at Racine Wisconsin 26–29 June 1970 (Cambridge, Mass., MIT Press, 1971) p. 234.
2. *De Ultracentrifuge, een Goudmijntje of een Gevaar Voor de Vrede*, Report of a working group of the Dutch Association of Scientific Workers, VWO, 1970.
3. Wakerling, R. K. and Guthrie, A., eds., *Electromagnetic Separation of Isotopes in Commercial Quantities* (Berkeley, University of California Press, 1949).
4. Abelson, P. H., Hoover, J. I., in Kistemaker, J. *et al.*, eds., *Proceedings of the International Symposium on Isotope Separation* (Amsterdam, Noordhollandse Uitgeversmaatschappij, 1958) p. 483.
5. Glasstone, S., *Sourcebook on Atomic Energy* (Princeton, Van Nostrand, 1967) p. 182.
6. Wright, W. J. K., "The Enrichment of Uranium", *Atomic Energy of Australia*, Vol. 15, January 1972, p. 2.
7. Beyerle, K., Groth, W., in Kistemaker, J. *et al.*, eds., *Proceedings of the International Symposium on Isotope Separation* (Amsterdam, Noordhollandse Uitgeversmaatschappij, 1958) p. 669.
8. Kelling, F. E. T., "Methoden Voor Uraanverrijking", *Atoomenergie*, Vol. 14, December 1972, p. 297.
9. Mohrhauer, H., "Stand der Urananreicherung in Europa", *Atomwirtschaft*, Vol. 17, June 1972, p. 300.
10. Becker, E. W. *et al.*, "Die Physikalischen Grundlagen der ^{235}U-Anreichung nach dem Trenndüsenverfahren", *Zeitschrift für Naturforschung*, Vol. 26A, No. 9, 1971, p. 1377.

11. Wick, G., "New Vistas for Isotope Separation", *New Scientist*, Vol. 51, 23 September 1971, p. 692.
12. Ashkin, A., "Acceleration and Trapping of Particles by Radiation Pressure, *Physical Review Letters*, Vol. 24, 1970, p. 156; "Atomic-Beam Deflection by Resonance Radiation Pressure", *Physical Review Letters*, Vol. 25, 1970, p. 1321.
13. Mayer, S. W. *et al.*, "Isotope Separation with the CW Hydrogen Fluoride Laser", *Applied Physics Letters*, Vol. 17, 15 December 1970, p. 516.
14. "Focus on an Optimistic Laser Market", *New Scientist*, Vol. 53, 17 February 1972, p. 379.
15. "Lower-Cost Conversion of ^{235}U to Fuel Sought in Laser Experiments at Avco", *Laser Focus*, Vol. 8, April 1972, p. 18.
16. Kilpin, D., "Isotope Separation Using Laser Excitation", *Nuclear Science Abstracts*, Vol. 26, (1972), No. 18, Abstract No. 43194.
17. Reported in *Atomwirtschaft*, Vol. 17, February 1972, p. 133.
18. Ćirić, M., "Séparation des Isotopes de l'Uranium à l'Aide d'Echangeurs d'Ions", *Energie Nucléaire*, Vol. 10, October 1968, p. 376.
19. "Separation of Uranium Isotopes by Chemical Exchange", JAERI-memo-3961, *Nuclear Science Abstracts*, Vol. 26, (1972), No. 20, Abstract No. 47760.
20. Bogaardt, M. *et al.*, "Objectives and Progress in the Centrifuge Enrichment Plant Industry", *Peaceful Uses of Atomic Energy* [Proceedings of the Fourth International Conference, Geneva, 6–16 September 1971] Vol. 9 (New York, Vienna, UN and IAEA, 1972) p. 63.
21. Avery, D. G. *et al.*, "Centrifuge Plants in Europe", *Peaceful Uses of Atomic Energy* [Proceedings of the Fourth International Conference, Geneva, 6–16 September 1971] Vol. 9 (New York, Vienna, UN and IAEA, 1972) p. 53.
22. Johnson, W. E., Sapirie, S. R., "Uranium Isotope Enrichment", *Peaceful Uses of Atomic Energy* [Proceedings of the Fourth International Conference, Geneva, 6–16 September 1971] Vol. 9 (New York, Vienna, UN and IAEA, 1972) p. 31.
23. Murphy, C. H., "Mainland China's Evolving Nuclear Deterrant, *Bulletin of the Atomic Scientists*, Vol. 28, January 1972, p. 28.
24. Quoted in reference [21], p. 58.
25. Griffith, D. R., "Review of Overseas Nuclear Power Development", *Atomic Energy of Australia*, Vol. 14, June/October 1971, p. 11.
26. Klusman, A., Völcker, H., "The Situation of the Nuclear Fuel Cycle Industry", *Atomkernenergie*, Vol. 17, May 1971, p. 149.
27. "L'Energie Nucléaire et le 6ème Plan Français", *Energie Nucléaire*, Vol. 13, July/August 1971, p. 284.
28. "Matériaux Nucléaires, Le Problème de l'Uranium Enriché", *Energie Nucléaire*, Vol. 10, January/February 1968, p. 39.
29. "A European Enrichment Plant", *Nuclear Engineering International*, Vol. 14, April 1969, p. 343.
30. *ENEA-Report of the OECD*, (OECD, 1968) figure 6.

5. Nuclear fuel fabrication plants

B. M. JASANI

Abstract

The basic principles of nuclear fuel fabrication techniques are briefly described; however, the details of these techniques are not always available. Fuel fabrication costs are also discussed and fabrication programmes and plants in various countries are described.

The rate of production of plutonium is expected to be about 100 000 kg per year by 1985; in some countries plutonium is stockpiled rather than recycled in thermal reactors. Moreover, in some countries highly enriched uranium is stockpiled for use in a high-temperature gas-cooled reactor; the fuel inventory of the reactor is 650 kg uranium enriched to 93 per cent uranium-235. The economics of such reactors are questioned and if decisions go against such reactors, there will be a substantial quantity of highly enriched uranium available.

I. *Introduction*

Unlike hydroelectric and fossil-fuelled plants, a number of very complex processes are involved before electricity is produced by a nuclear power plant. The first step, mining and milling of uranium, is performed by only a few countries which have large known reserves of low-cost uranium; these countries are Canada, South Africa, Southwest Africa and the United States. Australia may well join this group since recent explorations in this country indicate substantial reserves of uranium. The situation of the Soviet Union and the People's Republic of China is not very well-known. In figure 1, the world's reserves of uranium as of mid-1971 are shown and it can be seen that low-cost uranium (less than $10 per pound) amounts to a little under one million tons. [1]

After the uranium ore is removed from the mines, it is then processed in mills located near the mines to produce a concentrate known as yellow cake which contains 60 to 70 per cent uranium. If enriched uranium is required, yellow cake is further purified and converted into uranium hexafluoride in plants located some distance away from the mines. This process forms the second stage in the fuel cycle. Uranium hexafluoride is a solid at room temperature but forms a gas when the temperature is raised during the third stage in the nuclear fuel cycle which is known as the enrichment

Figure 1. Estimated world reserves of uranium, mid-1971

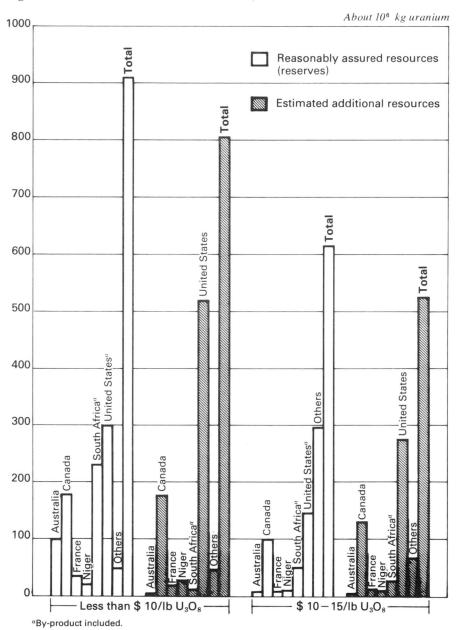

About 10^6 kg uranium

process. However, some reactors are operated with natural uranium, in which case, during the second stage of the fuel cycle, the yellow cake is converted into an oxide of uranium.

Enriched uranium in the form of uranium hexafluoride is not suitable for use in a nuclear reactor and is therefore first converted either into ura-

71

Table 1. Estimated fuel fabrication requirements for countries other than the United States[a]

Thousands of kilogrammes

Year	NAT & LWR UO$_2$	ATR & LWR mixed oxide	HTGR fissile	HTGR fertile	FBR Mixed oxide	Blanket
1972	2 500	0	0	0	16	8
1975	5 400	0	0	10	8	1
1978	7 000	144	0	2	8	1
1981	10 200	400	2	30	13	2
1984	13 500	830	4	73	91	25
1987	17 900	1 380	11	188	240	86
1990	21 900	2 200	21	310	970	340
1995	30 100	1 670	39	420	3 400	1 180
2000	36 600	2 100	60	760	7 100	2 600

[a] The analyses include plutonium recycling and 86 LMFBRs.

Source: Nuclear Power 1973–2000, US AEC Report WASH-1139(72), December 1972.

nium dioxide or uranium carbide. Most advanced countries have the capacity for performing this fourth stage in the fuel cycle which also consists of a process in which the final form of the reactor fuel is produced. It is this fuel fabrication process which will be considered in the following sections. From knowledge of the types of reactor used at present and those required in the future and the total electrical generating capacity forecast, it is possible to estimate the demand for fuel fabrication. The estimated fuel fabrication requirements for countries other than the United States are given in table 1. Details of fabrication techniques are not always available so that, in the following sections, only the basic principles are described briefly. Fuel fabrication costs are also discussed.

II. *Fuel fabrication processes*

Two forms of fuel have been developed for use in nuclear reactors—solid fuels fabricated into fuel elements of various shapes and liquid fuels in which the fuel is dissolved or suspended in the liquid coolant and in the moderator if one is used. The entire fuel fabrication process is practically eliminated if the fuel is incorporated in the coolant in this way. The heat is transferred directly to the coolant; there is no radiation damage to the fuel itself and new fuel can be added to the reactor continuously and fission products removed. The stability of both solutions and suspensions, however, is sensitive to temperature and flow conditions. Also the whole of the coolant system becomes highly radioactive so that there are extreme containment and maintenance problems in the primary system. Because of these problems, the development of reactors using liquid-metal fuel has been very slow. In the majority of reactors at present solid fuels are used so that, in the following sections, only the solid fuels are considered.

Generally the fuel material, either in the form of a metal or a ceramic, is placed in thin-walled metal tubes and sealed so as to prevent any escape of fission products into the coolant. Such a system also prevents corrosion of the fuel by the coolant. These tubes are called the fuel claddings. The choice of the cladding material is limited to beryllium, zirconium, magnesium and aluminium by the low neutron absorption requirements. The first two materials have not been widely used because they are expensive; aluminium has been used in water-cooled reactors in the United States whereas magnesium has been employed in the carbon dioxide-cooled reactors in Britain and France. With aluminium, however, special precautions are needed since it reacts slowly with uranium. At high temperatures aluminium and magnesium cladding corrode in water and in carbon dioxide respectively so that, for power reactors, zirconium is used as cladding. The advanced gas-cooled reactor (AGCR) in Britain uses stainless steel.

Pressurized water reactors (PWRs) and boiling water reactors (BWRs) use fuel assemblies which consist of prefabricated mechanical structures containing the fuel clads. Large numbers of reactors use fuel elements made of solid uranium in the form of either a metal or a ceramic. Natural uranium metal has been used for some time in reactors in which plutonium is specifically produced; uranium in this form is being used in the gas-cooled, graphite-moderated power reactors in Britain and France. Uranium alloy fuels, uranium dispersed in metals and ceramic fuels containing uranium have been extensively used in power reactors in the United States.

Uranium fuels

Natural uranium metal fuels

Natural uranium metal has been used widely in plutonium production reactors in which temperatures are relatively low and burnup is purposely kept low to obtain optimum plutonium production. Although natural uranium metal is used in many reactors because the fuel in this form is cheaper, its wide use in power reactors is limited because of the high temperatures and the required long burnups. High temperatures cause extensive dimensional changes in the fuel and, due to the nature of the structure of uranium metal, severe damage is often caused by radiation effects.

Natural uranium fuel elements are usually about 1 inch in diameter and the length can be between 6 and 40 inches. The fuel elements of gas-cooled natural uranium reactors have fins to improve heat transfer from the elements to the gas.

Uranium alloys

The adverse effects of high temperatures and radiation on the dimensions of natural uranium metal fuel are reduced considerably if other elements are added to uranium to form uranium alloys. The addition of small amounts

73

(2–5 per cent by weight) of molybdenum or zirconium improves the behaviour of the fuel elements. Also considerable dimensional stability and minimum corrosion effects have been achieved when small amounts of zirconium or niobium have been added to the uranium. If the proportions of such materials are increased (by about 10 per cent by weight) the effects of radiation at high temperatures on the fuel elements are considerably reduced although there is a greater wastage of neutrons because of the extra absorption. Such fuel elements have been used in Enrico Fermi and Hallam sodium-cooled reactors. Uranium-fissium alloy which contains uranium and mainly ruthenium with molybdenum has been used for the Experimental Breeder Reactor-2. Such a fuel element has been found to be highly resistant to radiation damage.

Uranium metal dispersed in metals

In such fuels, the uranium is dispersed in a sterile metal matrix, for example, in aluminium or zirconium. The use of a sterile metal matrix makes the fuel elements resistant to radiation damage and therefore high burnups are possible. There is high wastage of neutrons due to absorption and highly enriched uranium is needed in these elements. Often, these elements are not used in power reactors for economic reasons but they have been used in experimental reactors and reactors intended for military applications.

Uranium-magnesium dispersion elements have been used in some reactors in the Soviet Union. Such fuel elements are less susceptible to radiation damage and they have high thermal conductivity. The neutron wastage is low but fuel elements have relatively low melting points and they corrode when in contact with water.

Uranium-thorium alloys

Such a combination has two advantages. First, since thorium is a fertile material, a new fissionable isotope, uranium-233, can be produced. Thus there is a possibility of constructing a breeder reactor using the thorium-uranium-233 cycle; in any case, the use of thorium is expected to improve the conversion ratio in thermal reactors. Second, thorium can be used in reactors at higher temperatures than uranium. Uranium-thorium fuel elements, however, are not extensively used at present.

Uranium oxide

Uranium oxide in the form of pellets is widely used as a reactor fuel both in the enriched and natural uranium reactors; almost all the large pressurized and boiling water reactors use uranium-dioxide fuel. The Canadian heavy water reactors and the AGCRs in Britain and in the United States also use uranium-oxide fuel.

Uranium-dioxide powder is first compressed into cylindrical pellets from which it is then sintered at high temperature to form a ceramic-like solid.

Thin-walled tubes, made of an alloy of zirconium (the zinc alloy) or stainless steel, are then filled with such pellets stacked end-to-end. A fuel rod containing a 12-foot long column of stacked oxide pellets is usually about 13 feet long. The diameters of the pellets are accurately ground to provide a carefully controlled radial clearance space between the pellets and the cladding tube wall. Typical outside diameters of the fuel rods for a PWR are about 0.42 inches and the clad wall thickness is about 0.022 inches. The dimensions of a typical fuel rod of a BWR are 0.56 inches outside diameter with the clad wall thickness at about 0.032 inches. The fuel rods, arranged together in fuel "assemblies", stand vertically in the reactor in groups of 179 to 204 for a PWR and 49 for a BWR. All current PWR fuel rods are pressurized since the coolant water surrounding the fuel rods in a reactor is under substantial pressure.

Uranium fuel in this form has several advantages: the fuel does not easily corrode in water, steam or carbon dioxide; it can have long burnup without swelling; it has a high melting point and the retention of fission products within the fuel is good. However, the thermal conductivity of uranium dioxide is low so that the fuel rods must be small in diameter if the fuel temperature in the centre of the rod is to be kept below the melting point of the oxide. Also the heat loss through the gaps between the oxide pellets and the cladding becomes important. Usually this gap is minimal and is often filled with helium gas.

Uranium oxide in various combinations has also been used successfully in many reactors. Examples of various types of fuel are ceramic fuels containing mixtures of thorium oxide and uranium oxide, uranium-beryllium oxide and uranium oxide dispersed in graphite and metallic matrices such as stainless steel.

Uranium carbide

This type of fuel, a recent development, is particularly suitable for high-temperature gas-cooled reactors (HTGCR) or sodium-cooled reactors. The details of fabrication techniques are not available but the principle of the process is as follows. Uranium-carbide and thorium-carbide fuels are first prepared in the form of small spherical particles which are then coated with pyrolytic carbon and silicon carbide. These particles are then placed in fuel rods which are inserted into a graphite prismatic block having a number of holes for the fuel elements as well as for the coolant. [2]

Uranium carbide has several advantages: the thermal conductivity is comparable to that of uranium metal and about six to eight times that of uranium dioxide; it has a high melting point; it is less susceptible to radiation damage and its retention of fission products is high. However, it reacts with water so that the fuel has to be handled in an atmosphere of inert gas. Uranium carbide also reacts with most common metallic claddings.

Table 2. Estimated quantities of plutonium[a] and uranium-233 available from US facilities

Year	1970	1975	1980	1985	1990	1995	2000
Plutonium (10^3 kg/year)	2.5	6.6	28	60	100	160	240
Uranium-233 (10^3 kg/year)	–	–	0.8	7.8	11	12	12

[a] The estimates for plutonium assume 0.8 per cent plutonium in the chemically processed fuel; other estimates range from 0.45 to 0.74 per cent.

Source: Lotts, A. L. *et al.,* "The Status of Thermal Reactor Fuel Manufacture in the United States", *Peaceful Uses of Atomic Energy* [Proceedings of the Fourth International Conference, Geneva, 6–16 September 1971] Vol. 8 (New York, Vienna, UN and IAEA, 1972) pp. 201–14.

So far only uranium has been considered as a fuel but substantial amounts of plutonium-239 will become available after 1975 from commercial nuclear power plants (in operation and planned). In table 2 the estimated quantities of plutonium and uranium-233 from the facilities in the United States alone are given. If all of this plutonium is recycled in LWRs, it is estimated that there will be an annual refabrication requirement of 3 000 000 kg. The recycle fuel could amount to about 30 per cent of the fuel manufactured for LWRs and the recycle uranium-233 could be 50 per cent of the fuel for HTGRs in 1985. [2] It is therefore worth considering the plutonium fabrication technology briefly.

Solid plutonium fuels

Pure metallic plutonium is unsatisfactory as a reactor fuel because it exhibits six allotropic changes between room temperature and 1 190°F, its melting point. Therefore plutonium is first converted to an alloy or to a ceramic. This is complicated by the fact that plutonium is a highly toxic substance requiring extreme care in its handling which tends to increase the cost of fabrication of plutonium fuels in comparison to uranium fuels.

Plutonium alloys

The behaviour of plutonium-uranium alloys has been studied in some detail and it is found that up to 10 per cent by weight of plutonium in the alloy would make the fuel suitable for thermal reactors. At concentrations of plutonium higher than this that are required for the fast breeder reactors, the alloy is unsuitable because of some of its physical properties. Better results have been obtained with plutonium-uranium-molybdenum alloy and plutonium-uranium-fissium alloy.

Plutonium oxide

Plutonium oxide is isomorphic with uranium dioxide and thorium dioxide so that these form a continuous series of solid solution. Fuel elements containing uranium dioxide and plutonium dioxide in a mole ratio of 5 to 1 are possible fuels for fast breeder reactors. On the whole such fuels would have similar physical and radiation characteristics to those described for uranium-dioxide fuels. Plutonium-dioxide fuels have been used for the BR-5 fast reactor in the Soviet Union.

Plutonium dispersed in metals

Dispersion fuels of plutonium dioxide in stainless steel or niobium have been considered. Fuels with high plutonium-dioxide content (20 per cent) can be made that have similar physical and radiation properties to those of uranium-dioxide stainless-steel dispersion fuels. Such fuels are attractive for fast reactors but the high proportion of stainless steel is a disadvantage from the point of view of neutron economy.

Table 3. Comparison of fuel fabrication costs for Canadian power reactors and PWRs[a]

1970 US $/kg uranium

Items	PWR	Enriched uranium CANDU	Natural uranium CANDU
UO_2-powder[b] preparation	13.02	13.02 ⎫	8.00
Pelletization	15.10	8.80 ⎭	
Materials other than UO_2	29.65	13.58 ⎫	19.65
Encapsulation and assembly	17.62	7.97 ⎭	
Total	**75.39**	**43.37**	**27.65**

[a] Costs include allowance for working capital and overheads. Shipping charges are not included. In the cost calculations, it is assumed that all plants of about 1 000 kg U/day capacity are operating at 100 per cent load.
[b] The conversion from enriched uranium fluoride to uranium oxide is not required for natural-uranium CANDU fuel.
Source: Haywood, L. R. *et al.,* "Fuel for Canadian Power Reactors", *Peaceful Uses of Atomic Energy* [Proceedings of the Fourth International Conference, Geneva, 6–16 September 1971] Vol. 8 (New York, Vienna, UN and IAEA, 1972) pp. 185–99.

III. *Fuel fabrication costs*

It is not always easy to obtain data on the cost of reactor-fuel fabrication because the initial reactor-fuel loading and one or more reloads are usually included in the price of the nuclear power plants but as a rough estimate, for example for a BWR, about one quarter of the total fuel cycle cost is due to fuel fabrication. A comparison between the fuel fabrication costs for the Canadian heavy-water-moderated power reactors (CANDU reactors) and PWR has been made; this is shown in table 3.

A more recent study has compared the fuel fabrication costs for various types of reactor; the results are shown in table 4 from which it can be seen

Table 4. Fuel fabrication costs including fuel preparation for various types of nuclear power reactor

US $/kg

Reactor	Initial	Year 2020
LWR (W/O Pu Recycle)	83	42
LWR (Pu Recycle)	147	48
HTGR (with LMFBR)	243	89
LMFBR[a] (introduction in 1986)	303	115

[a] Includes core and blanket fuel.

Source: "Cost Benefit Analysis of the U.S. Breeder Reactor Program", US Atomic Energy Commission, WASH-1184, January 1972.

that the study has taken into account the effects of plutonium recycle.

The low costs of the CANDU fuels are due to the simplicity of the fuel design. By about 1990, it is predicted that these costs will decline to about half the present costs. From table 4 it can be seen that the same is true for the LWR but, if plutonium is recycled, the costs decline by one-third around the year 2020 although the initial costs of plutonium recycle are always high.

IV. *Fuel fabrication programmes and plants*

Almost all countries with a developed nuclear programme have some kind of fuel fabrication facility. It is, however, difficult to know the exact details of present capabilities and future plans. This is particularly true for plutonium fuel facilities since a good deal of initial production could be carried out in a well-equipped laboratory.

Argentina

The first nuclear reactor in Latin America was an Argonaut type built in Argentina. The reactor, RA-I, started operation in 1958 but the National Atomic Energy Commission (CNEA) had already begun the production of the first fuel elements in 1957. Since then all fuel elements for Argentina's research reactors have been produced by the CNEA laboratories. Fuels for PWRs have also been developed and there is an active interest in the production of plutonium fuels. There are plans for producing fuel elements for nuclear power stations and plans for a first fabrication plant are being considered. [3–4]

Belgium

In Belgium, the Centre d'Etude de l'Energie Nucléaire (CEN) and the Studie Centrum Voor Kernenergie (SCK) carry out the basic research in the fuel fabrication field and the Belgian industry concentrates on the production of uranium-oxide fuel. The CEN-SCK laboratories are situated at Mol near the Dutch border. A certain amount of work is devoted to the improvement of uranium-oxide fuel but the main effort concerns the development of mixed plutonium-uranium oxide fuels in cooperation with private industry. For example, considerable attention has been paid to the fabrication of fuels using vibration techniques to achieve the required fuel densities. The fabrication of fuels in the form of spheres of oxides and, more recently, some plutonium coated particles for use in the HTGRs have been produced for testing. Development of mixed uranium-plutonium-carbide fuels for use in the future is also being carried out. [5]

The second main fuel-study concern in Belgium is Belgonucléaire (BN) which is engaged in the development of plutonium-enriched uranium fuels for thermal and fast reactors. In collaboration with CEN, BN built a plutonium laboratory and in 1968 started a pilot unit for producing fuel rods. This unit processes about 100 kg of plutonium a year and manufactures 2 000 to 3 000 plutonium-enriched fuel rods annually. An additional plant for producing plutonium-enriched fuels is being constructed. While BN is engaged in fabrication of plutonium-enriched fuels, Métallurgie et Mécanique Nucléaires (MMN) fabricates enriched uranium fuels. Different types of fuel for both research reactors and power reactors are manufactured by MMN; examples of these are fuel elements with a core containing highly enriched uranium (90 per cent) alloy or fuels made of uranium metal or uranium-dioxide fuels. Uranium metal fuels have also been produced. An example is HARMONIE at Cadarache; the fuel contained uranium enriched to 93 per cent uranium-235. A large proportion of MMN's facilities are devoted to the production of uranium-dioxide fuels. The capacity of the plant may be about 200 000 kg of contained uranium dioxide in LWR fuel elements. [6]

Brazil

There has been some development work on fuel fabrication in Brazil at the Division of Nuclear Metallurgy of the Instituto de Energía Atomica where fuels using uranium and thorium oxides dispersed in aluminium for use in RE-SUCO subcritical assembly and for an Argonaut type of reactor are being developed. Ceramic fuels are also being investigated and there is a plan for a plant with a capacity of about 300 kg/month of uranium-dioxide pellets. [7]

Canada

In Canada the development of fuel fabrication began over a decade ago and now most fundamental research concerning fuel is being done by Atomic

Table 5. Some major contracts for Canadian fuel fabrication[a]

Reactor and country	Total order		Completed end-1970	
	About 1 000 kg U	Number of bundles	About 1 000 kg U	Number of bundles
NPD, Canada	16	1 200	16	1 200
Douglas Point, Canada	59	4 400	59	4 400
RAPP, India	24	1 800	24	1 800
KANUPP, Pakistan	40	3 000	40	3 000
Pickering, Canada	380	19 000	280	14 000
Gentilly, Canada	69	3 300	63	3 000
NPD,[a] Canada	13	1 000	13	1 000
Douglas Point,[a] Canada	56	4 200	45	3 400
Total	**657**	**37 900**	**540**	**31 800**

[a] Replacement fuel.

Source: Haywood, L. R. *et al.,* "Fuel for Canadian Power Reactors". *Peaceful Uses of Atomic Energy* [Proceedings of the Fourth International Conference, Geneva, 6–16 September 1971] Vol. 8 (New York, Vienna, UN and IAEA, 1972) pp. 185–99.

Energy of Canada Limited (AECL) while the manufacturing and designing is carried out by private industry. Some major contracts for Canadian fuel fabrication are given in table 5 and a forecast of the future Canadian demand is shown in table 6. Uranium-plutonium oxide fuel bundles and uranium carbide fuels have also been produced for testing in the NPD reactor. [8] There are four organizations offering fuel fabrication services: (1) Westinghouse Canada at Porthope, Ontario; (2) Canadian General Electric at Peterboro; (3) Combustion Engineering at Sherbrooke, Quebec and (4) a more recently organized firm, Moranda. [9]

France

While developing and producing fuels in its own specialized plants, the French Commisariat à l'Energie Atomique (CEA) has coordinated the activities of private industry in the manufacture of nuclear fuels. For a long time, work has been concentrated on fuels based on natural uranium metal

Table 6. Canadian fuel production and plant sizes

Year	Fabrication demand (about 1 000 kg U/year)	Maximum plant size (about 1 000 kgU/day)
1970	198	0.7
1975	493	1.6
1980	1 177	2.9
1985	2 735	5.0
1990	5 065	8.5

Source: Haywood, L. R. *et al.,* "Fuel for Canadian Power Reactors", *Peaceful Uses of Atomic Energy* [Proceedings of the Fourth International Conference, Geneva 6–16 September 1971] Vol. 8 (New York, Vienna, UN and IAEA, 1972) pp. 185–99.

for use in reactors abroad as well as within France. Zirconium-clad uranium-oxide fuels have been developed for use in nuclear submarine reactors. The CEA, in conjunction with several companies, is developing graphite-uranium-dioxide (or thorium-dioxide and uranium-dioxide) fuels for HTGRs. Work in progress on uranium-dioxide plutonium-dioxide fuels at the plutonium technology plant at Cadarache where the production capacity was initially about 4 kg per day with 25 per cent plutonium-dioxide content for the first Rapsodie cores. This has now increased to a capacity of 25 kg per day for the first core of Phénix on which production started in 1971. A considerable amount of automation has been introduced in the plant which has a potential capacity of about 20 000 kg/year of mixed oxide fuels for fast reactors. It is planned to extend this capacity further. All the fuel pins for Phénix will be produced at the Cadarache plant but the manufacture of the final assemblies will be shared between CERCA and SICN; the former carries out its own research, development and fabrication of all types of fuel elements. Uranium metal-cast fuel is fabricated at their Romans-Sur-Isère plant which has a capacity of about 600 000 kg/year of cast uranium elements. [10–11]

The Federal Republic of Germany

There are three major organizations in Germany (Alkem and Nukem at Wolfgang, Hanau at Bensberg and Interatom at Cologne) which are actively working in the field of fuel fabrication. Besides the fuel fabrication activities for the LWRs, these firms are engaged in the development of plutonium fuels for use in fast reactors as well as plutonium recycling in thermal reactors. The plutonium utilization in different types of fuels fabricated at the Alkem and Interatom plants are given in table 7. A new plant, established by Reaktor Brennelement GmbH at the beginning of 1971, fabricates uranium-dioxide fuel elements and has a capacity of about 400 000 kg/year. [12] A considerable amount of enriched uranium is accumulated at the Wolfgang site of Nukem facilities; some of this uranium is enriched to 93 per cent uranium-235 to be used in the thorium high-temperature reactor (THTR) fuels. [13] This is the "pebble-bed" designed reactor. Its core is a large tank which is filled with graphite spheres containing the highly enriched uranium fuel and thorium breeder material. The fuel is fabricated by the Nukem.

India

The main research and development on fuel fabrication for thermal and fast reactors in India is being carried out at the Bhabha Atomic Research Centre (BARC) where fuel elements for research reactors are manufactured. The BARC Atomic Fuels Division has fabricated half of the initial fuel for the Rajasthan Atomic Power Project (RAPP-1). Another plant, the Nuclear

Table 7. Comparison of plutonium utilization in different types of fuel

	Type of reactor		
	BWR	PWR	FB
Approx. capacity (kg/year)	40 000	40 000	10 000
Average pellet weight (g)	~20	~8	~1.5
Number of pellets per year	20×10^6	5×10^6	6.6×10^6
Plutonium content (per cent)	~2	~2	~20
Plutonium quantity corresponding to fuel capacity per year (kg)	800	800	2 000

Source: Höchel, J. *et al.,* "Fabrication and Irradiation of Plutonium-Bearing Fuel Pins for Thermal and Fast Reactors", *Peaceful Uses of Atomic Energy* [Proceedings of the Fourth International Conference, Geneva, 6–16 September 1971] Vol. 8 (New York, Vienna, UN and IAEA, 1972) pp. 281–94.

Fuels Complex (NFC) at Hydrabad, is now fulfilling the fuel replacement needs of Tarapur Nuclear Power Station and the initial requirements of the Kalpakkam Power Station. The NFC includes a ceramic fuel fabrication plant and a zircaloy fabrication plant. The plutonium-oxide fuel elements for the PURNIMA reactor at BARC were produced at BARC. [14–16]

Japan

In the long-range forecast prepared by the Electric Power Resources Development Coordination Council in 1970, the nuclear generating capacity in Japan was estimated to be 8 660 MW and 27 020 MW by the end of fiscal year 1975 and 1980 respectively. Anticipating this rapid growth of nuclear power plants, five private companies developed a significant fuel fabrication programme. The capacities of some of these firms are shown in table 8. [17] Japan Nuclear Fuel (JNF) plans to increase its capacity to about 490 000 kg/year while Mitsubishi Nuclear Fuel will operate in Tokai Mur at about 280 000 kg/year capacity. [18]

It is estimated that from the Japanese nuclear power plants about 15 000 kg of plutonium will be produced by 1980 and about 47 000 kg by 1985. Research and development on plutonium fuel is being carried out at the Japan Atomic Energy Research Institute (JAERI) facility. The Power Reactor and Nuclear Fuel Development Corporation (PNC) has established a Plutonium Fuel Development Laboratory to investigate the mixed oxide fuels. It is planned to recycle plutonium in thermal reactors until fast reactors become available. [19] Moreover the Nuclear Fuel Company plans to start fabrication of HTGR fuel for JAERI at the rate of 100 kg/year. [20]

The United Kingdom

In Britain, the United Kingdom Atomic Energy Authority (UKAEA), which is mainly concerned with research and development work, and British Nu-

Table 8. Nuclear fuel fabrication facilities in Japan

Facilities	Fuel type	Approx. capacity (kg/year)	Start
Sumitoma Electric	Plate type	–	August 1969
Furukawa Electric	Plate type	–	November 1969
Mitsubishi Atomic	Plate type	–	August 1969
Japan Nuclear Fuel (JNF)	Rod type for LWR	270 000	July 1970
Mitsubishi Atomic	Rod type for LWR	100 000	April 1970
Sumitoma Electric	Rod type for LWR	80 000	July 1972

Source: White Papers of Japan—1970–71, Annual abstract of official reports and statistics of the Japanese Government (Japan Institute of International Affairs, 1972) pp. 19–24.

clear Fuels Ltd. (BNFL) are the main organizations which fabricate nuclear fuel. In one of the BNFL's uranium metal fuel plants (at Springfields, Preston) fuels for the Magnox type gas-cooled reactors are fabricated in a plant that has a capacity in excess of about 2 500 000 kg of uranium per year as finished fuel elements. Uranium-dioxide fuel pellets, mainly for use in the UK MK II gas-cooled reactors (AGR's), are produced in another plant which has an annual throughput of about 300 000 kg uranium as uranium-dioxide pellets. There are three more plants which produce fuel pins: stainless steel pins are fabricated in one which has an annual output of about 500 000 kg uranium as finished fuel; in the other two, stainless steel and zirconium pins are fabricated. Each of these two plants has an annual capacity of about 100 000 kg uranium as finished fuel suitable for UK steam generation heavy water reactors, BWRs, PWRs, and fast reactors. A coated particle fuel plant has a capacity of about 5 000 kg per year and it is planned to increase this to about 20 000 kg uranium per year. A uranium-carbide fuel plant provides fabrications of fuels for the fast reactor programme and it is expected to have a capacity of 5 000 kg uranium per year. [21] A BNFL plant for the production of mixed oxide fuel at Windscale has a capacity for fuel fabrication of about 10 000 kg/year. This plant will produce recycle fuel for thermal reactors and the fuel capacity may amount to about 100 000 kg/year. It is planned to have a plant with a capacity of 120 000 kg to 180 000 kg/year for thermal recycle fuel. [11]

The United States

The estimated demands for fuel fabrication in the United States are given in table 9. At present there are nine industrial firms offering fuel fabrication for LWRs and one firm is offering fuels for the HTGR. Mostly uranium-dioxide-fuelled cores are fabricated at the moment, but as the plutonium stockpile from LWRs increases, mixed uranium-plutonium-oxide fuels will become available for recycle. The LWR fuel designs are based on an assembly of fuel rods containing ceramic fuel pellets; the HTGR fuel ele-

Table 9. Forecast for 1972 US fuel fabrication needs[a]

Thousands of kilogrammes

Year	LWR UO₂	LWR mixed oxide	HTGR fissile	HTGR fertile	FBR mixed oxide	FBR blanket
1972	750	0	1	11	0	0
1975	1 970	0	0	2	0	0
1978	3 300	400	3	62	0	0
1981	5 300	480	9	148	7	2
1984	7 400	1 000	19	300	19	4
1987	10 300	1 080	32	460	180	75
1990	14 000	168	44	580	850	310
1995	17 700	0	60	730	3 300	1 150
2000	19 700	0	70	830	6 900	2 500

[a] The analysis includes plutonium recycling and 86 LMFBR.

Source: Nuclear Power 1973–2000, US AEC Report WASH-1139(72), December 1972.

ments consist of a graphite block filled with spherical particles coated with pyrolytic carbon and silicon carbide.

Of the eight firms producing nuclear fuels for LWRs, about 95 per cent of the fabrication is performed by only the four which are listed in table 10. The figures for the fabrication demands given in the table may give an idea of the plant sizes since actual plant capacities are not known. The remaining four firms are the United Nuclear Corporation, the Atlantic Richfield-Numec, the Jersey Nuclear Company and the Gulf General Atomic (GGA). The fuel for HTGRs is offered by GGA. The current requirements for fuel are 20 000 kg of uranium-235 and thorium which means that there has to be a fabrication capacity of about 100 kg/day. There are no facilities for recycle of uranium-233 fuel but there is an extensive programme for the development of refabrication of uranium-233 at GGA and Oak Ridge National Laboratories. [19]

The development of plutonium fuels has been established at the Westinghouse Plutonium Fuels Development Laboratory and it is estimated that a plant with a capacity of about 10 000 kg/year would be sufficient for

Table 10. Demand for fuel fabrication from the four major US fabrication plants

Kilogrammes per day

Year	Babcock & Wilcox	Combustion Engineering	General Electric	Westinghouse
1970	100	300	1 300	700
1975	1 200	800	4 000	2 800
1980	3 100	2 200	9 200	7 100

Source: Lotts, A. L. *et al.,* "The Status of Thermal Reactor Fuel Manufacture in the United States", *Peaceful Uses of Atomic Energy* [Proceedings of the Fourth International Conference, Geneva, 6–16 September, 1971] Vol. 8 (New York, Vienna, UN and IAEA, 1972) pp. 201–14.

present needs. Other major plutonium plants are operated by General Electric and Babcock and Wilcox which has recently acquired the Numec organization which had built up a considerable plutonium facility at Leechburg, Pennsylvania. Other independent companies fabricating plutonium fuels are Jersey Nuclear and Gulf United Nuclear, which may, in the near future, plan for a major commercial plutonium facility since the fuel assemblies have been made for some German and British facilities. Nuclear Fuel Services has begun the production of mixed oxide fuels and is planning to construct a large plutonium fuel plant. Kerr-McGee has a plant for production of fuels for fast breeder reactors and commercial thermal power reactors. Finally, Atomics International has developed fuel production facilities and has an exchange agreement with the UKAEA on fast reactor fuel technology. [11]

V. *Conclusions*

The fuel fabrication programmes of only a few countries have been considered in the above discussion although it can be seen from table 11 that there are a number of other countries with significant nuclear programmes. Many of the countries shown in table 11 have fuel fabrication facilities on a smaller scale and there are some countries which may have extensive fabrication programmes without details of their plants being available, such as the People's Republic of China and the Soviet Union. What little is known about other countries indicates the increasing availability of large quantities of nuclear material, particularly those which may be diverted from peaceful uses to nonpeaceful uses. For example, the rate of production of plutonium in countries other than the Soviet Union, the People's Republic of China and the Eastern European countries, will rise to 6300 kg/year from its present rate of 1400 kg/year. By 1985 the rate is expected to be 100000 kg/year. In some countries plutonium is stockpiled rather than recycled in thermal reactors.

Another example is the case of highly enriched uranium used in high-temperature reactors. In the Federal Republic of Germany large quantities of such uranium are stockpiled for use in their 300 MW(e) (net) prototype demonstration THTR at Schmehausen (Ventrop); the fuel inventory of the reactor is 650 kg uranium enriched to 93 per cent uranium-235 and 6490 kg thorium, both fabricated in some 674000 fuel elements. [22] Although it is planned to construct a large 1200 MWe commercial THTR, the future of this pebble-bed THTR design is in some doubt because of the difficult technology. [23] The economics of such reactors is also questioned. [24] If the decision to build goes against the THTR, there will be a substantial quantity of highly enriched uranium available.

Table 11 a. Number of research reactors

Country	In opera- tion	Under con- struction	Planned
Arab Republic of Egypt	1	–	–
Argentina	5	–	–
Australia	2	–	–
Austria	3	–	–
Belgium	5	–	–
Brazil	3	–	–
Bulgaria	1	–	–
Canada	8	–	–
Colombia	1	–	–
Czechoslovakia	3	–	–
Denmark	3	–	–
FR Germany	28	3	–
Finland	1	–	–
France	23	–	–
Greece	1	–	–
Hungary	2	–	–
India	3	–	–
Indonesia	1	–	–
Iran	1	–	–
Iraq	1	–	–
Israel	2	–	–
Italy	16	–	–
Japan	21	2	–
Korea, Rep. of	1	–	–
Mexico	1	–	–
Netherlands	7	1	–
Norway	4	–	–
Pakistan	1	–	–
Philippines	1	–	–
Poland	3	1	–
Portugal	1	–	–
Romania	1	–	–
South Africa	2	–	–
Spain	5	–	–
Sweden	5	–	–
Switzerland	6	–	–
Thailand	1	–	–
Turkey	1	–	–
USSR	25	–	–
United Kingdom	23	–	1
USA	121	9	4
Uruguay	1	–	–
Venezuela	1	–	–
Viet-Nam, South	1	–	–
Yugoslavia	3	–	–
Zaïre, Rep. of	1	–	–
Chile	–	1	–
Cuba	–	1	–

Source: Power and Research Reactors in Member States, International Atomic Energy Agency, 1972.

Table 11 b. Number of power reactors

Country	Experimental reactors			Power reactors			
	In operation	Under construction	Shut down	In operation	Under construction	Planned	Shut down
Argentina	–	–	–	–	1	1	–
Australia	–	–	–	–	–	1	–
Austria	–	–	–	–	1	–	–
Bangladesh	–	–	–	–	–	1	–
Belgium	1	–	–	–	2	1	–
Brazil	–	–	–	–	1	–	–
Bulgaria	–	–	–	–	1	3	–
Canada	–	–	–	6	1	1	–
Czechoslovakia	–	–	–	1	–	4	–
DR Germany	...	...	...	1	1	1	–
FR Germany	3	–	–	12	5	14	–
Finland	–	–	–	–	2	1	–
France	–	–	1	11	3	3	–
Hungary	–	–	–	–	–	1	–
India	–	–	–	1	2	1	–
Israel	–	–	–	–	–	1	–
Italy	–	–	–	4	2	2	–
Japan	1	–	–	6	14	26	–
Korea, Rep. of	–	–	–	–	1	–	–
Mexico	–	–	–	–	–	1	–
Netherlands	–	–	–	1	1	–	–
Norway	–	–	–	1	–	1	–
Pakistan	–	–	–	1	–	–	–
South Africa	–	–	–	–	–	1	–
Spain	–	–	–	3	1	8	–
Sweden	1	–	–	2	6	5	1
Switzerland	–	–	1	3	–	8	1
Taiwan	...	...	...	–	2	2	–
Thailand	–	–	–	–	–	1	–
USSR	2	1	2	12	2	10	1
United Kingdom	1	–	–	15	6	–	–
USA	3	–	10	32	57	102	12
Yugoslavia	–	–	–	–	–	1	–

– = no reactors; . . . = data not available.

Sources: Power and Research Reactors in Member States, International Atomic Energy Agency, 1972. "Power Reactors '73", *Nuclear Engineering International,* Vol. 18, No. 203, April 1973, pp. 327–62.

References

1. Boxer, L. W. *et al.*, "Uranium Resources, Production and Demand", *Peaceful Uses of Atomic Energy* [Proceedings of the Fourth International Conference, Geneva, 6–16 September 1971] Vol. 8 (New York, Vienna, UN and IAEA, 1972) pp. 3–22.
2. Lotts, A. L. *et al.*, "The Status of Thermal Reactor Fuel Manufacture in the United States", *Peaceful Uses of Atomic Energy* [Proceedings of the Fourth International Conference, Geneva, 6–16 September 1971] Vol. 8 (New York, Vienna, UN and IAEA, 1972) pp. 201–14.
3. "Nuclear Power Programme in Argentina", *Nuclear Engineering International,* Vol. 16, No. 184, September 1971, p. 747.

4. "Development of Nuclear Energy in the Republic of Argentina", *Bulletin, IAEA,* Vol. 14, No. 6, 1972, pp. 3–9.
5. Goens, J., "The Nuclear Energy Research Centre CEN-SCK", *Nuclear Engineering International,* Vol. 16, No. 180, May 1971, pp. 331–34.
6. Maldague, P., "Activities and Associations of Belgonucléaire and MMN", *Nuclear Engineering International,* Vol. 16, No. 180, May 1971, pp. 334–36.
7. "Bold First Step in Brazil", *Nuclear Engineering International,* Vol. 16, No. 184, September 1971, p. 751.
8. Gray, J. L., "Canada, The CANDU and the Future", *Bulletin, IAEA,* Vol. 14, No. 6, 1972, pp. 11–15.
9. *Nuclear Engineering International,* Vol. 18, No. 203, April 1973, p. 281.
10. "Fuel Cycle Activities of the CEA", *Nuclear Engineering International,* Vol. 17, No. 196, September 1972, pp. 692–95.
11. Rippon S. E., "Plutonium—Problems and Possibilities", *Nuclear Engineering International,* Vol. 17, No. 189, February 1972, pp. 85–92.
12. *Nuclear Engineering International,* Vol. 16, No. 178, March 1971, p. 151.
13. *Nuclear Engineering International,* Vol. 16, No. 181, June 1971, p. 450.
14. "Nuclear Fuel", *Nuclear India,* Vol. 10, No. 9, May 1972, pp. 1–2.
15. "Fuel for PURNIMA", *Nuclear India,* Vol. 10, No. 10–11, June/July 1972, pp. 10–11.
16. *Nuclear Engineering International,* Vol. 17, No. 191, April 1972, p. 271.
17. *White Papers of Japan—1970–71,* Annual abstract of official reports and statistics of the Japanese Government (Japan Institute of International Affairs. 1972) pp. 19–24.
18. *Nuclear Engineering International,* Vol. 17, No. 189, February 1972, p. 76.
19. "Development and Utilization of Nuclear Energy in Japan", *Nuclear Engineering International,* Vol. 14, May 1969, pp. 398–401.
20. *Nuclear Engineering International,* Vol. 17, No. 198, November 1972, p. 904.
21. Royan, H. *et al.,* "Fuel Fabrication Processes at the Springfield Works of British Nuclear Fuels Ltd.", *Peaceful Uses of Atomic Energy* [Proceedings of the Fourth International Conference, Geneva, 6–16 September 1971] Vol. 8 (New York, Vienna, UN and IAEA, 1972) pp. 215–24.
22. "Power Reactors '73", *Nuclear Engineering International,* Vol. 18, No. 203, April 1973, pp. 327–62.
23. *Nuclear Engineering International,* Vol. 17, No. 194, July 1972, pp. 511–12.
24. Dahlberg, R. C. and Colby, L. J., "Th vs U Cycle", *Nuclear Engineering International,* Vol. 16, No. 187, December 1971, p. 965.

6. Nuclear fuel reprocessing plants

B. M. JASANI

Abstract

A considerable amount of fissile material will become available at nuclear fuel reprocessing plants. The technology involved in the reprocessing of spent fuels from nuclear reactors is, therefore, briefly described and reprocessing plants in various countries are also surveyed. Methods of storing nuclear waste products and the problems associated with them are indicated.

I. *Introduction*

After the fabrication of nuclear reactor fuel elements, the next stage in the fuel cycle is the use of fuel in power reactors. A fuel element in a reactor operating at a reasonable load factor has a life of about three years, after which, even though the fuel element may still have a considerable amount of fissionable material remaining, it is removed from the reactor for technical reasons. The spent fuel is transported from the reactor to a reprocessing plant where the fissionable material is separated from the radioactive wastes known as fission products. The reprocessing plants are specially designed facilities where not only are the uranium and plutonium separated and purified from fission products, but the plutonium is also converted to a form suitable for long-term storage. The problem of storage is a difficult one since the amount of radioactivity which will accumulate in time is very large and it will take a very long time before this amount decays.

Because a single reprocessing plant can handle the spent fuel from many reactors, only a few such plants exist at present; however, this situation may change rapidly as the number of power plants increases. This is evident from table 1 in which a forecast of the demands for reprocessing on a worldwide basis is given.

In the following section, the technology involved in the reprocessing of spent fuels is briefly described and reprocessing plants in various countries are surveyed.

II. *Reprocessing of spent fuels*

It can be seen from table 1 that substantial reprocessing of fuels from fast reactors will be required by about the year 2000. A method known as the

Table 1. Estimated world fuel reprocessing requirements[a]

Thousands of kilogrammes

Year	LWR Mixed oxide	HTGR Fissile	HTGR Fertile	FBR Mixed oxide
1972	95	0	0	0
1975	1 450	0	2	9
1978	3 520	0	4	9
1981	6 900	1	24	15
1984	11 400	3	85	65
1987	17 000	8	206	123
1990	24 100	16	401	377
1995	36 300	31	770	3 610
2000	46 300	45	1 100	10 800

[a] The analyses include plutonium recycling and 86 LMFBRs.

Source: Nuclear Power, 1973–2000, US Atomic Energy Commission, WASH-1139, December 1972.

Purex process for the recovery of uranium and plutonium for light water reactor (LWR) fuels is used in nearly all the major reprocessing facilities. The same process could be used, with some modifications, to reprocess fuels from fast reactors such as the liquid metal fast breeder reactor (LMFBR). Therefore, in describing the reprocessing of fuels for this paper, only the Purex process will be considered. However, nuclear fuel has to pass through a number of stages prior to the Purex process. These are described below.

Fuel cooling

Irradiated fuel is removed from a reactor and transported to the reprocessing plant by road or rail. There is still a considerable amount of heat produced within the fuel elements due to the presence of many radioactive materials. Several short-lived fission products are present; therefore, the fuel elements are kept either at the reactor site or at the reprocessing plant for a cooling period prior to reprocessing. This period varies with the different fuels used. For example, in table 2, the amount of heat still generated after 30-day and 150-day delays in fuels for LWR and LMFBR are shown. For economic reasons, short cooling periods for LMFBR fuels are often preferred, but it increases the problems of handling the LMFBR fuels because some of the volatile short-lived fission products such as iodine, xenon, krypton and tritium are also present in large amounts.

Fuel element preparation

Before uranium, plutonium and the fission products can be separated, it is essential to remove the fuel cladding. Two methods are used: one is to dissolve the cladding in chemicals; the other to remove the cladding mechanically by automatic decladding machines. The chemical decladding methods

Table 2. Comparison of fuel discharged from LWRs and future LMFBRs

	Typical LMFBR		Typical LWR	
	Ore	Mixed core-blankets	Pu recycle	Enriched UO_2
Burnup, MWd/metric ton fuel	80 000	30 000	33 000	33 000
Average specific power, kW/kg fuel	150	58	30	30
Decay heat, W/kg fuel				
30-day decay	200	80	50	50
150-day decay	75	30	20	20
Plutonium content, g/kg fuel	190	86	27	9

Source: Ferguson, D. E. *et al.,* "Recovery of Liquid-Metal Fast-Breeder Reactor (LMFBR) Fuels—Development of Techniques", *Peaceful Uses of Atomic Energy* [Proceedings of the Fourth International Conference, Geneva, 6–16 September 1971] Vol. 8 (New York, Vienna, UN and IAEA, 1972) pp. 395–410.

are generally not preferred because they have capacity limitations and large volumes of liquid wastes are produced. The mechanical method may consist of one of the following techniques: (1) The cladding may be stripped off by means of manipulators but this is an awkward operation and occasionally loss of fuel occurs. (2) The fuel-containing portion of the fuel-pin is cut into small lengths and placed in a leach liquor containing nitric acid and some ferric nitrate and, after leaching the fuel, the cladding hulls are removed. (3) The fuel element is sheared into small pieces of one to five centimetre lengths and the sheared pieces are collected into canisters which are then placed into leach liquor. [1–3] The last two methods are in general use and are basically similar for fuels from thermal reactors and fast reactors. An alternate method for removing cladding from fast reactor fuels is to dissolve the stainless clad in zinc. This process is still in the experimental stage.

Separation of fissile materials

After the fuel solution is formed it is treated chemically to separate uranium and plutonium by a Purex solvent-extraction process. The solvent used is tributyl phosphate in either n-dodecane or odourless kerosene. During the

Table 3. Cost of reprocessing fuels, including conversion, from different types of reactor *US $/kg*

Reactor	Initial	Year 2020
LWR (without Pu recycle)	34	22
LWR (with Pu recycle)	53	22
HTGR (with LMFBR)	69	34
LMFBR (introduction in 1986), including core and blanket fuel	38	30

Source: Cost-Benefit Analysis of the U.S. Breeder Reactor Program, US Atomic Energy Commission, WASH-1184, January 1972.

Table 4. Reprocessing plants

Country/ name of plant	Type of fuel reprocessed and separated	Capacity 1 000 kg/ year	Starting date
Argentina			
A pilot reprocessing plant;	–	–	–
A small chemical separation plant	Plutonium	–	1969
Belgium			
Eurochemic	Natural and slightly enriched uranium—MTR elements	100	1966
Czechoslovakia			
Uranium Industry Chemical plant (Mydlovary);	–	–	–
Nuclear Fuel Institute (Zbraslav)	–	–	–
France[a]			
Marcoule	Natural uranium	900–1 200	1958
La Hague	Natural metallic uranium;	800	1966
	(slightly enriched uranium oxide)	900	1975
FR Germany			
Karlsruhe (WAK)	Slightly enriched uranium oxide	35–50	1971
GWK	Slightly enriched uranium oxide	40	1964
India			
Chemical separation plant	–	–	–
Italy			
Eurex-1	Slightly enriched fuels;	10	–
	MTR, natural uranium	25	1970
ITREC	Uranium–thorium fuels	4	1969
Japan			
Tokai	Slightly enriched uranium oxide and natural uranium	260	1974
Spain			
Small chemical separation plant	–	–	–
UK			
Windscale	Natural metallic uranium;	2 500	1964
	Slightly enriched uranium oxide;	300	1970
	Slightly enriched uranium oxide;	800	1977
Dounreay	Highly enriched fuels	5–10	1958
USA			
West Valley (NFS)	Uranium oxide and uranium–plutonium oxide up to about 5 per cent enrichment	~130	1966
Morris (MFRP)	Fuels enriched to about 5 per cent in U-235 or equivalent plutonium reactivity	300	1971
South Carolina (BNFP)	Fuels enriched to about 5 per cent in U-235 or equivalent plutonium reactivity	1 500	1974
South Carolina (ARC)	Fuels enriched to about 3 per cent in U-235; also capable of processing mixed oxide (UO_2–PuO_2) fuels and higher enrichment fuels up to 5 per cent U-235	–	1976

[a] It is planned to discontinue activities on natural uranium at the La Hague plant.

Sources:
Albonetti, A., "Europe and Nuclear Energy", *The Atlantic Papers* 2 (Atlantic Institute for International Affairs, 1972) pp. 57–58.

first stage of the solvent extraction process, uranium and plutonium are separated from each other and almost completely from the fission products. Two more stages follow to complete purification of the uranium product. Final purification of plutonium is achieved by an anion exchange treatment. The reprocessing of fuels from fast reactors is essentially the same; the differences are due to higher plutonium content in the fuel solutions and their greater amount of radioactivity because of shorter cooling times. The radionuclides contributing to the radioactivity are mainly the volatile fission products tritium, iodine, krypton and xenon. These are removed by a process called voloxidation in which uranium-dioxide plutonium-dioxide fuel is heated in an oxidizing atmosphere. When oxidation occurs, volatile fission gases are released. [1–3]

Reprocessing costs

Very little information is available on the costs of reprocessing. However, in a recent analysis made by the United States Atomic Energy Commission, the reprocessing costs for fuels from various types of reactor have been compared. The results are shown in table 3.

III. *Reprocessing plants*

The amount of fuel from power reactors is, at present, relatively small but most countries are active in developing plans and reprocessing technology for both thermal reactor and fast reactor fuels. A brief survey of some of the existing plants is given below and summarized in table 4.

Argentina

Reprocessing plants on an industrial scale are not contemplated for the near future but three pilot plants have been built. [4] Information on the capacity of these plants is not available.

Boyle, J. E. *et al.*, "Operating Experience with the United Kingdom Fuel Reprocessing Plants at Windscale and Dounreay", *Peaceful Uses of Atomic Energy* [Proceedings of the Fourth International Conference, Geneva, 6–16 September 1971] Vol. 8 (New York, Vienna, UN and IAEA, 1972) pp. 525–34.
"Fuel Cycle Activities of the CEA", *Nuclear Engineering International*, Vol. 17, No. 196, September 1972, pp. 692–95.
Huges, T. G. *et al.*, "Development Design and Operation of the Oxide Fuel Reprocessing Plant at the Windscale Works of British Nuclear Fuels Ltd.", *Peaceful Uses of Atomic Energy* [Proceedings of the Fourth International Conference, Geneva, 6–16 September 1971] Vol. 8 (New York, Vienna, UN and IAEA, 1972) pp. 367–73.
International Atomic Energy Agency, *Annual Report*, GC (XVI)/480, 1 July 1971–30 June 1972, p. 52.
Nuclear Engineering International, Vol. 16, No. 186, November 1971, p. 895, 899.
Nuclear India, Vol. 10, No. 9, May 1972, p. 2.
Nuclear Engineering International, Vol. 17, No. 188, January 1972, p. 10.
Sinclair, E. E. *et al.*, "Existing and Projected Plants and Processes for Thermal Reactor Fuel Recovery: Experience and Plans", *Peaceful Uses of Atomic Energy* [Proceedings of the Fourth International Conference, Geneva, 6–16 September 1971] Vol. 8 (New York, Vienna, UN and IAEA, 1972) pp. 445–58.

Belgium

Belgonucléaire has a facility for reprocessing irradiated fuels, particularly the fuels from fast reactors. Research on volatization by fluoridation of uranium and plutonium is being carried out in collaboration with Centre d'Etude de l'Energie Nucléaire. [5] A major facility, the European Company for the Chemical Processing of Irradiated Fuels (Eurochemie) was started in 1966 as a joint undertaking sponsored by the OECD Nuclear Energy Agency. This plant, with a capacity of about 100000 kg per year, is capable of reprocessing different types of fuel. [6]

France

The French Commissariat à l'Energie Atomique (CEA) has two main fuel reprocessing plants designed mainly to reprocess metal fuels from the natural uranium gas-cooled graphite-moderated reactors. These plants are situated at Marcoule in the south of France and La Hague near Cherbourg. Both the plants were originally designed to meet the needs of the French military programmes. The Marcoule plant has been in operation since 1958 and was designed to reprocess large amounts of very slightly irradiated uranium to satisfy the military requirements. The plant is now also reprocessing highly irradiated metal fuels and fuels from "materials testing" reactors (MTRs). The plant has a capacity of about a million kilogrammes per year. The La Hague plant has been in operation since 1967 and it is similar in design to the Marcoule facility. It is being modified to allow processing of fuels from fast breeder reactors and LWRs. This plant also has a capacity of about a million kilogrammes per year. [7–8]

The Federal Republic of Germany

In 1967 the construction of a prototype reprocessing plant began at the Karlsruhe Nuclear Research Centre. The plant, with a capacity of about 40000 kg per year, began treating irradiated fuels in September 1971. It is operated by the Gesellschaft zur Wiederaufarbeitung von Kernbrennstoffen (GWK). A new concern, the United Reprocessors GmbH, has been jointly organized by British Nuclear Fuels (BNFL), the CEA and Kernbrennstoff-Wiederaufarbeitung-Gesellschaft GmbH (KEWA) to process low enriched uranium dioxide. [9]

India

At Tarapur, construction of the main plant for reprocessing fuels from power reactors has been completed. There is a plutonium processing facility at the Bhabha Atomic Research Centre (BARC) where the processing of irradiated thorium for the recovery of uranium-233 is also carried out. At the Reactor Research Centre, Kalpakkam, work is being done to start a reprocessing development laboratory. [10]

Japan

The first reprocessing plant built by Power Reactor and Nuclear Fuel Development Corporation (PNC) in Tokai may start operation in 1974 with an expected capacity of about 7 000 kg per day. However, as there will be an added requirement of about 3 000 kg per-day capacity by 1982, the Japan Atomic Energy Commission (JAEC) is making plans for a reprocessing plant to be organized by private industry. This plant may be built outside Japan. [11]

The United Kingdom

There are two reprocessing plants in Britain, one at Windscale and the other at Dounreay. The latter plant processes fuels from MTRs and from the Dounreay fast reactor. The Windscale plant processes fuels from thermal reactors. The capacities of these plants are shown in table 4. [3, 12]

The United States

Here there are two commercial reprocessing plants in operation. The first plant to be built in the United States was the Nuclear Fuel Services (NFS) plant at West Valley, New York, which started in 1966. The capacity of this plant is about one thousand kilogrammes per day but there are plans to increase this to two or three thousand kilogrammes per day of LWR fuel. The second reprocessing plant, the construction of which was completed in 1971, is General Electric's Midwest Fuel Recovery Plant (MFRP) at Morris, Illinois. The capacity of this facility is about one thousand kilogrammes per day of fuels from LWR. General Electric is planning to expand its nuclear fuel reprocessing capacity probably by constructing one or more large plants. [13] A third plant, the Allied-Gulf Barnwell Nuclear Fuel Plant (BNFP) near Barnwell, South Carolina, is designed to reprocess about 5 000 kg per day of LWR oxide fuel. [2]

The Soviet Union

Similar methods to those described above are used in the Soviet Union for reprocessing reactor fuels; however, no information is available on the number of plants, their capacities or locations.

Table 5. Expected waste accumulation in the USA during the next 50 years

	Half-lives (years)	Amount of radioactivity (10^6 curies)	
		Conventional thermal reactors	Fast breeder reactors
Total accumulated wastes (mainly shortlived)		142 700	523 300
Longlived components of above:			
Strontium-90	28	13 900	15 500
Caesium-137	27	18 900	38 600
Plutonium	24 400	0.438	8.01

Source: Tinker, J., "Breeders: Risks Man Dare Not Run", *New Scientist,* 1 March 1973, pp. 437–76.

IV. *Nuclear waste*

A considerable amount of radioactive waste is produced when fuel is burnt in a nuclear reactor. In table 5, for example, the expected waste accumulation in the United States during the next 50 years is shown. After reprocessing the fuel, radioactive wastes are, at present, stored either in nitric acid or in neutralized solutions in specially constructed tanks. These containers have to be cooled because a considerable amount of heat is produced by the radioactive materials. In the United States considerably more than 300 million litres of such liquid wastes have been collected during the past 30 years. [14] The possibility of converting liquid wastes into solids is also being investigated.

The problem of storage has not been solved satisfactorily. A number of suggestions have been made but difficulties arise because of the considerable quantity of accumulated radioactive products, some of them having half-lives of 20 years or more. This means that it would take several centuries before they decay to a safe level. Even longer periods are necessary for fuels from fast breeder reactors since, as is shown in table 2, these contain a greater amount of plutonium-239 than that produced in thermal reactors. This plutonium, with a half-life of 24 400 years, will remain dangerous for perhaps 200 000 years. Therefore, if waste is stored, the storage method not only has to be safe but it has to survive for a very long time. The waste also has to be under surveillance. Several methods of storage have been considered: one is to place the waste in deep rock caverns, another is to place it in deep unused wells and yet another is to put the waste into bedded salt. Serious thought has been given to the last-mentioned in the United States and the Federal Republic of Germany. Suggestions have also been made for storing the waste under the Antarctic icecap. [15]

Alternatively, waste could be disposed of by such means as casting it permanently into outer space or onto the sun. However, the method is not without dangers and the cost of electricity could increase by 0.2 to 2 mills/kWhr(e). [16]

V. Conclusions

Efforts are now being made to improve the reprocessing techniques. These have met with some success but there remain problems for which solutions have not been found, such as finding a satisfactory way to transport the irradiated fuels from reactors to reprocessing plants. It is estimated that with a million megawatts of nuclear power (one-third of which may be due to the breeder reactors) there will be 7 000 to 12 000 annual shipments of spent fuels between reactors and reprocessing plants. Each shipment may contain some 75 megacuries of radioactive substances. At present about seven megacuries from LWR fuels may be carried by each shipment. [17] Such large quantities of radioactivity have to be provided with radiation shields and containers which can withstand natural and unnatural disasters. The question of nuclear waste storage or disposal needs considerable thought.

References

1. Ferguson, D. E. *et al.*, "Recovery of Liquid-Metal Fast-Breeder Reactor (LMFBR) Fuels—Development of Techniques", *Peaceful Uses of Atomic Energy* [Proceedings of the Fourth International Conference, Geneva, 6–16 September 1971] Vol. 8 (New York, Vienna, UN and IAEA, 1972) pp. 395–410.
2. Sinclair, E. E. *et al.*, "Existing and Projected Plants and Processes for Thermal Reactor Fuel Recovery: Experience and Plans", *Peaceful Uses of Atomic Energy* [Proceedings of the Fourth International Conference, Geneva, 6–16 September 1971] Vol. 8 (New York, Vienna, UN and IAEA, 1972) pp. 445–58.
3. Boyle, J. G. *et al.*, "Operating Experience with the United Kingdom Fuel Reprocessing Plans at Windscale and Dounreay", *Peaceful Uses of Atomic Energy* [Proceedings of the Fourth International Conference, Geneva, 6–16 September 1971] Vol. 8 (New York, Vienna, UN and IAEA, 1972) pp. 525–34.
4. International Atomic Energy Agency, *Annual Report,* GC (XVI)/480, 1 July 1971–30 June 1972, p. 52.
5. Maldague, P., "Activities and Association of Belgonucléaire and MMN", *Nuclear Engineering International,* Vol. 16, No. 180, May 1971, pp. 334–36.
6. Albonetti, A., "Europe and Nuclear Energy", *The Atlantic Papers 2* (Atlantic Institute for International Affairs, 1972) pp. 57–58.
7. "Fuel Cycle Activities of the CEA", *Nuclear Engineering International,* Vol. 17, No. 196, September 1972, pp. 692–95.
8. Anchapt, P., "Adaptation des Usines Françaises de Retraitement à de Nouveaux Types de Combustibles Irradiés, *Peaceful Uses of Atomic Energy*

[Proceedings of the Fourth International Conference, Geneva, 6–16 September 1971] Vol. 8 (New York, Vienna, UN and IAEA, 1972) pp. 547–57.

9. *Nuclear Engineering International,* Vol. 16, No. 186, November 1971, pp. 899, 895.

10. *Nuclear India,* Vol. 10, No. 9, May 1972, p. 2.

11. *Nuclear Engineering International,* Vol. 17, No. 188, January 1972, p. 10.

12. Huges, T. G. *et al.,* "Development Design and Operation of the Oxide Fuel Reprocessing Plant at the Windscale Works of British Nuclear Fuels Ltd.", *Peaceful Uses of the Atomic Energy* [Proceedings of the Fourth International Conference, Geneva, 6–16 September 1971] Vol. 8 (New York, Vienna, UN and IAEA, 1972) pp. 367–73.

13. *Nuclear Engineering International,* Vol. 18, No. 203, April 1973, p. 286.

14. Holden, C., "Nuclear Waste: Kansas Riled by AEC Plans for Atom Dump", *Science,* Vol. 172, 16 April 1971, p. 249.

15. Zeller, E. J. *et al.,* "Putting Radioactive Wastes on Ice", *Bulletin of the Atomic Scientists,* Vol. 29, No. 1, January 1973.

16. Weinberg, A. M., "Social Institution and Nuclear Energy", *Science,* Vol. 177, 7 July 1972, pp. 27–34.

17. Inglis, D. R., *Nuclear Energy: Its Physics and Its Social Challenge* (Addison-Wesley Publishing Company, 1973) p. 325.

7. Uranium enrichment and the proliferation of nuclear weapons

P. BOSKMA

Abstract

Uranium enrichment plants on an industrial scale, still limited to the territories of the nuclear-weapon states, can be expected to proliferate to non-nuclear-weapon states in the next 15 years. Because of the expected shortage of enriched uranium by the end of this decade, new plants must be built and the monopoly position of the USA in the capitalist world will certainly be challenged. Non-nuclear-weapon countries like FR Germany, Japan, India, Australia, Canada and Zaïre have economic interests in this field, partly because of their level of nuclear reactor technology, partly because of their resources in natural uranium.

The access to uranium enrichment is also important for countries that want to keep an option open on nuclear weapons, especially thermonuclear weapons. It could be speculated that this aspect plays a role for some political groups in countries like FR Germany, India and Japan.

The Non-Proliferation Treaty does not hinder the proliferation of uranium enrichment facilities to non-nuclear-weapon states. Moreover it does not safeguard the spread of enrichment technologies. Of the countries indicated, FR Germany, Japan and Zaïre have so far signed but not ratified the treaty, while India and South Africa have not signed the treaty at all.

I. *Introduction*

This chapter discusses the present state of affairs with regard to the spread of uranium enrichment facilities around the world and the implications for the proliferation of nuclear weapons. Until now enrichment plants on an industrial scale have been limited to the territories of the nuclear-weapon states. The present situation constitutes practically a monopoly position for the USA in the capitalist world as a supplier of enriched uranium for nuclear fission reactors. This position will almost certainly be challenged during the next decade. Although quite a number of contacts between countries and big industrial companies about joint ventures on uranium enrichment are kept secret because of the commercial interests involved, a rather clear picture emerges. Several currently near-nuclear countries will almost certainly get direct access to the enriching of uranium, the only sector of nuclear technology still kept secret. Moreover, as has been discussed in the chapter, "Uranium enrichment technologies and the demand for enriched uranium", several new technologies not under the control of the nuclear-weapon states are in development. The centrifuge and jet nozzle processes are in the pilot plant stage and laser techniques and the use of rotating plasma are still in the laboratory phase but are promising as second generation enrichment techniques.

The Non-Proliferation Treaty, concluded in 1970, is an attempt to differentiate between the military and peaceful applications of nuclear technology. In its philosophy it tries not to discriminate between nuclear-weapon and non-nuclear-weapon countries as far as peaceful applications are concerned. It is even intended to stimulate cooperation in the nuclear energy field with due consideration for the needs of underdeveloped areas of the world. Until now only 77 countries have ratified the treaty. Several of the non-ratifiers are near-nuclear-weapon countries.

In section II of this chapter, some remarks relevant in this context are made on the NPT. Section III describes the plans of several countries for the enrichment of uranium and section IV discusses some possibilities for strengthening the NPT.

II. *The NPT*

It is outside the scope of this chapter to analyse the NPT in detail. Apart from concern about the proliferation of nuclear weapons, several more concrete political objectives may have been important in relation to the position of many countries to the treaty. Some points relevant in this context will be reviewed here.

The NPT makes a distinction between nuclear- and non-nuclear-weapon countries. However, according to article IV.2 of the NPT:

all parties to the treaty undertake to facilitate the fullest possible exchange of equipment, materials and scientific and technological information for the peaceful uses of nuclear energy. Parties in a position to do so shall also cooperate in contributing alone or together with other states or international organizations to the further development of the application of nuclear energy for peaceful purposes, especially in the territories of non-nuclear weapon states party to the treaty, with due consideration for the needs of the developing areas of the world.

This article can be looked upon as a stimulus for the spread of uranium enrichment facilities to many countries. One could question the real possibilities of countries to implement effectively such types of cooperation, especially in situations where the interests of big private multinational companies are at stake. In any case, the development of the spread of enrichment plants, already in progress, will certainly not be hindered by the

100

NPT. Due to the Janus-like characteristics of such facilities, many countries will get a physical capability for uranium based nuclear weapons.

The control measures to prevent a diversion of the peaceful applications of nuclear energy to weapon production are outlined in article III. They consist of a system of safeguards to be applied on all source and special fissionable material in all peaceful nuclear activities within the territory of non-nuclear-weapon states under the jurisdiction of the NPT or carried out under its control anywhere. Within a country the safeguards are only to prevent the diversion of nuclear energy to nuclear weapons or other nuclear explosive devices. The transfer of enriched uranium to other military purposes, such as nuclear submarine reactors, is not safeguarded by the treaty.

For international transactions, the parties to the treaty undertake in article III.2:

not to provide (a) source or special fissionable material or (b) equipment or material especially designed or prepared for the processing, use or production of special fissionable material, to any non-nuclear weapon state for peaceful purposes, unless the source or special fissionable material shall be subject to the safeguards required by this article.

The safeguards system operated by the IAEA consists essentially of a material accountancy system of source and special fissionable material, complemented by measures of containment and surveillance. According to article III.3, the system should not hamper

international cooperation in the field of peaceful nuclear activities, including the international exchange of nuclear material and equipment for the processing, use or production of nuclear material for peaceful purposes.

Bookkeeping of the quantities of uranium and plutonium in circulation gives a fair picture of today's nuclear technology. The system can be developed to a higher sophistication by the introduction of system analysis techniques for complete fuel cycles. Such a procedure could possibly also lead to a better understanding of the significance of material unaccounted for.

The safeguards system, however, does not control the proliferation of nuclear technologies. Both fuel reprocessing technologies and uranium enrichment technologies are safeguarded by indirect means: bookkeeping of the source and special fissionable material. The complex network of industrial companies operating on the international scene can easily divert, for example, the ultracentrifuge technology to another country without any safeguards. The problem has similarities to the conventional weapon trade among countries.

Moreover, in transferring nuclear material to military purposes, safeguards are no longer required except in the case of nuclear weapons. In principle nuclear material and equipment could be exported without safeguards to another non-nuclear-weapon state for a military research programme that was not producing nuclear weapons. An example could be the export to another country of a small centrifuge plant designed for the production of enriched uranium for nuclear submarines. Another interesting example would be the export of a small centrifuge plant for the isotope separation of other heavy elements. Although in most cases the IAEA safeguards system, prior to the NPT arrangements, will cover such situations, the NPT as such does not deal with them.

Countries can withdraw from the NPT when they decide that extraordinary events, related to the subject matter of the treaty, have jeopardized their supreme interests. The concept of "extraordinary events" is rather undefined. Moreover it is the country itself that defines the situation as such. In the US view, the dissolution of an existing military alliance might be such a case:

If NATO were to dissolve, this might well be interpreted by some countries as one of those events affecting their vital interests which could raise the question of the withdrawal clause under the treaty. [1]

Although on several points a kind of minimum interpretation of the NPT, which could be considered as conflicting with the intention of the treaty, is given above, the NPT, based upon the concept of promoting nuclear energy, is obviously still a rather weak instrument. Two conclusions can be formulated:

1. The NPT is an instrument for the promotion rather than the hindrance of the proliferation of uranium enrichment facilities.

2. The proliferation of uranium enrichment technologies is not safeguarded by the NPT.

III. *Countries with enrichment plans and their attitudes towards the NPT*

In this section the plans of several countries for uranium enrichment facilities are reviewed. It is certainly not complete, as many contacts are kept secret. However, the picture is sufficiently accurate to demonstrate the existing trends.

In the second half of the section the positions of various countries with regard to the NPT are outlined. A much more complete discussion on the policies of these countries can be found in reference [1].

Existing plans

The USA

The three existing diffusion plants are expected to operate at full capacity (17 100 tons SW/year) by about 1978 but planned improvements in technology are expected to enlarge this capacity to 26400–28000 tons SW/year. Decisions to build new plants by about 1982 will be taken during the coming years. The existing plants are operated for the US AEC by private contractors: it is AEC policy to sell them to private industry. The AEC "will afford American industry the opportunity to determine realistically the role it desires in the enrichment phase of the nuclear fuel cycle" [2] and it believes "that the private sector of our economy will make a major contribution to new enriching capacity on the time scale that we now believe will be necessary". [2] Customers abroad are guaranteed that existing contractual interests will be protected. The AEC is also doing research on centrifuge technology but this has not yet arrived at a stage of industrial deployment.

The USA is ready to let other countries participate in the building of multinational enrichment facilities outside the USA. Nixon's second annual review of US foreign policy of February 1971 states:

Having carefully weighed the national security and other factors involved, we have undertaken consultation with the Joint Committee on Atomic Energy of the Congress concerning ways in which the USA might assist our allies to construct a multinational enrichment plant to help meet future world demands. [3]

This includes a sharing of the technological secrets with other countries in a gradual process of cooperation with agreements on the governmental level. Classified technology will in the course of such multinational cooperation become available to the participating industries in the countries involved. [4] Recently the AEC decided that contractors should make the arrangements for enriched uranium 10 years in advance to get better information for the extension of US enrichment facilities. This could strongly influence the plans of other groups or countries.

Within the USA the AEC is already releasing information on enrichment to industry so that industry can evaluate the technology and put forward proposals for privately operated uranium enrichment facilities. [5] Several large companies are participating: Good Year Rubber Company has stated it is specifically interested in selling full-scale centrifuge plants [6] and General Electric has launched an intensive study that could lead to its becoming a major supplier to the world's uranium market. [7]

The tripartite centrifuge cooperation (FR Germany,
the Netherlands and the United Kingdom)

Research on centrifuge technology in these countries has been going on for a long time. A major breakthrough resulted in a US request in 1960 to keep the technology classified. In 1970, the UK, the Federal Republic of Germany and the Dutch government agreed to cooperate in the enrichment of uranium, using the centrifuge technology. Three pilot plants are in use by now, two of them located at Almelo (Holland) and one at Capenhurst

(UK), each with a capacity of 25 tons SW/year. Private companies of the three countries are participating in both the construction plants for the centrifuges and the enrichment plants.

The tripartite companies estimate the separative work demand in the world, excluding the USA, the USSR, the People's Republic of China, the Eastern European countries and excluding the Capenhurst plant, at approximately 5000 tons SW/year in 1980 and 13000 tons SW/year in 1985. [8] The capacities of the plants are planned to be 400 tons SW/year in 1976 and about 1000 tons SW/year around 1980. [9] Other estimates are even more optimistic: 3000 tons SW/year in operation by 1980 and 3000 tons SW/year under construction by that time. [4]

The tripartite organization founded a study group in 1972, the Association for Centrifuge Enrichment, which will provide information about the project to organizations which would like to participate. The studies could result in joint ventures with other countries for building enrichment facilities. General Electric (USA) and other companies from the UK, the USA, Belgium, Canada, Australia, Switzerland and Sweden have already shown interest in this study group. [9]

France

France has plans to expand its own enrichment facilities by building a new gaseous diffusion plant with a capacity of 6000–8000 tons SW/year. Production should start in 1978 and the plant should be in full operation by 1980. [10] France is looking for other countries to participate in the venture. A serious competition is going on inside the Euratom group of countries between this French plan and the centrifuge plans of FR Germany, the UK and the Netherlands. Apart from a multinational approach in Western Europe, France is prepared to cooperate with Japan and Australia. Plans of Japan and France have been reported for a joint gaseous diffusion plant either in Europe or Australia [11] and for cooperation in the exploitation of uranium in Niger. [12]

The Federal Republic of Germany

Apart from the tripartite cooperation, FR Germany is very active in uranium enrichment technology. The need of FR Germany's enrichment capacity has been estimated at 4000 tons SW/year by 1980. [13] The Karlsruhe Nuclear Research Center has a jet nozzle experiment of two tons SW/year in operation that is reported to have been sold to India. [14] The use of lasers is also under study.

Japan

Japan's need for enriched uranium is estimated at 8000–12000 tons SW/ year by 1985. [15] Japanese nuclear interests are pressing the government to build a 5000 ton SW/year enrichment plant for operation by 1980. Plans for cooperation with France, Australia and Canada have also been reported.

Japan is doing research on at least three enrichment methods: ion exchange technology, gas centrifuges and membranes for the gaseous diffusion method. [16–17]

South Africa

The demand for enrichment capacity in South Africa is estimated at about 2000 tons SW/year by the year 2000 and there are rich uranium supplies there.

South Africa claims to have developed a new enrichment technology which is strictly classified. A pilot plant has been built at Pelindaba near Pretoria [18–19] and there is much speculation about its technology. According to some reports it is probably the centrifuge method; [19] however, according to other reports, [20] the energy consumption is higher than for the gaseous diffusion process. South Africa plans to be able to meet 14 per cent of the world's need for enriched uranium by 1980 which would correspond to a capacity of about 6000 tons SW/year. [21]

Australia

Australia has substantial uranium fields and is prepared to participate in a multinational enrichment plant on its territory. Although this would essentially be a commercial enterprise, the government would take responsibility for government-to-government agreements in relation to the transfer of technology and safeguards. [22] Discussions with the UK, FR Germany, France, the USA and Japan are still continuing. [23] The capacity of the plant has been reported as about 6000 tons SW/year [22] but a decision about the technology has not as yet been taken.

India

India has important resources of uranium. It plans to build a prototype enrichment plant which, according to the chairman of the Indian Atomic Energy Commission, will not be designed on a conventional pattern but rather on a "centrifugal sorting method", presumably the jet nozzle process which has been pioneered in FR Germany. [14] Although this may be too speculative as to the technology involved, India's plans for a national enrichment facility seem very firm.

Canada

Canada is also rich in uranium and it has a policy similar to Australia's. The government of Canada would like to participate in a multinational undertaking to build a plant on its territory. Plans for cooperation have been reported with countries like FR Germany and Japan. [25] The capacity of the plant is expected to be about 5000 tons SW/year by 1980.

105

The People's Republic of China

According to reports, China plans to enlarge its uranium enrichment capacity from 80 to about 160 tons SW/year. [26] The enriched uranium will probably be needed totally for weapon production.

Zaïre

Zaïre has substantial resources of natural uranium. It has presented a plan for a uranium enrichment plant near the hydroelectric station at Inga on the Congo river. The power station would supply very cheap electricity for a gaseous diffusion plant of about 8000 tons SW/year. The plans are being studied in cooperation with the Belgian Syndicat d'Etude de l'Industrie Atomique. [27–28]

Countries interested in uranium enrichment and the NPT

Of the countries discussed, the USA, the UK, Canada and Australia have ratified the NPT: Japan, Zaïre, the Federal Republic of Germany and the Netherlands have signed the NPT; and France, South Africa, India and China have not even signed the treaty. We will shortly review the various positions of the non-member states.

Japan signed the NPT after a long hesitation. There was opposition from the nuclear industry with respect to the application of safeguards which they feared would create a risk of industrial espionage and possibly affect the industries' competitive position because of the extra costs. Japan finds itself in a very fluid political position due to changing relations among the USA, the USSR and China. It will possibly keep an option open on nuclear weapons for the future.

Japan has developed a high level of missile technology for civil purposes. Access to uranium enrichment would certainly be an important component of the nuclear option, especially with regard to the construction of a ballistic-missile nuclear-powered submarine force for an invulnerable second strike capacity.

The position of FR Germany and the Netherlands, both members of the European Atomic Energy Community (Euratom) of which France is also a member, is rather complex. Euratom owns all enriched uranium present in the community except the material explicitly reserved for military purposes. Now that the discussion between Euratom and the IAEA about the safeguards system has led to an agreement, FR Germany and the Netherlands will certainly ratify the treaty. The Netherlands is strongly in favour of it. A long discussion has been going on in FR Germany about signing the treaty. Before joining NATO it declared it would not produce nuclear weapons on its own territory. Due to the state of its present nuclear technology FR Germany will always have a nuclear option. The future will be strongly influenced by the development of the NATO treaty, Western European integration and the European security talks now under way. The participation of FR Germany in an integrated Western European nuclear force would not be impossible in the long run. Such a force could eventually be built up on the basis of the existing French and British nuclear forces, resulting in a submarine-based (invulernable) second strike capability.

The tripartite agreement on uranium enrichment among the UK, FR Germany and the Netherlands will be subjected to IAEA safeguards. However the UK can, within the terms of the NPT, divert enriched uranium from its own enrichment plant to weapon production.

India has been a major critic of the NPT which it would not join because it felt the treaty discriminates between nuclear-weapon and non-nuclear-weapon countries. The main factor influencing India's position is probably its security situation, especially with regard to China. A uranium enrichment facility and knowledge of enrichment technologies would provide India with physical access to thermonuclear weapons. Because of the costs involved, an Indian nuclear capabilitiy would possibly consist of a somewhat sophisticated kind of "force de frappe".

Both China and France are already nuclear-weapon countries. China would possibly enlarge its uranium enrichment capabilities because of a perceived threat from the USSR. China has stated that every socialist country has to rely primarily on its own defence capability. France has declared that it will behave exactly like the states adhering to the treaty. It is rather unclear, however, how far France will demand safeguards on possible cooperation with other countries in the field of uranium enrichment technology.

South Africa has said that it strongly supports the objectives of the NPT. It did not sign until now because of the danger of industrial espionage with regard to secret enrichment technology and the interference of the safeguards system with the normal operation of private industry. There are no external threats to South Africa's security and it is difficult to imagine how nuclear weapons could be of any help for internal racial problems. If, however, neighbouring countries like Zambia and Tanzania would provide facilities for guerrilla warfare in a South African regional conflict, it is imaginable that nuclear weapons could be used as blackmail.

Summarizing the present situation, we may conclude that India and Japan are two examples of countries for which the access to uranium enrichment technologies is of importance with regard to nuclear weapon proliferation. The know-how of a technology applicable on a small or medium-sized scale, like the centrifuge technology, would open a route to them for a national nuclear capability with thermonuclear weapons.

Concluding remarks on plans for uranium enrichment facilities

Table 1 summarizes the plans of various countries for new enrichment plants. Although most decisions have still to be made and several plans will

Table 1. Present and future uranium enrichment capabilities

Country	Process	Capability (tons SW/year)	References
USA	gaseous diffusion	10 000	[5]
France	gaseous diffusion	6 000–10 000[b]	[29]
UK[a]	gas centrifuge	1 000[b]	[4]
Netherlands[a]	gas centrifuge	1 000[b]	[4]
FR Germany[a]	gas centrifuge	1 000[b]	[4]
Japan	unknown	5 000	[15]
Australia	unknown	6 000	[22]
South Africa	secret	6 000[b]	[11]
Canada	unknown	5 000	[25]
People's Republic of China	gaseous diffusion	80	[26]
Zaïre, Rep. of	gaseous diffusion	8 000	[27–28]
FR Germany	jet nozzle	500–1 000	[13]

[a] Tripartite cooperation.
[b] Expected to reach these capacities by about 1980.

be interdependent, the trend is quite obvious. As has been described in chapter 4, a shortage of enriched uranium will develop at about the end of the decade. This will lead to the establishment of several new facilities, some of them probably as multinational enterprises. A substantial number of plants will probably be located in non-nuclear-weapon countries. The countries with substantial resources of natural uranium are especially interested in such developments. The monopoly position of the USA on the enriched uranium market will then be broken.

Three of the nuclear-weapon countries, the USA, France and the UK, are inclined to share their still classified technology with the new countries that are candidates for enrichment plants. The same holds for the non-nuclear-weapon countries participating in the tripartite agreement, FR Germany and the Netherlands.

This development will most probably result in a proliferation of enrichment technologies to many of the near-nuclear countries. Although the actual organization of a plant for the production of low enriched uranium differs from the organization for the production of weapon-grade uranium, it would not take much technological know-how or time to reorganize the plants if a country desired to do so.

In the longer run new technologies can be expected to emerge. Because the economic features of these technologies are still impossible to evaluate, it is difficult to estimate how much this would change the situation for smaller countries. However, the centrifuge technology already provides an attractive way for medium-sized countries to enter the business of uranium enrichment.

The proliferation of uranium technology will provide the physical capability for participating countries to have uranium-based nuclear weapons.

The dynamics of a free competitive market in this field lead almost inevitably to this situation, even if afterthoughts about military options and security problems were practically absent in decision making. The implications point to a world with a great number of uranium-based near-nuclear-weapon countries.

IV. *Nuclear energy and the NPT*

The problem of the proliferation of nuclear weapons around the world has been one of the major concerns of many people since 1945. Accelerated by a huge propaganda campaign on the benefits of nuclear fission as a practically unlimited energy resource in a situation of rapidly declining supplies of fossil fuel, participation in the nuclear energy business has become a policy objective for many countries. This holds especially for the industrialized countries whose standards of living are very sensitive to the availability of cheap energy. Quite a number of them (for example, Western European countries and Japan) are highly dependent in this respect on foreign resources and are prepared to pay for a more secure source of energy.

In recent years the earlier estimates of fossil fuels have turned out to be too pessimistic. The prospect of unlimited nuclear energy resources has already started a technological development in the nuclear energy sector; however, as huge investments and advanced technologies are involved, industry itself has been and still is an important promoter of such a development. It has withdrawn its attention from developments and technologies focusing on other energy sources such as solar energy and from those stressing a much more efficient use of energy. In most developed countries a continuing exponential growth of energy consumption is taken for granted. Only in recent years have some critical voices been heard pointing out the necessity of a limitation on energy consumption.

In such a climate the problem of the interference between nuclear weapon developments and the use of nuclear power provided only limited policy alternatives. Apart from the countries who want to have an option for nuclear weapons and thus have security interests in the nuclear technology field, many other countries have adopted a policy against the proliferation of nuclear weapons but favourable to the development of nuclear energy. The range of policy alternatives would possibly have been much broader if the whole problem of nuclear fission as an energy source had been more thoroughly studied and critically evaluated.

Possible measures for strengthening the NPT

In this concluding section some suggestions will be made for strengthening the NPT.

1. The treaty as it stands restricts itself to a non-proliferation of nuclear weapons or other nuclear explosive devices. As has been discussed in section II of this chapter, the proliferation of, for example, enriched uranium to other military purposes has not been forbidden. Adding such a prohibition would be very positive. It would create a better distinction between the military and peaceful applications and prevent a step-by-step proliferation to nuclear weapons.

2. The existing system of safeguarding only source and special fissionable material is an unsatisfactory situation. The treaty would be strengthened if some types of equipment crucial for obtaining a nuclear weapon capability would also be safeguarded. This holds in particular for fuel reprocessing and uranium enrichment equipment. Objections to such a measure could be expected specifically from industry because of their expected dangers of industrial espionage. However this problem could certainly be resolved if governments were seriously pressing for it. Similar objections have also been raised in the context of the present treaty. No problems have arisen as yet, according to our knowledge, but some experiments in this field might lower the barriers for such an expansion.

3. A much better situation would be reached if the nuclear fuel cycle were to be taken out of the national context. One could imagine a situation in which, for example, the IAEA would operate the fuel reprocessing and uranium enrichment plants and no other plants (either national or private) would be allowed. An even better solution would be a treaty in which the IAEA would be the only allowed proprietor of fuel reprocessing and enrichment plants. Such a solution seems utopian at present but would have a number of advantages, especially concerning the proliferation of the crucial technologies. It would take a much longer time for a country to develop its own technology. Moreover the economic incentive for a proliferation of enrichment facilities would be taken away and many companies would find it much less attractive to compete in this field.

Such an arrangement would mean that countries would deliberately decide not to develop certain technologies because of a common interest in not doing so. It is essentially the same as the objective behind the strategic arms limitation talks, although SALT I did not succeed in stopping the technological arms race.

The NPT as it stands does not prohibit the proliferation of crucial technologies like the uranium enrichment methods. It needs rather radical improvements to realize this objective. Such improvements may seem utopian but are simply a common interest of all countries. To quote Emelyanov:

The achievements of science and technology, and the speed with which these achievements are being put into practice, make it urgently necessary that the basic conceptions which have hitherto determined international relations should be revised. It is impossible to establish mutual relations between nations in the age of

110

atomic energy on the basis of the conceptions of a former epoch when civilization developed slowly and dependent upon a source of energy which did not threaten the destruction of civilization. [30]

References

1. Quoted in Willrich, M., *Non-Proliferation Treaty: Framework for Nuclear Arms Control* (Charlottesville, The Michie Company, 1969) p. 165.
2. Johnson, W. E. and Sapirie, S. R., "Uranium Isotope Enrichment", *Peaceful Uses of Atomic Energy* [Proceedings of the Fourth International Conference, Geneva, 6–16 September 1971] Vol. 9 (New York, Vienna, UN and IAEA, 1972) pp. 31–41.
3. *Ibid.,* p. 41.
4. Mohrhauer, H., "Stand der Urananreicherung in Europa", *Atomwirtschaft,* Vol. 17, June 1972, p. 300.
5. "US Nuclear Industry Demands Enrichment Data", *New Scientist,* Vol. 56, 30 November 1972, p. 509.
6. "Uraanverrijking in de VS", *De Ingenieur,* Vol. 85, 1 March 1973, p. 185.
7. "US Company Sets Up Gas Centrifuge Enrichments Study", *New Scientist,* Vol. 57, 1 February 1973, p. 250.
8. Avery D. G. *et al.,* "Centrifuge Plants in Europe", *Peaceful Uses of Atomic Energy* [Proceedings of the Fourth International Conference, Geneva, 6–16 September 1971] Vol. 9 (New York, Vienna, UN and IAEA, 1972) p. 53.
9. "Ruim 17 Miljard Dollar Voor Wetenschappen in de Verenigde Staten", *Atoomenergie,* Vol. 15, April 1973, p. 78.
10. Fréjacques C. *et al.,* "Développement Prévu par la France dans la Domain de la Séparation Isotopique de l'Uranium", *Peaceful Uses of Atomic Energy,* [Proceedings of the Fourth International Conference, Geneva, 6–16 September 1971] Vol. 9 (New York, Vienna, UN and IAEA, 1972) p. 43.
11. *World Armaments and Disarmament, SIPRI Yearbook 1972* (Stockholm, Almqvist & Wiksell, 1972, Stockholm International Peace Research Institute) p. 319.
12. *Keesings Historisch Archief* (Kleynsham Bristol, Keesing's Publications Limited) June 1972, p. 25292.
13. Klusman, A. and Völcker, H., "The Situation of the Nuclear Fuel Cycle Industry", *Atomkernenergie,* Vol. 17, May 1971, p. 149.
14. "India Buys German Route to Enriched Uranium", *New Scientist,* Vol. 53, 9 March 1972, p. 546.
15. Griffiths, D. R., "Review of Overseas Nuclear Power Development", *Atomic Energy in Australia,* Vol. 14, June/October 1971, p. 1.
16. Reported in "Kernbrenn-, Bau- und Betriebsstoffe", *Atomwirtschaft,* Vol. 16, February 1971, p. 108.
17. "Enrichissement en Europe, *Energie Nucléaire,* Vol. 11, November 1969, p. 572.
18. "More Uranium in South Africa", *Nature,* Vol. 215, 1967, p. 232.
19. "Verrijking in Zuid Afrika", *Atoomenergie,* Vol. 15, January 1973, p. 3.
20. "Enrichment Processes", *Nuclear Engineering International,* Vol. 16, March 1971, p. 301.
21. *World Armaments and Disarmament, SIPRI Yearbook 1972* (Stockholm, Almqvist & Wiksell, 1972, Stockholm International Peace Research Institute) pp. 283–365.

22. "Government to Release Information on Uranium Enrichment", *Atomic Energy in Australia,* Vol. 15, Ocotober 1972, p. 1.
23. Rowe, S., "Australia Rejects Nuclear Weaponry", *New Scientist,* Vol. 57, 8 February 1973, p. 314.
24. "Australian-Japan Atomic Energy Agreement" *Atomic Energy in Australia,* Vol. 15, April 1972, p. 2.
25. "New Master Policy for Fuel Supply", *Nuclear Industry,* Vol. 19, March 1972, p. 11.
26. Murphy, C. H., "Mainland China's Evolving Nuclear Deterrent", *Bulletin of the Atomic Scientists,* Vol. 28, January 1972, p. 28.
27. Reported in "Kernbrenn-, Bau- und Betriebsstoffe", *Atomwirtschaft,* Vol. 16, June 1971, p. 501.
28. Simonovitch, G., "Le Cycle du Combustible", *Energie Nucléaire,* Vol. 13, November/December 1971, p. 403.
29. "L'Energie Nucléaire et le VIeme Plan Français", *Energie Nucléaire,* Vol. 13, July/August 1971, p. 293.
30. Emelyanov, V. S., "Nuclear Reactors Will Spread", in Barnaby, C. F., ed., *Preventing the Spread of Nuclear Weapons,* Pugwash Monograph I (London, Souvenir Press, 1969) p. 71.

8. Nuclear weapon technology

J. C. HOPKINS

Abstract

Several aspects of nuclear weapon technology are discussed. The design requirements for simple fission weapons can be met by a modest effort. This is not true, however, in the case of the engineering design and fabrication which requires a much wider range of expertise and a considerably larger commitment of technical and financial resources. Thermonuclear weapons are more complex than fission devices and the design requires experience in fission weapon development. Fissionable material costs and requirements are briefly discussed and it is pointed out that it may be possible to use reactor-grade plutoniun in nuclear explosives.

In considering the capability to develop nuclear weapons, the general technical expertise of a country should be examined. Finally, it is noted that while the political impact may be substantial, the possession of a few simple fission weapons does not necessarily constitute a credible and effective military capability.

I. *Introduction*

The purpose of this article is to discuss several aspects of nuclear weapon technology that have frequently been overlooked. It is intended to supplement the general arms control literature rather than to serve as an overall review. Nuclear weapon technology will be confined, in this context, to the research, development and production associated with nuclear warheads; the much broader subjects of weapon systems and delivery vehicles will not be discussed. Finally, some comments will be made on the potentialities of the near-nuclear-weapon states to develop nuclear weapons.

II. *Nuclear weapon research and development*

Fission weapons

The theoretical design of simple fission weapons can be accomplished provided a few general requirements are met. The first is the assurance that the basic concept will work. This was proved by the USA in 1945 and has subsequently been confirmed by the UK, the USSR, France and China. The second requirement is the possession of the appropriate nuclear data such as critical masses, the number of neutrons per fission, and so on. While never as accurate as one would like, these data are nevertheless usable. The third requirement is the possession of the appropriate data relating to the pressure, temperature and volume of the fissile material. Again these data are either well known or can be approximated with reasonable accuracy. The fourth requirement is a means of estimating efficiency so that the yield can be calculated. In this case, the physics is at hand and available to all. Fifth is the theoretical description of the chain reaction and the numerical means to calculate the neutron distributions, criticalities and multiplication. Much of the standard reactor technology is suitable for this. Using the standard reactor technology for these theoretical descriptions shows it is incorrect to assert that there is no carry-over from reactor to weapon technology. The sixth requirement is the theoretical and numerical means to calculate the hydrodynamics involved. It turns out that, at least for the primitive fission weapons, such calculations are almost textbook examples. The seventh requirement is the possession of computing equipment which is now commercially available. Today one could easily find the required number of first-rate physicists necessary for the theoretical design of simple fission weapons. This completes the final requirement—staff to accomplish the task—which in the early days when the first devices were being contemplated was almost the only one which could be filled.

If these requirements are met, and I believe that they can be by all of the so-called near-nuclear-weapon states, a simple fission device can be designed with a high degree of confidence that it would give a yield in the kiloton range.

The engineering design and fabrication, on the other hand, require a much wider range of expertise and a considerably larger commitment of technical and financial resources. First of all they require high explosive development and the associated hydrodynamic research. The engineering design also requires detonator development, material studies, critical assembly work, mechanical design and, finally, actual fabrication. While information on all of these subjects is available in the open literature and most industrial nations have research in these areas or in closely related fields, it should be stressed that nuclear weapon development requires a higher degree of competence in physics, chemistry and nuclear, mechanical and chemical engineering, plus more highly skilled technicians, machinists and health physicists than are required in most other industries.

After the devices are designed and built, field testing, if done underground, requires scientists and engineers in the fields of geology, hydrology and rock mechanics. Work in these fields is necessary to ensure that containment of the test is adequate to comply with the objectives of the government and with the Limited Test Ban Treaty if the nation is a party to the treaty. In addition, the drilling technology, if the devices are tested in holes as is done in Nevada, is not possessed by many countries. This is because weapon tests require deep holes, frequently with considerably larger diameters (six to eight feet) than are associated with most civilian activities such as oil-well drilling. Nuclear weapons can, of course, be tested in mines or tunnels; this would probably be the most sensible approach for a modest test programme.

In addition, the field testing diagnostics, while performed by conventionally trained nuclear physicists, chemists and electronic engineers, are quite specialized and have required extensive research to develop. Although much of the necessary information on the experimental techniques is in the open literature, actual field test experience is necessary to achieve a high degree of scientific sophistication. Another very important consideration, of course, is that in weapon tests the scientist gets only one opportunity to obtain data in each experiment.

Thermonuclear weapons

Essentially no unclassified information is available on the research and development of thermonuclear weapons. It can be said, however, that these devices are a major step-up in complexity from simple fission weapons. No nation has yet developed such devices without extensive testing of fission weapons.

III. *Nuclear weapon costs*

There are at least two complementary approaches that can be taken to arrive at an estimate of the nuclear weapon costs. One approach is to sum up the costs of the separate tasks involved, such as the costs of the fissile material, the fabrication costs and so on. Another approach is to take known overall costs, such as those from France, Great Britain or from the USA, for approximately known strength levels and to work backwards to obtain warhead costs. Much effort has, of course, been devoted to both types of study.

Annex IV of the 1968 UN study lists the estimated costs of both small and moderate programmes for the development of 20 kiloton devices over a 10-year period. [1] The results of the UN analysis are given in table 1. It should be noted here that the UN study and others [2] have concluded that a 20-kiloton warhead can be produced with about 8 kg of plutonium or 25 kg of uranium-235. The US value for plutonium-239 (3 per cent plutonium-240) is $60 000/kg while the value for uranium-235 is $11 800/kg. Consequently, using these figures, the fissionable material in a 20-kiloton plutonium device is worth approximately $480 000 while in a 20-kiloton uranium-235 device, the uranium-235 value is approximately $300 000. Plowshare device costs have been quoted at $350 000 for a 10-kiloton fission de-

Table 1. The cost of nuclear weapon production   *US $ million*

	Small programme 10–20 kiloton weapons over 10 years	Moderate programme 100–20 kiloton weapons over 10 years
Plutonium meta 1	70	151
Design and fabrication	18	18
Testing	12	15
Total	**100**	**184**
Cost per nuclear weapon	10	1.9

vice and $600 000 for a 2-megaton device.[1] Generally devices with a larger yield use more material and cost more money while devices with a smaller yield use less material and cost less money.

When considering the costs, several points should be mentioned. The first is that the material is not expended if the weapon is not used. At a later date the weapon material could be used in a newer, more modern weapon or it could be used for reactor fuel or for peaceful nuclear explosives and much of the original investment could be recovered. The second point is that there are civilian spin-offs of the weapon programme. Expenditures for basic research are frequently justified on the grounds that there is a sizable practical payoff. This is, of course, true and the same arguments apply, though to a lesser extent, to nuclear weapon R&D. The weapon programme in the USA has made major contributions in the fields of biology and medicine, the practical applications of mathematics and computing techniques, astronomy, environmental sciences and in many more areas. Fortunately, these civilian spin-offs of the US weapon programme are available to all people everywhere.

IV. *Fissile material requirements*

It is commonly recognized that uranium-235 and plutonium-239 are the principle fissile materials used in nuclear weapons. It is also realized that both of these materials are very difficult to obtain in the quantity and purity needed for weapons. The separation of uranium-235 from uranium-238 requires large diffusion plants or centrifuge facilities while plutonium-239 is made in reactors. Weapon-grade plutonium (that is, plutonium-239 with very little contamination of plutonium-240) is made by exposing the uranium-238 for a relatively short period of time to prevent plutonium buildup, while plutonium that is normally produced in a power reactor has a relatively large amount of plutonium-240 due to the neutron capture in the plutonium-239. It has been stated that reactor-grade plutonium (that is, with a few

---

[1] These figures do not reflect the development costs included in table 1.

116

tens of per cent of plutonium-240) is not suitable for the production of nuclear weapons. If this were true, then there would be little worry about the hundreds of thousands of kilogrammes of plutonium that will be produced by the world's power reactors of the future. However, it may well be possible to use reactor-grade plutonium in nuclear explosives.

While reactor-grade plutonium may work, it does have several severe disadvantages. In addition to the more or less obvious weapon design problems due to the spontaneous fission of the plutonium-240, the α-decay might produce a requirement for adequate cooling of the device. Moreover, the radioactivity could result in serious health physics problems during fabrication and maintenance operations. The last problem could well be the most serious, particularly for assembly line operations.

For many years the technological difficulties and large financial outlays involved in preparing weapon-grade nuclear material have contributed to the decision of various nations not to pursue a nuclear weapon capability. Indeed, this is understandable considering the problems involved in separating uranium-235 from normal uranium or of producing plutonium-239 in nuclear reactors. However, should any new technique be developed that would permit the production of uranium-235 or plutonium-239 more easily or cheaply this situation might change.

Another area for concern involves the production of uranium-233 from thorium. Although thorium is about three times more abundant than uranium, at present there is not much evidence of it being used for weapon applications, but it is possible that it could be so used.

V. R&D capabilities

There are many excellent studies on the availability of fissionable materials and on plutonium production capabilities and, while these are undoubtedly the most important considerations, general technical expertise is also extremely important. For example, what are a country's resources in mathematics, experimental and theoretical physics and chemistry, material sciences, electronics, and engineering? A nation that lacks experience in these areas is seriously handicapped in nuclear weapon production. This aspect has been neglected in many of the analyses of a country's potential for developing nuclear weapons. The same comments, of course, apply to the development of sophisticated weapon delivery systems.

VI. Conclusion

In conclusion, it can be said that all of the major states with civil nuclear industries do possess the technical expertise required to develop simple fission weapons. It should be borne in mind, however, that the costs in scientific manpower and technical resources to establish even a minimal nuclear capability are very high. Finally, it should be realized that, while the political impact may be substantial, the possession of a few simple fission devices does not necessarily constitute a credible and effective military capability.

References

1. *Effects of the Possible Use of Nuclear Weapons and the Security and Economic Implications for States of the Acquisition and Further Development of These Weapons,* UN document A/6858, 1968.
2. *World Armaments and Disarmament, SIPRI Yearbook 1972* (Stockholm, Almqvist & Wiksell, 1972, Stockholm International Peace Research Institute).

9. Nuclear miniweapons and low-yield nuclear weapons which use reactor-grade plutonium: their effect on the durability of the NPT

J. K. MIETTINEN

Abstract

Miniweapons, a new generation of tactical nuclear weapons, are presently being introduced in Europe. They have smaller yields than the earlier types (possibly as low as a few tons of TNT equivalent), produce little blast and almost no radioactive residue. Being laser-guided they are highly accurate. Nuclear shells of 155-mm and 8-inch howitzers, and possibly artillery rockets and atomic demolition munitions (ADMs) are being miniaturized. The main drawback of such modernization is an increased probability of the real use of nuclear weapons in case of crisis. In addition, this modernization is contrary to the spirit of the NPT.

Another type of low-yield nuclear weapon can be made with plutonium produced in civilian power reactors. Since such weapons may soon be available to many countries, the NPT, which is regrettably one-sided and tentative, should be reinforced to guarantee its survival.

I. Miniaturization of nuclear weapons and its significance for the NPT

Soon after the NPT came into force, demands were published in the USA for the development of a new generation of tactical nuclear weapons which would produce less radioactive residue and have smaller yields than the presently existing ones. Probably the first to clearly express these demands in the military literature was Robert M. Lawrence who, in an article evidently written in 1969 but not published until 1971, described "fission weapons of extremely low yields, of the order of several tons of TNT equivalent" as well as small "enhanced radiation weapons—neutron bombs" which release 80 per cent of their energy in the form of prompt neutrons, produce very little blast and yield almost no radioactive residues. [1] Lawrence points out that the military usefulness of these weapons would be great, since they could be employed close to home troops, they would produce little radioactivity or collateral damage and would possess a high death-to-injury ratio (3:1, while conventional weapons have a ratio of 1:3).

Pressure for the development of such weapons has come partly from US military circles and partly from the AEC weapon developing laboratories. The first indication that such weapons were actually being developed came from former US Secretary of Defense Melvin Laird in an interview on 13 April 1972. [2] Mr Laird announced that the US goverment had been developing and improving its tactical nuclear weapons for a number of years. The main purpose of this modernization programme was to obtain smaller yields and less radioactive residue as well as improved accuracy, flexibility and safety. Mr Laird stressed in the interview that a successful conclusion of SALT would result in greater emphasis being placed upon the role of tactical nuclear weapons. "One approach gaining momentum calls for the smaller, cleaner tactical nuclear weapons . . . designed to localize damage to the immediate target area." In this background information, the reporter who interviewed Laird writes that "in addition, the services are emphasizing much more accurate delivery systems, involving artillery shells, air-to-surface missiles and glide bombs, all of which home in on a laser beam illuminating the target". Advocates of modernization maintain also that enhanced radiation weapons would be sufficiently different, in a qualitative sense, to permit the establishment of a firebreak between them and present-day tactical nuclear weapons, that is, that they could be used like conventional weapons without the risk of escalation. The present author does not accept this argument. They would be nuclear enough to trigger the use of old-type tactical nuclear weapons by an adversary lacking the modern type. A larger proportion of energy released as blast and heat is not militarily such a disadvantage on the battlefield that it would prevent use of the old-type weapons in retaliation. A true firebreak exists only between conventional and nuclear weapons. The adversary has no need to respect the rule of cleanliness self-imposed by the modernizers. World opinion would unambiguously charge the first-user of enhanced-radiation weapons with the guilt of triggering nuclear war. The political disadvantages caused by the introduction of such clean weapons would be much greater than the possible military advantages. Such an attempt to eliminate the nuclear threshold by means of technological "development" is, in the minds of most Europeans, just the thing not to do.

Unfortunately, recent news gives the impression that such modernization is already occurring. According to an article by John W. Finney in *The New York Times*, "the Army has ordered several thousand new nuclear shells for its large cannons in Europe. The cost of the Army's nuclear ammunition modernization program is being kept secret by the Pentagon but congressional sources who have been briefed on the plan say that it will run into "millions and millions of dollars". [3] (The cost was disclosed by Major General Edward B. Giller at a testimony by the US Joint

Congressional Atomic Energy Commission on 14 July 1973 to be $800 million.) [4] Finney's article continues:

. . . the purpose is to replace the atomic ammunition produced 10 to 15 years ago for two of the Army's largest artillery pieces—the 155 mm howitzer and the 8 in. howitzer. The new ammunition will provide increased simplicity, greater capability and better reliability. The purchase is financed through the US AEC budget for production of weapons which in recent years has been slightly under $1 billion annually.

The budget has been so secret that not even Senator Stuart Symington, the second-ranking Democrat on the Senate Armed Services Committee, had information regarding it before he recently became a member of the Congressional Joint Committee on Atomic Energy. Former Defense Secretary Elliot L. Richardson was similarly uninformed at a hearing of the Senate Foreign Relations Committee on 8 May 1973. This modernization, which has vast political implications, is evidently proceeding so secretly that even most members of the US Senate have not been aware of it.

Although Finney's article does not expressly state that the modernization mentioned includes miniweapons, taken together with Laird's interview of a year ago, it cannot but be believed that this is so.[1] Indirect evidence is also found in British Parliamentary debate on 10 May 1973:

Commenting on a report that the Pentagon are pressing NATO on "mini-nukes" —a new generation of miniature nuclear weapons for the battlefield", he (Mr Gilmour, Minister of State Defence) said: "The US has not put such a proposal to the alliance. I would expect, if they did so, there would be full consultation through the nuclear planning group of NATO." [5]

The article continues:

Smaller nuclear weapons raised (in the Parliament) a number of fascinating intellectual questions such as when was a nuclear weapon not a nuclear weapon and what system of political control should govern their use. [5]

Such debate is indirect evidence that modernization of the US Army's nuclear shells signifies the introduction of miniweapons, although this modernization has not yet been extended to the allies. The French nuclear tests in Mururoa in July 1973 are also said to include miniweapons. This is quite a depressing development and in sharp contrast to the spirit of the NPT.

Low-yield howitzer shells provided with a homing device do not necessarily represent the most typical miniweapons. By nuclear miniweapons we usually understand low-weight and low-yield one-man devices that can be carried in a handbag and launched by a mortar or bazooka, or dug into a pit as an atomic demolition munition (ADM) and discharged from a distance. They would be developed for every conceivable purpose and de-

---

[1] News in the world press on 16 July 1973 about General Giller's testimony expressly stated the deployment of miniweapons.

ployed in large numbers by the front-line units and commandoes. They would be intended for real use, and their use would probably be unavoidable in the case of war.

Such typical miniweapons are feasible and evidently have been developed, but it is not yet known to what extent they have been deployed.

Their deployment is a double-edged sword. They would certainly be useful and decrease the amount of collateral damage, which is good, of course. But the trouble is that their usefulness would simultaneously guarantee their deployment in case of war. This, again, would almost certainly trigger a process of escalation, which would lead to a full-scale nuclear war. There are several inbuilt escalation mechanisms in the use of nuclear weapons which make the restriction of their use extremely difficult. Because of the effectiveness and vulnerability of these weapons, both sides are under tremendous pressure to use their own nuclear weapons for destroying those of the adversary before he can use them. This may lead to large-scale pre-emptive strikes. Use of nuclear weapons soon destroys target acquisition and communication possibilities. Radio and radar connections may be cut for hours or days. This leads to escalation of yields, since lower accuracy must be compensated by higher yields. Furthermore, one is always more liberal regarding the weapon yields intended against the enemy than those which one has to absorb oneself. Therefore, the two sides can be expected to increase the yields alternatively in each salvo. Finally, the bitterness of war leads to the desire to punish and destroy beyond any strategic or tactical need, as shown by the terror bombardment of Dresden in World War II.

One factor which may have speeded up the miniaturization process is the reluctance of the Western European allies to plan for the use of nuclear weapons in their territory because of their destructiveness.

Miniaturization of one's own weapons helps of course, but it does not solve the problem, because one cannot miniaturize one's adversary's weapons. And there is, indeed, no indication that such a process would also take place in the East.

Use of tactical nuclear weapons in a major clash in Europe is unlikely because it would lead to nuclear war which would be so destructive that it would be irrational. Everything should be done to avoid this. The nuclear threshold should remain as high as possible. The lowering of this threshold would be the most dangerous aspect deriving from the development of nuclear miniweapons.

II. *"Primitive miniweapons" using reactor-produced plutonium*

Plutonium is produced by nuclear reactors from the non-fissionable uranium isotope 238. By absorbing one neutron, U-238 yields Np-239 which, by beta-decay, produces Pu-239. This is a fissionable nuclide like U-235 and can be utilized for weapon production.

Reactor fuel elements are quite expensive to manufacture. When civilian power reactors are employed in the production of electricity, the elements are kept in the reactor for as long as possible, usually for more than one year, in order to yield the best economy. During this time, up to 30 per cent of the Pu-239 reacts further. By absorbing an additional neutron, it produces the plutonium isotope Pu-240, which is spontaneously fissionable.

Weapon-grade plutonium should contain no more than 10 per cent Pu-240 and preferably less (4 per cent is a common figure). Military plutonium-producing facilities achieve this by removing the fuel elements from the reactor after only a few weeks' use. The so-called burnup value of the uranium fuel is thus limited to less than 1 000 megawatt-days per ton of uranium. In natural uranium reactors, the fuel elements can be removed without shutting the reactor down but this is not possible with the most common type of civilian power reactor, the light-water reactor, which must be shut down for several weeks in order to remove the fuel rods. The fact that plutonium containing as much as 30 per cent Pu-240 can be utilized in the production of low-yield nuclear weapons has become widely known only quite recently. The *SIPRI Yearbook 1972* states: "Even though contaminated with up to 30 per cent Pu-240, the plutonium normally produced in nuclear power reactors would still be usable as the fissile material for more primitive, but still effective nuclear weapons. A relatively larger amount of this plutonium would have to be used for a given explosive yield and consequently the physical size of the weapon would be larger. Steps would have to be taken to prevent the device from overheating due to the spontaneous fission of Pu-240". [6]

The most important problem regarding high Pu-240 content is not the slightly higher critical mass nor the overheating (mainly due to α-radiation) but the high density of spontaneous neutrons which tend to initiate the chain reaction too soon, before a high degree of over-criticality is attained. Therefore, the yield tends to remain low, in most cases below one kiloton according to Swedish researcher and physicist, Nils Gyldén. [7] Since spontaneous fission follows the Poisson Law of statistics, however, higher yields are also occasionally obtained. Improving technology may render it possible to obtain yields of up to 0.5 kiloton, perhaps even more, with a high degree of probability. Such a weapon would be almost ideal as a low-yield nuclear device, provided that safety to the home troops is always considered along with the maximal theoretical yield. Military commanders often consider a yield greater than that required as a bonus. An unexpected extra yield would be problematic only under certain conditions, for example, when the target is too close to areas having a dense civilian population.

The regeneration of plutonium from spent fuel elements is a well-known technology. There are presently about 20 regeneration plants in 11 countries and the number is rapidly increasing. Any technologically advanced country can construct a regeneration plant and most probably will as soon as it becomes economically feasible, that is, sometime during the 1980s.

Approximately one-third of the world's nations have not yet joined the NPT. Those that have power reactor programmes without bilateral safeguards agreements are free to do as they please with the plutonium produced by their reactors. Even those countries which have signed the NPT can legally keep their nuclear option open, that is, prepare for weapon production but not actually assemble or test warheads. It appears likely that many countries are going to do just this, should the nuclear-weapon countries continue to modernize their tactical nuclear weapons and should the NPT not be essentially reinforced at the first five-year review conference. Since the power reactor programme requires plutonium production in any case, the establishment of a military miniweapon system would be a cheap and attractive bonus. Calculations have demonstrated that, at the beginning of the 1980s, that is, before the fast breeder programme can begin, there will be an overproduction of plutonium. Fissionable material will thus be freely available. The weapon programmes of the present nuclear-weapon countries were expensive since it was necessary for them to construct gas diffusion plants in order to separate U-235 for their reactors. If plutonium is readily available, then the only costs of a nuclear weapon programme are, essentially, those of warhead design and assembly. Although these expenses must not be underestimated, they form only a small portion of the total cost of a full-scale nuclear weapon programme based upon enriched uranium. Gyldén estimates the warhead design and fabrication costs for a series of 20 minibombs having less than one kiloton yields to be as low as 30 million Swedish crowns (approximately $7 million). U Thant's well-known report estimates the cost as $18 million. Thus, the availability of power reactor plutonium will open a new chapter in the history of nuclear weapon development and render it possible for many countries to cheaply produce their own low-yield tactical nuclear weapons.

III. *Comparison of miniweapons and low-yield weapons which use plutonium produced in power reactors*

Miniweapons which have been developed by the US Atomic Energy Commission represent the ultimate result of technological development. They are smaller in size and yield, safer, more accurate and considerably more expensive than the previous models. They are made of weapon-grade plutonium and, in a way, they represent waste of material, because in them only part of that energy is released which could be released from the critical mass present in the weapon.

The low-yield weapons which use reactor-grade plutonium would be considerably different. The critical mass for plutonium containing around 30 per cent Pu-240 is approximately 10 per cent greater than that of the weapon-grade plutonium. Such a device also requires a somewhat greater explosive than a corresponding device made of weapon-grade plutonium. The former would therefore be somewhat bigger and clumsier. Perhaps the greatest difference would be the unpredictability of the yield. Yet another difference is that the "primitive" low-yield weapons are only theoretical at the moment (and hopefully will remain so) while the former, advanced type of miniweapons are a reality, as was disclosed by General Giller on 14 July 1973.

IV. *Effect of miniweapons on the durability of the NPT*

The Non-Proliferation Treaty, which on 5 March 1973 had been in effect for three years, obligates the non-nuclear-weapon states not to acquire or manufacture nuclear weapons. The non-nuclear signatories, which might have planned to acquire nuclear weapons in the absence of the treaty, might have contemplated in most cases acquiring small tactical weapons of the kiloton level. The treaty has prevented this development.

However, the treaty also contains article VI which obligates the signatories "to pursue negotiations . . . for cessation of the nuclear arms race . . . and nuclear disarmament . . ."

Development of a new generation of nuclear weapons (more flexible, more useful in battle, smaller and better) by one signatory, while the treaty has been in force preventing other signatories simultaneously from acquiring similar weapons, clearly violates the spirit of this article which requires progress towards nuclear disarmament, not nuclear arms development. It is true that the wording of the article is very vague: "arms race", for instance, is not defined, and it might be maintained that miniweapons are not a part of the arms race since they are not more effective than previously known weapons. But this is untrue. Since they are smaller and better and since they constitute a step in the technological development, they are more effective in some ways and thus can well be considered a part of the arms race. The worst thing is that the non-nuclear-weapon states must now be prepared to defend themselves against such new weapons which are much more likely to be used against them than were the earlier variety. Thus, the non-nuclear signatories can justly consider themselves to have been deceived. This dubious modernization therefore has grave consequences for the durability of the NPT.

While the SALT negotiations and the Nixon-Brezhnev pact of 22 June 1973 do promise some hope that a strategic nuclear holocaust is becoming less probable, the development of a new generation of nuclear weapons, the miniweapons, shows that the nuclear powers have no intention of giving up their nuclear weapons. It is evident that application of technological development for weapon production cannot be barred. In view of the possibility of using reactor-grade plutonium for production of low-yield tactical nuclear weapons by virtually any state in the near future, one cannot but be pessimistic regarding the longevity of the NPT.

References

1. Lawrence, R. M., *General Military Review*, January 1971, pp. 46–63; February 1971, pp. 237–63.
2. *New York Times*, 16 April 1972.
3. Finley, J. F., "US Army's Guns in Europe to Get New Nuclear Shells", *New York Times*, 10 May 1973.
4. *The Daily Telegraph*, 16 July 1973.
5. *Ibid.*, 11 May 1973.
6. *World Armaments and Disarmament, SIPRI Yearbook 1972* (Stockholm, Almqvist & Wiksell, 1972, Stockholm International Peace Research Institute) p. 366.
7. Hallén, S., *Dagens Nyheter*, 15 May 1973.

Article III

1. *Each non-nuclear weapon State Party to the Treaty undertakes to accept safeguards, as set forth in an agreement to be negotiated and concluded with the International Atomic Energy Agency in accordance with the Statute of the International Atomic Energy Agency and the Agency's safeguards system, for the exclusive purpose of verification of the fulfilment of its obligations assumed under this Treaty with a view to preventing diversion of nuclear energy from peaceful uses to nuclear weapons or other nuclear explosive devices. Procedures for the safeguards required by this article shall be followed with respect to source or special fissionable material whether it is being produced, processed or used in any principal nuclear facility or is outside any such facility. The safeguards required by this article shall be applied on all source or special fissionable material in all peaceful nuclear activities within the territory of such State, under its jurisdiction, or carried out under its control anywhere.*

2. *Each State Party to the Treaty undertakes not to provide: (a) source or special fissionable material, or (b) equipment or material especially designed or prepared for the processing, use or production of special fissionable material, to any non-nuclear-weapon State for peaceful purposes, unless the source or special fissionable material shall be subject to the safeguards required by this article.*

3. *The safeguards required by this article shall be implemented in a manner designed to comply with article IV of this Treaty, and to avoid hampering the economic or technological development of the Parties or international cooperation in the field of peaceful nuclear activities, including the international exchange of nuclear material and equipment for the processing, use or production of nuclear material for peaceful purposes in accordance with the provisions of this article and the principle of safeguarding set forth in the Preamble of the Treaty.*

4. *Non-nuclear-weapon States Party to the Treaty shall conclude agreements with the International Atomic Energy Agency to meet the requirements of this article either individually or together with other States in accordance with the Statute of the International Atomic Energy Agency. Negotiation of such agreements shall commence within 180 days from the original entry into force of this Treaty. For States depositing their instruments of ratification or accession after the 180-day period, negotiation of such agreements shall commence not later than the date of such deposit. Such agreements shall enter into force not later than eighteen months after the date of initiation of negotiations.*

1. Introduction

The greater use of various types of nuclear reactor for the production of electricity will make available large quantities of highly enriched uranium, plutonium and uranium-233. The possibility of diversion of these materials from the nuclear fuel cycle for military purposes will then increase.

Initially, national controls over fuel cycle activities were established to prevent any diversion of nuclear materials into nonpeaceful uses. However, since national systems varied from country to country and since diversion of nuclear material from peaceful to nonpeaceful uses could be adopted as a national policy, such control systems were inadequate. Bilateral, multilateral and regional safeguards arrangements were then established to prevent diversion but it became evident that there was a need for a uniform international safeguards system.

In 1957, the International Atomic Energy Agency (IAEA) was created, one of its tasks being to establish and administer a safeguards system for nuclear material provided by or through the IAEA or through any bilateral, multilateral or national nuclear activities for which the application of international safeguards had been requested. The procedures of this early IAEA safeguards system are described in IAEA document INFCIRC/66.

The Treaty on the Non-Proliferation of Nuclear Weapons, which came into force on 5 March 1970, established the framework within which international safeguards, specifically those of the IAEA, were to operate. Under the treaty the IAEA was given the special responsibility of providing safeguards for ensuring that non-nuclear-weapon countries do not engage in the manufacture of nuclear weapons or other nuclear explosive devices. All non-nuclear-weapon states party to the NPT were required to conclude an agreement with the IAEA for the application of safeguards on all nuclear materials used in all peaceful nuclear activities. The IAEA Board of Governors, therefore, set up a Safeguards Committee which made recommendations for the structure and content of the agreements [1] to be concluded between the IAEA and the non-nuclear-weapon states, parties to the NPT.

The IAEA carries out its verification activities by making use of the national accounting and control system. The agency applies its safeguards so as to enable it to verify the findings of the national system. There are three basic components of NPT safeguards: material accountancy, containment and surveillance.

The term material accountancy is applied to a collection of measurements and other determinations which enable the state and the IAEA to know the location and movement of nuclear material. Diversion of nuclear material for use in nuclear weapons can take place at the outputs of two stages in the nuclear fuel cycle, that is, in a uranium enrichment plant or in a reprocessing plant. The latter is a more sensitive area since not only uranium but also plutonium can be available in pure form at this stage. Although these are the most important stages in the nuclear fuel cycle from the viewpoint of safeguards, the flow of nuclear material through all the peaceful nuclear activities is monitored under the NPT system. This material is followed and measured or, alternatively, the measurements which have already been made are verified. This is done for movements of nuclear material not only within a particular plant but also for movements from plant to plant within a country or between different countries. The nuclear material is checked up to the fuel fabrication plant, for example, where once the fuel elements are produced, they are sealed and registered and each element is then given an identification mark so that it can be traced through to the reprocessing plant. Each plant is subdivided into sections called material balance areas[1] (MBAs) and safeguards are applied at key measurements or stategic points.[2] In a reprocessing plant the strategic points are the input and output stages where fissionable material such as plutonium is measured before either storing it or sending it to a fuel fabrication plant. Afterwards, the verification is quantified: the IAEA makes a statement for each MBA of the amount of material unaccounted for[3] (MUF) with the limits of accuracy.

The other two components of NPT safeguards, containment and surveillance, are designed as complementary measures to accountancy. Containment is a measure to prevent movements of materials whereas surveillance is the detection of movements of nuclear materials. Containment is provided for, in most cases, by the nuclear facilities in the form of, for example, tanks or pipes; such measures may be reinforced by the use of a lock or a seal on storage containers. Surveillance is achieved by using cameras or

[1] " 'Material balance area' means an area in or outside of a *facility* [where]:
(a) The quantity of *nuclear material* in each transfer into or out of each 'material balance area' can be determined; and (b) The *physical inventory* of *nuclear material* in each 'material balance area' can be determined when necessary, in accordance with specified procedures, in order that the material balance for Agency safeguards purposes can be established." [1]
[2] " 'Strategic point' means a location selected during examination of design information where, under normal conditions and when combined with the information from all 'strategic points' taken together, the information necessary and sufficient for the implementation of safeguards measures is obtained and verified: a 'strategic point' may include any location where key measurements related to material balance accountancy are made and where containment and surveillance measures are executed." [1]
[3] " 'Material unaccounted for' means the difference between 'book inventory' and 'physical inventory'. 'Book inventory' of a 'material balance area' means the algebraic sum of the most recent *physical inventory* of that 'material balance area' and all inventory changes that have occurred since that *physical inventory* was taken. 'Physical inventory' means the sum of all the measured or derived estimates of *batch* quantities of *nuclear material* on hand at a given time within a 'material balance area', obtained in accordance with specified procedure." [1]

other devices placed at strategic points so that both the containment measures and the inventory changes are monitored. If surveillance is carried out by IAEA personnel, the inspection access constraints set forth in the Facility Attachment are observed. The Facility Attachment, which describes procedures to be applied to a particular plant, is based on information given to the IAEA by the country in control of that plant. The information is based on a questionnaire which the IAEA sends out. An important element of the Facility Attachment is the verification procedure of which essential factors are the frequency and duration of inspections. Under normal circumstances inspections are carried out by the IAEA and their frequency and duration depend on the efficiency of the national accounting and control system.

The NPT safeguards distinguish between routine inspections and special inspections by explicit "action levels". Normally the inspector will confine his visits to selected points in the plant. However, if a large amount of material cannot be accounted for, the inspector may have access to additional points in the plant. However, this right of access will only be exercised after consulting the government concerned. If after detailed inspection, the IAEA and the operator of the plant conclude that there was no satisfactory explanation of the loss of nuclear material, the matter may eventually be reported to the agency's Board of Governors.

The application of safeguards could become easier if a nuclear facility were designed carefully. For example, if the design of the facility were such that appropriate surveillance equipment could be installed at locations which were important from the point of view of safeguards, then inspections could become less intrusive. Also the physical protection and security of nuclear materials and facilities could be better provided for if physical barriers, facility isolation, secure nuclear materials storage methods, communications and intrusion alarm systems were carefully designed and installed. Another important aspect of the nuclear facility design when safeguards procedures are applied is the availability of adequately designed equipment and laboratory facilities to measure with acceptable accuracy the amount and composition of all nuclear material in the plant.

The effectiveness of NPT safeguards depends on having reliable methods of detection, identification and analysis of nuclear materials which may be in different chemical forms and physical assays. Until recently verification techniques consisted of conventional chemical or physio-chemical analysis of samples taken from strategic points in a plant. Such techniques, known as destructive techniques, are very accurate but they are costly, time consuming and, above all, they require destruction and some consumption of the sample. Moreover, it is not always easy to obtain a representative sample, particularly from heterogeneous sources.

These limitations have been overcome, to some extent, by the development of new assay techniques using direct physical measurement methods.

The new techniques, known as nondestructive techniques, use portable or semiportable instruments which give rapid and sufficiently accurate information for safeguards. With such nondestructive techniques, interference with the normal plant operation is minimized. There are two types of nondestructive assay methods: the passive assay, in which gamma rays and/or neutrons from fissionable materials are measured and the active assay, in which an external gamma-ray or neutron source is used and the secondary gamma rays and neutrons are measured. Of the two the passive assay technique is preferred. Although some of these techniques are used in practice, most are still in the development stage.

There are two unsolved problems related to safeguards which need some consideration. The first one concerns paragraph two of article III of the NPT. According to this,

each State Party to the Treaty undertakes not to provide: (a) source or special fissionable material, or (b) equipment or material especially designed or prepared for the processing, use or production of special fissionable material, to any non-nuclear-weapon State for peaceful purposes, unless the source or special fissionable material shall be subject to the safeguards by this article.

Paragraph one of this article defines "the safeguards by this article" as safeguards "applied on all source or special material in all peaceful nuclear activities". Thus, according to the letter of the NPT, supplies to states which do not have a new safeguards agreement are not allowed. In practice, the supplies have not been halted.

The second problem concerns diversion of nuclear material by terrorists, organized criminals and other nongovernmental groups. Since there is no doubt that, under certain circumstances, the possibility of such diversion exists, it is necessary to evaluate the risks involved to the growing nuclear industry and to note that NPT safeguards, which are aimed at detecting governmental diversion, have no provisions for dealing with nuclear diversion on a nongovernmental level.

Reference

1. IAEA Document INFCIRC/153.

2. The IAEA's NPT safeguards—national control and international safeguards

R. RAINER AND B. SANDERS

Abstract

The safeguards system applied by the IAEA pursuant to article III.1 of the NPT includes the new concept of a relationship between national control and international safeguards. It provides for the establishment of national systems of accounting and control of nuclear material. The IAEA will make full use of such systems in carrying out its verification activities and it will take account of the efficiency of the state's system in determining its inspection effort. The precise relationship between the national system and agency safeguards, and the degree of coordination between control activities of the state and of the IAEA, depend on many factors. Arrangements for coordination in the application of safeguards are part of the NPT agreement between the IAEA, Euratom and the latter's non-nuclear-weapon state members. Some technical elements of these arrangements might be relevant to agreements with individual states that have technically developed national systems, including national inspections. The coordination between international and national inspections might also be a useful precedent to follow in verifying arms control measures.

The IAEA's present safeguards operations are based on two principal legal instruments which in turn find their main support in the IAEA statute. The first instrument was the agency's Safeguards System 1965 (which was extended in 1966 and 1968) and, since 1970, there has been a system that was devised to define the agency's safeguards activities pursuant to the Treaty on the Non-Proliferation of Nuclear Weapons (NPT).

The objective of safeguards under the Safeguards System 1965, in the terms laid down in the agency's statute, was to "ensure, so far as it is able, that assistance provided by it or at its request or under its supervision or control is not used in such a way as to further a military purpose".[1] The only limitation to this responsibility lies in the phrase "so far as it is

---

[1] Article III.A.5 of the statute also authorizes the agency "to apply safeguards, at the request of the parties, to any bilateral or multilateral arrangements, or at the request of a State, to any of that State's activities in the field of atomic energy". Article XII lists the safeguards, rights and responsibilities which the agency is to have to the extent relevant to the project or arrangement.

able". Taken literally, this might be read to mean that the agency should make absolutely certain, by all means at its disposal, that none of the items under its safeguards are used, even indirectly, in a way that would further any military purpose. It is relevant to note that the safeguards operations that are governed by the Safeguards System 1965 still constitute the largest share of the agency's safeguards work, being applied at present in 27 out of a total of 41 states where the agency has safeguards responsibilities. It is evidence of the excessive scope of this objective and of the inability to define within that scope exactly what it is that the agency should do, that in reporting to governments on the outcome of its operations, the agency has so far had to limit itself to a statement that its inspections had not divulged a violation of the relevant agreement.

It was the experience the agency gained in applying its safeguards under the original system that prompted the drafters of the NPT to choose the agency as the instrument for applying safeguards under that treaty. When the NPT entered into force, however, steps had to be taken to adapt the agency's safeguards system to NPT conditions, particularly in view of the open-ended character of the 1965 system. Shortly after the entry into force of the NPT, on 5 March 1970, the agency's Board of Governors set up a committee to advise it on the agency's responsibilities in relation to safeguards covered by article III.1 of the NPT[2] and, in particular, on the content of the agreements to be concluded pursuant to that treaty. The committee met for almost a year and, at the end, recommended to the board a series of provisions that together form our present document INFCIRC/153, the so-called Blue Book. On the technical side, this was based on conceptual studies made by consultants, recommendations by panels and expert working groups and results from development and systems studies in member states of the agency. On the nontechnical side, model agreements were worked out. All this material was incorporated into working papers which were considered by the committee and which resulted in the Blue Book. One of the main results of this concerted action was a more precise definition of the objective of agency safeguards when used for the purpose of the NPT. This was formulated as

the timely detection of diversion of significant quantities of nuclear material from peaceful nuclear activities to the manufacture of nuclear weapons or of other nuclear explosive devices for purposes unknown, and deterrence of such diversion by the risk of early detection.

According to document INFCIRC/153 this objective could be achieved by the use of material accountancy as the safeguards measure of fundamental importance, with containment and surveillance as important supplemen-

---

[2] The board only considered safeguards requirements arising from article III.1 of the NPT. The question of safeguards requirements under article III.2 of the NPT was not dealt with by the board and is not considered in this chapter.

tary measures. The document further provides that the technical conclusion of the agency's verification activities shall be a statement.

. . . of the amount of material unaccounted for over a specific period . . . Furthermore, the sanctions provided in the Agency's Statute can now be called forth . . . if the Board upon examination of relevant information . . . finds that the Agency is *not* able to verify that there has been no diversion of nuclear material required to be safeguarded under the agreement to nuclear weapons or other nuclear explosive devices.

This new verification approach has introduced some new concepts into the safeguards philosophy. In this chapter the authors discuss one of the principal concepts involved, the interplay between national control and international safeguards.

The Blue Book provides that:

The Agreement should provide that the State shall establish and maintain a system of accounting for and control of all nuclear material subject to safeguards under the Agreement, and that such safeguards shall be applied in such a manner as to enable the Agency to verify, in ascertaining that there has been no diversion of nuclear material from peaceful uses to nuclear weapons or other nuclear explosive devices, findings of the State's system. The Agency's verification shall include, *inter alia*, independent measurements and observations conducted by the Agency in accordance with the procedures specified in Part II below. The Agency, in its verification, shall take due account of the technical effectiveness of the State's system.

In carrying out its verification activities, the agency is to make full use of the national system and should avoid unnecessary duplication of the state's accounting and control activities. Some elements of the national system are described in the Blue Book. They include, for example, a system for measuring quantities of nuclear material together with a system for evaluating the precision and accuracy of measurements; procedures for inventory taking and evaluation of accumulations of unmeasured inventory and losses; a records and reports system, and measures to ensure that the accounting procedures are operated correctly. How far some of the actions listed are fulfilled by the plant operator, or, in some cases, by the state itself, naturally depends to a large extent on the specific situation in the country. Summarizing, one might say that the national system of accounting for and control of nuclear material should serve as the infrastructure for the application of the international safeguards system.

The 1965 agency safeguards system did not specifically assign a role to the national system. It was necessary, of course, for each state which had concluded a safeguards agreement with the agency to establish the internal machinery needed to meet its international obligations; however, there were no specific requirements for the organization of the system, and its components and operation were, consequently, determined exclusively by the state. Conversely, the agency's system operated to a large extent independent of the state's system and the intensity of agency safeguards and, in particular, the agency's inspection effort—which under the new system is influenced by the effectiveness of the national system and the quality of its findings—had no formal relationship with any activities of the state. The formal statement that there should be a national control system and the definition of its role within the international system has only been developed as part of the NPT safeguards system.

Discussion of this interesting concept of a control system to ensure compliance with treaty obligations, consisting of national measures brought into relationship with international safeguards, may be of substantial relevance for the future development of nuclear safeguards. One consequence of applying this concept might be a possible decrease in specific safeguards costs for the agency. It is becoming more important, given the continuous increase in nuclear activities and, therefore, safeguards work, that the agency ensure optimum cost effectiveness.

The definition of the technical objective of safeguards in the Blue Book has been an important step in dissipating possible apprehensions about the potential open-endedness of international safeguards. The development of effective national control systems and their systematic coordination with international safeguards will help to assure accomplishment of the technical objectives within the constraints governing the international system.

The Blue Book defines the relationship between the national system and agency safeguards in a flexible manner. It is also clear from the Blue Book that in verifying the findings of the national system, the agency not only checks the measurements and observations made by the state, but also makes its own independent measurements and observations. The magnitude of the independent activity is related, *inter alia*, to the uncertainties in the findings of the state's system. The Blue Book postulated a common objective for the national system and for the agency's safeguards. A formal (quantified) statement setting forth the technical conclusion is only required for the agency's verification acitivities. This should be a statement, within each material balance area, of the amount of nuclear material unaccounted for over a specific period and the limits of accuracy of the amounts stated.

Besides providing the basis for the application of agency safeguards, the national system has the task of guarding against diversion of nuclear material at the subnational level (that is, by individuals, groups or even by the operator himself). Appropriate measures by the state to ensure the physical security of nuclear material will be a desirable and necessary supplement to the three safeguards measures: nuclear material accountancy, surveillance and containment. Primarily, however, the national system should ensure that the required accounting data are available as records, open to inspection by the agency and transmitted to the agency in the form of reports. Also, the national system should evaluate these data, together with accumulations of unmeasured inventory and unmeasured losses. The Blue Book does not specifically require a state to establish a full-fledged inspection apparatus. For a state to do so, it must consider the nature and size of the nuclear activities on its territory and the concomitant degree of complexity of its accounting and control measures. The existence of national inspection reflects the efficiency of the national system and the extent to which the operators of facilities are functionally independent of the state's control system, a factor which the agency has to take into account in the determination of its own inspection effort. However, the task of national inspectors (who may have other functions besides those specifically connected with the application of a safeguards agreement) and their method of work may well differ from those of agency inspectors; consequently, to coordinate the two, special arrangements will be required.

There is yet insufficient experience regarding the extent to which a national system can be integrated into international safeguards work. The protocol to the NPT agreement signed on 5 April 1973 by the agency, the European Atomic Energy Community (Euratom) and the non-nuclear-weapon states, members of Euratom, contains specific provisions on the coordination of the safeguards activities of both organizations. Although these were developed in a different situation, some of the technical elements of the agreed coordination may also be relevant for the relationship between a highly-developed national system and agency safeguards. The major difference between the Euratom system and individual national control systems is the very high degree of functional independence of plant operators from the Euratom Commission. This may not exist elsewhere between operators and the national authority. The commission, as the authority for implementing the security control provisions of the Euratom treaty, is independent from the governments of member states in carrying out this task; accounting and other data are collected directly from plant operators. In addition, Euratom has a safeguards objective comparable to that of the agency. These particular aspects have to be fully recognized. As discussed below, some of the technical procedures agreed upon may equally apply to the coordination of a national system with the agency's system, provided a number of criteria are met by the national system.

The agency's NPT safeguards system—and, therefore, also the arrangements with Euratom—comprises the traditional components of the 1965 system (review of design information of plants, the requirement to maintain records on nuclear material, the obligation to transmit reports to the agency and the carrying out of inspections by the agency). The design information is used to prepare the technical document setting forth in detail how safeguards are applied at a particular plant (this is the so-called facility attachment which forms part of the Subsidiary Arrangements to the Safeguards Agreement). The collaboration in the evaluation of design information provided for reflects existing practice; subsidiary arrangements are always negotiated between the agency and the state. In the field of nuclear material accounting, a state may choose to establish a central nuclear material accounting system which would involve analysis and evaluation of the data received from nuclear plants. An evaluation by the state of these accounting data, involving also investigations of random and systematic measurement errors, or enquiries into causes of nuclear material unaccounted for, would considerably facilitate the verification task of the agency.

The nub of any coordination arranged between the IAEA and the state would lie in the national system's criteria and procedures for the acceptance or rejection of the operator's measurements and the way these are verified by the international safeguards system. The accuracy is a function of the kind and quantity of the material involved in a given material balance area and the measurement capability associated with it. The design information should give the figures for throughput and inventory at the key measurement points together with the accuracy with which measurements can be carried out. This information would enable the national system of accountancy and control—if it wishes to go that far—to design a verification plan which would permit it to make a statement on the quantities of material unaccounted for and their limits of uncertainty. As the actual throughput and inventory change, the magnitude, scope and nature of the verification effort should be adjusted; this is an iterative process which must continue as long as the safeguards are applied and which probably should be renewed for each material balance period, that is, each period for which, after the physical inventory is taken, a material balance is struck. At the same time the national system would verify the actual performance of the measurements by the operator. This process of national verification is also a continuing one. The international safeguards authority in turn has the task of drawing its own technical conclusions on the material unaccounted for and on the limits of uncertainty, and for this purpose, it has to use the results of its independent measurements. To this end, it has at its disposal the entire range of safeguards procedures including: the analysis of design information and of the on-going operational process; the independent verification of the operator's accounting and operating records; the analysis of the reports made by the operator; the taking and analysing of samples; the observation of physical inventory-taking, and the use and verification of means of surveillance and containment. Whatever the extent to which the international authority makes use of the findings of the national system, it must, under any circumstance, receive full design information, accounting reports and the information obtained by the national system in the application of its inspection, if any. The nature, intensity and scope of the independent verification by the international system will obviously depend on the kind of technical process involved, the quality of the operator's measurements and his measurement methods, the level of control applied by the national system and the latter's capacity to make statements that are independent from those of the operator. Thus, the extent and nature of the international verification is always subject to variation and the way it dovetails with the national system must be continuously reviewed.

The most important point in the coordination of national control activities and international safeguards concerns the coordination of inspections. Article 80 of the Blue Book states figures for the maximum routine inspection effort to be applied by the agency for categories of facilities, expressed in terms of man-years of inspection. There are no maxima for individual plants. Article 81 lists the criteria to be taken into account in determining the actual number, intensity, timing and mode of routine inspections of a plant; however, these criteria are neither susceptible to easy quantification nor does the Blue Book indicate the relative value to be assigned to each of them. Panels of experts have already achieved results in further defining these matters and in quantifying the technical conclusions to be reached in an iterative process. In the subsidiary arrangements there is usually a figure for the estimated actual routine inspection effort to be applied by the agency at a particular plant under normal conditions; for individual states these figures have had to be calculated without taking into account the impact national inspections may have once they are established.

Under the protocol to the IAEA/Euratom-NPT agreement, the estimates of the respective inspection efforts by Euratom and the agency for each nuclear plant will be worked out in advance according to agreed rules and methods. Similarly the verification approach and inspection procedures will be laid down in advance. The calculation of the inspection effort and the coordination of the inspection activities of the two organizations constituted the crucial part in the negotiations. The coordination arrangements, which take up 12 of the 25 articles of the protocol, involve:

1. A statement of principle that account will be taken of the community inspection effort in determining the actual number, intensity, duration, timing and mode of agency routine inspections.

2. Estimates of the actual routine inspection effort per facility will be agreed upon. These estimates are based on examples for specific types of facilities. (The examples are based on rules and methods for calculating routine inspection effort, agreed between Euratom and the agency.) These estimates will constitute actual maxima, subject to normal operating conditions and provided that a number of conditions continue to be met, such as: the continued validity of the information on community safeguards and of the design information provided; regular reports; application of the coordination arrangements for inspections, and the application by the community of its stipulated inspection effort.

3. Agency inspections will be carried out simultaneously with community inspections and the agency will implement its inspection rights by observing community inspection activities whenever it can so achieve the purposes of its routine inspections, as laid down in the agreement. This requires agree-

ment on planning and scheduling of inspections, on technical procedures, and advance coordination in the carrying out of each inspection. Equally, advance knowledge by the agency of the number, types and contents of the items to be inspected at a particular community inspection is necessary.

4. The agency must be fully informed of the work performed by community inspectors and on the results of community inspections; the "inspection working papers" for inspections at which agency inspectors were present and inspection reports for all other inspections have to be made available to the agency.

5. Techniques for random selection of statistical samples of nuclear material have to be agreed upon since samples for the agency are normally taken together with community samples.

6. An institutional machinery composed of representatives of the community and of the agency (liaison committee) is established to facilitate the application of the agreement and, in particular, of the coordination arrangements.

An analysis of these coordination arrangements shows that they are based predominantly on the existence of a technically effective and functionally independent control system (which will, in addition, be adapted to meet all the requirements resulting from the agreement, the protocol and the subsidiary arrangements) and on a willingness to undertake substantial additional obligations. It follows that certain elements of these arrangements could also be relevant to agreements with an individual state, provided that the state has a technically developed national system and is prepared to undertake substantial additional obligations in organizing and operating its national system, which, in turn, would enable the agency to take account of the national inspection effort.

The extent to which national inspections would be valuable in the context of an NPT-type agreement would depend on a number of factors. Among these are such considerations as: whether the national system is geared to obtain the same technical conclusions as the agency's system; the extent to which it provides for impartial and independent verification of operators' nuclear material accountancy; the adequacy of the quality control by the state of operators' measurement systems; the analysis of samples and checking of standards used for testing; whether the state's verification of physical inventories of nuclear material is compatible with agency requirements in both intensity and procedure, and whether the national inspection procedures meet agency standards. If these conditions were met, it should be possible to carry out national and agency inspections in such a way that the agency has full knowledge of the results obtained through national inspections and can use them for its own verification. All this would, obviously, require a very efficient (and possibly costly) national control system. The agency should, of course, always be in a position to carry out a substantial independent verification effort and to obtain a basic amount of data for itself. This implies that the agency should have direct access to all the information on which the national system bases its findings. If all these requirements were fulfilled, and appropriate coordination arrangements could be worked out, then the agency should be able to keep its routine inspection effort below the level at which it would have to perform otherwise, without this resulting in a lower credibility of the agency's statements on the results of its verification.

Safeguards consist basically of a bookkeeping system for nuclear material. As Dr Rometsch, the present head of the IAEA's Department of Safeguards and Inspection, put it in his paper for the 1971 Geneva Conference:

That in practice bookkeeping can really be the backbone of a safeguards system is related to the simple fact that today's nuclear technology centers around the fission of the nuclei contained in only two chemical elements which are used almost exclusively for nuclear purposes—uranium and plutonium.

One has to examine very carefully, therefore, whether a comparable situation exists for other agreements in the field of arms control and whether there is a comparable relationship between the obligations to be verified and the proposed verification system. Nevertheless, it should be recognized that the NPT safeguards agreements assign for the first time a substantial role to national control measures; that they foresee a defined relationship of the international system with the national system in flexible terms, and that they have opened the possibility for the coordination of international inspection activities and national inspections.

3. NPT safeguards

W. HÄFELE

Abstract

Safeguards of nuclear material have been a major point of concern since the early days of nuclear power. The first part of this chapter covers historical development of such safeguards and analyses the driving forces that led to that development. Special attention is given to the period of the early 1960s when peaceful applications of nuclear power became a category of its own for both nuclear-weapon as well as non-nuclear-weapon states. The establishment of a civilian nuclear fuel cycle and the flow of nuclear material in it are its most obvious characteristics.

This was the scope of the problem when the NPT came up, as negotiations had to embrace military considerations, alliance problems and questions on the civilian applications of nuclear energy. An analyses of this complex interweaving is attempted. It culminates in an assessment of the present situation and the accomplishments of NPT safeguards.

The final part deals with the problem of physical protection and more general applications of safeguards techniques that have been developed in the past years. Finally, the general context of the NPT is more explicitly considered in order to obtain a longer-range outlook.

I. *The first phase of the safeguards problem*

If an assessment of the present state of nuclear safeguards is to be made, it is useful to consider, at least briefly, the short history of safeguards in the use of nuclear energy. One can distinguish three phases in their history. The first phase began in 1945. At that time there was only one nuclear-weapon state, the United States of America, and on the surface the situation looked simple. The USA proposed from the beginning an international authority which would own or have managerial control of all nuclear material from the processing of ore in the mine to the end uses of such material. It was proposed to give the international authority the power to impose sanctions for minor violations, and to have a veto-free Security Council to deal with major violations. It was also suggested that a control system be set up after which the stockpile of nuclear weapons in the possession of the USA would be disposed of. This plan is known as the Baruch plan [1] after the US Ambassador to the United Nations at that time.

This plan did not materialize. The Soviet Union made a counterproposal that left nuclear resources in national hands and gave the international authority only the power to conduct certain inspections. It then became impossible to agree on control and inspection procedures and the arms race began. It was really only the military use of nuclear energy that was of interest. The term "military use" refers here to both the design and construction of weapons and the nuclear propulsion devices for submarines and ships. By 1955 the stockpiles of nuclear weapons had grown so large that it seemed impossible to give satisfactory assurances of their elimination no matter what the procedures would be. Because of this problem the United States also officially dropped the Baruch plan. It is noteworthy that this was as late as September 1955. Of course, the problem of the stockpile of nuclear weapons persisted. International negotiations on arms control and disarmament since 1955 have been characterized by the problem of fissionable material production cut-off and transfer.

II. *The US Atomic Energy Acts, the second phase of safeguards and the Treaty of Rome*

Complementary to the international development of safeguards is their development within the United States. The Atomic Energy Act of 1946 placed a strict embargo on the export of nuclear information and material with the explicit hope that such a policy could halt the proliferation of nuclear weapons. The atomic bomb explosions by Great Britain and the Soviet Union, however, demonstrated that this policy had failed. By 1953 the nuclear monopoly of the USA no longer existed and the problem of non-proliferation became much more complex. The US side then established a new approach to the problem which marked the beginning of the second phase of safeguards.

The principal idea of that second phase was to encourage the peaceful uses of atomic energy by providing an incentive for the transfer of fissionable material from the military domain to the civilian domain. This idea was enhanced by the growing recognition of the fact that the peaceful uses of atomic energy might indeed become important one day. The starting point for this new policy was the famous speech of President Eisenhower before the UN General Assembly in December 1953. Accordingly, inside the USA a new Atomic Energy Act replaced the one of 1946. It is useful to recall the senate report on the envisaged 1954 atomic energy legislation.

Today we are not alone in the drive to achieve peacetime atomic power. Eight years ago, besides the United States, only the United Kingdom, Canada, and—as we have recently come to find—the Soviet Union had major atomic energy projects in being. The possibility of cooperation with other nations to gain mutual advantage in the areas of peacetime power appeared far in the future. As against

143

this, however, more than 20 countries now have vigorous atomic energy programs, and several of them are pressing toward the construction of atomic power plants to turn out useful amounts of electricity. [1]

The resulting 1954 Atomic Energy Act did provide for international cooperation in the field of the peaceful uses of atomic energy. Against the background of what has been said about the first phase of the history of safeguards it is natural that this new legislation insists on inspection and verification of the peaceful uses of the atom in international cooperation.

In order to expedite this plan, the USA brought forward the idea of creating the International Atomic Energy Agency (IAEA). It was hoped that all cooperation, specifically the transfer of nuclear material, would be channelled through this agency. The IAEA was therefore expected to be the principal instrument for the transfer of nuclear material from the military to the civilian domain.

The third big event that got the programme for the peaceful uses of atomic energy started was the first International Conference on the Peaceful Uses of Atomic Energy at Geneva in 1955. The success of this conference was overwhelming and in response there was a truly worldwide enthusiasm for the development of the peaceful uses of atomic energy.

The IAEA in Vienna grew slowly. Many partners were uncertain about their eventual success but many bilateral contacts developed. Most of them were between non-nuclear-weapon states and nuclear-weapon states, chiefly the USA, because at that time high posture in the field of military uses of nuclear energy was synonymous with high posture in the field of peaceful uses of atomic energy. Other instances of bilateral cooperation were the Dutch-Norwegian and the Canadian-Indian programmes.

The transfers of nuclear material that were made through the IAEA were limited. Today it is clear that those transfers did not have the impact on the arms race that was hoped for at the time of the foundation of the IAEA. Nevertheless, the agency developed steadily and became a major instrument in helping lesser developed nations make use of the benefits of the atom, especially in the application of radioactive isotopes. The importance of that development and its significance for the underdeveloped countries is sometimes underestimated.

The agreements on cooperation that were concluded by the USA provided for: the exchange of information, the transfer of nuclear material and the transfer of equipment including complete reactors. The idea of safeguards was relevant to all three areas. Safeguards adhered to the elements that came from the nuclear-weapon states.

In many cases the safeguards required by the Atomic Energy Act of 1954 were to be implemented by the IAEA; it was therefore necessary for this agency to set up a safeguards system. In the early years of the 1960s the non-nuclear-weapon states, while receiving cooperation from the USA and other nuclear-weapon states, had nevertheless developed elements of the peaceful uses of atomic energy of their own. The original safeguards system of the IAEA therefore distinguished sharply between nuclear material to be safeguarded that came from nuclear-weapon states via the IAEA and nuclear material not subject to safeguards. Further, in the early 1960s the isolated nuclear facility was the focus of interest. In many cases this was a research reactor, say a swimming pool reactor, which had no fuel cycle. The power of such facilities was too small to produce something like a technical flow of fissionable material since 1 g/day of nuclear material corresponds with 1 MW(th). Accordingly, the safeguards provisions of the early IAEA system concentrated on these isolated nuclear facilities as such. The impact of large power reactors and their related fuel cycle was not yet felt. The document that describes the procedures of this early IAEA safeguards system is IAEA Document INFCIRC/66 with its revisions 1 and 2. [2] The procedures there are described in fairly broad terms that allow for a wide spectrum of interpretation. The peaceful uses of atomic energy were not yet commercially and industrially significant when the original document was conceived and adopted by the Board of Governors of the IAEA.

During the second phase of safeguards the Treaty of Rome was signed, thus constituting the European Community in general as a part of the European Atomic Energy Community, Euratom. The concept of that community was very broad; nothing less than the unification of Europe. The peaceful uses of atomic energy therefore had a very broad scope politically, geographically and technically. The treaty that constitutes Euratom has article 7 on safeguards as a cornerstone of the whole arrangement. It is preceded by article 6 on the supply of nuclear material. Supply and safeguards of nuclear material as key components of the discussion on arms control and disarmament indeed reappear in the Treaty of Rome. Their inclusion in that treaty is important as a matter of principle. The signatory states abandon their sovereign rights in respect to safeguards of nuclear material in a legally binding form, permanently and not only on the occasion of special transfer of such material. The safeguards provision of the Euratom treaty are, accordingly, very universal. Similarly, according to that treaty there is no ownership of nuclear material; the various users of nuclear material only process that material, the ultimate title being with the Euratom Supply Agency.

This powerful and far reaching concept of ownership and safeguards of nuclear material within Euratom developed parallel to the IAEA under the assumption that the peaceful industrial and commercial uses of atomic energy would come at a time when the concept of the common market had fully materialized.

The practical implementation of the peaceful applications of atomic energy was more complex. Enriched uranium and plutonium were available in larger quantities only from the United States. According to the basic ideas of the Atomic Energy Act of 1954, a far-reaching agreement of cooperation was made which included the aspects of safeguards. Safeguards required by the Atomic Energy Act were identified with Euratom safeguards and this led to the concept of their verification by the USA. The practical situation that evolved can be described by saying that it was a cross between the Euratom Treaty of Rome of 1957 and the US Atomic Energy Act of 1954.

III. *The early 1960s*

The slow but steady evolution of arms control and disarmament led to the third phase of the history of safeguards. Plans for a General and Complete Disarmament (1962) to be negotiated by an Eighteen Nations Disarmament Committee (ENDC) had been arrived at after several intermediary stages including: the Western proposal for a certain package deal in 1957, the Ten Nations Disarmament Committee of 1960, the US Program for General and Complete Disarmament of 1961, the Swedish UN resolution on the creation of a non-nuclear club of 1961 and an Irish resolution also of 1961. The idea not to transfer nuclear weapons from nuclear-weapon states to non-nuclear-weapon states and to freeze the existing strategic situation was the concept for the start of the ENDC. All this appears very similar to what had been attempted in the 1950s but the points of principle arose from some strategically relevant developments in weapon technology:

(a) The technological possibility of having hardened missile silos was demonstrated and implemented.

(b) The software for that hardware, that is the strategic concept, was provided for by a number of outstanding thinkers in the USA. The name of Jerome Wiesner has to be mentioned here.

(c) Technology had reached a point where reconnaissance, delivery and the nuclear warhead established a consistent weapon system that was capable of reaching any point on the globe. The globe was no longer "unlimited"; it had become small.

These technological developments had changed the world at a fundamental level. Moreover, arms control and disarmament problems were no longer those of the 1950s; they, too, had changed.

The ENDC started its work in 1962 but it was 1964 when a proposal of President Johnson introduced the concept of non-proliferation and freezing that stimulated the work of the ENDC so clearly. It was also at that time that the peaceful applications of the atom experienced a breakthrough from the state of R&D to the stage of industrial and commercial build-up. I refer to the Oyster Creek event. In December 1963 the Jersey Central Power and Light utility ordered a boiling water reactor from General Electric on purely commercial grounds. A boom of ordering LWRs followed in

146

the USA. Today the capacity of nuclear power plants that are firmly ordered, under construction or in operation totals roughly 100 000 MW(e).

The salient point is that shortly thereafter, in 1966, two nuclear power stations were ordered in Germany (Stade and Würgassen) also on purely commercial grounds.

In a number of industrialized non-nuclear-weapon states the development of the peaceful applications of nuclear energy grew more and more successful. The development was never conceived as an extension of a basically military development but was conceived and implemented as a development on its own grounds and merits. The cheap production of electricity was only the peak of an iceberg. In the 1950s and 1960s it became obvious what modern technologies meant to an industrialized nation. Strong impulses for innovation were obtained by the development of such technologies. Nuclear energy was the forerunner and a prototypical venture. What weapon development was for the nuclear-weapon states, the development of civilian major technologies was for the non-nuclear-weapon states: ventures for innovation and progress. The worldwide debate and reflection on big science of these years is indicative of that. On the meaning of big science and its impact on modern industrialized non-nuclear-weapon states, a book written by Ryukichi Imai serves as an example of these far-reaching considerations. [3] Among other things this also meant that no longer was a high posture in the field of the peaceful uses of atomic energy synonymous with a high posture in the field of military uses of atomic energy. The peaceful uses had started to become a category on their own. This is the background against which the advent of the NPT has to be seen.

IV. *The third phase of safeguards*

In the mid 1960s, the NPT safeguards presented two main problems, one political and the other technical.

The political problem is obvious if one considers the original drafts of the NPT. The US draft required in article III, IAEA or equivalent international safeguards, thus permitting Euratom safeguards to be on an equal footing with IAEA safeguards. One has to bear in mind that the size and experience of the Euratom safeguards were larger than those of the IAEA, at least in the second half of the 1960s. Also the political embedding of Euratom safeguards in the Treaty of Rome was more comprehensive. In the years that were politically characterized by the key word of the bipolar strategic equilibrium, the whole problem was, apart from one of prestige, a question of the structure of alliances. This political problem was emphasized by the fact that both safeguards systems were not very specific. It was not clear to what extent they were complementary to one another or simply parallel.

The other problem was equally complex. The word technical hardly describes it adequately. It was mentioned before that the peaceful application of nuclear energy had much matured both in nuclear-weapon states and in industrialized non-nuclear-weapon states. All non-nuclear-weapon states were possibly ready to admit that the global security question indeed required an inequality in the military domain. Of course, military inequalities have always occurred in history. But there had never been a demand to legalize such inequalities on a worldwide basis and to perpetuate them indefinitely. This demand was unique; even so the non-nuclear-weapon states were eventually ready to accept that, but they insisted on not establishing by the same token, an inequality in the civilian domain. Recall that in the 1960s it began to be possible to have a high posture in the peaceful applications of the atom with no posture whatsoever in military applications. A sharp decoupling of the military and peaceful applications of the atom was the issue at stake.

This debate sometimes took unexpected directions, for instance concerning the problem of fallout or spin-off. It was argued that this spin-off would be significant and would put the nuclear-weapon-states into a technologically superior position in the civilian domain forever. Such a claim was not without substance although it turned out that this was again a complex problem. On the surface there was no tangible evidence for such spin-off. But one must realize that the low price for separative work that was, and still is, offered by the USA and other nuclear-weapon states was possible only because the diffusion plants were larger, and they were large because of military requirements. Without such low prices for separative work the commercial breakthrough of the light water reactor would not have been possible that early. It was therefore more a capacitive fallout than a straightforward technical fallout. The whole debate was highlighted by the debate on the technological gap.

Another problem was that of competition between a nuclear-weapon state and a non-nuclear-weapon state in the field of commercial applications of the peaceful atom. Nuclear-weapon states should not have an advantage there simply because there was inequality in the military domain. That this should be appropriately expressed in the final text of the NPT was therefore demanded, as well as that safeguards of nuclear weapons be applied to all partners equally, irrespective of their weapon status. This whole argument is somehow highlighted by the insertion of article IV in the final text of the NPT. This follows from the idea of the equality of all states in the civilian domain. To some extent this is also true for article V. Both articles were not contained in the various early drafts of the NPT. In my judgement the existing form of the NPT is much more balanced than before.

A third aspect of the problem in connection with NPT safeguards was the global nature required for such safeguards by the NPT. NPT safeguards were rightfully expected to be universal. They should embrace political parties that are not within the same political grouping. Up to then safeguards had been executed only within such political groupings and not across.

This made it obvious that the existing IAEA safeguards as described in INFCIRC/66 and its revisions were not designed to meet this new situation. A much more detailed description and design of safeguards was required to do this. Or more precisely, a much greater formalization was required. A strong formalization allows one to more safely predict what safeguards are up to. Further, it was necessary to make the whole safeguards procedures more objective. Not the subjective feelings of those who inspect, but objective findings that can be proven and demonstrated must be the basis for NPT safeguards. This then leads among other things to a predetermined answer to the question: when will the inspector be satisfied? Is he searching for a kilogramme, for 10 grammes, for a gramme or for a milligramme of nuclear material? This must be answered in advance so that the signatories of the NPT know what to expect. Finally, NPT safeguards must be rational. Otherwise it would be impossible to have truly global safeguards simply for financial reasons.

V. *Safeguards and the NPT*

One can summarize by saying that the universal nature of NPT safeguards requires such safeguards to be *formalized, objective* and *rational*. These were the considerations that led to the establishment of the principles for NPT safeguards. In the NPT (preamble and article III) this principle is described as follows:

the principle of safeguarding effectively the flow of source and special fissionable materials by the use of instruments and other techniques at certain strategic points. [4]

This description points to a technical situation. It is the flow of nuclear material through the fuel cycle. In the commercial application of nuclear energy many thousands MW(th) are produced and many kilogrammes per day are flowing through the cycle accordingly. The universal nature of NPT safeguards also covered all processes involved in the fuel cycle, that is, reactors, chemical reprocessing, fabrication, transport and storage. This is in contrast with the earlier situation of IAEA INFCIRC/66 where it was the isolated nuclear facility for which that early IAEA system was designed. The difference can be illustrated by examining the part of the fuel cycle that connects the reactor and the reprocessing plant. If one considers the reactor as an isolated facility it is necessary to calculate the build-up of plutonium in that reactor. This is a tedious and still insufficiently accurate job. If on the other hand the reactor is considered to be part of a fuel cycle, all one has to do is to make sure that the irradiated fuel elements reach the dissolver of the reprocessing plant. There the fuel is then open and accessible for direct measurement. Measurement becomes the most important tool in a modern safeguards system such as that of the NPT. This also helps to expedite the search for objectivity and formalization. Measurements result in figures and figures can be dealt with objectively, at least in principle, and the procedures can be formalized. It is now natural to consider instruments and other techniques that measure the flow through the fuel cycle. For that, certain points have to be identified. They then become strategic points. For instance, the dissolver of a reprocessing plant is obviously such a strategic point in the fuel cycle. On the other hand, most of a nuclear power station is not of interest for measuring the flow of material through the fuel cycle. It is therefore not necessary to expose most of such a power station to safeguards procedures. The IAEA has given a definition of a strategic point:

Strategic point means a location selected during examination of design information where, under normal conditions and when combined with the information from all "strategic points" taken together the information necessary and sufficient for the implementation of safeguards measures is obtained and verified; a "strategic point" may include any location where key measurements related to material balance accountancy are made and where containment and surveillance measures are executed. [5]

The principle of NPT safeguards defines safeguards procedure in a predictable way as necessary and sufficient procedures. It thus also helps to make safeguards rational. The IAEA definition of a strategic point also makes explicit what the three principal components of NPT safeguards are: material balance accounting, containment and surveillance.

The containment which exists, in most cases anyway, provides a conduit function for the flow of nuclear material through the fuel cycle and surveillance helps to make the system complete where necessary. Storages may be a good example of that.

The NPT safeguards principle concentrates on the nuclear material. Indeed, it is the nuclear material that establishes the link between the civilian and the military domain. If the civilian domain could be made completely tight against the military domain the whole safeguards problem would be taken care of. Of course, the nuclear material has to be somewhere, mostly in nuclear facilities and to that extent NPT safeguards also touch the nuclear facilities. But the fact that NPT safeguards have as their subject the nuclear material and not the peaceful applications as such establishes a subtle but sometimes decisive distinction. It is then natural to have accountability of nuclear material as the main component of NPT safeguards. Surveillance, where required, makes the safeguards system complete.

The NPT safeguards principle brought new, mostly technical, substance into the procedure of negotiating the NPT. It was felt that the technical

150

weight of such substance is large enough to resolve the above mentioned difficulties of NPT safeguards. In 1967 the IAEA started a whole sequence of working groups that brought together a limited but capable group of experts who worked hard to analyse the problem in greater depth and to spell out, in an iterative fashion, solutions to the various subproblems. This cautious and wise approach was in my judgement outstandingly successful. In the summer of 1970 it was possible to hold the first large international symposium on safeguards techniques at Karlsruhe, Germany. The Board of Governors of the IAEA established the Safeguards Committee that negotiated in great detail the procedures for NPT safeguards during the second half of 1970 and the early part of 1971. In spite of its large membership this committee was very successful. Its results are contained in IAEA Document INFCIRC/153 which has served as a base document ever since.

It was necessary to install various levels of safeguards. The INFCIRC/153 document distinguishes the level of the operator of a nuclear facility. The operator keeps certain predetermined records and forwards form sheets as reports to the safeguards authorities. Inspections are conducted by a national or regional safeguards authority and the IAEA verifies these procedures by making sure that the inspection of the national or regional safeguards authority is properly executed by a limited amount of inspections of its own. A certain structuring of the safeguards procedures was thus necessary in order to make the whole safeguards process feasible.

VI. *The NPT, the Treaty of Rome and the nuclear-weapon states*

From the outline given above it can be seen that safeguards procedures should be applied to the peaceful applications of nuclear energy regardless of whether the peaceful applications take place in nuclear-weapon states or in non-nuclear-weapon states. It is the principle of equality in the civilian domain that leads to this request. The whole approach and the provisions of the NPT can easily become a precedent for future non-proliferation problems. Therefore it is more than ever necessary not to let the idea of non-proliferation apply to the civilian domain. During the negotiations of the NPT this approach led the industrialized non-nuclear-weapon states to ask the nuclear-weapon states to apply NPT safeguards also to their peaceful applications of the atom. The USA and Great Britain basically agreed and made a formal offer to IAEA to do just this. In the case of France, which is not a signatory of the NPT, it was argued that France is a signatory of the Treaty of Rome and to that extent subject to Euratom safeguards. This throws additional light on the question of IAEA versus Euratom safeguards.

The sequence of events started in March 1970 when the NPT came into effect. The NPT requested the non-nuclear-weapon states adhering to the treaty to start their negotiations with the IAEA 180 days after the original entry into force of this treaty. This would have been September 1970. However, the Safeguards Committee of the Board of Governors of the IAEA revealed their results only in May 1971. The text of the NPT requests the conclusion of the negotiations between the IAEA and the non-nuclear signatory not more than 18 months later. This leads then to November 1972, at the latest, as the starting date for NPT safeguards to become operative. However, this schedule applies to those non-nuclear signatories for whom the NPT entered into force in March 1970. The Euratom non-nuclear weapon countries insisted on having the Euratom safeguards continue in a way that satisfied both NPT requirements and the provisions of the Treaty of Rome. In order to assure this they signed, but did not yet ratify, the NPT. This means that at least formally the clock has not yet started to run.

To give the desired assurance it was necessary to start negotiations between the IAEA and Euratom. This in turn required Euratom to have a mandate from the Council of Ministers but here the complex problem of the nuclear weapon status of France came up which took some time to resolve. The Treaty of Rome does not make a distinction between nuclear-weapon states and non-nuclear-weapon states but the NPT does. On the other hand, France is not a signatory of the NPT. It was possible to resolve that problem within Euratom by compromise and the negotiations between the IAEA and Euratom started. They were successfully concluded in March of this year. It was possible to reconcile the Treaty of Rome and the NPT. If, on a *de facto* basis, safeguards in the Euratom countries were in the past a cross between the Treaty of Rome and the US Atomic Energy Act of 1954 they will probably, in the future, be a cross between the Treaty of Rome and the NPT.

It is reasonable to expect ratification of the NPT by the non-nuclear-weapon states of the European Community in the course of 1973: NPT safeguards can then become effective in turn. One should realize that even this way one arrives at November of 1973, the date that was calculated above as the latest date to make NPT safeguards effective for those signatories that had ratified early. The accumulation of practical NPT safeguards experience in larger amounts therefore might actually start in 1974. In my judgement it will take two or three years after that before a review of existing NPT safeguards experience can be meaningful. The text of article VIII of the NPT, however, provides for a first review conference five years after entry into force of the NPT, that is, in 1975. In view of the very elaborate work that went into the preparation and build-up of NPT safeguards and in view of the size and complexity of the matter, only a thorough evaluation of a sufficient amount of practical field and headquarter experiences makes sense, in my judgement. I therefore express the personal view that a first review conference in 1975 is definitely too early so far as the problem of safeguards is concerned.

VII. *Physical protection*

There is one more point that must be dealt with. The Safeguards Committee of the IAEA Board of Governors has made it explicit that IAEA Safeguards are aimed at the early detection of a diversion of nuclear material. Paragraph 28 of INFCIRC/153 reads accordingly:

. . . The objective of safeguards is the timely detection of diversion of significant quantities of nuclear material from peaceful nuclear activities to the manufacture of nuclear weapons or of other nuclear explosive devices or for purposes unknown, and deterrence of such diversion by the risk of early detection. [6]

Earlier in this chapter we dealt with the fact that it is nuclear material that is subject to safeguards and not the peaceful applications as such. Paragraph 28 also says that it must be a significant quantity. That means that not each individual milligramme as such can be subject to safeguards but it also says that timely detection is the objective. It is the concern that a state could be going nuclear. It was not the single accident but rather the planned long-range preparation of a government for the production of nuclear weapons that was at stake when the NPT was designed. It is only consistent then that the IAEA deals officially only with governments, not with individuals. It is the government of a signatory state that undergoes the obligation of NPT safeguards and all the legal steps required to do this are imposed on the operator of a nuclear facility by its government, not the IAEA. By comparison, Euratom deals directly with the operator. The signatories of the Treaty of Rome have impowered Euratom with the necessary sovereign rights.

But let us go further. Paragraph 28 says that deterrence of such division is also aimed at. The logical extention of deterrence is prevention. On the level of a state this deterrence might be expected to work in many cases although certainly not in all cases. The sequence: detection, deterrence, prevention leads then naturally to physical protection.

Physical protection is not the explicit objective of NPT safeguards. One has to realize however that much of the protection can be covered by safeguards that are aimed at detection. Apart from material accountancy and surveillance, it is the measure of containment that makes up for the three principle components of safeguards. This is the case at least for most of the large power reactors. It is natural therefore that the IAEA has recently issued "Recommendation for the Physical Protection of Nuclear Material". [7] These recommendations were published in June 1972 and the IAEA gives these recommendations to the governments. This is consistent with the fact that physical protection is in practically all cases aimed at individuals or groups. Following an article of Ralph Lapp [8] let us call such a group "group X". The problem of group X is not within the scope of the NPT. The basic feature of the NPT is the distinction between nuclear-weapon

Table 1. Physical protection of nuclear material

Possesser of material	Detection of diversion	Protection against diversion
State	Taken care of by NPT and other safeguards	Mostly taken care of by NPT and other safeguards (de facto)
Group X	Taken care of by NPT and other safeguards	Open

states and non-nuclear-weapon states and it is obvious that this distinction cannot be made for the problem of group X. Group X can operate in all countries regardless of whether they are nuclear-weapon states or not. Any international arrangement that may be envisaged must therefore cover all states equally. It may be helpful to summarize that situation as is done in table 1, above.

VIII. *The context of the NPT and future tendencies*

The final section of this chapter will deal with the context of the NPT. The fact is often overlooked that there are today as many as eight treaties that may be called non-proliferation treaties. [9]

The Antarctic Treaty of 1959

This treaty is aimed at the non-proliferation of military activities into the Antarctic. It contains provisions for inspections. But it also contains provisions that we would today call environmental or ecological provisions.

The Treaty Banning Nuclear Weapon Tests in the Atmosphere, in Outer Space and Under Water (1963)

This treaty is aimed at keeping the atmosphere, outer space and under water clean and "to put an end to the contamination of man's environment by radioactive substances".

The Treaty on Principles Governing the Activities of States in the Exploration and Use of Outer Space Including the Moon and Other Celestial Bodies (1967)

This treaty is designed to avoid the proliferation of military activities into outer space. It contains provisions that one could call environmental provisions, that is to keep the outer space clean. It also contains a provision that can be interpreted as belonging to the safeguards domain.

154

**The Treaty on the Prohibition of Nuclear Weapons
in Latin America (1967)**

This treaty is aimed at keeping Latin America free from nuclear weapons.

The Treaty on the Non-Proliferation of Nuclear Weapons (1968)

**The Treaty on the Prohibition of the Emplacement of Nuclear
Weapons and other Weapons of Mass Destruction on the Sea-Bed
and the Ocean Floor and in the Subsoil Thereof (1971)**

This treaty is aimed at the non-proliferation of nuclear and other large
scale weapons into the sea-bed. Safeguards and verification measures are
an integral part of the arrangements.

**The Convention on the Prohibition of the Development,
Production and Stockpiling of Bacteriological (Biological)
and Toxin Weapons and on Their Destruction (1972)**

This convention is aimed not only at the non-proliferation but even more
at the elimination of biological weapons. It also distinguishes sharply between the military and peaceful applications of biological techniques and
the wording is obviously influenced by the NPT. This goes as far as having
a review conference every five years. Safeguards measures are not mentioned, probably because there is no direct possibility for the implementation of meaningful safeguards.

**The Treaty between the USA and the USSR on the
Limitation of Anti-Ballistic Missile Systems.
The Interim Agreement between the USA and the
USSR on Certain Measures with Respect to the
Limitation of Strategic Offensive Arms. The
Protocol to the Interim Agreement (1972)**

It is a common opinion that the complex of SALT Agreements probably contain the greatest relevance. It is my personal opinion that the
SALT Agreements would not have been possible outside the context of the
above mentioned sequence of non-proliferation treaties and in particular
the NPT. It is this context that has led to an overall situation that made the
SALT approach a feasible one. Much can be said about the details and the
implications of the various provisions of SALT but this one point must be
made: article XII of the SALT Agreement provides for verification by the
use of national technical means, that is satellite reconnaissance. Paragraph
3 of article XII puts the obligation on both parties not to use deliberate

concealment measures which impede verification by national technical means.

Having considered this sequence of non-proliferation treaties and the constant evaluation of the various provisions one is led to a number of comments:

1. The incompleteness and deficiencies of the NPT are indeed a drawback but this drawback is much less severe if the NPT is looked upon in a broader context and not in an isolated fashion.

2. Arms control and safeguards were in most cases linked together and expressed two sides of the same thing.

3. Arms control and environmental control are closely connected. Both aspects already appear in many of the eight non-proliferation treaties.

Originally many groups looked at safeguards as an intrusion into and a burden on the peaceful applications in question. But it becomes more and more apparent that safeguards—if adequately implemented—can induce the operator to keep his house in good order. It is particularly the safeguards element of accountability of nuclear material that tends in that direction. It is now obvious that such good housekeeping is a necessity for the prudent protection of the environment too. Large amounts of plutonium and fission products in the fuel cycle constitute indeed a potential danger to the environment. Prudent management can therefore be, at least to some extent, an answer to both the challange of safeguards and the challenge to protect the environment. Furthermore, nuclear materials are the only class of substance for which global accountability is now being established. This leads to the possibility of control in its original meaning, that is to have the atom safely in hand. I am convinced that it will be a necessity of the near future to have global accountability of many more substances, for instance: CO_2, SO_2, NO_x, aerosols, the temperature of the oceans, DDT and oil spills. Such accountability is often referred to as monitoring, but the term accountability reaches further than monitoring. It is the control of the environment and the climate that leads to such requirements.

Such a viewpoint reveals the fact that the ultimate reason for control by safeguards and verification is the limitations of the globe. Nuclear weapons are too far-reaching for the small globe so they must be under control. Civilian technology is too far-reaching and heavy for man's environment so certain aspects of that civilian technology must be kept safely in hand. It is my personal view that these civilization problems will readily bypass the problem of arms control. The SALT Agreements may, some decades from now, be looked upon as the turning point where the priority changed from the military domain to man's civilization in general. We all have to live on spaceship earth; neither bombs nor poisons can be tolerated on board. This, to me, is the ultimate meaning of safeguards.

References

1. Hall, J. A., "Atoms for Peace, or War", *Foreign Affairs*, Vol. 43, No. 4, July 1965, p. 602.
2. *The Agency's Safeguards System* INFCIRC/66 (1965), INFCIRC/66/Rev. 2 (1968), Vienna, IAEA.
3. Imai, R., *Science and the State*, Tokyo, 1968.
4. Treaty on the Non-Proliferation of Nuclear Weapons, INFCIRC/140 (1970), Vienna, IAEA.
5. *The Structure and Content of Agreements between the Agency and States Required in Connection with the Treaty on the Non-Proliferation of Nuclear Weapons*, INFCIRC/153 (1971), Vienna, IAEA.
6. *Ibid.*, Paragraph 28.
7. *Recommendations for the Physical Protection of Nuclear Material*, Vienna, IAEA, 1972.
8. Lapp, R. E., "The Ultimate Blackmail", *The New York Times Magazine*, 4 February 1973, p. 12.
9. *Treaties in Force, A List of Treaties and Other International Agreements of the United States in Force on January 1, 1973*, Department of State, Publ. 8697, New York, 1973.

4. Arguments for extended NPT safeguards

J. PRAWITZ[1]

Abstract

Developments in the implementation of safeguards and the growth of the
nuclear industry provide the basis for a discussion of what improvements
and amendments could be proposed at the NPT Review Conference to be
held in Geneva in 1975. This chapter discusses the possibility of extending
the application of IAEA safeguards as opposed to the agreed provisions
of the 1968 non-proliferation treaty. Nuclear activities left uncovered by
the compromise in the treaty as well as new safeguard needs are analysed
and the need for additional measures of physical security is pointed out.
The necessity of treating weapon-grade plutonium in the same manner
as reactor-grade plutonium and plutonium in the same manner as uranium
is also disucussed. A maximum proposal regarding the strengthening of
the NPT concludes the chapter.

I. *Introduction*

When the Treaty on the Non-Proliferation of Nuclear Weapons (NPT)
was negotiated in the mid-1960s, the question of safeguards was always
considered an important and difficult one. In August 1967 it moved into
the focus of world politics when the USA and the Soviet Union put forward identical draft treaty texts with blank space left for the control article. This left safeguards as the only issue separating them from complete agreement. Half a year later, compromise language was proposed
and on 12 June 1968 the General Assembly of the United Nations passed
the NPT. [1] It is natural that the resulting control article could not take
into account all wishes and suggestions expressed. However, the article
was accepted and became the basis for the implementation of control.
Detailed principles of such implementation were later worked out by the
International Atomic Energy Agency (IAEA) in IAEA document INFCIRC/
153 (the Blue Book) [2] and a number of bilateral safeguards agreements
were concluded between the agency and individual NPT parties as prescribed in the treaty.

This process has by now produced a certain amount of experience. In

[1] The views and opinions expressed in this paper are those of the author and do not imply
the expression of any position on the part of the Swedish Ministry of Defence.

addition, the continued negotiations to stop the nuclear arms race (SALT) can be expected to create some inspiration for further strengthening the NPT. Moreover, the growth of the civil nuclear industry and the expected build-up of plutonium stockpiles are easier to assess today than they were five years ago. However, it is also apparent that a number of important states have not become parties to the NPT and will not become parties in the near future. The possibility that weapon-grade nuclear material would be stolen by terrorists and guerillas for blackmail purposes was not taken seriously in 1968 but is now considered a reality. These developments provide the basis for a discussion of what improvements and amendments could be proposed at the Review Conference to be held in Geneva in 1975 in accordance with NPT article VIII.3.

Possible amendments to the NPT can be divided into two political categories. One includes issues which were discussed before the NPT agreement in 1968 and which might be raised again at the Review Conference. The other category includes new issues not discussed at that time, such as protection of plutonium against theft by terrorists. In the latter case some measures will probably be of interest to all governments and successful negotiations may be possible in a reasonable time. However, in the former case it might be much more difficult to change old compromises and rehash past issues.

II. *The scope of the present provisions*

The NPT introduces safeguards in two ways: first by stipulating that non-nuclear-weapon states, parties to the treaty, apply safeguards on "all (its) source or special nuclear material in all peaceful nuclear activities" and secondly by stating that all parties to the treaty should not provide, except under safeguards, nuclear material and certain other specified equipment and material to any non-nuclear-weapon state, whether a party to the treaty or not.

This latter provision, enforcing some arms control on nonsignatories who import nuclear material and equipment from states party to the treaty, together with corresponding provisions in treaty articles I and II makes the NPT an international scheme for cooperative prevention of proliferation rather than a treaty for individual abstentions from the nuclear option. The behaviour of nonsignatories will of course be of fundamental importance from the point of view of non-proliferation; therefore, the possibility of influencing them in this respect is very important. This approach might also be politically realistic because there seems to be a deep and general consensus among all states, (including those who hesitate to subscribe to the treaty themselves) that non-proliferation is good for others.

Safeguards will thus apply to all peaceful nuclear activity in non-nuclear-weapon states, parties to the treaty, and to such nuclear activity in non-signatory non-nuclear-weapon states, that is connected with imports from signatory states.

Uncovered by safeguards will be the remaining peaceful nuclear activities in nonsignatory states, all nuclear activities in nuclear-weapon states, and all nonpeaceful nuclear activities other than bomb-making in non-nuclear-weapon states.

III. *Possible voluntary application of safeguards*

Due to unilateral undertakings and requests by suppliers, there might be an additional area covered by safeguards in nuclear-weapon states and in nonsignatory countries. For example, the United States has announced that when the NPT comes into force, IAEA safeguards will be applied to all its nuclear activities, excluding only those with direct national security significance. [3] Great Britain has made the same offer in relation to its nuclear activities. [4]

It is also reasonable to assume that many non-nuclear-weapon states, on an individual basis, wish not to be connected with any actual or potential nuclear weapon programme, and, therefore, may include a provision in their individual safeguards agreements for the "continuation of safeguards" with respect to nuclear material transferred out of the country.[2] Such a provision would assure that all nuclear material transferred from the country and any subsequent generation of special fissile material derived from such transferred materials would never support any nuclear weapon production.

This would be specifically true in three cases not covered by the NPT; namely, material transferred to a nuclear-weapon state, to a nonsignatory non-nuclear-weapon state after passing through a nonsignatory nuclear-weapon state and to a signatory non-nuclear-weapon state that withdraws from the non-proliferation treaty and terminates the related safeguards agreement when the material is present there.

IV. *Military non-nuclear weapon activities*

As safeguards, according to the NPT, shall apply to nuclear activities for *peaceful purposes* only and as the manufacture of nuclear weapons and other nuclear explosive devices is the only use of fissile materials which the treaty forbids a non-nuclear-weapon country, there will be a category

[2] Basic provisions for the continuation of safeguards are laid down in the IAEA statute article XII.A.5 and in the IAEA Safeguards System (1967). [5]

of uses for such material which is not forbidden but which a state might declare nonpeaceful and which, therefore, could be exempted from safeguards. One example of such use is fuelling reactors for the propulsion of submarines, aircraft carriers and other naval vessels. In general, this category would include all material used or intended for use in any nuclear activity that is not the manufacture of explosive devices but is declared to be nonpeaceful, or material intended for export to nuclear-weapon countries for any nonpeaceful purpose.

It is clear that the NPT control machinery would lose a great deal of its significance if such permitted activities, which might also include handling of weapon-grade materials, are left free of control. The existence of this independent nuclear area in signatory states could quickly violate the aim of the non-proliferation treaty. Therefore, it is encouraging that the safeguards agreements prescribed by the NPT will put certain restrictions on the possibilities of exempting material from control.[3]

V. *Hidden facilities*

According to Blue Book paragraph 62, parties shall provide the agency "with an initial report on all nuclear material which is to be subject to safeguards". This applies both to material used for peaceful (NPT article III.1) and nonpeaceful (Blue Book paragraph 14) purposes. However, to verify that *all* material has really been declared poses a problem, as the IAEA is not able to scan a country for material and facilities which may not have been declared.

This dilemma was solved in articles 11–18 of the Treaty for the Prohibition of Nuclear Weapons in Latin America (the Tlatelolco Treaty) by means of a special agency to carry out "special inspections", if a party to the treaty were to make reasoned requests for such inspections. How this would be done in practice has not yet been worked out. One suggestion is that if one party suspected that a specific unsafeguarded installation or building on the territory of another party was of the kind that should have

---

[3] These restrictions are outlined in the Blue Book, paragraph.14 which prescribes that a state wanting an exemption from safeguards on nuclear material for a permitted nonpeaceful purpose shall inform the agency of the activity, making it clear "that the use of the nuclear material in a non-proscribed military activity will not be in conflict with an undertaking the State may have given and in respect of which Agency safeguards apply and that during the period of non-application of safeguards the nuclear material will not be used for the production of nuclear weapons or other nuclear explosive devices". The state and the agency shall in addition make an arrangement so that, only while the nuclear material is used in such an activity, will the safeguards provided for in the agreement not be applied. The safeguards provided for in the agreement shall apply again as soon as the nuclear material is re-introduced into a peaceful nuclear activity. The agency shall be kept informed of the total quantity and composition of such unsafeguarded nuclear material in the state of any exports of such material. Each arrangement shall be made in agreement with the agency.

been declared for control, the regional agency mentioned could invite the IAEA to go to the place and carry out a special inspection.

VI. *Physical security*

It should be appreciated that the IAEA safeguards system is only a fact-finding machine. There is nothing prohibiting a country from sending home the inspectors and using safeguarded materials for bombs. Safeguards will detect but not prevent that. There is also the possibility that weapon-grade material could be stolen by subnational terrorist and guerilla groups for blackmail purposes or by agents of other states. The present wave of hijacking and terrorism must not escalate to the nuclear level. However, many of the bilateral agreements for nuclear material supply already stipulate rules intended to improve the physical security of safeguarded material. The main ones are:

1. An option can be made for buying back plutonium produced with the supplied fuel if it is not needed by the consumer, provided that the plutonium not being utilized in reactors be located in storage facilities designated by the supplier. Although there are economic reasons for this policy, the main purpose is to stockpile surplus plutonium in the most secure places from the supplier's point of view. In addition, the IAEA[4] statute and the Euratom treaty[5] provide for distributed stockpiling of special fissionable material.

2. Supplier nations also frequently reserve a right to pre-approval of any reprocessing of supplied fuel. The purpose of this provision is to avoid the use of facilities where accounting for extracted plutonium is difficult and, consequently, diversion easy.

3. A request can also be made for specifications of any project involved before fuel delivery is approved.

4. As a consequence of provision 3, the right is reserved to approve beforehand any resale of supplied fuel and equipment to third countries. The prime purpose of this is to get assurance that reactors using supplied fuel are power, and not dual purpose or plutonium production, reactors.

---

[4] The relevant provision is included in article XII.A.5 of the IAEA statute, which makes it possible to "deposit with the Agency of any excess of any special fissionable materials recovered or produced as a by-product over what is needed in order to prevent stock-piling of these materials, provided that thereafter at the request of the member or members concerned, special fissionable materials so deposited with the Agency shall be returned promptly to the member or members concerned for use" as may be permitted.

[5] Article 80 of the Euratom treaty prescribes that the Euratom Commission "may require that any excess of any special fissionable materials recovered or produced as a by-product, not being actually in use or ready for use, be deposited with (its) Agency or in storage premises which are or can be controlled by the Commission. The special fissionable materials so deposited shall, at the request of the parties concerned, be returned to them without delay".

5. Shipment schedules can be restricted in order to avoid unnecessary stockpiling of nuclear fuel awaiting use in reactors.

6. Most countries apply general and strict secrecy to certain technical information and know-how, mainly concerning design of nuclear explosive devices and methods for separation of uranium isotopes.

It has also been claimed that some suppliers have sold fuel and equipment cheaper than the production costs in order to spread the application of safeguards. Most supplier nations exercise some or all of the above-mentioned policies.

Some of these provisions will be obsolete when the IAEA safeguards system comes into full operation. The Blue Book provides for design information (paragraphs 8, 42–48) but a system for dispersed stockpiling would probably be very desirable to reduce the risk that fissionable material would be used in contradiction with international agreements. Buying-back plutonium may cause small countries with large uranium deposits great financial problems if they are going to buy all the plutonium that happens to be produced with the uranium they export. Clearly, an international scheme for administration of plutonium flows and dispersed stock-piling would be very helpful, at least for small suppliers, in the same way as the IAEA safeguards system is helpful for countries not having the necessary resources to organize a worldwide network of bilateral safeguards to watch exported material.

The selection of places where plutonium deposits can be optimally guarded introduces a dilemma: which organization is strong enough to protect the stockpiles effectively and at the same time is unable itself to seize the stockpiled material? Particularly sensitive from a security point of view is transportation of nuclear materials both between countries and within countries. Guarding material in stock and in transit may possibly be a task for a special UN or IAEA guard force. The problems of physical security to protect fissionable material from diversion by governments require especially careful study.

A different problem is to protect stockpiles from unauthorized use by individuals and groups. That would be the responsibility of governments and it is a question of physical security in its real sense. Practical measures to protect nuclear material in use, storage and transit were recommended by the IAEA in June 1972 (the Grey Book).[6] A binding international commitment to apply such measures would reduce the general risk for diversion of material. Recognizing the possible dimensions of the effects of

---

[6] While these ''Recommendations for the Physical Protection of Nuclear Material'', produced by a panel of experts working under IAEA sponsorship in Vienna from 6–10 March 1972, ''are not binding upon States, they represent the conclusions of the experts for an optimized system and they are recommended for use by States as required in their physical protection systems''.

such diversions, an international agreement to prevent them seems adequate, while the practical management of relevant measures could be a task for national governments.

VII. *The plutonium-240 problem*

According to paragraphs 79–80 and 104 of the blue book, the inspection intensity at a certain nuclear facility would be related to the number of effective kilogrammes of nuclear material in that facility. This concept focuses more attention on highly enriched uranium than on the same amount of a lower grade material. No similar discount is envisaged for reactor-grade plutonium containing a higher concentration of the isotope 240 as compared to weapon-grade qualities containing only a few percent.

From time to time it has been suggested that plutonium should be treated in the same manner as uranium, which would considerably reduce the burden of safeguards in the future. This idea has consistently been resisted by representatives of the nuclear powers without explanation and qualifications due to the secrecy applied to nuclear weapon technology. The credibility of similar statements from representatives of non-nuclear powers is of course less.[7]

A suggestion, made at a scientific symposium in 1970 by this author, that it would be possible to produce a nuclear explosion from essentially any grade of reactor-produced plutonium was then confirmed in the written statement of an experienced Los Alamos scientist.[8]

In a recent public statement [8] the Swedish scientist Dr Nils Gyldén said that use of reactor-grade plutonium for bombs may give a yield that is lower and more difficult to predict, but it would probably give a yield of nuclear size. The higher the Pu-240 concentration, the less predictable the yield. For a sophisticated military purpose, weapon-grade plutonium

---

[7] An early discussion of this problem took place in the so-called Randers committee in 1964. [6]

[8] Dr C. J. Mark said in a lecture at the 10th Pugwash symposium in Racine, Wisconsin, 26–29 June 1970, "I should like to mention a comment of Dr Prawitz of the National Research Institute of Defence in Stockholm to the effect that a colleague of his has become persuaded that he could produce a nuclear explosion from essentially any grade of reactor-produced plutonium that might be available. I am not familiar with the details of the calculations of Dr Prawitz's colleague, and I can only assume that by "nuclear explosion" he means what I would mean, which is an explosion of at least three orders of magnitude more energy per pound than would be available from high explosives. From my own considerations of this problem, I have no reason to question such a conclusion, and I would like to warn people concerned with such problems that the old notion that reactor-grade plutonium is incapable of producing nuclear explosions—or that plutonium could easily be rendered harmless by the addition of modest amounts of the isotope Pu-240, or "denatured" as the phrase used to go—that these notions have been dangerously exaggerated." [5]

would be necessary. For demonstration purposes, reactor-grade material may very well do and that is the essential fact with respect to the NPT.[9]

An independent study by the Finnish phycisists P. Jauho and J. Virtamo arrived at the conclusion that even in the "worst" case, a device using heavily Pu-240-contaminated fuel, the explosion yield may range up to one kiloton. [10] This problem is also discussed by Professor J. K. Miettinen and Dr John Hopkins in their respective chapters.

VIII. *A maximum proposal*

In order to strengthen the NPT several measures extending the safeguards procedure may be envisaged. These extended safeguards may also require a matching extension of the scope of NPT articles I and II.

One such measure might be the prohibition of any party of the NPT from assisting any other country in acquiring nuclear weapons. At present the nuclear countries are forbidden to transfer nuclear weapons to any recipient whatsoever and to assist non-nuclear states in acquiring nuclear weapons, while they are permitted to assist each other. In addition, non-nuclear-weapon states are not formally prohibited from assisting other countries who want to make the bomb. These possibilities could be closed by means of amending treaty articles I and II.[10]

Most nuclear powers, and indeed the USA and the USSR, do not co-operate with each other in the field of nuclear weapon design. Only the USA and Britain have a special relationship in this respect, and it was to provide for the continuation of that relationship that cooperation between nuclear powers was permitted in article I of the treaty. The prohibition of that relationship is not desirable but if the political integration of Western Europe could reach the point where a country could inherit both the nuclear power status of France and Britain and the special relationship between Britain and the USA it would constitute an opportunity for rapid

---

[9] The views of Dr Gyldén were confirmed in an authoritative statement by the Swedish Research Institute for National Defence (FOA) on 25 June 1973. [9]

[10] Articles I and II may be amended to reflect the suggested ban on all cooperation in nuclear weapon technology between all states in the following way:

I. Each State Party to the Treaty undertakes not to transfer to any recipient whatsoever nuclear weapons and other nuclear explosive devices directly or indirectly; and not in any way to assist, encourage, or induce any other State to manufacture or otherwise acquire nuclear weapons, or other nuclear explosive devices, or control over such weapons or explosive devices.

II.a. Each State Party to the Treaty undertakes not to seek or receive the transfer from any transferor whatsoever of nuclear weapons or other nuclear explosive devices or the control over such weapons or explosive devices directly or indirectly; or any assistance in the manufacture of nuclear weapons or other nuclear explosive devices;

b. Each non-nuclear weapon State Party to the Treaty undertakes not to manufacture or otherwise acquire nuclear weapons or other nuclear explosive devices.

proliferation. Moreover, that country would become the greatest single new nuclear power that could be envisaged.

As time goes on and the understanding and potential capability of weapon making spreads, measures to stop cooperation in nuclear weapon technology between countries that are now non-nuclear will become more urgent. A loophole in article II was discovered by the United Arab Republic delegation in Geneva before the treaty was concluded but it was not removed for procedural reasons. There are authoritative statements to the effect that this loophole should not be considered to exist but its formal closing would be preferable.[11]

It would also seem necessary to remove the possibility of exempting nuclear material used for nonpeaceful purposes. Safeguards should apply to all nuclear material whatsoever in a non-nuclear-weapon state party to the treaty and the qualification "peaceful" in article III.1 should be deleted.

Furthermore, the safeguards clause should be amended to provide for "the continuation of safeguards" on all nuclear material transferred to and from a party. Nuclear-weapon states should also gradually start applying safeguards on their peaceful nuclear activities in addition to those covered by the transfer rule mentioned earlier. These measures would greatly improve the possibilities of accounting for the world stockpile of fissionable material and also provide certain arms control effects such as the suggested amendments to articles I and II.

In addition, the possibility should be explored of providing for special inspections, if requested by a party which suspects that some prohibited activity has been carried out in another state.

Finally, provisions for improved physical security should be added to article III. These may include obligations to use the services of the IAEA for dispersed stockpiling of excessive special fissionable material and to establish effective protection of material in stock and under transportation by special guards, possibly by the IAEA.

---

[11] On 26 September 1967, the United Arab Republic representative in the ENDC suggested that a special sentence should be added to the draft article II saying that non-nuclear-weapon states "should not in any way assist, encourage, or induce any non-nuclear-weapon State to manufacture or otherwise acquire nuclear weapons or other nuclear explosive devices, or control over such weapons or explosive devices". [11] However, the Soviet representative on 27 February 1968 argued that such an extra provision was unnecessary because it was already covered by "the meaning of Article II and the preamble to the Treaty. If a non-nuclear-weapon State Party to the Treaty were to assist another non-nuclear-weapon State to manufacture and acquire nuclear weapons, such a case would be regarded as a violation of the Treaty". [12] The US representative, on the same occasion, argued that "it seems clear that a non-nuclear-weapon State which accepts the Treaty's restrictions on itself would have no reason to assist another country not accepting the same restrictions to gain advantage from this fact in the field of nuclear weapon development. If a non-nuclear-weapon Party did nevertheless attempt to provide such assistance in the territory of a non-party, the presumption would immediately arise that these acts had the purpose of developing nuclear weapons for itself, in violation of the Treaty". [13]

References

1. United Nations Document A/RES/2373 (XXII).
2. *The Structure and Content of Agreements between the Agency and States Required in Connection with the Treaty on the Non-Proliferation of Nuclear Weapons*, IAEA Document INFCIRC/153 (the Blue Book).
3. Document ENDC/206 5 December 1967.
4. Document ENDC/207 5 December 1967.
5. IAEA Document INFCIRC/66/Rev. 1, section 16, 1967.
6. IAEA Document GOV/COM. 14/OR. 6–7.
7. Mark, C. J., "Nuclear Weapons Technology", in Feld, B. T. *et al.*, ed., *Impact of New Technologies on the Arms Race* (Cambridge, Mass., MIT Press, 1971) p. 137.
8. *Dagens Nyheter*, 15 May 1973.
9. FOA 4 Dnr 4660-45.
10. Jauho, P. and Virtamo, J., "The Effect of Peaceful Use of Atomic Energy upon Nuclear Proliferation", Paper presented to the Helsinki Arms Control. Seminar, June 1973.
11. Document ENDC/197.
12. Document ENDC/PV. 370, paragraph 59.
13. Document ENDC/PV. 370, paragraph 83.

5. Nongovernmental nuclear weapon proliferation[1]

M. WILLRICH

Abstract

The use of nuclear energy to generate electric power will result in very large flows of material that could, if successfully diverted, be used to make fission explosives or radiation weapons. While most attention has thus far been focused on the possibilities for governmentally authorized diversion of strategic materials from a nuclear power industry to a clandestine nuclear weapon programme, this paper focuses on the problem of unlawful diversion by nongovernmental groups. The possible reasons and options for diversion by individuals acting alone, profit-oriented criminal groups, terrorist groups, nuclear enterprises and political factions are discussed. The safeguards required to keep nongovernmental diversion risks as low as practicable are considered. Unlike international safeguards which are designed to detect governmentally authorized diversion, national safeguards should be designed to prevent unlawful nuclear diversion. Different measures are required to prevent thefts by employees of nuclear industries and thefts by outsiders. Strict access controls combined with material accountancy are necessary to prevent employee thefts, while a combination of physical barriers and special security forces are required to deal with potential external threats. The governments of nuclear-weapon and non-nuclear-weapon states have a common interest in the effectiveness of national safeguards systems to prevent nongovernmental nuclear weapon proliferation.

I. Introduction

Nuclear weapons are relatively easy to make assuming the requisite nuclear materials are available.[2] Fission explosives can be made with a few kilogrammes of plutonium, high-enriched uranium or uranium-233. The design and fabrication of a simple, transportable, fission explosive device is not a difficult task technically. A variety of radiation weapons are also conceivable, and they are simpler to make than fission explosives. More-

---

[1] The views expressed are the author's and do not necessarily reflect those of any institution or governmental agency.

[2] This statement is controversial although I believe it is in accord with the majority opinion of those who are technically competent to judge.

over, what appears to be one of the most effective types of radiation weapon, a plutonium dispersal device, requires only a few grammes of plutonium to make. The effects of the use of a nuclear weapon depend on the characteristics of the device and of the target area. The effects of a relatively simple, low-yield fission explosive or a plutonium dispersal device involving hundreds of grammes can be sufficiently intense and widespread to kill tens of thousands of people and cause hundreds of millions of dollars in property damage.

In this chapter, the term "nuclear weapon material" means plutonium, high-enriched uranium (containing 20 per cent or more uranium-235) or uranium-233 in forms that could be used directly to make fission explosives.

The use of nuclear energy to generate electric power will result in very large flows of nuclear weapon material through various fuel cycles. By 1980 several thousand kilogrammes of nuclear weapon material will be present in civilian fuel cycles in a number of countries with large nuclear power industries. Thereafter, the amount of nuclear weapon material involved in nuclear power industries throughout the world is expected to increase rapidly for many years. There are, however, significant differences in the possibilities for diversion of nuclear weapon material related to each of the major power reactor types. Nuclear weapon material unlawfully diverted from the nuclear power industry in one country might be used in nuclear weapons to threaten people or governments in other countries. The incentives for nongovernmental diversion from nuclear industries depend heavily on the future development of terrorism on a transnational scale and on the future attitudes of governments toward the possession of nuclear forces. Major nuclear diversions could significantly and adversely affect the international political climate within which the nuclear power industry is developing on a worldwide basis.

A great deal of effort has already been devoted to internationally administered safeguards, and especially to the development of the system administered by the International Atomic Energy Agency (IAEA) under the Treaty on the Non-Proliferation of Nuclear Weapons (NPT). The role of international safeguards is primarily limited to *detection* of nuclear diversion that is governmentally authorized, although it is hoped that the risk of detection may actually deter this kind of diversion.

For international safeguards to be effective, however, they must be based on strong national control systems, especially in countries with large nuclear industries. National safeguards systems are necessary to *prevent* diversion of nuclear weapon material from nuclear power industries by nongovernmental groups or individuals acting alone. It is noteworthy that the IAEA/NPT safeguards system fully recognizes the importance of national systems. Indeed, the IAEA took a commendable initiative in 1972 by convening a panel of experts which developed recommendations for the physical protection of nuclear material.

With this background in mind, the remainder of this paper considers two interrelated topics: the risks of nongovernmental nuclear diversion and the safeguards required to keep those risks as low as practicable.

II. *The risks of nongovernmental diversion*

The analysis of nongovernmental diversion possibilities which follows is mainly intended to provide readers with a more informed basis for making their own judgements concerning the credibility of the risks involved— judgements necessarily based on their own views of human nature.

Diversion by one person acting alone

Reasons for diversion

The possible reasons for one person to steal nuclear weapon material from the nuclear power industry comprise a broad spectrum. On the rational end of this spectrum is financial profit and on the irrational end is a psychotic expression of extreme alienation from society as a whole. In between lie such motives as settling a grudge against the management of a nuclear plant or a strong conviction that nuclear weapon proliferation is a good thing. Profit appears to be by far the most sensible general motive for an individual to steal nuclear material. (The "rational" terrorist would normally be operating as part of a group rather than alone.)

More specifically, the lone person who contemplates unlawful diversion of nuclear weapon material may do so with any of a large number of particular uses for the material in mind. These would include the following.

Black market sale. The entire amount of stolen material might be sold in one transaction if a large quantity of nuclear material would bring a premium price. Alternatively, small amounts might be sold over long periods of time in separate transactions if the thief viewed his ill-gotten gains as something like a very precious metal, to be liquidated in installments as income is needed.

Ransom of stolen material. If carefully worked out, the thief might be able to obtain at least as high a price for return of the stolen material as he would be able to get by sale in a black market. The enterprise from which nuclear material was stolen would be one possible target of such a blackmail scheme; another could be the national government involved. The nuclear enterprise, the government and, depending on his tactics, the thief, might all have strong interests in keeping from the public any information about a nuclear diversion incident. This possibility raises two questions: (1) Does the general public in the country where a nuclear theft occurs have a right or a need to know about the occurrence? (2) Do other governments have a right or a need to be informed about such a theft if circumstances indicate the stolen materials has been taken out of the country?

Fabrication of a weapon and actual nuclear threat. Manufacture of a fission explosive using high-enriched uranium would seem to be within the capabilities of one person working alone, assuming he possesses the requisite technical competence. Due to plutonium's toxicity, an individual would find it much more difficult to work safely alone with plutonium than uranium. But a lone individual might not care for his personal safety, or might be quite sophisticated technically, or willing to settle for a very crude explosive design, or he might want a radiation weapon.

But what would the individual do with his fission explosive or radiation weapon? As with the stolen material, he might sell the device on the black market or ransom it. The government concerned would be a likely target for blackmail of this type, and it might be prepared to pay a very high price to gain possession of the device. It would, of course, be necessary to establish the credibility of the nuclear threat, but this would not seem difficult. One easy way to do so would be to send the authorities a design drawing of the device, perhaps together with a sample of the nuclear material used and photographs of the actual device.

As with the ransom of stolen nuclear material, the thief could make his demands and conduct the entire transaction in secret, or he might from the outset or at some stage in the negotiations make his demands known to the public. The governmental authorities would probably wish to keep the matter secret, at least until an emergency evacuation became necessary. If the nuclear weapon problem were disclosed to the public, serious panic could result.

Nuclear weapon bluff. This leads to a further question. If a design plus a sample of nuclear material would establish the credibility of the thief, why would the thief actually have to fabricate and emplace a fission explosive or radiation weapon in order to obtain satisfaction for his demands? If government authorities were willing to pay off a nuclear bluff, the potential profit or political utility of a little nuclear weapon material would be increased enormously. Moreover, a series of such bluffs would enormously complicate the problems a government faces.

Scope of the risk

Fortunately, every person in a society need not be considered a potential thief of nuclear material. Assuming minimal safeguards are required by the government concerned, the risk of nuclear theft by one individual acting alone exists primarily with respect to persons (mainly nuclear industry employees) who have authorized access to nuclear material at facilities and the persons who have authorized control over nuclear material during transport between facilities in various fuel cycles. This considerably narrows the scope of the risk of individual theft. However, it also means that somone who is in a position to steal nuclear material by himself may well possess the technical knowledge required to handle it safely.

Individual diversion options

The individual thief who is an employee in a nuclear facility or in the transportation system for nuclear material has two basic options for acquiring material for fission explosives or radiation weapons: (1) he can attempt to steal a large amount of material at one time, or (2) he can take a small amount each time in a series of thefts. Perhaps the most likely scenario for a large theft by an individual from a nuclear facility would be to fake a criticality accident or some other emergency condition which requires immediate evacuation of all persons from the facility. The thief might be able to make off with a significant quantity of material through the safety exit.

The possibility and significance of a series of thefts of small amounts of nuclear material would depend on the detection threshold in the material accountancy system and the elapsed time between the event and knowledge of the event. It seems that a material accounting system would provide little protection against small thefts by a plant employee given the limit of error of material unaccounted for (LEMUF) in any such system and the knowledge the employee would normally have of what the LEMUF was.

Individual acts of theft of nuclear material in transit or in storage during transit would be likely to result, if successful, in the loss of much larger amounts of material than could be stolen from material being processed. For example, if a truck containing a nuclear shipment were driven by a single individual, the risk of theft could be very large. The truck driver himself might decide to steal the shipment or another individual might hijack the truck.

Diversion by a profit oriented criminal group

Reasons for diversion

There are two reasons why a profit oriented criminal group might want nuclear weapon material. One is obvious: the realization of large profits in black market or ransom dealings. The other reason is less obvious: the possession of a few nuclear explosives or radiation weapons might place a criminal group effectively beyond the reach of law enforcement authorities. A criminal organization might use the threat of nuclear violence against an urban population to deter police activities directed specifically against nuclear theft. A criminal group might also use nuclear weapons to coerce from the police a tacit or explicit grant of immunity from law enforcement for a broad range of other lucrative criminal operations.

172

Scope of the risk

To what extent would profit oriented criminal groups become interested in the potential for financial gains from illicit trade in nuclear material? On the one hand, it may be argued that the potential gains are so large that a wide variety of criminal organizations would attempt to exploit the possibilities of nuclear diversion. On the other hand, it may be argued that criminal groups interested in financial profits would not develop a black market in a commodity such as nuclear material which has revolutionary implications, and the theft of which might prompt a public outcry and result in a major governmental reaction.

Diversion options

It seems clear that a criminal group would be able to develop a capability to apply sophisticated means, including substantial force if necessary, in order to carry out a successful nuclear theft. Therefore, the analysis which follows focuses on the technical capabilities a group might have to deal with nuclear material, not its capabilities to use force or stealth to obtain it.

Minimal nuclear capability. At a minimum, a group contemplating nuclear theft would have to be capable of recognizing precisely the material it wanted and of understanding the procedures required for safe handling. A criminal group with such a minimal nuclear capability would have two basic tactical options. (1) It could attempt to infiltrate nuclear industrial or transport facilities through which nuclear material passes, and then steal very small quantities of material without being detected. (2) It could attempt to burglarize a nuclear facility or hijack a vehicle carrying a nuclear shipment and take a large amount at one time. If successful with a series of small nuclear thefts or a single large one, a criminal group with minimal technical competence would possess material that it could sell to others or use to blackmail the enterprise from which it stole the material. These are basically the same options available to one person acting alone. However, an organized group would have greater capabilities than one person to make arrangements for either the black market sale or ransom of stolen material.

The development of a black market in nuclear material would seem to require a subtle organizational structure, possibly composed of several loosely affiliated groups. A nuclear black market would probably become transnational and global in scope since demands for stolen nuclear material would not necessarily exist close to, or in the same country as, the sources of supply. Moreover, material processing or weapon fabrication, if part of the black market operations, might take place in especially remote areas or places where a government was prepared to look the other way. A profit oriented criminal group might thus target its efforts on especially vulnerable nuclear fuel or facilities anywhere in the world. The material stolen might then be sold to purchasers in other countries far from the scene of the crime.

Capability to manufacture nuclear weapons. A criminal group could acquire the technical competence to fabricate nuclear weapons in a number of ways. A group member with a well developed scientific and mathematical talent could develop the required competence on his own without formal training; a group member with some aptitude and a college education might be sent to a year or two of graduate school, or the group might recruit or kidnap and coerce someone already possessing the requisite technical skills. Alternatively, someone with the requisite skill might decide to pursue a career in crime rather than lawful industry and take the initiative to form his own criminal group.

A favourable location could be selected for the manufacturing facilities in the midst of an intensively industrialized area or in a remote and inaccessible region. A national government might even be willing to host a clandestine manufacturing operation. Governments strongly opposed to nuclear weapon proliferation may find it extremely difficult to deal with such a criminal group if its manufacturing facilities were located on territory under the jurisdiction of a government that was congenial or passive to proliferation.

A profit oriented criminal group with a capability to manufacture nuclear explosives could, if it wished, maintain a small stockpile of weapons for its own protection. Having willingly engaged in the manufacture of nuclear explosives for others to use, the group would have long since resolved within its membership any doubts regarding the morality or expediency of the use of a nuclear threat to protect its own members or their illegal activities.

A number of factors could create incentives or disincentives for a profit oriented criminal group to develop the capability of manufacturing nuclear weapons. The capabilities and preferences of potential buyers could be decisive. For example, national governments interested in the clandestine acquisition of nuclear weapons might well prefer to purchase nuclear material in order to manufacture in their own facilities, weapons which were tailored to their particular requirements. However, terrorist groups might provide a ready market for fabricated nuclear weapons.

Capability to manufacture nuclear weapon material. It seems very unlikely that a criminal group could develop its own capability to produce significant amounts of plutonium. The operations required are too numerous and complicated, and the scale is too large. There are a number of reasons why it is also very unlikely that a criminal group would be capable of enriching uranium, at least in the near future. Gas centrifuge technology, the most likely method, is being developed under conditions of secrecy. The operation of centrifuges would be a technically demanding task. In order to acquire a capability to produce high-enriched uranium from low-enriched or natural uranium, the criminal group would have to steal a sufficient number of centrifuges. Given the cost of one centrifuge, inventory controls capable of detecting the theft of one or more centrifuges would seem justified. If a theft were promptly detected, there would seem to be a reasonable amount of time to track down the group and recover the stolen centrifuges.

Diversion by a terrorist group

Reasons for diversion

While financial gain should not be excluded entirely, the dominant motive of a terrorist group which might attempt to divert nuclear material would probably be to enhance its capabilities to use or threaten violence. An important, though secondary, purpose might well be to provide itself with an effective deterrent. In these respects, a terrorist group which possessed a few nuclear explosive devices would be in a qualitatively different position offensively and defensively than one with only conventional arms. Diversion could place nuclear weapons in the hands of groups that are quite willing to resort to unlimited violence.

Scope of the risk

The scope of the risk of diversion by terrorist groups would seem to depend largely on how widespread terrorist behavior becomes in the future. Although any assessment in this regard is highly speculative, present trends appear discouraging. (1) The incidence of violence initiated by various terrorist groups seems to be increasing in many parts of the world. (2) Terrorist groups are increasing their technical sophistication, as evidenced by the armaments and tactics they use. (3) Terrrorist groups are rapidly developing transnational links with each other in order to facilitate the flow among countries of arms and ammunition and even of terrorist personnel. (4) Whatever works as a terrorist tactic in one part of the world is likely to be picked up and possibly repeated elsewhere. These trends appear discouraging, especially if they are not reversed in the near future as nuclear power industries develop and material flows rapidly increase.

Diversion options

Terrorist groups might become one potentially large source of black market demand for nuclear weapons. However, a terrorist group may prefer, for various reasons, to develop its own capabilities to divert and use nuclear materials. A terrorist group may wish to be independent of any profit-making criminal enterprise; it may believe that a spectacular act of diversion would serve its own purposes, or it may be able to obtain the material it wants more cheaply by stealing it than by buying it on a black market.

The diversion options of a terrorist group would not differ substantially from those available to a profit oriented criminal group. However, there appear to be a number of important differences in the implications from the exercise of certain diversion options by the two types of potential diverter.

Whereas there may be incentives working on all sides to keep the fact of theft by a profit oriented criminal group secret from the public, there may be incentives for a terrorist group to want the fact of a successful nuclear theft to be well publicized. Theft of a large amount of nuclear material would not only acquire for the terrorist group a significant capability but it could also itself generate widespread anxiety among people in the country where it occurred and in countries against which the group's activities might ultimately be aimed. On the other hand, one reason why a terrorist group might prefer to conduct its nuclear theft operations secretly, at least initially, would be its own vulnerability to swift and forceful government action during the period between nuclear theft and completion of the fabrication of fission explosive devices or radiation weapons.

The ability of a concerned government to deal with an emergent terrorist nuclear threat would depend on the location of the group's base of operations, and in particular the location of its weapon manufacturing facilities. These may be unknown and hard to locate, although believed to be within the national territory of the government concerned, or they may be located on territory subject to the jurisdiction of a government that was for some reason not prepared to take decisive action against the terrorist group.

Once a terrorist group possessed fission explosives or radiation weapons, the group's options for their coercive use, both aggressively and to deter enforcement action, cover the complete range discussed previously for an individual acting alone and for profit oriented criminal groups. However, if a terrorist group were involved, doubts concerning the credibility of many options previously considered would be substantially removed, and the inner logic of the possibilities for nuclear coercion would predominate. These possibilities would be exploited by a group of people who were quite free of the intellectual or emotional restraints that tend to inhibit the use of violence by other groups.

If a terrorist group decided to enter the nuclear field, the incentives to acquire the capability to manufacture its own explosive or radiation devices would seem very large. Whether a group would acquire such a capability becomes largely a question of how difficult it would be. Since one nuclear scientist or engineer could provide the key to solving this problem, it is difficult to imagine that a determined terrorist group could not acquire a nuclear weapon manufacturing capability. Here again a terrorist's willingness to take chances with his own health or safety should be contrasted with the possibly more conservative approach of a person engaged in crime for financial profit.

Diversion by a nuclear enterprise

Diversion options

We consider here only the risk of diversion by the managers of a nuclear enterprise of some of the material flowing through facilities under their own operational control. The most likely diversion option would be for the managers of processing facilities to manipulate material balances within the margins of uncertainty in the accountancy system. The exact nuclear material input of a fuel reprocessing or fabrication plant is not known to anyone. Therefore, the input could be stated to be at the lower limit of the range of uncertainty, or, in other words, at the lower end of the limit of error of material unaccounted for (LEMUF). The output could then be stated to be either at the lower or at the upper limit of the LEMUF. If the material output were stated to be at the lower limit, the excess material, if any, could be diverted and kept. If, however, the output were stated at the upper limit, the plant management might be able to charge its customers for more material than was actually present.

Reasons for diversion

The managers of a nuclear enterprise may desire, or be required, to co-operate with government authorities in the diversion of nuclear material from their own facilities for use in a broad range of governmental programmes. They may want to divert material in order to cover up for material losses which are known to the management, but which have not yet been discovered by the regulatory authorities of the government concerned. They may want to have some clandestine material on hand simply as a convenient way to remove material accountancy anomalies as they arise—an easy way to balance the books. Finally, the managers of a nuclear facility may view manipulation of material balances as a way to increase slightly the profitability of the enterprise.

Scope of the risk

The risk that managers of a nuclear enterprise would manipulate material balances to their own advantage would seem inherent in the nuclear power industry because of the high intrinsic value of the material involved and the fact that no one will know exactly how much nuclear material is actually flowing through a major facility. In addition to the presumed honesty of nuclear plant managers, there are limitations on the scope of this particular diversion risk. (1) If an "arms length" economic relationship exists between the operators of distinct steps in the fuel cycle, the possibilities for diversion by material balance manipulations are lessened. (2) Since one man could probably not get very far in a manipulation process, a conspiracy within the plant is necessary, and this increases the risk of detection.

Government material accountancy requirements could arguably have the effect of either increasing or reducing incentives within industry to manipulate nuclear material balances. Given the inherent uncertainties involved, vigorous government enforcement of stringent requirements might increase the incentives for plant managers to cheat the system in order to keep their facilities operating efficiently. However, a lax governmental attitude towards material accountancy would lead to a breakdown of discipline within industrial operations and an opening up of opportunities for much larger manipulations of material balances and perhaps to large-scale undetected diversions by criminal or terrorist groups.

Diversion by a political faction within a nation

Scope of the risk

The government of a nation is normally not of one mind. The possession by a political faction within the government of enough nuclear material in a suitable form to make a few weapons might significantly affect the internal balance of political forces within a nation. This particular risk of nuclear diversion would seem confined to nations where there is access to nuclear weapon material in civilian industry, and where armed force is commonly used as a means of transferring governmental power and authority. In a nation with a small nuclear industry where there was no immediate access to material from which nuclear weapons could be made directly (only natural uranium or low-enriched uranium-fuelled reactors without reprocessing or plutonium storage facilities) the risk of nuclear diversion by a political faction would seem negligible. It should also be noted that in countries where force is a frequently used instrument for political change, the line between a political faction and a criminal group would sometimes be difficult to draw.

Reasons for diversion

The overriding reason why a political faction might want to divert nuclear weapon material would be to achieve its own immediate or future political objectives. Pre-emptive diversion by a political faction to shore up its power base seems quite credible; so does protective diversion by a faction fearing it was about to be suppressed or outlawed. In either of these circumstances, diversion would not necessarily mean subsequent use of the diverted material in acts of violence. Rather, the reason for nuclear diversion would be to deter violence. It seems more difficult to establish the credibility of diversion of material by a faction in order to threaten or use nuclear violence in a *coup d'état*. Would the use of nuclear explosives to blow up a king's palace appear to some political groups to be a symbol of the ultimate triumph of modern technology over an archaic government?

Whether or not to acquire nuclear weapons is an issue that is likely to be on the agenda of many non-nuclear-weapon nations from time to time in the future. Adherence to the NPT and acceptance of IAEA safeguards cannot be expected to settle the issue permanently, although such governmental action should substantially strengthen the position of those who oppose the acquisition of nuclear weapons. Those who favour the acquisition of such weapons may view diversion of material from nuclear industry as a convenient and effective way to confront the government with a *fait accompli*, and to reverse in fact the non-nuclear-weapon decision.

Diversion options

A political faction planning nuclear diversion might have two options not available to criminal groups. (1) It might be possible for the political faction to carry out diversion with the cooperation of an industrial enterprise with an inventory of nuclear material. This enterprise might also provide the faction assistance in weapon manufacturing. (2) The armed forces, or particular units of the armed forces, might be persuaded to participate in the plot and to seize the nuclear material that the faction wanted.

In a country where violence is considered to be a necessary catalyst for political change, a political faction may decide to drop out of the government for a while, take to the hills and begin the process of civil war. A group which carried a significant quantity of nuclear weapon material with it into the hills would be in a far different political position than one which took with it only conventional arms and chemical explosives. Faced with an outlawed political faction in possession of nuclear material, the government would have two choices. (1) It might condemn the nuclear theft in the strongest possible terms, brand those responsible as criminals of the worst sort, and promise effective action. (2) It might immediately move to suppress public disclosure of the theft and quickly open negotiations with the leaders of the faction with a view to agreeing upon a political accommodation. In either case, the main justification for the action taken would be the same; namely, the preservation of internal security and political stability.

III. *Safeguards against nongovernmental diversion*

Safeguards functions

Safeguards are necessary to provide assurance against acts of nuclear violence carried out with material unlawfully obtained from the nuclear power industry. To provide this assurance, national safeguards systems as a whole should perform four interrelated functions:

1. prevention of unlawful diversion;

2. detection of unlawful diversion;
3. recovery of diverted material;
4. response to threats of nuclear violence.

"An ounce of prevention is worth a pound of cure." The relevance of this old saying to a nuclear safeguards system is already apparent from the preceding discussion of nongovernmental diversion risks. Nevertheless, by far the most effort has been devoted to the development of means to detect nuclear diversion after it has happened. Moreover, the detection method that has received the most attention thus far has been accountancy—record keeping, inventory controls, reports and independent audits—which, unlike other possible methods of detecting diversion such as continuous surveillance, makes little contribution to the related function of preventing diversion.

With respect to the prevention of diversion, attention has been focused primarily on such well-known and widely used means as physical barriers, locks, alarms, and so forth. Relatively little effort has been devoted so far to the development of more advanced technological methods. This is in marked contrast to the large efforts that have been devoted to various sophisticated techniques for the assay of nuclear materials, especially the nondestructive measurement of the fissile material content of fuel elements, scrap storage drums, and so on—measurements related to the detection of diversion after it has happened.

The need for means to recover material after it has been unlawfully diverted is now recognized. Governments have disclosed very little, however, about what, if anything, has been actually done to provide for such recovery. Furthermore, governments have not yet publicly recognized the need for contingency plans to respond to nongovernmental nuclear threats.

The extent to which the recovery and response phases of a nuclear safeguards system should be revealed to the public is a difficult question. Revealing the details to these parts of the system in order to produce public confidence would in itself substantially reduce their effectiveness. However, the general public and, what is more important, any potential diverters must believe that governments have planned carefully about what will be done to recover any diverted material and to respond to any nuclear threat.

It should be recalled that there are two very different ways in which material may be unlawfully diverted from the nuclear power industry. One involves the use of stealth by persons with authorized access to nuclear material. The other involves the use of force by persons not authorized to have access to the material taken. Safeguards measures to deal with the internal threat are very different from those designed to deal with the external threat. With this overview of the functions of safeguards against nongovernmental diversion in mind, we consider hereafter specific measures to prevent such diversion.

Prevention of employee thefts

Access controls

Access to nuclear weapon material may be limited to those whose jobs require it. Included in this category are jobs in uranium enrichment, fuel fabrication, chemical reprocessing, material storage facilities, and, for certain types of reactor, nuclear power plants. Jobs in the transportation of nuclear weapon material in certain stages of the fuel cycle would also be included in this category because the employee holding such a job may be in a position to divert the vehicle or the container in which the material is being shipped.

The design of jobs in nuclear industry is thus important. It appears desirable from a safeguards standpoint to clearly separate jobs requiring access to nuclear weapon material from other jobs in the industry. In order to increase the satisfaction and productivity of workers in other industries, steps are being taken to redesign jobs so that the simple reiteration of one task is avoided and the integration of a variety of tasks is involved. Would designing jobs in nuclear industry so as to keep the number of employees requiring access to nuclear weapon material to a minimum adversely affect the productivity of workers in that industry?

Employee security clearance

There are three major reasons why a security clearance may be justified for jobs in the nuclear power industry which involve handling large amounts of nuclear weapon material frequently over long periods of time. (1) Such a clearance would be the only way to guard against internal sabotage of nuclear facilities which would be extremely costly to the target enterprise. (2) Prior security clearance may be the best control measure to deal with the risk of employee diversion of very small quantities of plutonium for use in radiation weapons. (3) Prior security clearance of employees in the most sensitive jobs would help to ensure that links do not develop between the inside of a facility and any outside group planning a forcible theft.

If a security clearance were required, jobs could be denied to various employees on grounds that had nothing to do with merit or technical qualifications. The denial of clearance to an employee may prejudice his subsequent career anywhere in the nuclear power industry, even in less sensitive positions. Therefore, requiring special clearance of employees authorized access to nuclear weapon material may conflict with the rules and employment practices in agreements between trade unions and the managements of various nuclear enterprises and, in the United States, raise problems related to compliance with equal employment opportunity laws. In any event, an employee security clearance requirement raises issues concerning the appropriate extent of a government's authority to investigate persons who are neither prospective government employees nor working on classified contracts nor suspected of having committed a crime. These issues will be more substantial in some countries than in others.

Employee surveillance

There are many possibilities for monitoring the activities of employees who have access to nuclear weapon material. At least two employees may be required to be present whenever such material is handled in a facility. It would seem that a two-person rule would not impose an undue burden on industry since many of the operations involved would probably require the presence of at least two people for health and safety reasons. Beyond a two-person rule, employees who are handling nuclear weapon material could be kept under continuous surveillance by stationing security personnel at locations to observe the work or by closed-circuit television monitoring. Among the most cost-effective measures may be inspections upon entry to and exit from places where nuclear weapon material is located. Of course, employees and any parcels they are carrying may be searched with varying degrees of thoroughness. To ensure detection of very small quantities of nuclear weapon material (especially plutonium) exit doorway monitoring instruments could be used.

Preventing employee theft during transportation

Preventing employee theft in the transportation of nuclear weapon material raises special problems. A person driving a truck or piloting an aircraft containing a shipment of nuclear weapon material has perhaps the greatest opportunity of anyone to steal such material. Moreover, the firms that transport nuclear weapon material are essentially part of the transportation industry which serves all kinds of other industries and activities in addition to the nuclear power industry. Theft from the transportation industry is itself a major criminal enterprise in many countries. Since many of the measures intended to deal with employee thefts during transportation are the same as those that may be used to prevent hijacking by outsiders, we will defer further discussion at this point.

Measures to prevent theft by outsiders

Physical containment

Nuclear weapon material may be stored in a variety of ways to make it difficult to steal. The container may be so heavy that it cannot be moved without a crane and the crane may itself be inoperable without a special key. Containers may in turn be located in a vault or a special building with very thick walls and flooring. If nuclear weapon material is in process areas outside of special storage facilities, the building itself may be specially constructed to withstand attempted thefts. Alarms can also be installed to bring an attempted theft to the attention of persons who can prevent it.

The location of a facility will also be a factor in determining the vulnerability of nuclear weapon material within it to theft by outsiders. Health and safety considerations require most nuclear facilities to be located at remote sites. This may also have advantages from a safeguards point of view. An offsetting consideration would be the effect a remote site would have on the risk of theft of nuclear weapon material during lengthy transportation to and from the facility.

Security forces

Physical barriers alone cannot adequately protect nuclear weapon material. Given enough time, a group of men with modern tools could penetrate any series of physical barriers that could be erected at a reasonable cost. Investments in stronger physical barriers may be more cost-effective than the investment of an equivalent amount of money in security forces up to a point, and care should be taken to design a system which will reach that point. However, the capability to use force under human direction and control is an essential part of the safeguards necessary to prevent nuclear diversion.

This requirement raises a variety of difficult issues, but two have decisive importance. (1) What postulated capabilities should the security force be designed to defeat? (2) Who should have responsibility for the use of force if necessary to prevent nuclear theft?

Security force requirements. The credible capabilities of those attempting a nuclear theft range from a well-armed individual acting alone to a well-armed paramilitary group of substantial size.

In designing a safeguards system, on-site and off-site security forces may be considered as a whole. Of critical importance are the means used to bring to bear any off-site forces relied on. Unarmed watchmen cannot be expected to deter a determined thief or criminal group, though they may sound the alarm. However, the capabilities of armed guards to do much more than unarmed watchmen should not be overestimated. Here is the dilemma: can we expect armed guards at nuclear facilities to give their lives in defence of nuclear weapon material? It would seem that armed guards should be relied on to prevent nuclear theft only to the extent that they are superior in numbers and firepower to the criminal forces arrayed against them. The precise capabilities of off-site law enforcement authorities to deal with nuclear thefts may be similarly questioned.

A special on-site security force with sufficient capability to prevent any credible nuclear theft has several advantages over the alternative of relying on a combination of on-site and off-site capabilities. (1) Responsibility for security and theft prevention can be centralized and clearly fixed rather than diffused among disparate authorities. (2) The precise methods of protecting nuclear weapon material may be specialized and made as efficient as possible within the limits of the financial resources available for this purpose. (3) Investments in special training and equipment would pay off. (4) It is even reasonable to expect that the members of such a specialized security force would be willing to substantially endanger their lives in order to protect the nuclear weapon material within their charge.

Responsibility for providing security forces. To what extent should the nuclear power industry have the duty of and be held responsible for the protection of society against nuclear thefts? There are reasons why the use of force to prevent nuclear thefts and the development and deployment of effective capabilities for this purpose might not be viewed as an appropriate burden to impose on the nuclear industry itself, whether that industry is privately owned or government owned. The effectiveness of many different security forces, for which each nuclear facility operator would be individually responsible, could be doubtful since recruiting, training and equipping would be on a decentralized basis. Moreover, the public could not be expected to have as much confidence in a multiplicity of security forces maintained by various enterprises as in a single security force embracing the entire nuclear power industry and operated by the national government. Moreover, the costs of one centrally controlled force for the entire nuclear power industry would be substantially less than a multiplicity of forces developed by nuclear enterprises themselves. Finally, such a force could make a major contribution to all the other safeguards functions: detection, recovery of stolen materials, and response to nuclear threats.

Transportation

The prevention of diversion of nuclear weapon material during transportation deserves special analysis because of the amount of material being transported and its potential vulnerability. Nuclear weapon material may be shipped by train, truck, ship or aircraft; depending on the circumstances, they may be shipped together with other goods or in exclusive-use vehicles. Exclusive-use trains, ships and aircraft are impractical, while exclusive-use trucks are feasible and economical in most commercial circumstances. The opportunities to hijack a ship or a train are small, while the opportunities to hijack an aircraft or a truck are relatively large. Perhaps the greatest vulnerability of nuclear weapon material to theft, however, exists during inter-vehicle transfers from one mode of transportation to another, such as from ship to truck or truck to aircraft.

Special measures may be necessary to ensure that: *(a)* the location of the vehicle used is known at all times; *(b)* a substantial deviation from a prescribed route or speed of travel will be detected by anyone on board the vehicle; *(c)* it takes more time to break and enter the shipping containers in which nuclear weapon material is carried than for adequate help to

184

reach the vehicle; *(d)* sufficient force can be brought to bear in a timely manner to prevent a successful hijacking. Though expensive, the means to provide such assurance are available with existing technology. It would seem that an armed escort from a special security force should accompany shipments of significant amounts of nuclear weapon material.

Co-location of nuclear facilities

It is sometimes suggested that the vulnerability to theft of nuclear weapon material from the various fuel cycles could be reduced if nuclear facilities were co-located so that transportation from the site were eliminated. For example, we might visualize a large 4 000–5 000 megawatt nuclear power station with four or five light water reactors. Enrichment (by means of centrifugation), fuel fabrication (plutonium-bearing as well as low-enriched uranium) and reprocessing services might be furnished to the reactors by facilities built on the same site as the nuclear power station. Hence, the nuclear feed material to the site would be in the form of uranium hexafluoride and the output would be radioactive waste for permanent storage. The fuel cycles for other reactor types may lend themselves more readily to co-location of facilities than light water reactors.

The main advantage in co-location of fuel cycle facilities at power plant sites would be the reduction in transportation of nuclear weapon material. However, the total number of fuel fabrication, reprocessing, storage and possibly enrichment facilities that would be required would be substantially greater with such co-location than if a large number of nuclear power plants were supported by a relatively few facilities providing fuel cycle services. Moreover, the co-location of nuclear fuel cycle and power generating facilities would result in the loss of important economies of scale in very large fuel fabrication and reprocessing plants. Finally, there are few sites where as many as four or five 1 000 megawatt nuclear reactors can be located within environmental constraints.

Although the location of fuel cycle facilities at power stations may not be practical in most circumstances, co-location of nuclear fuel cycle facilities themselves should be seriously considered. The transportation of fresh fuel assemblies to, and irradiated fuel assemblies from, a reactor are not the most vulnerable transportation links. Rather the greatest diversion risks exist during the transport of high-enriched uranium from an enrichment plant to a fuel fabrication plant and of plutonium from a reprocessing plant to a fuel fabrication plant for recycling. These links could be elimated, for example, if a centrifuge enrichment plant were co-located with a plant to fabricate high-enriched uranium fuel for high-temperature gas-cooled reactors, or if a reprocessing plant were located on the same site as a plant to fabricate fuel for light water reactors or fast breeder reactors. Moreover, co-location of these facilities would substantially reduce the total number of places where nuclear weapon material is present.

IV. *Conclusions*

Nongovernmental nuclear weapon proliferation could adversely affect the security of governments and people generally and the prospects for the future development of nuclear power. Nuclear-weapon and non-nuclear-weapon states have a common interest in the effectiveness of national safeguards systems to prevent this type of nuclear proliferation. Thus, close international coordination and cooperation is needed urgently to develop and implement national systems. In the design of national safeguards, the use of the best available technology and institutional mechanisms is justified in view of the dangers of nongovernmental nuclear weapon proliferation.

References

1. The material for this paper is drawn primarily from an in-depth study recently completed and not yet published by myself and Theodore B. Taylor, *Nuclear Diversion: Risks and Safeguards,* conducted for The Ford Foundation's Energy Policy Project. The study examines the risks of diversion from the nuclear power industry in the United States and evaluates present US Atomic Energy Commission safeguards requirements to prevent unlawful diversion.
2. This paper also draws upon relevant portions of an extensive study of the IAEA safeguards developed to implement the NPT, conducted under the auspices of the American Society of International Law with support from the National Science Foundation by a group composed of Bernhard G. Bechhoefer, Bennett Boskey, Victor Gilinsky, Edwin M. Kinderman, Lawrence Scheinman, Henry D. Smyth, Paul C. Szasz, Theodore B. Taylor and Mason Willrich, as project director. Mason Willrich (ed.), *International Safeguards and Nuclear Industry* (Baltimore, The Johns Hopkins University Press, 1973).

6. Nuclear power: a Trojan horse for terrorists

D. KRIEGER

Abstract

Nuclear power is developed in a society in the belief that it will provide a relatively cheap energy source and reduce dependency on external energy sources. This form of energy, however, presents grave risks not only from reactor accidents and the storage of waste products, but also from the release of radioactive material by terrorist sabotage or conventional warfare. Societies cannot effectively protect the nuclear fuel cycle against sabotage short of converting to a garrison state; this is a problem which will only increase as nuclear reactors proliferate. The diversion of plutonium by terrorists for conversion to atomic or radiological weapons presents additional risks since unidentified or unlocated terrorists cannot be deterred by threat of retaliation. It is suggested that the nuclear Trojan horse can only be harnessed by a worldwide moratorium on the use and development of nuclear fission energy and a crash programme to develop alternative energy sources including solar, geothermal and fusion.

I. *Introduction*

The Trojan horse of the atomic age is nuclear energy which will ensure a radioactive future for mankind and present as serious a hazard to public safety as do nuclear weapons. The construction of nuclear power plants ensures that a country will be as vulnerable to mass destruction from conventional weapons as it would be from atomic weapons. With a fully developed nuclear power industry, it will be possible for even a small power or terrorist group to destroy a major power; it will be necessary for the attacking state or organization to use only conventional weapons to release into the atmosphere the radioactivity generated in nuclear power reactors. Each nuclear power plant located near a major city represents the potential demise of that city.

In addition, the possibility of radioactive material being stolen or hijacked by disaffected foreign or domestic groups—which might use the material for political blackmail, terrorism or retaliation—will increase as the nuclear power industry expands. The purpose of this chapter is to argue that nuclear energy undermines the national security of even major powers and represents a serious hazard to humanity. Nuclear power, in other words, is a Trojan horse which undermines not only national security but human security. My remarks in this paper will apply primarily to attacks by foreign or domestic terrorist groups. These groups may be able to attack undetected or, because of their mobility and/or mind-sets, would not be inhibited by the same fears of retaliation which would act upon a government.

II. *The "energy crisis"*

What is known in the developed world as the "energy crisis" is, in reality a crisis of dependency brought on by increasing demands for energy and decreasing availability of inexpensive energy sources. The United States, for example, could develop its known 200 years' reserves of coal—but not in an environmentally satisfactory way—at less expense than it can import Middle Eastern oil. Thus, it has increasingly opted for the latter, and in the process has become increasingly dependent on supplies from this politically volatile region.

In 1965 the United States imported only 20 per cent of its oil demand with only 2 per cent coming from sources other than Canada and Venezuela which are considered dependable. In 1972 imports rose to 27 per cent and are expected to reach 35 per cent in 1973, and jump to 40–60 per cent by the end of this decade. The proportion of oil imported from the Middle East has continued to rise, and thus the dependency of the United States.

Japan and Western Europe are also dependent on Middle Eastern supplies for meeting their energy demands. Japan imports 85–90 per cent of its petroleum from this area, and Western Europe is dependent upon Middle Eastern imports for approximately 50 per cent of its petroleum needs.

In monetary terms, it is expected that by 1975, the Middle East and North Africa, including Iran, will receive annual revenues from oil of almost $20 billion; by 1980 they are expected to reach $63 billion. By 1980 it is expected that the United States will be spending approximately $18–24 billion for energy imports; Europe will be spending $23–31 billion, and Japan, $12–16 billion.

The crisis of dependency can be solved in only two ways: the reduction of energy demand (conservation) or the development of domestic energy supplies. The former policy is advocated persuasively by Stewart Udall, former US Secretary of the Interior. He suggests the following measures for reducing future fuel demands by as much as 50 per cent:

In transportation, gasoline consumption should be reduced 50 per cent by cutting auto travel in half. It will take time to achieve this objective, but for the present, rationing, car pooling, and/or doubling of gas prices at the pump would force changes in Americans' extravagant travel habits. Crash efforts to develop cheap, pleasant, convenient mass transit and intercity passenger services would also lead to enormous economies.

The minicar is a must. By imposing stiff taxes on oversized autos (a practice already in effect in some Western European countries) and by forcing reductions in the weight, size, and horsepower, we can double the miles-per-gallon performance of private vehicles. By building fast trains between major urban centers, we can make big reductions in interurban traffic, eliminate short-haul airline service, and thereby achieve major energy savings. Additional fuel savings are possible if we insist that airplanes fly with nearly full loads, thus paring wasteful duplication by competing airlines. The point here, as in other areas of the energy problem, is that personal convenience must be sacrificed to conservation.

In electric power we can increase the efficiency of generating plants at least 20 per cent with combined cycles and magnetohydrodynamics—two engineering advances that will stretch the effective use of steam. We can also invert and prod gluttonous users into scaling down their fuel requirements . . .

On the residential front we should use natural gas, not electricity, where supplies of gas are available; gas, being a fuel burned directly, is twice as efficient. We can adopt stiff tests that will force all energy-wasting appliances off the market. We can provide a safe substitute for gas pilot lights, which use nearly half the gas consumed in homes, and we can even eliminate such extravagances as central heating . . .

Our houses need much better insulation to keep the energy-supplied warm or cool air inside. The glass boxes that we now use for office buildings require year-round, artificial "climate control", largely because the windows cannot be opened; merely opening windows would allow us to "control" our inside climate naturally on perhaps one-quarter of the annual workdays. [1]

Proponents of nuclear energy, such as Chauncey Starr, founder of the American Nuclear Society, describe conservation as "the politically risky, distasteful course of rationing". [2] Perhaps because it is politically risky, conservation has not been treated as a serious solution to the crisis of dependency. The answer has been sought rather in the development of alternative energy sources. Dr Starr, for example, in a paper distributed by the Department of State as background information "in view of the national interest in the energy crisis", concluded: ". . . I would very much rather accept the minimal risks of large scale nuclear power than the already evident risks of international tensions from foreign oil". [2]

Dr Starr's opinion is apparently widely shared in high places. Richard Nixon, in his Energy Message to the Congress of 18 April 1973, stated: "The major alternative to fossil fuels for the remainder of this century is nuclear energy . . . It is estimated that nuclear power will provide more than one-quarter of this country's electrical production in 1985, and over one-half by the year 2000." Western Europe expects to have one-third of its electrical output supplied by nuclear energy in 1985, and in Japan the figure is expected to rise to 30 per cent by 1980 and 44 per cent by 1985.

Alternative energy sources to nuclear fission, have been severely hampered in their development by underfunding. In fiscal year 1972, the United States spent over \$300 million on nuclear fission R&D while spending less than $50 million on fusion, less than $10 million on solar energy and fundamental energy policy studies and less than a million dollars on geothermal energy. In fiscal 1973 the United States plans to spend over $400 million for fission R&D, $65 million for fusion, $13.4 million for solar energy and fundamental energy policy studies, and $2.5 million for geothermal. For fiscal 1974, the United States administration has requested approximately $563 million for R&D on nuclear fission, $70 million for fusion, and $15 million for solar energy.

These inequities in funding continue to exist despite the fact that in December 1972 extremely positive reports were issued by the National Science Foundation on both geothermal and solar energy. The panel on geothermal energy, headed by Walter Hickel, recommended an expenditure of $684.7 million on geothermal R&D and indicated that this could lead to the generation of more geothermal energy by the year 2000 than the total electricity generating capacity of the USA today. The second report, *Solar Energy as a National Energy Resource*, indicated that solar energy "is an inexhaustible source of enormous amounts of clean energy" and "there are not technical barriers to wide application of solar energy to meet US needs".[1]

Despite these recommendations, the United States, as well as Western Europe and Japan, seems set on solving the crisis of energy dependency by the development of nuclear fission energy.

III. *Nuclear power safety*

It is by no means certain that nuclear power plants would be safe even were it not for the possibilities of conventional attack, sabotage or diversion of nuclear material. Scientists have disputed the safety of nuclear reactors on technical grounds and even AEC scientists have admitted that no satisfactory means exist for calculating the probability of an accident. [6] The failure to adequately test the emergency core cooling system (ECCS) is an important variable in the evaluation of claims of nuclear plant safety. A report by *Aerojet* issued in August 1971 listed 28 areas of knowledge or capability critical to effective operation of the ECCS; in seven areas it found techniques for dealing with the problems to be completely missing, and in the remaining 21 areas it described the status as incomplete, unverified, inadequate, imprecise or preliminary. [7]

The storage of radioactive wastes is a second major safety problem. The radioactive poisons cannot be disposed of; they can only be stored so as to keep them from contact with the environment. But some of the radioactive wastes will remain poisonous for a quarter of a million years. Man,

[1] For a general discussion of alternative energy sources see references [3–5].

of course, has no way of knowing whether the environment can be protected from these poisons for many times the length of recorded history.

The reasonable estimate under the circumstances would be the conservative estimate of man's capabilities. Hannes Alfvén, Nobel Laureate in Physics, has argued:

Fission energy is safe only if a number of critical devices work as they should, if a number of people in key positions follow all their instructions, if there is no sabotage, no hijacking of the transports, if no reactor fuel processing plant or reprocessing plant or repository anywhere in the world is situated in a region of riots or guerrilla activity, and no revolution or war—even a "conventional one"—takes place in these regions. The enormous quantities of extremely dangerous material must not get into the hands of ignorant people or desperados. No acts of God can be permitted. [8]

Yet, despite the warning that even "acts of God" cannot be permitted, the decisions are now being made—by the political leadership of today—that it is worth the risk of creating those long-lived poisons to increase the supply of energy. These decisions represent either an ignorance of the risk involved or an arrogance toward humanity unprecedented in human history; they are decisions which subject not only the present generation but the next 100000 generations as well, to the risks of radioactivity released into the environment.

IV. *Consequences of a major accident*

John Gofman, a former Associate Director of the Lawrence Radiation Laboratory and leading critic of the AEC, has estimated that in one year a nuclear power plant of 1000 MW(e) would produce as much strontium-90 and cesium-137 as would 23 megatons of atomic fission bombs. He has also estimated that the combined atmospheric testing of nuclear weapons by the United States, the United Kingdom and the USSR through 1963 amounted to a total of 250 megatons. [9] Atmospheric testing led, of course, to the arousal of scientific and public opinion against the hazards of radioactive fallout and to the signing of the Partial Test Ban Treaty prohibiting such testing. Nevertheless, in 10 years the situation is such that 12 nuclear power plants in one year create as much radioactive waste as all atmospheric testing through 1963;[2] by the year 2000, the United States alone expects to have some 1000 nuclear power plants.

[2] Linus Pauling, Nobel Laureate in Chemistry and Peace, estimated 600 megatons of bombs in atmospheric testing up through 1963. On this basis he reached the following conclusions: "It is my estimate that about 100000 viable children will be born with gross physical or mental defects caused by cesium-137 and other fission products from the bomb tests carried out from 1952 to 1963, and 1500000 more, if the human race survives, with gross defects caused by the carbon-14 from these bomb tests. In addition, about 10 times as many embryonic, neonatal, and childhood deaths are expected—about 1000000 caused by the

In addition to strontium-90 and cesium-137, nuclear power plants create as a byproduct plutonium-239 which has a radioactive half-life of 24 400 years, thus making it radioactively dangerous for some 250 000 years. This element is largely man-made, as it is extremely rare in nature. Donald Geesaman, a physicist at the Lawrence Radiation Laboratory, has estimated that about half a kilogramme of plutonium-239 represents the *potential* for 9 billion cases of human lung cancer. [9] This is certainly more damage than would be caused in a short time frame, but even if only one particle in a million were ingested, half a kilogramme of plutonium-239 could cause 9 000 cases of lung cancer. Thirteen tons of plutonium were produced in 1971; by 1980 it is estimated that there will be about 130 000 kg produced annually and, by the year 2000, 750 000 kg produced annually. The consequences of even a small release of this substance into the atmosphere would be catastrophic.

A major accident at a nuclear power plant which involved a meltdown of the reactor fuel core would lead to consequences of disaster magnitude. The United States Atomic Energy Commission estimated in a 1957 study, the Brookhaven Report, that a major accident could cause 3 400 immediate fatalities, 43 000 injuries and $7 billion in property damage. [11] A whole city might need to be evacuated within 12 hours to keep fatalities and cancer cases to the foregoing levels and an area of 150 000 square miles might remain contaminated and uninhabitable for decades. Needless to say, the evacuation of a large city would create economic chaos, and unprecedented social problems in dealing with possibly millions of nuclear refugees. In an AEC update of this report, WASH-1250, which was begun in 1965 but not released until 1973, the estimates were raised to 45 000 deaths and $19 billion in property damage. [12]

US government response to potential damage
caused by nuclear accidents

It would appear that the damage caused by a major nuclear accident in a nuclear power plant would be comparable in destructiveness to a nuclear attack—the difference between the two being that the government at least *attempts* by means of deterrence to protect against nuclear attack, while it supports the construction of nuclear power plants. Congress, in

fission products and 15 000 000 by carbon 14. An even larger number of children may have minor defects caused by the bomb tests: these minor defects which are passed on from generation to generation rather than being rapidly weeded out by genetic death, may be responsible for more suffering in the aggregate than the major defects . . . It is my opinion that the bomb test strontium-90 can cause leukemia and bone cancer; iodine-131 can cause cancer of the throat, and cesium-137 and carbon-14 can cause these and other diseases. I make the rough estimate that because of the somatic effect of these radioactive substances that now pollute the earth about 2 000 000 human beings now living will die five or ten or fifteen years earlier than if the nuclear tests had not been made." [10]

the Price-Anderson Act, has in fact provided an enormous subsidy to the nuclear power industry by limiting its liability in the case of an accident to $560 million;[3] the difference in liability between this figure and the $19 billion damage figure estimated in WASH-1250 is the responsibility of the citizen who must not only accept the risk of nuclear accident but the major liability as well.

Further signs of United States government generosity to the nuclear power industry are found in AEC regulation 50.13 which states that nuclear licence applicants "are *not required* to provide for design features or other measures for the specific purpose of protection against the effects of attacks and destructive acts, including sabotage, directed against the facility by an enemy of the United States, whether a foreign government or other person . . . ." [14]

Considerable protection against the threat of external attack on a nuclear power plant would be provided by burying the plant underground in the same way that nuclear missiles are placed in hardened underground silos. This has not been required, however, and all presently built US nuclear reactors are above ground, and all currently planned reactors will also be built above ground. Were the reactors to be safeguarded by underground construction, the price of nuclear energy would increase substantially, and for this reason this option has been declined by the nuclear power industry. Their purpose is profit, and if they are not effectively regulated by government, they will opt for the most profitable, rather than the safest, route.

V. *The vulnerability of the nuclear fuel cycle*

The nuclear fuel cycle is subject to destructive attack or theft of nuclear material at a number of key points. High-level radioactive wastes, including plutonium-239, are found in nuclear power plants, fuel reprocessing sites and in liquid storage sites. Any of these sites are vulnerable to destruction and radioactive release by conventional weapons.

Terrorists have already threatened to dive-bomb the Oak Ridge National Laboratory in a hijacked plane. [15] Dismissing the possibility of a kamikaze-type attack on a nuclear power plant plays into the hands of the first suicidal terrorist who decides to attempt to destroy a city through this method.

The transportation of nuclear material between points in the fuel cycle

---

[3] For a discussion of the Price-Anderson Act, see reference [13]. The authors state: "If the Price-Anderson Act were repealed, as assuredly it should be, it is extremely doubtful that any future nuclear electricity generating plants would be built above ground. Indeed, it is extremely doubtful that any electric utility company would be so foolhardy as to continue operation of nuclear electricity plants already built."

presents opportunities for the theft of nuclear material. Sam Edlow, a consultant on nuclear material transport, has pointed out that ". . . the transportation industry is so thoroughly infiltrated by the Cosa Nostra that any cargo which organized crime determines to obtain will be obtained". [16]⁴

Since nuclear material for civilian uses is shipped with few or no guards or extensive precautions, it is likely that even well organized and determined "non-professionals" will eventually be able to lay their hands on nuclear materials. Theodore Taylor, president of the International Research and Technology Corporation, has stated:

The levels of physical security now applied to fissionable materials for civilian use, in the United States and other countries, are considerably lower than those overcome in many successful thefts of other valuables in the past. Many situations now exist where quantities of fissionable materials sufficient for several nuclear explosives are not protected by armed guards, major physical barriers, or intrusion alarms. [17]

VI. *Nuclear theft and nuclear weapons*

Once possession is obtained of plutonium-239 or enriched uranium, it is presumably not technically prohibitive to construct atomic weapons the size of those which destroyed Hiroshima and Nagasaki. One needs only approximately 6 kg of plutonium or 20 kg of enriched uranium and the knowledge of how to construct the bomb. Representative Craig Hosmer, a member of the Joint Committee on Atomic Energy, has stated:

nuclear weapons designs are only an incidental facet of the general antiproliferation effort. This is because the laws of physics from which nuclear weapons are designed have become so universally understood that any effort now to suppress the data would be absurd. The cat has been out of the bag for a long, long time. A potential proliferator enterprising enough to lay hands on illicit supplies of fissionable material is certain to be smart enough to know how to weaponize them. [18]

Hosmer has also pointed out, correctly it would seem, that "the potentiality for diversion remains low not primarily because the [safeguards] systems are working well but because the major flow of materials into them is yet to come." [18]

According to the Stockholm International Peace Research Institute (SIPRI), in 1971 there were some 128 nuclear power reactors in 16 countries which produced some 13 000 kg of plutonium. But by 1977 there are expected to be some 325 nuclear reactors in 32 countries producing about 65 000 kg of plutonium, and by 1980 the total is expected to rise to an annual production figure of about 130 000 kg of plutonium. [19] One-third of this plutonium would be accumulating in non-nuclear-weapon countries.

⁴ The article concludes: "To sum up—the environment of the transportation industry is one of incompetence, criminality, and unreliability." [16]

194

The supply in these countries alone would be sufficient for the *weekly* production, in theory, of some 100 nuclear weapons of Nagasaki size (20 kiloton range). This does not mean, of course, that anything near this number would be produced, but with an annual world accumulation rate of about 130 000 kg, a loss rate of one-tenth of one per cent would still supply sufficient fissionable material for 20 Nagasaki-size weapons.

It should be pointed out that "efficient" nuclear weapons generally require plutonium that contains some 90 to 95 per cent Pu-239. The plutonium which is extracted from nuclear reactors generally contains about 70 per cent Pu-239 and the remainder is Pu-240 and other non-fissionable isotopes. This difficulty can be overcome, however, simply by relying on "inefficient" weapons. According to SIPRI:

Even though contaminated with up to 30 per cent Pu-240, the plutonium normally produced in nuclear power reactors would still be usable as the fissile material for more primitive, but still effective, nuclear weapons. A relatively larger amount of this plutonium would have to be used for a given explosive yield and consequently the physical size of the weapon would be larger. [19]

Even without constructing an atomic bomb, the threat of releasing plutonium into the atmosphere in a public place should compel governments to accede to almost any terrorist demand. Released in the atmosphere as fine particles, the radioactive effects of less plutonium than would be needed for a bomb could render a metropolitan area uninhabitable, or destroy a major portion of a nation's agricultural produce.

VII. *Terrorists and their motives*

Douglas DeNike, a psychologist at the University of Southern California Medical School, has prepared a list of persons who might attempt nuclear sabotage, theft and/or blackmail and also a list of possible motives for nuclear malfeasance. [20] These are shown below.

Possible Malefactors
1. Foreign governments and their agents, acting under orders.
2. Sub-units of foreign governments and their agents or military forces, acting with or without official sanction.
3. Individuals or groups engaged in domestic subversive activity: extremists, terrorists, nihilists.
4. Criminals—highly organized, loosely associated, or individual.
5. Psychopaths, severe neurotics, and psychotics, harboring sadistic, homicidal, or suicidal motives.
6. Mercenaries in the pay of others, or who need the money to pay off debts, support a heroin addiction, etc.
7. Disgruntled employees seeking to sabotage an installation for revenge, or out of casual vandalism.
   (Note: Any of these categories may contain persons who, out of ignorance, may do much greater damage than they intended.)

8. Otherwise normal persons who act opportunistically and impulsively. They may act on the spur of the moment due to momentary life stress from troubles with loved ones, bereavement, divorce, job failure, ill health, etc. Also, opportunistic thieves who might attempt theft of radioactive material with only vague plans of what they might do with it.

Motives for Nuclear Malfeasance
1. International enmity or rivalry.
2. Sectional or factional enmity, such as civil war, terrorism.
3. Desire to create panic or interrupt electrical power, either for its own sake or secondary to some other design, such as looting under cover of darkness, etc.
4. Desire to establish credibility of later threats of repetition, demands for blackmail payments, etc.
5. Desire to obtain special nuclear materials for bombs.
6. Desire to obtain radioactive waste materials for terror, homicide, blackmail, or resale. Motives 6 and 7 may also subsume the desire to control such materials in order to secure immunity from persecution or prosecution for the thieves or for others as stipulated in threats to the authorities.
7. Sadistic motivation—merely to cause suffering. This might take the form of a specific grudge against particular persons likely to be killed or injured in a nuclear incident, such as employer, spouse, rival, etc.
8. Suicidal/homicidal motivation—to die spectacularly, take other lives at the same time.
9. Publicity motivation, to get one's name in the papers, or to publicize some specific cause (a frequent motive for aircraft hijacking and terrorism).
10. Psychotic motivation. This can take various forms, depending on the nature of the delusional system involved.

VIII. *Harnessing the nuclear Trojan horse*

There is only one method available for harnessing the nuclear Trojan horse; a total worldwide moratorium on the use and development of nuclear fission energy. This will not be a popular alternative for the industries which are heavily invested in nuclear power, nor an easy solution to arrange at the international level. Nevertheless, a moratorium provides the only assurance possible against the sabotage of nuclear facilities or the diversion of nuclear materials by terrorists.

No technical solution is capable of harnessing the nuclear Trojan horse. To place the facilities in hardened underground sites and increase significantly the police protection of nuclear material shipments will lessen the probabilities of sabotage or diversion, but never eliminate the possibility entirely. The United States could turn itself into a garrison state to protect its nuclear material and facilities, but not adequately control the diversion of nuclear material in other countries. The only way the United States and other developed countries can even hope to achieve a global moratorium is by accepting the leadership in declaring and enforcing a moratorium.

It must be emphasized that the "energy crisis" is a crisis of dependency rather than a crisis of resources. Rather than sending $40–60 billion to the Middle East annually by 1980, the United States, Japan and Western Europe should immediately join with all other countries in a full-scale, fully funded effort to develop alternative energy sources including fusion, geothermal and solar.

It is a false dichotomy to argue that either we must become increasingly dependent on oil imports from the Middle East or develop nuclear fission energy. The employment of coal gasification techniques could make the United States an energy exporter over the next few decades, and the development of geothermal, fusion or solar energy sources could provide virtually an infinite supply of energy. These energy technologies and resources could be provided to developing countries in return for their foregoing the option of nuclear fission to meet their energy needs.

What holds the United States back from development of even its coal resources is the financial cost, but this is a fundamentally anti-human form of accounting. The dollar cost is given greater weight than the risk to human life created by the development of a plutonium future from nuclear power plants.

Nuclear Trojan horses are already scattered around the United States and many other nations; it is not too late to call for a complete moratorium on nuclear power plants, but it must be done soon. What is needed is a global effort to develop and distribute non-poisonous forms of energy throughout the globe.

While the global energy development effort is taking place some energy conservation may be needed; in this regard the developed world, which uses the majority of the world's energy resources, may learn a significant lesson about living styles from China and other underdeveloped countries. Stewart Udall has stressed the following figures in arguing for energy conservation:

Two hundred nine million Americans use about as much energy for air conditioning alone as the 800 million mainland Chinese use for all purposes—and Americans waste each year almost as much energy as the Japanese (105 million people) consume annually. [1]

The nuclear Trojan horse will only be harnessed when human risks and concomitantly national security are given a higher priority than financial profit for the nuclear power industry. Without an immediate moratorium on nuclear energy, it is only to be hoped that radiation release—from a major nuclear accident, caused by sabotage or otherwise, or the threat or explosion of a nuclear weapon by terrorists—will not become a necessary precondition for realizing the basically anti-human nature of a nuclear fission approach to solving the crisis of energy dependency.

References

1. Udall, Stewart, "The Energy Crisis: A Radical Solution", *World Magazine,* 8 May 1973, p. 35.
2. "International Realities of the Energy Crisis", US Department of State News Release, April 1973, p. 5.
3. Wilford, John Noble, "Energy Crisis: The Quest for New Sources Becomes Urgent", *New York Times,* 18 April 1973, p. 21.
4. "Federal Energy Research and Priorities", statement by Senator Mike Gravel before the Senate Interior Committee, 30 June 1972.
5. O'Connor, Egan, "A Sunshine Future or a Radioactive One?" (New York, Committee for Nuclear Responsibility, April 1963).
6. "Accident Rate at Atom Plants Unpredictable, AEC Aide Says", *Los Angeles Times,* 10 March 1973.
7. "The Clear and Present Danger, A Public Report on Nuclear Power Plants", (Los Angeles, California, the Environmental Protection Group, April 1973) p. 37.
8. "Energy and Environment", *Bulletin of Atomic Scientists,* May 1972, p. 6.
9. Gofman, John, "Time for a Moratorium", *The Case for a Moratorium,* (Washington, DC, Environmental Action Foundation, 1973) p. 7.
10. Dr Linus Paulning's Nobel Peace Prize Lecture, in *Science and Peace,* an Occasional Paper of the Center for the Study of Democratic Institutions, 1964.
11. *Theoretical Possibilities and Consequences of Major Accidents in Large Nuclear Plants,* USAEC Report WASH-740, March 1957.
12. *The Safety of Nuclear Power Reactors and Related Facilities,* USAEC Report WASH-1250, June 1973.
13. Gofman, John and Tamplin, Arthur, *Poisoned Power,* (Emmaus, Pennsylvania, Rodale Press, 1971) pp. 177–80.
14. USA EX, 10 CRF Part 50, Licensing of Production and Utilization Facilities, as amended through 28 July 1972, p. 5 sec. 50.13.
15. Ingram, Timothy, H., "Nuclear Hijacking: Now Within the Grasp of Any Bright Lunatic", *Washington Monthly,* January 1973.
16. Geesaman, Donald (compiler), "And Now for a Little Diversion", *Environment,* Vol. 14, No. 8, October 1972.
17. Taylor, Theodore, "The Need for National and International Systems to Provide Physical Security for Fissionable Materials", Paper delivered to the 138th meeting of the American Association for the Advancement of Science, 28 December 1971.
18. "Keynote Remarks", in Leachman, Robert and Altoff, Philip *et al., Preventing Nuclear Theft: Guidelines for Industry and Government* (New York, Praeger, 1972) pp. 6–8.
19. *World Armaments and Disarmament, SIPRI Yearbook 1972* (Stockholm, Almqvist & Wiksell, 1972, Stockholm International Peace Research Institute) pp. 288, 366.
20. DeNike, H. Douglas, "Nuclear Safety and Human Malice", mimeographed paper, University of Southern California School of Medicine, 1972.

Part III
Cooperation in the
peaceful applications
of nuclear energy

Article IV

1. *Nothing in this Treaty shall be interpreted as affecting the inalienable right of all the parties to the Treaty to develop research, production and use of nuclear energy for peaceful purposes without discrimination and in conformity with articles I and II of this Treaty.*

2. *All the Parties to the Treaty undertake to facilitate, and have the right to participate in, the fullest possible exchange of equipment, materials and scientific and technological information for the peaceful uses of nuclear energy. Parties to the Treaty in a position to do so shall also co-operate in contributing alone or together with other States or international organizations to the further development of the applications of nuclear energy for peaceful purposes, especially in the territories of non-nuclear-weapon States Party to the Treaty, with due consideration for the needs of the developing areas of the world.*

Article V

Each Party to the Treaty undertakes to take appropriate measures to ensure that, in accordance with this Treaty, under appropriate international observation and through appropriate international procedures, potential benefits from any peaceful applications of nuclear explosions will be made available to non-nuclear-weapon States Party to the Treaty on a non-discriminatory basis and that the charge to such Parties for the explosive devices used will be as low as possible and exclude any charge for research and development. Non-nuclear-weapon States Party to the Treaty shall be able to obtain such benefits, pursuant to a special international agreement or agreement, through an appropriate international body with adequate representation of non-nuclear-weapon States. Negotiations on this subject shall commence as soon as possible after the Treaty enters into force. Non-nuclear-weapon States Party to the Treaty so desiring may also obtain such benefits pursuant to bilateral agreements.

1. Introduction

The peaceful apsects of nuclear energy are dealt with in articles IV and V of the NPT. The former encourages all parties to the treaty to facilitate and participate in the fullest possible exchange of equipment, materials and scientific and technical information for the peaceful uses of nuclear energy, whereas the latter is concerned with peaceful nuclear explosions. The non-nuclear-weapon states are prohibited from developing the technology for such explosions but benefits from the applications of nuclear explosives are to be made available to them "under appropriate international observation and through appropriate international procedures".

Article IV complements the preceding articles of the NPT by encouraging cooperation in the development of nuclear energy for peaceful purposes by the exchange of equipment, materials and scientific and technological infor-mation with particular consideration for the needs of the underdeveloped areas of the world. However, the needs of the underdeveloped areas remain to be defined. Often underdeveloped countries could benefit more from assistance from non-nuclear technologies. On the other hand, cooperation can take place between nuclear-weapon countries and non-nuclear-weapon countries which have some peaceful nuclear programme. In the latter coun-tries the conventional industry should be sufficiently advanced so that they can at least produce components for reactors if not participate in many steps of the nuclear fuel cycle. The major steps are uranium mining, uranium en-richment, the construction and the development of nuclear reactors and fuel fabrication and reprocessing, of which a number yield themselves quite well to this type of cooperation.

The first of these, uranium mining, has become a highly commercial enterprise. In the United States, most uranium was initially imported from Canada and South Africa but as military requirements were fulfilled, the remaining imported and indigenously produced uranium has accumulated. A considerable amount is being stockpiled by the five largest uranium pro-ducers (Australia, Britain, Canada, France and South Africa) to maintain prices and commercial interests. These stocks and the uranium produced by the above mentioned countries in the next few years will amount to about four times more uranium than will be required. It is difficult to visualize how article IV can influence the uranium market under these cir-cumstances.

The next step in the fuel cycle is the uranium enrichment process which is the only part of the fuel cycle that has been kept under strict secrecy. When article IV was included in the NPT, many believed that the uranium enrichment process would become available to others under safeguards. The countries which have so far monopolized enrichment technology are the United States, the Soviet Union, the People's Republic of China and France. The willingness to share this technology with others is of prime importance for the implementation of article IV. So far there has been no real relaxation of secrecy. On the contrary, many countries are developing their own technology for enriching uranium and in some cases this development is based on international cooperation. Britain, the Federal Republic of Germany and the Netherlands have a trilateral agreement for the joint development of the gas ultracentrifuge process and the Euratom countries have started a study of the diffusion, centrifuge and jet nozzle processes. South Africa has developed its own, as yet undisclosed, process and recently it has been reported that there may be some cooperation between South Africa and the Federal Republic of Germany. This suggests that the South African enrichment process may include a variation of the German jet nozzle process. [1]

The problem with the next stage of the nuclear fuel cycle—fuel fabrication for reactors—is that most countries, certainly in Western Europe, have bought light water reactors (LWRs) from the United States and one of the conditions for the sale of reactors is that the first generation of fuel elements must also be bought from the USA. This may not be practicable since many countries have recently started to build their own fuel fabrication plants which can be built on a relatively small scale with modest investment. As far as reprocessing of the spent fuel is concerned, there is some cooperation among countries such as Britain, the Federal Republic of Germany and France but this is purely from a commercial and economic point of view rather than as a result of article IV. In most cases, the ideal of cooperation expressed in article IV seems to have disappeared due to the vast commercial interests in the field of nuclear reactors.

Considerable interest has been shown in the peaceful applications of nuclear explosions. An important advantage of using such explosives is the availability of a very large amount of energy within a relatively small volume. These explosives cannot be developed indigenously by the non-nuclear-weapon states party to the NPT, since this is prohibited by the treaty. However, under article V, all the potential benefits from any peaceful applications of nuclear explosions should be made available to the non-nuclear-weapon states party to the treaty.

Basically there are two types of peaceful nuclear explosion: cratering explosions and contained explosions. The former can be used, among other things, to break and remove large quantities of earth in uncovering mineral deposits and for the construction of canals, dams, water reservoirs and the building of roads and harbours. Contained explosions, on the other hand, can be used, for example, to release oil and natural gas deposits and to create underground cavities for the storage of natural gas and oil products or biologically dangerous industrial wastes.

202

Economic advantages of nuclear explosives have been predicted but are controversial. Another important consideration is the effect of the radiation produced by the explosion. Radiation hazards are present in both types of peaceful nuclear explosion: in the case of cratering explosions, through the release of radioactive products into the environment and in the case of contained explosions, through the use of products which may have become radioactive in the explosion. Radionuclides having relatively long half-lives, such as tritium, carbon-14 and kripton-85, are of particular concern. It was reported recently that silver mined in the Soviet Union with the use of nuclear explosives was radioactive. [2] Clearly these are some of the problems that should be studied under a programme of international cooperation in the peaceful uses of nuclear energy.

References

1. "German-S. African Enrichment Talks", *Nuclear Engineering International*, Vol. 18, No. 208, September 1973, p. 667.
2. Linder, L., Britikman, G. A. and Schimmel, A., "Appearance of Low-level Radioactive Silver on the World Silver Market", *Nature*, Vol. 240, No. 5382, December 1972, pp. 463–64.

2. International nuclear collaboration and article IV of the Non-Proliferation Treaty

B. GOLDSCHMIDT

Abstract

Various forms of international nuclear collaboration and the conditions under which these are possible are discussed. Successively studied are the problems of assistance to underdeveloped countries, collaboration among advanced nations and cooperation in the still secret key sector of uranium enrichment. It is shown that the philosophy of article IV of the non-proliferation treaty has up to now had practically no influence on international nuclear collaboration. It is concluded that since the economic stakes are large, international nuclear dealings will be carried out more and more between industrial firms according to the standard rules of commerce, competition and national interests. It can, nevertheless, be considered that implementing an international inspection of all nuclear activities in non-nuclear-weapon countries, parties to the treaty, forms the political foundation enabling each one, alone or in collaboration with others, to embark on the production of enriched uranium. Therefore, in the near future the last top-secrecy stronghold of this technology will also yield. International collaboration will have played an important role in this evolution, probably less through article IV of the NPT than through the generalization of its safeguards system.

I. Introduction

The entry of atomic energy into the industrial age has been so quick and far-reaching that existing structures, as well as ways of thinking and acting consistent with the former situation, have all become suddenly outdated.

This applies to international nuclear collaboration which, during the earlier phases of scientific (sometimes military) and pre-industrial development, took place mainly between governments and through the atomic commissions of the leading countries. These multidisciplinary state organizations have played a very important part but have difficulty today in adapting to what could be called the vulgarization of the atomic enterprise.

As the economic stakes are huge, international atomic dealings, now largely protected against the threat of proliferation of weapons by the extension of international inspection, will be carried out more and more between industrial firms according to the standard rules of commerce, competition and national interest.

Such a realistic situation seems hardly compatible with the idealistic philosophy of article IV of the non-proliferation treaty, by which the parties involved agree to collaborate among themselves, to aid less-developed members and to promote as wide an exchange as possible of scientific and technical equipment, materials and information.

Under present circumstances, article IV is no more than a pious vow having no practical application, which tries to present in more palatable terms a treaty not always subscribed to with enthusiasm.

A backward glance will show the extraordinary rate at which the atomic enterprise has developed since the war.

After the 1947 defeat at the United Nations of the Lilienthal-Baruch plan, according to which a supranational authority would have been responsible for the utilization and development of atomic energy on behalf of all nations, the US government pursued a policy of secrecy and monopolization of nuclear materials which paralyzed international nuclear collaborations during the years following World War II.

It was only after the explosion of the first Russian hydrogen bomb exactly 20 years ago, during the summer of 1953—a major event in the history of the atomic age—and its detection by the US radiological survey network, that the United States government decided to abandon this policy.

President Eisenhower's speech of December 1953 before the United Nations crystallized this change and resulted in the creation of the International Atomic Energy Agency; this led, subsequently, to a partial lifting of the veil of secrecy. Had at that time a non-proliferation treaty also been proposed, then article IV would have been one of its key elements. It would have led to the abolition of secrecy and to the free exchange of nuclear materials and equipment. However, this has since been achieved gradually, as a few typical examples show.

In 1949 the transfer by the US Atomic Energy Commission of one millicurie of radionuclides of iron to the Norwegian Defence Institute was the subject of a violent disagreement between two men—Robert Oppenheimer and Lewis Strauss—a disagreement undoubtedly not irrelevant to one of the great human tragedies of the atomic adventure, the Oppenheimer affair. The free circulation of radioisotopes throughout the world is now a firmly established reality and international trade can be estimated in terms of thousands and even hundreds of thousands of curies.

If some 10 000 kg of uranium oxide, hidden since 1939 by a far-sighted Dutch university professor, had not been available in 1950, the first Scandinavian pile could not have been built in 1951. Yet today the stock of uranium on the world market amounts to thousands and even hundreds of thousands of kilogrammes. It is true that this is a temporary glut, which, unfortunately, slows down prospecting and will inevitably be followed by a shortage towards the beginning of the next decade.

In the same way, the name of the miracle solvent, tributyl phosphate, was not publicly announced until the 1955 Geneva Conference. For more than 20 years this advent has played an essential part in the fuel cycle, not only for the purification of uranium but also after irradiation for the separation of uranium from plutonium and fission products. Until 1955 its properties were a state secret.

Even heads of state played the atomic secrets game with one another. Just 15 years ago, in 1958, the British Prime Minister, Harold MacMillan, wrote a top-secret personal letter to General de Gaulle telling him that British scientists considered the cooling-gas input temperature of the large graphite piles at Marcoule to be dangerously low. In fact this was not the case, but the French scientists were obliged as a result to explain to de Gaulle the existence of energy stored in irradiated graphite and the Wigner effect.

Very few traces of the secrecy policy are left now and these are restricted to the principle of the methods themselves; to the H-bomb theory and the South African uranium-isotope separation process, and to the knowledge of the precise technology of the submarine propulsion engine, the A-bomb mechanism and the enrichment of uranium by gaseous diffusion or ultra-centrifugation. This secrecy about uranium isotopic separation is, in fact, responsible for the present near-monopoly of uranium-235 production.

Apart from these few zones still covered by scientific secrecy, nuclear energy is now part of the standard industrial scene and any shades of secrecy encountered are due to normal protection of the know-how of each industry. This means that in the nonmilitary field only one bastion of secrecy and only one monopoly are left; that of enriched uranium. For all the rest, the rules of technical assistance or international collaboration are becoming more and more standard and, for the most part, commercial.

II. *Assistance to underdeveloped countries*

Advanced techniques have a special attraction for many underdeveloped countries. This prestige still surrounds the applications of nuclear energy, especially in the less-industrialized countries where it is not yet tarnished by accusations of pollution. It is somewhat arbitrary to classify countries according to their degree of development, but in this case it is reasonable to divide them into two categories: on the one hand, those able to parti-cipate industrially in a phase of the fuel cycle (apart from the extraction and initial concentration of uranium ore) or in the construction of certain reactor or power station components; and on the other hand, those not yet advanced enough to take part in these industrial stages.

Countries in this latter category, which are not sufficiently developed to have a national industrial activity in the fuel cycle or in the manufacture of important reactor components, are those farthest removed from the arms manufacturing stage. For these countries the fact of subscribing to the NPT involves no true renunciation, at least for the time being, apart from the purely theoretical right to receive arms from a nuclear power. It can, therefore, be said that the NPT does not even inflict a moral obligation on advanced countries to increase their technical assistance to developing parts of the world, and indeed the existence of the treaty and its article IV has led to no such increase during recent years whether bilaterally or through an international body such as the International Atomic Energy Agency.

According to the degree of development of the country this assistance can take different forms, briefly described later. In all cases it can include help in the prospecting and eventual mining of uranium. The countries concerned should be aware that there will be a glut of uranium until almost the end of this decade but, in any event, it is necessary to count about six years between the discovery of a large deposit and the start of the output of the mines.

The least-advanced countries, those with a hospital system too primitive to allow for the medical use of radio-elements, can profit by some agricultural applications of radioisotopes: chemistry; physics and the fertility of soils; the release of sterilized insects; food preservation and plant improvement.

It should, nevertheless, be noted that, although these applications seem attractive, agricultural experts such as those of the Food and Agriculture Organization sometimes disagree with their colleagues of the International Atomic Energy Agency, claiming that the sums devoted to nuclear applications could be used more profitably for more traditional projects.

It must also be pointed out that the use of food sterilization by irradiation, however attractive, is blocked by the inability of international organizations to take the responsibility for guaranteeing its harmlessness.

For countries medically in a position to use radioisotopes and radiation, this application can play an important part in diagnosis, clinical research and therapy. Here again the choice may be difficult in the case of countries which still lack the basic necessities: antibiotics, child care and so forth.

In applications of radio-elements to both agriculture and medicine (and, of course, hydrology, sedimentology and industry for more advanced countries) the training of specialists in their use is one of the indispensable aspects of technical aid, as is the loan of experts and the supply and maintenance of the correspondingly delicate electronic equipment.

The next stage in technical assistance for more developed countries is the sale of favourably priced reactors, ranging from the demonstration reactor unable to produce artificial radio-elements, through the low-power research reactor capable of producing certain radioisotopes, to the research reactor for nuclear physics experiments.

Here again, prestige questions may be involved since even a very low-power reactor undeniably needs laboratory infrastructure, implies the difficult definition of an interesting work programme, and employs a team of specialists, all leading to high maintenance costs. The purchase of such a reactor results from a choice of priorities made occasionally at the expense of the general scientific development of the country. Cases are even known of reactors inaugurated with great ceremony and hardly used afterwards.

Five to ten years from now the economy of low- and medium-power reactors derived from the submarine engine will have progressed parallel to the increasing need for electricity in underdeveloped countries. A number of these countries will probably be as anxious to possess a first nuclear power station in the 1980s as they were to own a research reactor in the 1960s; and, here again, the competition between the industries of supplier countries will be keen.

Very spectacular and much advertised projects such as nuclear desalination plants or the creation of agro-industrial complexes are still very premature at this stage, but their first applications, which can be expected to materialize during the next decade, will undoubtedly be extremely valuable for the less fertile parts of the world.

III. *Collaboration among advanced countries*

The problems of international collaboration are different for highly developed countries participating, or preparing to participate, industrially in the fuel cycle and the construction of power stations and their components.

There are, on the one hand, the five nuclear powers which for the first time have a special status proclaimed by the non-proliferation treaty which limits the category to these five alone; and on the other hand, nations for whom the signing of the treaty represents or would represent a true renunciation since it is they who could embark now or shortly on the manufacture of nuclear armaments. According to article IV of the treaty, these latter countries should benefit especially from international collaboration aimed at the further development of civil applications of atomic energy.

We are not dealing now with international collaboration along the lines of the "Atoms for Peace" programme (which cost very little in the sense that the technique made available had been developed for national, and often military, uses while the facilities and equipment for the supply of essential materials already existed) but with gigantic commercial and political interests. The issue is a growing share of the world energy market at a time when the problem of energy is becoming crucial. Already the construction of nuclear power stations throughout the world represents an annual investment of some $10 000 million, a market dominated by the United States and the Soviet Union in their respective spheres of influence. It is true that during the 1950s five other industrialized powers embarked on independent national programmes: Czechoslovakia and particularly the United Kingdom, France, Sweden and Canada. These last four countries realized too late that they were out of the running and that their only chance to compete on the world market was by forming technical and industrial alliances.

While these countries were engaged in the reactor war, the United States, taking advantage of its achievements in the field of nuclear submarine propulsion, chose to try out the first large nuclear power stations (derived from the smaller submarine engine) in Europe where the cost of electricity was then higher than in the United States.

Hence, through the USA-Euratom programme, with financial backing from Eximbank, the US nuclear industry was able, sometimes at the expense of European electricity producers, to test the supposedly proven light water, enriched uranium power stations. The US utilities consolidated on a large scale towards the end of the 1960s and firmly established this system, undoubtedly destined to become the main source of world nuclear electricity until the end of the century.

Of the five countries mentioned above, Canada alone is still in the race with its pressurised heavy water, natural uranium system adopted by Canadian electricity producers and exported to Pakistan and to India where it is being developed independently. It has just won its laurels in an international competition in Argentina. If the Canadian programme had been able to develop more quickly and on more powerful industrial and geographical grounds, it would certainly have enabled the production of nuclear electricity to be achieved on a larger scale outside the monopoly of the big enriched uranium producers. It would, thus, have become a strong rival to the US and Soviet systems whose main strength is the large number of stations in operation, under construction or being planned. These give electricity producers all over the world the confident feeling that if they still take a risk today in choosing this type of nuclear power station, the same can be said of all their rivals.

At the present development stage of nuclear electricity production and for stations considered to be economically proven, article IV of the non-proliferation treaty encourages world trade. It therefore favours the two large nuclear powers which dominate world exports.

For nuclear power systems still under study such as the high-temperature reactor or the fast-neutron breeder—which is the hope of the future—international collaboration no longer takes the form, as in the past, of a gratuitious surrender of knowledge, chiefly by the great powers; instead, it consists of agreements between industrial firms through which the sphere of influence of the leading countries is generally extended.

In the fuel cycle field the philosophy prevailing over article IV of the non-proliferation treaty seems irrelevant under present circumstances. The natural uranium market has been dominated by the Soviet Union and the United States who have monopolized all the uranium available in their respective spheres of influence. During the 1960s, once its armaments programme was saturated, the USA switched to a new policy and in 1964 Congress placed an embargo on the importation of foreign uranium in order to protect the local mining industry. This is one of the reasons for the temporary glut, the present low prices and the difficulties encountered by Australian, British, Canadian, French and South African producers to support the uranium market. International coordination is essential in this field and steps should be taken immediately to avoid a predictable shortage at the beginning of the 1980s.

The manufacture of fuel elements is one important stage in the cycle and it requires relatively low investments. Many companies have sprung up in Europe as a result but are handicapped because US firms generally guarantee their nuclear power stations only on the condition that they themselves supply the first load of fuel. These European firms should join together if they are to survive economically and large power station constructors should certainly try to obtain substantial shares in the groups formed. Here again the operation will be dictated by commercial interests alone. This is illustrated by the case of United Reprocessors, who are economically organizing the Western European spent-fuel processing market. Before beginning construction of a large plant in Germany, they intend to saturate the existing British and French plants of Windscale and La Hague.

IV. *Uranium enrichment problems*

Finally there is the main question of uranium enrichment, the last stronghold of atomic secrecy, and of the monopoly held by the nuclear powers, the favourite ground of nuclear rivalries not only during the 1970s but also since the beginning of the atomic age.

Even during World War II the gaseous diffusion method of isotope separation created difficulties between Roosevelt and Churchill. It was first thought of by the British but then developed independently by the Americans. The US plant was built without the participation of the British who were obliged after the war to develop their technology alone and build their own plant at Capenhurst.

When, however, at the beginning of 1955, after the start-up of the first stages of the Capenhurst plant, the French asked the British to build a similar plant in France, the United Kingdom had to forego this industrially important project because the United States objected outright, calling on the 1943 Quebec Anglo-American agreements concerning the secrecy of any atomic data liable to have a military application.

Less than a year later, during the first negotiations of the Six, which were to lead to the creation of Euratom, the building of an isotope separation plant was considered the main task to be accomplished in common; a working group was set up at the beginning of 1956 to study this venture without waiting for the treaty to come into force.

I was asked to preside over this working group which was later transformed into a Research Association for the Construction of a European Plant and was extended to include Denmark, Sweden and Switzerland. Several processes were already under consideration: centrifugation recommended by the Dutch and Germans, who were also studying the jet nozzle process; and the gaseous diffusion method which was backed by the French. The latter campaigned at the end of 1957 for the immediate construction of an enrichment plant, but the forces working to delay the operation were too strong. The issue touched directly on the interests of the USA which was not in favour of the production of enriched uranium abroad. The United States, therefore, chose to supply the Euratom nations with the uranium-235 necessary for their future nuclear power stations. These were the conditions which led France to decide on the independent construction of its Pierrelatte Plant and to assign the output preferentially to military applications; now that these needs are partially satisfied, some civil production is starting to take place and this will tend to increase.

The next stage in this international imbroglio was not a treaty of collaboration but almost the opposite; worried about German and Dutch progress in the matter of ultracentrifugation in 1960, the US government obtained an undertaking from the Federal Republic and the Netherlands to keep the work secret. This agreement, touching on the danger of proliferation, implied no exchange of knowledge between the partners.

At the end of 1966, the Germans and Italians brought up once again in different European circles the idea of a common separation plant. At this time neither the British nor the French allowed the Germans access to their gaseous diffusion technologies but the British had offered to Germany, who refused, a solely economic and commercial share in an eventual enlargement of Capenhurst.

Two years later, in November 1968, came the sensational announcement by the German, British and Dutch governments of their decision to co-operate in the ultracentrifugation field on the basis of progress made independently by these three countries on this method. Ultracentrifugation has the advantage of consuming much less electricity than gaseous diffusion and should probably, therefore, become economically competitive when the technological and industrial problems which still arise have been solved.

The so-called Troika agreement was signed in 1971 and provided for a series of three pilot plants starting in 1973, one at Capenhurst and the other two at Almelo in the Netherlands. These units would be followed in about 1976 by a relatively modest production plant, containing nevertheless from 50 000 to 100 000 centrifuges. This would be gradually enlarged to reach, by about 1985, some two million centrifuges—the dimensions anticipated for future large plants.

This process is also being actively studied in Japan. It was developed in the USA by certain firms and at the US Atomic Energy Commission, which has increased its financial effort in this field. The economy of centrifugation is much less bound up with the size of the plant than that of the gaseous diffusion process. On the other hand, it depends on a very large centrifuge production plant with a capacity of several hundred thousand units a year and which, to be paid off, must sell its output over a period of many years.

In 1972 the Commissariat à l'Energie Atomique with European industries from the Six, Great Britain, Sweden and Spain set up an economic partnership, "Eurodif", to examine a project for a gaseous diffusion plant in Europe. A Franco-Australian group was created at the same time to study an enrichment plant project in Australia. Similarly, a Franco-Japanese group is investigating the economics of gaseous diffusion plants.

Following this example, the Troika is bringing together a large number of firms from European industrialized countries, Canada, the USA and Japan to work out the economics of the ultracentrifugation process.

At the end of 1971 the USA had announced the conditions under which their technology could be made available to a multinational plant built outside their own territory, but these conditions were sufficiently stringent to cast doubt on the willingness of the USA to help or hasten the inescapable loss of their monopoly.

This point of view is reflected in an official study on "Commercial nuclear energy in Europe" prepared in December 1972 by Mr Warren Donnelly for the Chamber of Representatives and which concluded with the following questions:

Past U.S. policy determinations have judged as advantageous the strong position of the United States as the principal supplier of enriched uranium or enrichment services in the free world market. To what extent should U.S. diplomacy and foreign policy seek to preserve this position? To what extent should the U.S. attempt to prevent, limit, or control the development and use of alternative enrichment technologies that might threaten U.S. facilities with technological obsolescence, or increase the possibilities of proliferation of foreign capabilities to produce nuclear weapons materials?

The US commercial policy, moreover, progressively stiffened; the period of low prices due to commerical expansion and to amortization on the military programmes of large facilities was over. In a few years the price

212

per isotope separation unit went from $26 in 1970 to $36 in 1973, while new contract conditions oblige customers to sign an undertaking about eight years before the first delivery with a down payment of about one-third of the total sum. The order must continue over 10 years beyond the first delivery and the penalty for cancellation is at least 50 per cent, the price being fixed unilaterally only on the day of delivery. Such conditions are aimed, among other things, at catching the foreign markets in advance and thus helping finance new US plants due to start production in the early 1980s. The first of these should be settled before 1976 and could be partly financed by Japan which will still not have access to the technology, only to the production.

In 1970 the Soviet Union also entered the market, offering less exacting conditions than the USA, as shown by the contract with France signed the following year. This offer applies to all non-nuclear countries that have subscribed to the non-proliferation treaty. Uncertainty over the production capacity of the Soviet plants affects the date at which, allowing for their output and in the absence of new plants, the shortage of enriched uranium will be felt.

It seems beyond question that several large plants costing at least $1 000 million each will have to come into operation between 1981 and 1985, and the European market should enable one of these to be set up in Europe in 1981. It is not certain whether centrifugation, in spite of its attractive long-term prospects, will be able to provide an adequate answer by the start of the next decade and partisans of gaseous diffusion are convinced that only a large European project based on their own method can meet European needs with all the safety and diversity desired by consumers.

The next 18 months will be decisive and will show whether Europeans can overcome their political and technical rivalries or whether, because of their differences of opinion, they will have to be resigned to confirming the US and Soviet monopolies.

The affair is of fundamental importance for the international development of atomic energy. However, it will hardly be solved on the basis of commitments made by the leading countries in applying article IV of the non-proliferation treaty, even though uranium enrichment was one of the fields which the non-nuclear industrial powers subscribing to the treaty considered probably to be most relevant to this article.

Although the secrecy policy has scarcely been relaxed in this key sector, commercial, and even monopolistic interests prevail over the philosophy of technical assistance in working out new projects.

It can, nevertheless, be considered that implementing an international inspection of all atomic activities in non-nuclear countries, parties to the treaty, forms the political foundation enabling each one, alone or in collaboration with others, to embark on the production of enriched uranium, a field so far reserved for the five nuclear powers alone. Formerly, such an undertaking would have been suspected of being in favour of proliferation.

Thus, unavoidably the time will come, a few years from now, when the last top-secrecy stronghold, the technology of uranium enrichment, will yield in its turn. Then the last stage in the vulgarization of nuclear techniques will have been reached. International collaboration will have played an important part in this evolution, helped probably less by article IV of the NPT than by the generalization of its safeguards system.

3. On the peaceful use of nuclear explosions

V. S. EMELYANOV

Abstract

The possibilities of using nuclear explosions for civil purposes have been studied mainly in the United States and the Soviet Union. Both countries have been examining the feasibility of using nuclear explosions for exploiting oil and gas deposits, for opening up ore fields, for building water reservoirs in arid regions, for earth-moving operations in canal construction and so on. In the United States the Plowshare Program was established to implement a number of such projects; the Soviet counterpart is "The programme of use of commercial underground nuclear explosions". Such studies have so far been largely theoretical, and although much useful data has been obtained from test explosions, none of the projects under investigation has yet reached the stage of wide practical application. The advantages of using nuclear explosions for such projects lie chiefly in saving labour and therefore money. However, the danger of subsequent radioactive contamination of the environment is very real; the problem of designing a "clean" explosive has still not been solved. It is concluded that, at present, peaceful nuclear explosions are advisable only for exceptionally urgent problems which cannot otherwise be solved.

I. *Introduction*

In September 1958 a report, issued by the second international conference convened by the UN in Geneva on the peaceful uses of atomic energy, told the international public for the first time about the possibility, importance and advisability of using nuclear explosions for nonmilitary purposes. It was pointed out that energy from the explosions can be used to move considerable amounts of earth or rock, to construct large canals and harbours, as well as to uncover shallow coal and ore deposits prior to open-cast mining. The potentials of nuclear explosives in connection with increasing the production of gas and oil, constructing large water reservoirs in arid regions and underground reservoirs for natural gas were also mentioned. At the same time, discussion following this report revealed deep concern about the dangerous contamination of the environment by radioactive debris produced in nuclear fission processes.

The writer of the report, David Johnson, himself claimed that these projects were to be carried out using "clean" nuclear explosives. The day before Mr Johnson delivered his report, Edward Teller had told the conference about the possibility of producing these clean nuclear explosives.

As things stand now, 15 years later, the problem of a clean explosive has still not been solved. Moreover, it was suggested in 1970 at the Pugwash symposium in Racine, Wisconsin, USA, that it would probably not be solved within the next few decades. Nevertheless, some studies of the possible use of nuclear explosions for civilian purposes have been made during this period but they have failed to come to any satisfactory conclusion. Such research, which has only been carried out in the USA, France and the USSR, is limited mainly to calculations and experimental type explosions. Very few explosions are aimed toward practical ends.

Major programmes worked out in the USA, such as the construction of a second Panama canal and harbours in Alaska and Australia, have not been implemented. It seems that this can be explained mainly by the fear of subsequent radioactive contamination that threatens all projects of that kind.

The first working group's report on the problems of disarmament and control of weapons, delivered at the Pughwash conference in Ronneby, Sweden, in September 1967, contained the following statement on civilian use of nuclear explosives:

While there might be a long term economic advantage in employing nuclear explosions for recovery of oil, construction of canals etc., there does not seem to be any significant present advantage in using nuclear explosives as compared with other means of realising the same objectives.

Indeed, we believe even the potential advantages of nuclear explosives for peaceful purposes to be sufficiently small, so that such programmes should be suspended if they appear to conflict with progress in arms control and disarmament. [1]

The problem of the use of nuclear explosions was also treated in reports and discussion at the International Conference of Non-nuclear Powers held in 1968 in Geneva.

A special report on civil use of nuclear explosions was presented by Professor David R. Inglis at the Pugwash Symposium on preventing the spread of nuclear weapons, held in London in 1969. In this report Professor Inglis stated:

Three general types of non-military uses of nuclear explosives are foreseen: (a) recovery of natural resources; (b) digging; and (c) scientific neutron experiments.

The first two are in the developmental stage and have not yet produced any useful products. [2]

He continued:

The nuclear cratering experiments showed that a surprisingly high fraction of radioactivity is contained beneath the bottom of the crater being buried by the rock that is ejected almost vertically high into the air and falls back into the crater. Still, some radioactivity does escape, its amount depending on the design of nuclear explosive. It appears that much of the nuclear-explosive research carried out with

216

testing in the United States in recent years has been aimed at reduced radioactivity (developing a so-called "clean" explosive) with this application in mind. [3]

In the discussion of the paper "Comparative Economics of Nuclear and Conventional Fuel" by Professor I. T. Rosenquist at the same symposium, much attention was paid to the problems of using nuclear explosions for oil and gas stimulation as well as for carbonate shale retorting.

Much research and testing, mostly in the USA and USSR, has been done since the first report by Johnson in 1958. In the USA, four national symposia (in 1955, 1959, 1964, 1970) were held and a substantial amount of scientific and technical documentation was published. Study of these publications makes it possible to conclude that the main results, as well as the general attitude to the problem, are nearly identical in these two countries. This idea was affirmed by Professor N. Hillberry, former director of the Argon National Laboratory who said in 1959, "If a question is put correctly, the answer will be unambiguous irrespective of who it was put by—American or Russian".

The research and tests performed both in the USSR and the USA followed the same trend; that is, examining the possibility of using nuclear explosions for recovering oil and gas, for opening up the ore fields, and for earth moving in the construction of canals and the like.

In the USA a large-scale general programme called the Plowshare Program was established, which envisaged the implementation of a number of nuclear projects. A similar programme, including theoretical and experimental research as well as major tests and pilot commercial projects, was undertaken in the USSR. Its title was "The programme of use of commercial underground nuclear explosions".

The interest in civil nuclear explosions was considerably heightened by discussions of the draft treaty for the non-proliferation of nuclear weapons. According to article 5 of this treaty, nuclear-weapon powers party to the treaty undertake to ensure that the benefits of applications of peaceful nuclear explosions will be made available to non-nuclear-weapon states party to the treaty.

What are the benefits of civil use of nuclear explosions? Preliminary results of the experiments carried out in the USA during certain projects make it possible to answer this question and evaluate the difficulties and dangers which cannot be neglected in the implementation of large-scale commercial projects.

II. Projects dealing with natural gas recovery stimulation

A number of projects aimed at investigating the feasibility of increasing the rate of natural gas extraction from gas fields have been performed in the USA.

In the course of one of these projects, Gasbuggy, the amount of ex-

217

plosive and depth of burial were varied and measurements were taken of temperature, gas pressure and radioactivity in a well and the distribution of such isotopes as krypton-85, iodine-131, xenon-133 and tritium. Six months after the explosion, krypton-85 and tritium were still present in gas samples, but according to the Atomic Energy Commission (AEC), the radio-activity level was not a threat to health.

At the symposium of the Oil Engineers Society held in Houston, September 1968, the engineers who had taken part in the Gasbuggy project and evaluated its results estimated that gas yields after a nuclear explosion would be eight times greater, and for a longer period, than if conventional methods had been used. Before the project started, engineers expected that with five experimental wells yielding a total of 566 m³ a day, in 20 years time they would be able to extract only 10 per cent of the gas stored in the field. However, after a nuclear explosion a single well was able to yield up to 21 200 m³ a day. At this rate, 80 per cent of the total gas reserves of this field are expected to be withdrawn in 20 years.

Following the favourable results of Gasbuggy, shot mining companies in the USA asked the AEC to speed up the nuclear explosion experiments within the Plowshare program and displayed a keen interest in using nuclear explosions for recovering gas and other mineral reserves.

SER Geonuclear Corporation and consortium oil companies started preparations for a nuclear explosion in oil-bearing shale, and Kennecott Copper Company suggested using a nuclear explosion for breaking up a copper ore deposit. The Columbia Gas System Service Company made plans to create a huge underground gas reservoir by exploding a 200 kiloton nuclear charge at a depth of 1 500 m, but because of strong opposition from the public, had to abandon its site in Pennsylvania and look for a new site in another state.

Many other projects are underway as well. Recently a number of experimental single and group explosions for dam construction in canals and harbours as well as for ore recovery were carried out. Distribution of radio-isotopes in fallout was studied during these tests.

The results indicate that before the commercial utilization of nuclear explosions is mastered, it is urgent to continue developing nuclear charges fit for production use. Moreover, it is necessary to study in further detail the effects following nuclear explosions—dependence of the size and shape of the crater or cone on the depth of burial, strength and chemical composition of rock and other parameters. The Plowshare experiments have shifted from the research stage to development and to practical utilization and demonstration tests.

In the USSR favourable conditions for the successful practical use of nuclear explosions include a number of major deposits of minerals in sparsely populated areas and a great deal of construction work requiring earth moving and rock excavation.

Research in this field resulted in new information on the mechanical, seismic and radiation effects of nuclear explosions. This information reveals the main possibilities for the utilization of nuclear explosives:

(a) oil and gas recovery stimulation,

(b) creation of underground reservoirs for natural gas and oil products,

(c) creation of underground storage for wastes harmful to living organisms,

(d) extinction of runaway gas and oil fountains,

(e) underground methods of ore recovery.

By using cratering nuclear explosions it is possible to carry out the following projects:

(a) preparation of mineral deposit sites for open-cast mining; that is, dead rock baring, drainage, rock crushing and construction of access tracks for taking out ore or coal,

(b) canal construction,

(c) construction of dams for hydroelectric power stations,

(d) construction of water reservoirs for technical water supply,

(e) excavation of cuttings and construction of embankments for railways and roads.

Those are the trends of research and development in the USSR. Work along these trends falls into three stages:

(a) theoretical and laboratory research,

(b) experimental explosions aimed at studying useful effects and specific features of nuclear explosions,

(c) pilot and production explosions fulfilling a particular task with simultaneous research and refinement of explosion energy. [4]

Much attention during this work is, of course, paid to safety provisions.

Extensive research is being carried out in the USSR to find new ways to lessen or eradicate harmful seismic and radiation effects of nuclear explosions. Some experimental explosions have already been carried out and a number of projects on gas and oil stimulation and on underground storage construction as well as underground ore recovering and bleaching, have been worked out. [5]

III. *Projects dealing with the construction of under-ground reservoirs for natural gas, gas condensate and oil products*

The rate of growth of the oil and gas industry strongly depends on the progress in reservoir construction. Conventional methods of construction of artificial reservoirs are either labour-consuming (well drilling) or non-universal and requiring special geological conditions (dissolving of rocksalt with water). The latter method requires, in addition, a vast supply of water and the possibility to remove biologically harmful salt brine. That has made it urgent to develop new, more efficient ways of creating underground reservoirs. [6]

Preliminary economic estimates showed that construction of underground gas reservoirs by nuclear explosions

would be six times cheaper in comparison to storing beforehand condensed gas in surface reservoirs and three times cheaper than storing it in voids created by dissolving rocksalt. [6]

Let us look more closely into the creation of underground storage space with nuclear explosions.

It is necessary to create a reservoir for gas condensate with a total volume of 300 000 m³ with a geological section showing a thick bed of rock-salt overlaid by a sandstone layer. The maximum yield of explosion determined from seismic safety of ground buildings was 35 kiloton. The total cavity volume after such an explosion was about 150 000 m³.

To form the cavity of required volume it is necessary to make two explosions in succession. The depth of burial is 850 metres. The maximum separation of nuclear explosions securing the stability of the cavity under influence of compression wave is 800 metres. [7]

The cavities produced were to be broken through by drills a month after the explosions. The tests showed no traces of radioactivity in the gas taken up from the cavity 120 days after the explosion.

Nevertheless,

the full understanding of the optimum of operating reservoirs constructed by nuclear explosions providing minimum radioactive contamination of the stored product has not yet been attained. [7]

The first nuclear explosions for recovering oil were performed in the USSR some years ago. The results obtained through underground explosions at the test oil field served as a basis for a programme of commercial exploitation of other oil fields.

Due to natural conditions, the oil yield when using conventional recovery methods is very low and the process is long which causes high capital and operating costs. Experimental research indicates that using nuclear explosions makes it possible to increase oil and gas yield rates and reduce the time involved in exploitation.

Two methods of exploitation have been worked out. In the first one a nuclear explosion takes place within the oil and gas reservoir while the natural interconnection between the production and the aquiferous zones is preserved. According to the experimental plan, three 40-kiloton nuclear explosions at a depth of 1 600 meters are to be detonated, each producing intensively fissured zones with 270 meter radii. Hydrodynamic calculations permit us to expect production to increase to 3 000 000 m³ per day as compared to the 250 000 m³ per day with conventional technology. The resulting commercial effect would be a production time reduction to one-eleventh of the original and a tenfold increase in the annual output of gas and condensate.

The second method involves breaking the interconnection between the thick oil-bearing zone and the aquiferous zone. That should result in forcing the aquiferous system throughout the oil-bearing formation by means of a high head of water to sustain the oil pressure. The most promising results are expected from exploding 20–30 kilotons of nuclear charges in the centre of the deposit below the water-oil contact. Both oil-bearing and aquiferous beds are to be shattered by the explosion. [8]

Runaway oil and gas fountains often emerge at oil and gas fields and in the most serious cases can hardly be controlled by conventional means. To seal off such uncontrollable fountains a method using nuclear explosives has been developed. The idea is to explode a nuclear charge placed in a slanting hole close to the uncontrolled well, thus causing displacement of rock and sealing the well. Uncontrolled fountains at two fields have been handled by this method.

IV. *Ore crushing for the exploitation of underground mineral resources*

There are ore deposits in the USSR where the use of nuclear explosives for the fragmentation of ore rock is advisable. It should be kept in mind that by exploding two or three nuclear charges of 1–1.5 kilotons, it is possible to break up 1.5–2 million tons of ore otherwise needing 0.3–0.4 kilometres of mine working. According to rough estimates, the use of powerful nuclear explosives could cut down the cost of ore production one and a half to two times.

V. *Cratering nuclear explosions*

The useful effect of a cratering explosion arises from its ability to crush and displace huge amounts of rock. Theoretical and experimental studies of cratering explosions have enabled the USSR to gain experience in their performance, get initial data for calculating the parameters of their placing and predict useful results as well as adverse consequences of the explosions. The use of such explosions, especially for large-scale excavation work, has proved to be both possible and efficient.

To investigate some practical uses of nuclear explosions, single cratering shots of various yields (0.2; 1.1 and over 100 kilotons) have been set off in different rocks. An evaluation of the results revealed, in particular, the feasibility of the construction of water reservoirs in arid regions of the country. There is a constant lack of water in arid regions of the central

Asiatic republics of the USSR, so that the use of nuclear explosions for construction of water storage areas in this region would considerably speed up the solving of an important problem.

For certain projects broader prospects can be opened by using group rather than single cratering explosions. They can be used for uncovering major ore or coal deposits near the surface, digging canals and so on. A group explosion using three charges of 0.2 kilotons has produced some useful data for production companies.

An important project under consideration is aimed at re-routing the waters of the northern rivers into the Volga river. Climate irregularities, increasing water demand and construction of a number of reservoirs at the Volga, the Kama and other tributaries of the Volga caused the Caspian sea level to drop 2.5 metres in the past 35 years. That inflicted considerable losses to fishery, sea transport and other aspects of the coastal zone economy.

One version of this project involves digging a deep 112.5 kilometre-long canal between the north-flowing Pechora River and the Volga. Plans are being made to excavate with nuclear explosions, a 65 kilometre-long section of the canal crossing predominantly rock formations.

According to preliminary estimates, the use of nuclear explosions would reduce construction costs to such a level that the cost of conventional methods would be three to three and a half times greater.

VI. *Concluding remarks*

As far as can be judged from the outside, the situation in the USA now is not favourable to building new nuclear power plants nor to using nuclear explosions.

A number of anxious articles appeared in the US press claiming that nuclear plants are dangerous because of the resulting radioactive contamination of the environment and the possibility of disaster in the event of failure.

Professor Inglis wrote in a foreword to Gene Bryerton's book *Nuclear Dilemma:*

A reactor may have a large and locally very lethal accident. Here the costs would not be hidden. Moreover if it should occur in only one reactor, distrust might cause a shutdown of all others producing a lasting nationwide blackout . . . [9]

In his book, Bryerton wrote that among the ever increasing number of books, articles and speeches criticizing nuclear power stations, some authors mention a small paper which is referred to as WASH-740 or the "Brookhaven Report". The full title of this report reads, "Theoretical Possibilities and Consequences of Major Accidents in Large Nuclear Power Plants". The report was prepared by a group of about 20 leading scientists and engineers of Brookhaven National Laboratory and in March 1957 was presented to the US Joint Atomic Energy Committee.

In the report the most serious possible accident considered assumes that 50 per cent of fission products escape into the atmosphere. The analysis of such an accident shows that 3 400 persons would be killed, 43 000 suffer injuries, and the losses from damage would amount to $7 billion. People within a 15 mile radius would be killed and within a 45 mile radius would be wounded; about 150 000 square miles of soil would be contaminated by radioactivity. [10]

The Brookhaven Report is widely used in propaganda raised against nuclear plant construction. Though it is well-known that modern nuclear reactors are equipped with reliable control and safety means, this propaganda finds its way to many people.

Although in a reactor the process of nuclear fission is strictly controlled, in nuclear explosions it is, in essence, uncontrollable. Furthermore, as many authors pointed out, the nuclear explosion technology itself has still not been completely refined.

While, in principle, nuclear plant reactors can be completely protected against the release of radioactivity, peaceful nuclear explosions are inevitably followed by fallout which ranges a considerable distance from the point of the blast. Thus, Yu. Israel and V. Petrov, having studied the spread of radioactive debris of underground explosions to great distances, wrote:

Cratering nuclear explosions eject some amount of radioactivity into the atmosphere.

Parts of the radioactive products of nuclear explosion fall back down into the crater. The rest of the radioactive products are distributed in the basic blast wave and the cloud formed by the explosion. Radioactive products associated with comparatively small earth particles become airborne and are carried by the wind rather far from the shot point, causing radioactive contamination of the environment. [11]

Despite successful experiments by the USA and USSR on the use of nuclear explosions for gas recovery stimulation, underground gas reservoir construction and excavation works, the main problem hindering wide use of peaceful nuclear explosions is the danger of radioactive contamination of the environment with fission products and this has not yet been resolved.

Therefore it seems that the peaceful use of nuclear explosions today can be considered advisable only in exceptional cases when an urgent problem crops up which cannot be solved by alternative means. Nuclear explosions may be used mainly for experimental production purposes under close scientific observation.

Only when nuclear explosives are developed to be truly clean and avoid triggering fission devices which produce radioactive fission products can they be put to wide use. As it has already been said, this problem is not yet solved and it is not even known when the solution can be found.

References

1. *Proceedings of the Seventeenth Pugwash Conference of Science and World Affairs* Ronneby, Sweden, 3–8 September 1967, p. 40.
2. Barnaby, C. F., ed., *Preventing the Spread of Nuclear Weapons,* Pugwash Monograph I (London, Souvenir Press, 1969) p. 79.
3. *Ibid.,* p. 81.
4. "Nuclear Explosions for Peaceful Use", *Atomizdat* (Moscow, 1970) pp. 5–7 (in Russian).
5. *Ibid.,* p. 11.
6. *Ibid.,* pp. 14–15.
7. *Ibid.,* p. 15.
8. *Ibid.,* pp. 27–28.
9. Bryerton, Gene, *Nuclear Dilemma* (New York, Ballantine Books, 1970) p. XV.
10. *Ibid.,* p. 28.
11. "Nuclear Explosions for Peaceful Use", *Atomizdat* (Moscow, 1970) p. 87 (in Russian).

Part IV
Security problems of
non-nuclear-weapon states

Article VI

Each of the Parties to the Treaty undertakes to pursue negotiations in good faith on effective measures relating to cessation of the nuclear arms race at an early date and to nuclear disarmament, and on a treaty on general and complete disarmament under strict and effective international control.

1. Introduction

During the 1960s, there was general agreement that the further proliferation of nuclear weapons would jeopardize world security; therefore, non-proliferation was seen to be to the advantage of all states. However, some states argued that a treaty which did not provide for actual nuclear disarmament was undesirable and even counterproductive. The main objection was that a treaty which prevented non-nuclear-weapon states from acquiring nuclear weapons while allowing the nuclear-weapon states to retain and even improve their nuclear arsenals would contain such unbalanced obligations that it would become nonviable in the long term. Article VI, which obligates the nuclear-weapon powers to "pursue negotiations in good faith on effective measures relating to cessation of the nuclear arms race at an early date and to nuclear disarmament", was included in the treaty in an attempt to overcome this objection.

A number of non-nuclear-weapon states requested that the nuclear-weapon powers commit themselves not to use nuclear weapons against them. UN Security Council resolution No. 255 of 19 June 1968 which deals with security assurances for non-nuclear-weapon states, was adopted for this purpose. The implications of article VI of the NPT and of the Security Council resolution are discussed in chapters 2 and 3 of Part IV.

In the final analysis, the success of the NPT will depend on the attitudes of the so-called near-nuclear countries towards their security problems. Some of these countries have been selected as case studies and their attitudes towards the NPT are discussed in chapters 3–7 of Part IV.

2. The non-proliferation of nuclear weapons and the security of the non-nuclear states

A. N. KALIADIN

Abstract

The Treaty on the Non-Proliferation of Nuclear Weapons has marked an encouraging trend towards international peace and cooperation; it is the fruit of prolonged effort by various persons and organizations. In it, provision is made to counter, through the UN, threats of nuclear aggression. The NPT, despite its limitations, has inhibited the proliferation of nuclear weapons, while pressure for nuclear-weapon use has lessened due to factors such as the realization (in Viet-nam) of the futility of imperialism and the increased tempo with which various agreements are being negotiated. The NPT could be broadened by giving further security advantages to the non-nuclear-weapon states which would facilitate their advances in the peaceful uses of atomic energy. A strengthening of UN peacekeeping machinery is the key to lasting security for the non-nuclear states.

Five years ago the Treaty on the Non-Proliferation of Nuclear Weapons was opened for signature. Subsequent developments—the adherence of an overwhelming majority of states to the treaty and substantial positive changes in the international environment—have confirmed the necessity and importance of this undertaking for the strengthening of international peace and security.

Current favourable developments in world politics serve as convincing proof of the correctness and foresight of those in the 1950s and 1960s who pressed for a peaceful alternative in international relations, carried out an insistent fight for their improvement and worked to curb the arms race and the nuclear threat.

The broad concept of non-proliferation of nuclear weapons was put forward by the USSR and a number of other socialist states as early as the mid-1950s. Propositions included were: a complete, general and international ban on nuclear weapon testing; a prohibition of deployment of those weapons to foreign territories; the creation of non-nuclear zones, and a ban on transfer of nuclear weapons to other states or military blocs. According to the proposals by the Warsaw Pact nations, new states—

whether militarily aligned or non-aligned—would be unable to own, control or use nuclear weapons.

In contrast, the members of NATO evaded their commitments in the non-proliferation and non-dissemination field. Within the NATO framework, various projects for sharing control over nuclear forces had been worked out; as a result, progress on the non-proliferation of nuclear weapons was postponed.

Only after the control-sharing schemes had been put aside because of international pressure, was an agreement corresponding to the interests of international security possible.

The conclusion of the NPT was the result of the combined efforts of many nations, a broad international public and various peace movements. We now see that these efforts were not futile. They have reduced the danger of war, broadened international cooperation, created a more favourable climate for constraining the arms race and intensified cooperation in the peaceful use of atomic energy.

The NPT forms an integral part of the positive processes taking place in international life today. These are reflected in the signing of the ceasefire agreements in Viet-Nam and Laos, the decisive turn to détente and East-West cooperation on the European continent and the conclusion of a whole complex of treaties recognizing the principles of peaceful co-existence.

The security problems of states which had forsworn the acquisition of nuclear weapons took a prominent place in the negotiations for the NPT. The treaty itself and its system of guarantees reflect the solutions which were finally found.

The security problems are covered by provisions of the treaty regarding the non-transfer and non-acquisition of nuclear weapons (articles I and II); international control (article III); obligations of the participating states to carry out negotiations on the cessation of the nuclear arms race and on nuclear, general and complete disarmament (article VI); and the affirmation of the right of the non-nuclear-weapon states party to the treaty, to conclude regional agreements assuring the total absence of nuclear weapons in their respective territories (article VII).

The NPT was supplemented by UN Security Council resolution No. 255, adopted on 19 June 1968 and by the related individual statements of the USSR, the USA and the UK. The resolution and the statements contain commitments to provide or support immediate assistance to a non-nuclear-weapon state, party to the treaty, that faces a threat of aggression in which nuclear weapons are used. In their statements made in the Security Council, the USSR, the USA and the UK all proclaimed their intention to act immediately through the Security Council to stop the aggression or to remove the threat of aggression.

Resolution No. 255[1] states that any aggression accompanied by the

[1] No state voted against it; Algeria, Brazil, France, India and Pakistan abstained.

use of nuclear weapons would endanger the peace and security of all states. The Security Council

> recognized that aggression with nuclear weapons or the threat of such aggression against a non-nuclear-weapon state would create a situation in which the Security Council, and above all its nuclear-weapon-state permanent members, would have to act immediately in accordance with their obligations under the United Nations Charter,

that is, provisions of the charter regarding collective measures for the prevention or removal of the threat to the peace. In connection with the security of non-nuclear-weapon states, both resolution No. 255 and the three-party pledge confirm article 51 of the UN charter regarding the inherent right of individual and collective self-defence. In a situation in which the Security Council is unable to make a decision immediately on effective measures to suppress nuclear aggression or remove the threat of aggression, article 51 assures support to a non-nuclear nation, party to the NPT, that faces such a threat.

When resolution No. 255 and the three-party pledge were adopted, it was stated that they were designed to make it clear in advance to a potential aggressor that its actions would be effectively repulsed and that victims of the aggression would be given necessary assistance and support. It was understood that such a warning in advance would, by itself, serve as a deterrant.

Resolution No. 255 and the statements of the three nuclear weapon powers emphasize the central role of the Security Council in realizing the special guarantees given to non-nuclear nations party to the NPT. In addition, the resolution contains a specific reference to the actions necessary to counter nuclear aggression. Also, in both the resolution and the three-party statements, the necessity of prompt action and the importance of using the machinery of the Security Council for that end are emphasized.

It is of primary importance that resolution No. 255 and the statements of the three nuclear weapon powers also contain a condemnation of the aggressive use of nuclear weapons. It is, in effect, an admission that policies of nuclear pressure, threats or blackmail are inconsistent with the commitments assumed by the parties to the NPT. It has been strongly emphasized that the states which renounced the possession of nuclear weapons are fully entitled to rely on and receive the support and assistance of the UN in case of the threat of nuclear attack.

The above-mentioned statements, which describe the requirements of three nuclear-weapon powers to bring into effect the mechanism of security assurances to non-nuclear nations, may serve as an additional basis for possible collective action. Moreover, truly regional agreements and organs also lend themselves to these purposes.

Thus, according to the meaning of the NPT and the accompanying special documents, the security of non-nuclear-weapon nations party to the treaty, is to be assured by prevention of the further spread of nuclear weapons, progress in nuclear and general disarmament, cessation of the nuclear arms race and, finally, the special security guarantee and the effective use of the machinery of the UN.

Five years after the signing of the NPT and three years after its coming into force, one can draw some tentative conclusions concerning the changes in the security situation of the states banning the possession of nuclear weapons. As the changes have been brought about not only by the existence of the NPT, but also by general shifts in the international environment, both these factors should be taken into consideration.

Although the NPT is not yet universal in its membership (a number of the nuclear-weapon nations such as France and the People's Republic of China have not joined) there is definite progress in the assertion of the principle of non-proliferation of nuclear weapons. During the past five years, the number of the states party to the NPT, has doubled and the whole system of measures in the field of non-proliferation of nuclear weapons, including safeguards agreements between non-nuclear-weapon countries and the IAEA, has been brought into action.

Although some non-nuclear countries are still outside the NPT system, none have ventured to challenge the treaty. Since 1968 the situation with regard to ownership and possession of nuclear weapons has been stabilized. The number of countries possessing nuclear weapons has not increased and the spread of nuclear weapons has been suspended.

The NPT has contributed to the creation of conditions which inhibit the acquisition of nuclear weapons. It has become a stabilizing factor in relations among the non-nuclear-weapon nations themselves. It has helped to ease one state's suspicions of another concerning nuclear force. By containing the sphere of nuclear arms, the insecurity, fear and tensions associated with races in nuclear weaponry have been avoided.

In addition, existing nuclear armaments have remained unused. No nation has become a victim of the aggressive use of nuclear weapons or the object of the threat of such aggression. Consequently, no situation emerged which required the UN Security Council to convene to consider measures provided for in resolution No. 255.

Because of favourable changes in the international climate, the danger of nuclear conflict has receded. Also international developments have demonstrated that attempts to use nuclear power for pressure, intimidation or blackmail are futile.

The victory of the Viet-Namese people over imperialist aggression has shown that, under existing conditions, it is impossible to stop popular movements for national independence and social advance. The non-nuclear nations have demonstrated that they are in a position to uphold successfully their national rights and legitimate interests in the international arena and to counter effectively any imperialist military encroachments.

The avoidance of burdensome expenditure on nuclear arms and the concentration of efforts on problems of economic and social advance have become realistic and attractive alternatives for non-nuclear-weapon nations. Favourable changes in international relations on the European continent have contributed to the assurance of peace and have added to the security of these countries in Europe.

A whole system of treaties between socialist and capitalist states in Europe, based on the inviolability of the interstate boundaries and on non-use of force in mutual relations, has emerged. In this connection the treaties of the USSR, Poland and the GDR with the FRG, as well as the agreements on West Berlin, should be mentioned.

Efforts are being undertaken to make the European continent a region of secure peace and fruitful, stable and mutual cooperation and understanding. Some progress has been made in the creation of a more reliable system of security and cooperation in Europe. In this connection one should mention the convocation of the all-European Conference in the course of which the basis for a stable all-European security system will be laid with discussions on security and cooperation and multilateral consultations on the reduction of arms and armed forces in Europe.

The tangible achievements in implementing the principles of peaceful co-existence between the East and the West on the European continent have confirmed the validity of the European countries' adherence to the NPT. The conclusion of this treaty in conjunction with other factors made détente and peace in this area possible.

After the conclusion of the NPT, definite practical results in restraining the nuclear arms race were achieved, such as the Treaty on the Prohibition of the Emplacement of Nuclear Weapons and other Weapons of Mass Destruction on the Sea-bed and the Ocean Floor and in the Subsoil thereof, which came into force in 1972.

The 1972 Soviet-US agreements on the Limitation of Strategic Arms (SALT) have imposed ceilings on the deployment of ABM systems by both sides, and on numbers of ICBMs, SLBMs and modern missile submarines. These agreements materially and quantitatively limit the most destructive military capabilities of the USSR and the USA.

In the course of the continuing Soviet-US negotiations on further limitations of offensive strategic arms, the following tasks are under consideration: the turning of the interim agreement into a permanent one; the gradual reduction of strategic offensive weapons and the limiting of their qualitative improvement.

While assessing the treaty on the limitation of ABM systems and the Interim Agreement with respect to the limitation of strategic offensive arms, one should take into consideration other Soviet-US agreements and, in particular, the Document on Basic Principles of Soviet-US relations. This states that in a nuclear age there is no other basis for Soviet-US relations but peaceful co-existence. Both sides declared that they would do everything possible to avoid military confrontations and prevent a nuclear war. The Soviet-US agreements on the limitation of strategic arms and on prevention of nuclear war, when coupled with the principles of co-existence, become significant steps toward reducing the threat of nuclear war, restraining the arms race and allowing nuclear and general disarmament.

It should be noted that only the first steps toward limitation of nuclear arms have been taken. On the whole, the process of accumulation and perfection of armaments has not been halted. Other nuclear powers are not party to the existing treaties on limitation of strategic weapons. Nevertheless the existing treaties contribute to the lessening of the nuclear arms race and to eventual nuclear disarmament and, thus, strengthen the security of all nations.

The assurance of general security has been facilitated by recent measures taken in the UN, and directed toward creating more effective barriers against the use of force in international relations, and, particularly, against the use of nuclear weapons.

On the initiative of the USSR, the twenty-seventh session of the General Assembly of the UN adopted a resolution calling for the non-use of force in international relations and the prohibition of the use of nuclear weapons. The General Assembly solemnly declared on behalf of the member states its denunciation of the use of force or the threat of its use in all its forms and manifestations in international relations in accordance with the UN charter. This included a prohibition on the use of nuclear weapons. The resolution says, in particular, that denunciation of the use of force and of the threat of its use and the ban on the use of nuclear weapons should be fully complied with.

The security interests of the non-nuclear nations are also enhanced because the Soviet proposal is designed to provide greater security to all nations, including non-nuclear states, by increasing the guarantees against both nuclear and conventional aggression. But, primarily, it is the nations not possessing nuclear weapons and major conventional armaments that benefit from a strengthening of the legal and international guarantees against attack. A comprehensive ban also creates an additional barrier against the use of force by aggressors and colonizers.

Thus, the results of the NPT system vindicate the foresight of the non-nuclear nations in avoiding the nuclear-arms race. Their decision, as experience has shown, has led not to a lessening of their international security but, on the contrary, to tangible advantages. One cannot leave unnoticed the allegations discrediting the NPT and other agreements in the field of arms limitation and international détente but the positive developments in world politics, of which the NPT and the SALT agreements are a part, have exerted a favourable influence on the international security of all states, large and small, nuclear and non-nuclear. (This chapter does not deal with other benefits obtained by the participating states, for example, those in the sphere of peaceful uses of atomic energy.)

Regional activities, such as the efforts to reduce arms and armed forces in Europe, the search for a regional security system in Asia and the attempts to solve the Middle East conflict according to the Security Council resolution of 22 November 1972, are all broad, constructive trends toward international security. The further the world advances in this direction, the greater will be the international security of the non-nuclear-weapon nations.

It seems desirable, when planning for the future, to provide specific steps for the development of security systems of non-nuclear nations.

1. It is necessary to make the NPT a universal treaty. Of foremost importance is the participation of the countries well advanced in nuclear technology but not party to the NPT. That some of them are situated in areas of heightened tension also threatens international peace.

It is also most urgent to broaden the applications of the NPT and to implement its international safeguards in order to prevent international disputes from developing into nuclear confrontations. The universality of the treaty would contribute to the validity and efficiency of the security guarantees. It would increase their role as factors for assuring international security.

The concerted and purposeful actions of the participating states to secure the adherence of other non-nuclear states possessing a nuclear potential could have a considerable effect because of the interest of the latter in obtaining equipment, materials and technical know-how for developing the peaceful uses of atomic energy.

2. In the field of disarmament, which is of great importance to the security of the non-nuclear-weapon nations, the further limitation of nuclear-missile arms (stockpile reductions, qualitative improvement limits and so forth) is on the agenda.

The World Disarmament Conference should advance the cause of general disarmament, including nuclear disarmament, of states possessing nuclear weapons. A successful conference would exert a beneficial influence on the security position of all nations. The non-nuclear nations will have an opportunity at the World Disarmament Conference to make active contributions toward the attainment of major disarmament agreements.

3. It is necessary to implement the recommendation of the UN General Assembly banning the use of force in international relations and prohibiting the use of nuclear weapons. The next logical step is the adoption by the Security Council of a corresponding recommendation.

4. It is important to work out a generally accepted definition of aggression and of the norms and principles pertaining to the responsibility for

acts of aggression, violations of sovereign rights of a state and forceful continuous domination of colonial nations. It might be particularly worthwhile to solve the problem of responsibility for NPT violations which are especially serious and jeopardize international peace and security.

5. The consummation of the efforts for the creation of regional security systems in Europe and Asia, seems to be a very promising means of strengthening the security of non-nuclear nations.

6. Taking into consideration the responsibilities put on the UN in connection with the implementation of the security guarantees for the non-nuclear countries, it is very important to perfect the UN's function as an instrument for maintaining international peace by preventing any breaches of peace and by peaceful settlement of international conflicts.

Implementing the UN declaration on strengthening international security; coming to an agreement based on respect for the UN charter, on the question of UN peacekeeping operations; and solving international disputes by a wider use of peaceful means would all increase the UN's role in assuring the security of all nations and promoting the efficient use of UN machinery for upholding international peace.

The steps mentioned above do not exhaust the problem of increasing the security of non-nuclear countries. Nevertheless, their implementation would substantially facilitate the creation of a system of peace and international security which is not burdened by an arms race or interstate conflicts and tensions. The current favourable developments on the international arena present opportunities for the achievement of this aim.

3. The UN Security Council resolution of 19 June 1968 and the security of non-nuclear-weapon states

J. GOLDBLAT

Abstract

The non-nuclear-weapon states which under the non-proliferation treaty have renounced the acquisition of nuclear weapons are entitled to security guarantees on the part of the powers which have retained these weapons. However, UN Security Council resolution 255 of 19 June 1968, which was offered as a substitute for such guarantees, is devoid of practical value. It has not created new commitments beyond those already included in the UN charter; it has not established special procedures to deal with nuclear aggression; it cannot be put into effect as long as the nuclear power "club" consists of the permanent members of the Security Council enjoying the rights of veto over the Council's decisions.

The problem is bound to be raised again at a conference reviewing the operation of the NPT. One way of reducing the inequality of the parties under the treaty would be for the nuclear-weapon powers to accept a formal commitment not to use nuclear weapons against non-nuclear-weapon states.

Under the Treaty on the Non-Proliferation of Nuclear Weapons (NPT), non-nuclear-weapon states have renounced the manufacture or other acquisition of nuclear weapons. In lieu of security guarantees, they were offered a pledge of assistance contained in UN Security Council resolution 255 of 19 June 1968. The resolution welcomed:

The intention expressed by certain States that they will provide or support immediate assistance, in accordance with the Charter, to any non-nuclear-weapon State Party to the Treaty on the Non-Proliferation of Nuclear Weapons that is a victim of an act or an object of a threat of aggression in which nuclear weapons are used.[1]

The intention referred to above was expressed in identical formal declarations by the UK, the USA and the USSR, that aggression with nuclear

---

[1] See annex 1.

weapons, or the threat of such aggression, against a non-nuclear-weapon state would create a qualitatively new situation in which they, as permanent members of the Security Council, would have to act immediately through the Security Council, to take the measures necessary to counter such aggression, or to remove the threat of aggression in accordance with the charter. Any state which committed aggression with nuclear weapons or which threatened such aggression would be countered effectively by measures taken in accordance with the charter to suppress the aggression or remove the threat of aggression.

France, the fourth nuclear-weapon power, did not sponsor the resolution but declared that, in its opinion, the only solution to the nuclear menace lay in the cessation of production of nuclear arms and in the destruction of stockpiles.

The resolution was passed with a margin considered narrow for a document of that importance. Out of 15 Security Council members, 10 voted in favour: Canada, Denmark, Ethiopia, Hungary, Paraguay, Senegal, Taiwan, the UK, the USA and the USSR; and five abstained: Algeria, Brazil, France, India and Pakistan. The voting record reflected the doubts of a number of countries about the significance of the resolution. Indeed, the following questions could be asked:

1. Has the Security Council resolution created new commitments on the part of nuclear-weapon powers beyond those already contained in the UN charter?

2. Has it introduced new procedures to deal with what was termed a "qualitatively new situation" resulting from aggression with nuclear weapons or the threat of such aggression?

3. Who is the direct addressee of the resolution?

4. Most importantly, have the nuclear-weapon powers, parties to the NPT, themselves renounced the use of nuclear weapons against non-nuclear-weapon states?

The following is an attempt to answer these questions:

1. It will be recalled that chapter VII of the UN charter provides for collective measures, both nonmilitary and military, to prevent and remove threats to peace, and to suppress acts of aggression or other breaches of peace. Measures not involving the use of armed force may include complete or partial interruption of economic relations and of rail, sea, air, postal, telegraphic, radio, and other means of communications, and the severance of diplomatic relations. Measures of a military character may include such action by air, sea, or land forces as "may be necessary" to maintain or restore international peace and security.

Under the charter, assistance to a country attacked is not contingent on the type of weapon employed in aggression. It is obvious that assistance must be provided or supported, and an aggressor countered effectively, not only in case of attack with conventional weapons, but also, and with even greater reason, in case of attack with weapons of mass destruction. No new commitments have been created by the Security Council resolution beyond those already included in the UN charter. If anything, the resolution can be understood as restricting the right of *all* UN members to benefit from assistance, as it applies only to parties to the NPT.

2. Admittedly, an aggression with nuclear weapons would be qualitatively different from one carried out with conventional weapons, but the nuclear-weapon powers failed to draw proper conclusions from their own statements. The resolution stresses the urgent nature of action to be taken in case of nuclear aggression: it asks the Security Council to act "immediately". However, it is hardly possible to attach any weight to this requirement without detracting from the obligations of the Security Council to take appropriate measures with respect to other breaches of the peace, the element of haste being already implied in the provisions of chapter VII of the charter. In any event, no special procedures, other than those established by the charter, are envisaged. Thus, any decision concerning assistance to a nation attacked with nuclear weapons (as in the case of attack with conventional weapons) would have to have approval of all the permanent members of the Security Council which are also nuclear-weapon powers. Considering that only these powers could use nuclear weapons, it is unlikely that an aggressor would consent to a collective action being taken against itself.

3. The assistance clause, as it was phrased, would make sense if not all nuclear-weapon states were permanent members of the UN Security Council. Sanctions could then be applied against a guilty state with the concurrence of the permanent members.

When the Security Council resolution was adopted, the People's Republic of China, by then a nuclear power, was still not occupying its seat in the United Nations; thus at that time it was the only country which could be affected by the resolution. But now, and as long as the nuclear-weapon-power "club" is limited to those countries which are permanent members of the UN Security Council, the resolution could not be put into effect.

4. The Security Council resolution contains no "negative" assurances whereby nuclear-weapon powers would commit themselves never to use nuclear weapons against non-nuclear-weapon states. A reference has been made to charter article 51 concerning the exercise of self-defence until the Security Council has taken measures necessary to maintain international peace and security. This reference has little to do with the objective of the resolution—to assist non-nuclear-weapon nations attacked with nuclear weapons. But its inclusion can be interpreted as recognition of the right of nuclear-weapon states to resort to all possible means of warfare without constraint in all conflicts; that is, in conflicts with non-nuclear-weapon states as well, so long as the nuclear powers do not con-

sider themselves to be aggressors; and there exists, as yet, no internationally agreed definition of aggression.

UN General Assembly resolution 2936, adopted on 20 November 1972, on the renunciation of the use or threat of force and the prohibition of the use of nuclear weapons, could have similar effects. Since under this resolution, the non-use of nuclear weapons has been indissolubly associated with a UN charter provision regarding the non-use of force, a use of force might be taken by the attacked nation as freeing it from the obligation not to employ nuclear weapons. This would be tantamount to licensing the first use of nuclear weapons, under certain circumstances, against any nation.

Conclusions

Whatever were the motives of the UN members in 1968 in accepting a resolution devoid of practical value, the question of security guarantees is bound to be raised at a conference reviewing the operation of the NPT.

The balance of rights and obligations under the NPT is heavily tipped in favour of the nuclear-weapon powers. One way of reducing the inequality of the parties under the treaty would be for the nuclear-weapon powers to accept a formal commitment—as an adjunct to the NPT—not to use nuclear weapons against non-nuclear-weapon states. Although at present there is no immediate danger that a non-nuclear-weapon country would be attacked with nuclear weapons, there exists a lingering apprehension, at least in certain regions of the world, that in very critical situations this may happen. The rumours that the USA was weighing the possibility of having recourse to nuclear weapons during the war in Viet-Nam, although quickly dismissed, helped to dramatize the potential threat.

The proposed ban would have to be unconditional, that is, valid under any circumstances with respect to nuclear-weapon-free zones or countries. (Article VII of the NPT reaffirms the right of any group of states to conclude regional treaties in order to assure the total absence of nuclear weapons in their respective territories.) As a matter of fact, it is already partly in force as concerns the Latin American area under the Treaty of Tlatelolco. The UK and the USA have signed and ratified Additional Protocol II of the treaty, which provides for an undertaking by nuclear-weapon states to respect the statute of military denuclearization of the area, and China and France have recently decided to adhere to it. A similar commitment with regard to non-nuclear-weapon countries, in general, and with regard to the parties to the NPT, in particular (the latter being especially entitled to a *quid pro quo*) may pose problems only when nuclear weapons are stationed on the territory of such countries. In these cases, the undertaking would probably have to be hedged with reservations which could render the ban somewhat less than unconditional.

As in other international agreements relating to the rules of conduct in war, there can be no complete certainty that the banned weapons would not be used in violation of the undertaken commitments. But an obligation of the type described above would create a political, legal and moral barrier to the employment of the most devastating methods of warfare, at least against those states which do not possess adequate means of retaliation.

A non-use of nuclear weapons agreement may strengthen the determination of the non-nuclear-weapon parties to the NPT to abide by their option to remain non-nuclear; it may encourage wider participation in the treaty and also provide an inducement to setting up nuclear-weapon-free zones.

Postscript

On 22 June 1973, the USA and the USSR signed an agreement on the prevention of nuclear war. The main undertaking, as stated in article IV of the agreement, is as follows:

> If at any time relations between the parties or between either party and other countries appear to involve the risk of a nuclear conflict, or if relations between countries not party to this agreement appear to involve the risk of nuclear war between the United States of America and the Union of Soviet Socialist Republics or between either party and other countries, the United States and the Soviet Union, acting in accordance with the provisions of this agreement, shall immediately enter into urgent consultations with each other and make every effort to avert this risk.

The agreement reflects a policy consistently followed by the two big powers ever since the Cuban missile crisis of 1962, and their obvious interest in avoiding a nuclear confrontation between themselves, or an involvement in conflicts which may result in such a confrontation. But it does not meet the security requirements of non-nuclear-weapon states and cannot dissipate their apprehensions.

Annex 1. UN Security Council resolution 255, of 19 June 1968

The Security Council

Noting with appreciation the desire of a large number of States to subscribe to the Treaty on the Non-Proliferation of Nuclear Weapons, and thereby to undertake not to receive the transfer from any transferor whatsoever of nuclear weapons or other nuclear explosive devices or of control over such weapons or explosive devices directly or indirectly, not to manufacture or otherwise acquire nuclear weapons or other nuclear explosive devices, and not to seek or receive any assistance in the manufacture of nuclear weapons or other nuclear explosive devices,

240

Taking into consideration the concern of certain of these States that, in conjunction with their adherence to the Treaty on the Non-Proliferation of Nuclear Weapons, appropriate measures be undertaken to safeguard their security,

Bearing in mind that any aggression accompanied by the use of nuclear weapons would endanger the peace and security of all States,

1. *Recognizes* that aggression with nuclear weapons or the threat of such aggression against a non-nuclear-weapon State would create a situation in which the Security Council, and above all its nuclear-weapon State permanent members, would have to act immediately in accordance with their obligations under the United Nations Charter;

2. *Welcomes* the intention expressed by certain States that they will provide or support immediate assistance, in accordance with the Charter, to any non-nuclear-weapon State Party to the Treaty on the Non-Proliferation of Nuclear Weapons that is a victim of an act or an object of a threat of aggression in which nuclear weapons are used;

3. *Reaffirms* in particular the inherent right, recognized under Article 51 of the Charter, of individual and collective self-defence if an armed attack occurs against a Member of the United Nations, until the Security Council has taken measures necessary to maintain international peace and security.

4. Italy and the nuclear option

F. CALOGERO

Abstract

This chapter is intended merely to augment a paper prepared for the Arms Control and Foreign Policy Seminar in Santa Monica, California.

Although there are no major obstacles in the way of ratification of the NPT by Italy, a delay can be expected. The most effective way Italy and other countries can be discouraged from taking the nuclear option is by the reduction of the role of nuclear weapons in international relations. This option is unlikely to be taken by Italy but lack of reasoned, informed public opinion on the question could lead to a drastic, ill-advised policy change.

A rather thorough analysis of the problem of proliferation in the Italian context is given in a recent paper prepared for the Arms Control and Foreign Policy Seminar (Santa Monica, California) which bears the same title as this chapter. The discussion here will take that analysis for granted and omit all the factual information given there.

On 5 April 1973 an agreement was signed by the IAEA, Euratom and seven European countries (Belgium, Denmark, FR Germany, Ireland, Italy, Luxembourg and the Netherlands) which set up an accepted procedure for the harmonization of the Euratom and IAEA safeguards systems.

As far as Italy is concerned, there should therefore be no obstacle in the way of ratification of the NPT (achievement of the agreement mentioned above had been stated as a precondition for ratification when the NPT was signed by Italy in January 1969). It may, however, be anticipated that a considerable delay will occur before ratification, due to the low procedural efficiency of the Italian parliamentary system. Moreover, no political group appears at present particularly eager to press the issue which is, in fact, forgotten by everybody with the sole exception of a few professionals in the Foreign Ministry and the Nuclear Energy Agency (CNEN). This includes some who have been among the most vocal leaders of the opposition to the NPT and who are therefore not likely to press for speedy ratification.

Under the present circumstances, ratification of the NPT by Italy does not, however, appear to be an event of great significance. The general political mood concerning nuclear weapons and disarmament and European security is presumably much more important. It might therefore be unwise to mount a campaign for the speedy ratification of the NPT since past experience indicates that this is an issue on which the "hawks" have ample space for argument, given the extraordinary innocence of the public and of most political leaders on strategic matters, and the lack of progress in disarmament negotiations, especially at SALT.

We fully share the conclusion of the paper referred to above: that the most effective way to discourage Italy—or for that matter most other countries—from striving for a nuclear option is to reduce the role of nuclear weapons in international relations. The most important indication in this respect can and should come from SALT. A display of restraint and good sense there, resulting in a joint successful effort to break away from the arms race spiral, would indeed be of major importance not only in itself, but also for its worldwide impact on the motivations to "go nuclear". It would provide the strongest argument to those political forces within each country who argue in favour of restraint. For Italy in particular, the reliance of Great Britain and France on nuclear weapons, and the future role of the British and French "independent deterrent" are also matters of substantial relevance.

It is reasonable to predict that, at least for several years, responsible Italian political leaders are not likely to seriously consider acquiring a nuclear option—not even to the extent of playing a secondary role in influencing decisions concerning the civilian nuclear programme. This assertion is perhaps overoptimistic in that it does not take into consideration the possibility of a major political upheaval such as a breakdown of the constitutional government and the emergence of an authoritarian régime. It is based upon a survey of the contemporary Italian political scene, with none of the major parties ideologically or pragmatically bent on a "hawkish" course in foreign policy. It should be added that also at the highest technical level, such as the leadership of the Nuclear Energy Agency (CNEN), there now serve individuals who provide every guarantee that the agency will remain unsympathetic towards any ambition in the nuclear weapon field. This may not be so at some lower echelons of the bureaucratic and technological structure but the presence of some such individuals who, more or less openly, advocate the acquisition of an Italian nuclear option is not likely to have a decisive influence in the foreseeable future.

Undoubtably, the developments concerning European security in the Mediterranean sector will very largely determine the Italian attitude towards nuclear weapons. It is also worthwhile to re-emphasize that any use of military force in Europe in order to modify a political situation induces political leaders and public opinion to wonder whether additional reliance on the military might not be sought. In such a framework the action of those who advocate the development of an independent nuclear option is clearly made more easy. In view of the eventual achievement of a politically federated Europe, the example of the French and British nuclear forces will in the future probably be the determining factor in shaping Italian decisions in the nuclear weapon field.

It should finally be emphasized that while the political configuration outlined above suggests that, at least for the next several years, Italy will continue its policy of strict non-proliferation (not giving weight to factors leading to a nuclear option when making decisions relevant to the civilian nuclear energy programme), an element of uncertainty persists in that these matters have up to now been almost totally ignored by the Italian political debate. They have been briefly discussed—with much noise and chaff—only when the question of signing the NPT exploded but this discussion merely served to expose the widespread ignorance prevailing among decision-makers, journalists and the public. This situation contains an element of danger, especially in the context of the great revolution in strategic thinking associated with nuclear weapons. It might indeed happen that at some juncture ill-conceived arguments based on totally outmoded ways of thinking may be taken seriously, both by public opinion at large and by decision makers, with catastrophic consequences that could hardly be predicted much in advance. There is clearly an important educational task to be pursued, aiming both at the general public (through the mass media and the educational system) and at the political élite (including party, trade union and religious leaders).

In this respect even the action of a few sensible people, if they were dedicated and competent, could have a very significant effect. This action, however, must be directed to the proper goals (education rather than propaganda) and not wasted in improvised public sorties whose only results would be to discredit the people involved and decrease the payoff of any serious educational effort.

5. The non-proliferation treaty: the Japanese attitude three years after signing

R. IMAI

Abstract

Three years after signing the non-proliferation treaty, the nuclear world as seen from Japan does not present a very optimistic picture. Two important issues remain without major progress; namely, freeing nuclear technology's international exchange (article IV) and moving more rapidly toward meaningful arms control (article VI). On the other hand, international safeguards (article III) have been streamlined so that they are no longer regarded as the major obstacle toward NPT ratification, so long as satisfactory arrangements can be worked out with the IAEA.

Security considerations in post-Viet-Nam Asia are not the same as in 1970. Similarly, the meaninglessness of Japan's "nuclear option" is becoming better understood. If there is a discernible apathy among the Japanese about the NPT, it is because the treaty has so far failed to prove to be more than an intermediary step and political instrument for the assurance of European security.

At the forthcoming NPT Review Conference, further clarification of articles IV and V, as well as more tangible measures to identify nuclear weapon states' obligations under article VI, should be more carefully worked out. Japan, however, does not regard these to be preconditions for its ratification, but would rather like to participate in the international discussion in 1975.

I. Introduction

There are people in Japan, although not many in number, who oppose their country's ratification of the NPT and are not hesitant to express their view in public. On the other hand, there is an even smaller number of people who would actively promote ratification and take upon themselves the responsibility for preparing a safeguards agreement with the International Atomic Energy Agency (IAEA) and manoeuvre through the political entanglement of the National Diet. The remaining 99.999 per cent of the population would not object to ratification of the treaty. This illustrates the fact that the NPT is a non-issue in Japan today and that no one in the political parties, civil service or industry can expect to make political or other gains by publicly promoting the cause of the NPT.

However, failing to promote the NPT will lead to a great political loss. Although the opposition is small in number, it extends from the far left (Communist Party) to the far right (nationalist wing of the Liberal Democratic Party) obviously appealing to very different factions of national sentiment.

At the same time, it is not difficult to persuade most people that the loss to Japan from not joining the NPT will probably exceed the dubious gain of rejecting it. There has never been very much talk of active gain in becoming a party to the NPT, and the events of the past three years seem to support this attitude. One of the difficulties today is that due to rapid changes in world politics, the existence of an identifiable NPT bandwagon around the world is somewhat questionable.

II. *Three faces of the NPT*

It is possible to divide what NPT stands for into three separate categories. First, this treaty is an end product of all the past negotiations on nuclear disarmament and arms control since World War II which ended with two nuclear holocausts. East-West discussions came through many tedious processes: the UN Atomic Energy Committee; the ENDC (now CCD); the Partial Test Ban Treaty, the IAEA and finally, in January 1968, the agreed draft of the non-proliferation treaty. Today, there is a new and different set of negotiations, such as the SALT and MBFR talks. It is important to view the significance of the NPT within the stream of these events and to re-evaluate what it stands for today.

Second, the NPT symbolized the sort of world order worked out by the USA and the USSR after years of cold war nuclear confrontation. This détente is based on a balanced nuclear deterrence in which these two powers maintain law and order by excluding the possibility of a disturbance which might be caused by the emergence of a sixth nuclear power. While the basis of deterrence has been further fortified, the entrance of the People's Republic of China onto the scene has changed the situation a great deal. Today bipolarized centres of military gravity do not necessarily command the full control of the rest of the world. From the Japanese viewpoint, the future of US-Japanese relations and the security of post-Viet-Nam Asia need to be evaluated and analysed before a clear perspective can emerge.

Third, and very important, the non-proliferation treaty is, by definition, a treaty of principles and not necessarily the ideal in procedural arrangements. This is reflected in the manner with which the treaty is structured. For example, the NPT does not contain a section on definitions. No one has been able to define what is intended by "other nuclear explosive devices". This implies that one cannot precisely explain what it is that the countries agreed not to "manufacture or otherwise acquire". The same is true with regard to the nuclear weapon states' "undertakings to pursue negotiations in good faith on effective measures relating to cessation of the nuclear arms race" (article VI). Is SALT I a sufficient discharge of the nuclear-weapon states' obligation, or is SALT II also required? Non-nuclear-weapon states' obligations under article III are not very precisely defined either. During the summer of 1970 at meetings in Vienna to begin discussions of the safeguards agreement under the NPT, extensive debates took place about the difference between "concluding safeguards agreement with IAEA" and "accepting IAEA safeguards". The outcome of this debate was rather inconclusive and led to a badly defined relationship between the IAEA and Euratom. The text of the NPT is ridden with such problems. Some of them may be clarified by amending the language in the treaty but many of the problems have direct bearing on substantive matters. Some of the problems reflect the differences in political interests among the countries concerned and this leads one to wonder if vague wording was not adopted intentionally. Many other problems arise from mismatching political ideology and technical realities. After all, the NPT is the first attempt to coordinate political objectives with modern technology. The existing treaty text did not necessarily fully succeed in this attempt.

All three phases of the NPT as pointed out here are closely interrelated. Changes in evaluation of one category will immediately affect the meanings in the other two categories to the extent that it is difficult to treat the three separately. Progress in the technology of peaceful uses of nuclear power, or re-assessment of nuclear power as a source of energy in the context of the worldwide concern for the environment, is bound to produce changes and affect the manner and the extent of proliferation of potential nuclear capabilities around the world. Changes that were brought about during the past three years have had delicate but profound effects on each of the three areas. In some cases, what seemed to be the most critical issue at the time of the writing of the treaty has become less important. For example, it is less likely that the near-nuclear states of the world will find much value in becoming miniature-scale nuclear-weapon powers seeking to obtain political nuisance value, and, thereby, running the risk of endangering their own national security. Whether this is to be credited as an achievement of the NPT or regarded as an example of lack of understanding on the part of the architects of the treaty, is quite another matter.

III. *Disarmament negotiations*

The history of the ENDC in Geneva leading to the NPT is well known. The USA and the USSR agreed to limit horizontal proliferation of nuclear capabilities to the extent that non-nuclear-weapon states were asked to ac-

247

cept international safeguards. The basic logic seemed to be that while the two would negotiate the proper balancing of deterrent forces, they did not want to have "world peace" disturbed by the emergence of small or medium-sized nuclear powers. This world order, which has been arrived at after 20 years of negotiations, is supported by the tremendous growth of their own nuclear capabilities. Both the USA and the USSR must know very well that no third country can afford, either financially or technically, to challenge their powerful nuclear fortress on an equal footing. The USA has occasionally talked about Chinese nuclear armaments but that may have been motivated more by US domestic politics and a wish to influence the economy-minded US Congress than by the possibility of a real threat to their own security.

Of course, there has always been the underlying peace theme which is undeniable in any disarmament or arms control discussions. But it is also obvious that veteran negotiators in Geneva were not excessively naîve about the political realities of achieving peace. World peace commands all due respect in any discussion of the NPT but need not be mentioned every time.

SALT I revealed three very interesting things that can happen when disarmament negotiations are extended beyond the NPT. It has become very clear that the limitation of strategic nuclear arms is a subject for the USA and the USSR and is not within the capabilities of any other power. In other words, although the outcome of SALT will affect the entire population of the world, the negotiations themselves have been conducted bilaterally and in an atmosphere of well-kept secrecy. Although SALT is related to article VI of the NPT, none of the non-nuclear-weapon states, parties to the treaty, has been consulted by either the USA or the USSR about the negotiations. It has also revealed very distinctly that the SALT achievements could be related only to the keeping of balance and to items verifiable through the existing technical means and without on-site inspections. Thus, we have a strange situation in which MIRV nuclear warheads increase in number and in destructive capabilities as a result of a successful "disarmament treaty". SALT has also made it very clear beyond any doubt that the USA and the USSR will be very hesitant to resort to actual use of the tremendous nuclear arsenal in their possession. This has affected the credibility of the nuclear umbrella and, thus, has had a profound influence on the security structure throughout the world.

It may be too early to try to pass judgement of the significance of SALT while its second phase negotiations are in progress in Geneva. However, generally reported contents of SALT II do not seem to change the above-mentioned, and admittedly over-simplified, observations. It did not create an atmosphere in which non-nuclear-weapon states would want to adhere to the NPT at all costs, for SALT presented an example of the sort of nuclear world order which nuclear-weapon states can, and do intend to, bring about.

248

Non-nuclear-weapon states may be pleased that détente has been achieved between the two nuclear giants and that this has produced a favourable political climate but this is no reason to be grateful to the two countries. In this regard, it is doubtful that security guarantees to non-nuclear-weapon states against nuclear attacks or threats remain as big an issue today as in 1969.

What seems to be more significant in the context of the NPT is that today nations are capable of more realistic assessment of the military and political usefulness of nuclear armament in achieving their respective national goals. At the writing of the NPT, there seems to have been a tacit assumption that any country which was technically capable would go nuclear at the first opportunity. For the same reason as the decline of nuclear-umbrella credibility, many countries are losing interest in their own nuclear armament possibilities. For a country like Japan, nuclear armament does not present a real option. Japan is not interested in changing the global *status quo* by force and, therefore, nuclear weapons for offensive purposes are meaningless. Japan cannot afford to have, and sees no real national interest in having, an annual high expenditure level in order to build up and maintain a nuclear capability comparable to that of the USA or the USSR. Worldwide opinion to discredit the achievements of big science and technology in comparison with those of human welfare also has something to do with this conclusion. At the same time, whether a second strike capacity is really an effective deterrent against a determined nuclear attack is something worth reconsidering. It may be very wrong to assume that people will always behave like cold-blooded, rational "strategic men" in the case of national emergency. Real restraint on the use of nuclear weapons may not reside in the cold-blooded calculations of the "strategic man", but in the fact that no one is expected to gain very much by exercising so great a destructive power on anyone else. What one should fear and try to prevent is the case of a nation or a group of people who are less sophisticated in the appreciation of the global significance of nuclear arms and who are intensively interested in changing the *status quo* by getting hold of a small number of nuclear weapons. These people could then very effectively challenge the peace of the world.

IV. *Post-Viet-Nam Asian security*

The NPT has much less to do with the nuclear armament of advanced industrial countries than one would think. If one is looking for a nuclear option in peacetime, in many cases such an option does not really exist regardless of the NPT. If one is talking about the case of a real emergency involving "supreme interests" such as national survival, then article X provides for the right to withdraw from the treaty. Furthermore, the status of being near-nuclear is in itself sufficient prestige and a politically meaning-ful situation, as I have had occasion to discuss under the title of "Nuclear Power Minus Two Years". [1]

In the case of an advanced industrial country, the NPT represents a world order about which the following are some of the factors to be con-sidered. First, does the NPT contribute to national security? Once a country has decided that nuclear armament is not in its plans, it is obviously to its advantage that other countries refrain from nuclear armament; the clearest indication of such intention is for them to join the NPT. Unless there is a justifiable reason for the country to leave its intentions vague, it could avoid possible misunderstanding by also joining the NPT.

The next consideration concerns the advantages and disadvantages, jus-tice and injustice regarding which it is not necessary to go into detail in this chapter. Unless there are gross inconveniences or injustice which a na-tion feels is brought upon it by the treaty, it is rather unlikely that prob-lems of this nature will reverse the conclusion arrived at from analysis of other factors.

A more important consideration regarding the NPT is the country's evaluation of the "NPT world order" *vis-à-vis* its own posture in inter-national politics. In the case of Japan, changing Asian situations in the post-Viet-Nam era have to be carefully analysed. This includes in particu-lar, an attempt to forecast the future of US-Japanese relations, which is, by no means, a simple subject for a chapter of this length.

The first observation is that there does not seem to be a high probability of a recurrence of a US-Soviet or US-Chinese nuclear confrontation in Asia, that is, if there ever was one similar to that in the European theatre. The current concern is nuclear confrontation along the Sino-Soviet border, and this is a very different type of confrontation compared to that between two major nuclear powers. The present nature and future development of the border confrontation will have a profound effect on Asian security. The very important clue to this question is what we may assume to be the basic Chinese philosophy regarding strategic nuclear weapons or tactical nuclear defence. If this philosophy is different from what we are used to from exposure to the US type of strategic theories, we do not have the tools to forecast future Chinese behaviour regarding the use of nuclear weapons. China has been very reluctant to express in public its basic nuclear philos-ophy and it is likely that, for some time to come, Japan will have to base its policy on an uncertain understanding of what China's next move might be. It seems clear today, however, that China will favour Japan's ratifica-tion of the NPT in spite of China's hostility against a US-Soviet-dominated world order.

The significance and value of a US nuclear guarantee is not the same today as it was several years ago. The US-Japanese Mutual Security Treaty is under review in the absence of a strong and credible scenario of an invasion of Japan by an outside force. It is possible that the treaty contains a considerable risk for Japan to become involved in a US-Asian war, to which the USA itself will propose minimum military participation. This factor will have to be weighed against the uncertainty which China's nuclear posture may create.

In the area of trade, Japan and the USA are developing competitive positions which tend to breed uneasy feelings through day-to-day contact. There have been some indications of this trend already. At the same time, in many areas the two countries are natural partners. In the area of future energy resources, Japan has a very complicated problem regarding relations with the United States. There are the obvious problems of Middle Eastern oil and enriched uranium. Both cases indicate that Japan would be ill advised to take a posture which might displease its powerful neighbours across the Pacific unless there were specific reasons to do so. Thus, we can afford to pay due respect to the architects of the NPT world order, when and if it is required.

This seems to be in agreement with the general mood of the industrial sector of Japan. During the recent annual conference of the Japan Atomic Industrial Forum, Forum leadership came out fairly strongly urging the government to ratify the NPT as soon as possible. Needless to say, this is a reflection not only of the wishes of Japanese nuclear industry but of the industrial leaders of Japan in general who are more and more concerned about the rumour of deteriorating US-Japanese relations.

V. Problems of a procedural nature

Even though some of the shortcomings of the NPT regarding procedural matters concern substantive matters, they could well be taken up during the review conference and at least be identified as such although an actual amendment of the treaty's language may not be possible in all cases. What seems to be a serious fault in the non-proliferation treaty is the lack of definitions; this was rather extensively discussed in 1968 and 1969.

Because of the lack of definition of "other nuclear explosive devices", the question often came up as to whether a "fast critical assembly" (especially if it were to go into nuclear excursion) should belong to this class. The USA has indicated that it should not, but this is merely a US interpretation. It is certainly possible that a different interpretation regarding similar experimental facilities may be made.

Another problem is the case of article V which provides that the parties undertake "to cooperate to insure that potential benefits from any peaceful applications of nuclear explosions" will be made available to non-nuclear-weapon states. This means that non-nuclear-weapon states are not allowed to develop, possess or use nuclear explosives even when their value for peaceful uses has been demonstrated. Setting aside the argument as to whether this is indeed a feasible industrial technology or not, one can take this up as an example of an important problem concerning the rights of technically advanced countries.

There are still other complications with regard to article V in which it is stipulated that an appropriate international body may act as an inter-mediary for providing such a service. The membership of this international body is only one part of the issue. However it is set up, the international body ought to be capable of ensuring that only services and not know-how regarding nuclear explosives have passed from nuclear-weapon states to non-nuclear-weapon states because the latter would constitute a violation of article I. Will nuclear-weapon states be willing to disclose sufficient details about their weapons so that the international body can exercise this function with sufficient knowledge and confidence? At this point one realizes that although article III provides for ensuring that non-nuclear-weapon states will abide by their obligation under article II, there is no provision within the structure of the NPT to ensure that nuclear-weapon states will not violate the obligations in article I. Why should nuclear-weapon states be allowed to set their own rules regarding the observation of treaty obligations?

VI. *Problems of safeguards*

Regarding IAEA safeguards, I have presented a fairly extensive discussion in an Adelphi paper [2] published by the International Institute for Strategic Studies and I shall therefore limit my argument here to the general outline.

The concept of safeguards has undergone considerable change since its inception and through the actions of the IAEA Safeguards Committee in 1970. It started out with a fairly crude idea of a "cops-and-robbers" game which intended to catch diverters in the midst of their illegal act. This was equivalent to giving an unlimited search warrant to an inter-national organization. A further difficulty encountered by the investigators was the lack of a noticeable distinction between peaceful and military nuclear technology. Then there was a proposal that safeguards inspectors need not enter the nuclear facilities, but could instead keep continuous watch at the gates so that no diverted material could leave the premises unauthorized. This negated the charge that safeguards procedures violate commercial secrecy and reveal proprietary technical information, thus creat-ing unfair competitive positions between nuclear industries of non-nuclear-weapon states and those in nuclear-weapon states for which safeguards are not required. However, the concept of constant watch was very unpopular and, in addition, a fairly impractical proposition.

The systems analysis approach provided a solution to all these problems. The objective of safeguards was defined as "providing for timely detection of diversion of significant quantity of nuclear material from peaceful nuclear fuel cycle, and thereby, to deter such diversion". Terms such as "timely", "significant quantity", "diversion" and "peaceful fuel cycle" have been given rigorous definitions. The newly defined objective means that by providing such capabilities, it will make diversion impossible or impractical in view of the risk of being detected. By converting safeguards technology into a system, it became unimportant whether the diverted material would be directly converted into nuclear weapons or simply stored somewhere. The system is concerned only with unauthorized or unreported diversion as such. The term "detection" is defined in a statistical manner, partly in consideration of the inevitable inaccuracies in nuclear material measurements and calculations.

The NPT safeguards, as embodied in IAEA document INFCIRC/153, rely heavily on the national system of nuclear material control and propose to verify the national findings. This has created a number of new problems.

1. How does one determine the extent of reliability of different national control systems? To do so on other than purely technical grounds will produce clearly unacceptable political discrimination between countries.

2. A technical definition of effectiveness of a national system is not easy because, in reality, the nuclear industry is so diverse that simple simulation models cannot reflect the real movements of nuclear material within the fuel cycle.

3. "Material unaccounted for" may be assessed not in absolute kilogrammes but in percentage of nuclear material throughput. This is because any inaccuracies or standard deviation are expressed in terms of a ratio in order to be applicable to actual calculations. Countries with a larger nuclear industry will have to be given a larger allowance for detection of diversion.

4. It will be very difficult to relate the outcome of safeguards activities to a possible violation of the treaty obligations and ultimately to article II of the NPT. At least there will be considerable hesitation before applying any sort of international sanction.

5. In the case of nuclear facilities, it is a well-accepted practice that the superintendent of the plant has absolute authority to refuse access to an outsider in the name of health and safety. This is different from the usual case of harmony with domestic law and it will be very difficult to call such a case of non-cooperation, "non-compliance".

6. A much simpler way to divert a significant quantity of nuclear material is to declare that such material has been stolen during the course of international transfer. It would be extremely difficult to prove that the report is false unless each and every international transfer were escorted by representatives of the IAEA.

7. The actual level of safeguards activities of the IAEA will not be determined according to technically calculated needs but by the annual budget which is approved by its Board of Governors and supported by its member states.

In the process of writing safeguards agreements between the IAEA and Euratom, or between the IAEA and the United States for the latter's voluntary acceptance in accordance with the statement made at the time of signature of the NPT, many efforts were made either to solve these problems or to give preferential interpretations to suit different national interests. The results of such exercises seem to have simply proven that it is not possible to find a technical solution to political problems. To offer a political solution to technical problems, on the other hand, will only create biased and unfair practice in the actual application of safeguards.

As a way of resolving this impasse, Japan has proposed to the International Atomic Energy Agency the creation of a committee of technical experts to serve as adviser to the Board of Governors. This committee shall be entrusted with the job of giving technical interpretations to technical provisions of the safeguards agreement, and to offer technical analysis and evaluation regarding actual methods of safeguards application whenever it is called for. This seems to be the only practical way to provide maximum objectivity and fairness to the system. Other than this, most of the unresolvable portions of the seven problems enumerated above have no reasonable short-term solutions. It is much more realistic to accept them as intrinsic limitations of the safeguards concept, and to try to live with them. In other words, safeguards are not the "almighty technical arm" of the NPT, but safeguards technology and the IAEA system have been improved to the extent that they no longer remain a major NPT issue although they continue to be an important IAEA problem.

VII. *The free flow of technical information*

All signs indicate that a very important change is taking place in nuclear technology itself and the role it is expected to play in our society. For a long time nuclear power generation and the use of ionizing radiation had been the "peaceful uses" of nuclear energy; this term implied that the basic role of this technology is military. When one compared the size of expenditure both for production and R&D for weapon purposes and peaceful industry, the point was quite clear.

The situation is very different today. Although nuclear power is not the cleanest of energies (it still has problems of safety and radioactive contamination of the environment) it is considered as the only valid and feasible form of energy production to supplement fossil fuel. In many countries, including the USA, FR Germany and Japan, nuclear power is expected to produce one-third to one-quarter of all electric power by 1985.

One might be able to call this situation a change of emphasis from military production to energy production and industrial technology. The way nuclear energy and its technology is handled either within a country or between nations will have to change in accordance with its changed role and the NPT happens to be an appropriate tool to symbolize this change. This is a role which drafters of the treaty may have tacitly assumed but the point is becoming more clear and more important due to developments in the past years. As far as non-nuclear-weapon states are concerned, they are undertaking not to possess nuclear weapons and are accepting IAEA safeguards, thus providing the means to restrict military nuclear power in a manner as effective as may be feasible within the political and technical realities of today. At the same time article V exemplifies another restriction which non-nuclear-weapon states have been forced to accept.

What is necessary in return for such a restriction is to create an atmosphere in which peaceful nuclear technology can freely develop and expand in accordance with its own merit, and in order to meet the energy and technical needs of the world population. What seems to be most important in this regard is to make the international exchange of technical information as free as in any other technical area. Article IV of the NPT says that the parties to the treaty "have the right to participate in the fullest possible exchange of scientific and technological information for the peaceful uses of nuclear energy" and this provision should not be regarded as mere lip service. It is, in fact, one of the most important provisions in the treaty, the one which symbolizes the positive meaning of the NPT.

Today, it is well-known that a part of the technology of nuclear power is classified by several nuclear-weapon states on the grounds of national security. The case in point is the technology of uranium enrichment. It is said that the western world needs another large-scale uranium enrichment plant of the order of 10 000 tons of separative work capacity per year by the early 1980s and possibly additional plants of the same capacity every 18 months. Today, uranium enrichment technology and an assured source of supply of enriched uranium are considered the real key to the successful use of nuclear power to meet the world's energy requirements. On the other hand, there is always a danger that someone may make use of this technology, especially the technology of ultracentrifuge, to produce a small amount of highly enriched material in a clandestine manner and, thus, manufacture a bomb or two. A very effective argument against this is that the world has had that danger for years because plutonium is a much more readily available material, and any country with the level of technology and a small research reactor could have manufactured a small number of bombs. Unless someone is interested in the clandestine manufacture of hydrogen bombs, but not in plutonium bombs, no new risk is added by freeing enrichment technology from military classification. The hydrogen bomb is a fairly sophisticated technological product but it is strategic nonsense for a country with such a level of sophistication to want to possess a small number of clandestine hydrogen bombs. Besides, the safeguards arrangements should be able to detect such clandestine diversions.

In view of the other provisions of the NPT, there is less and less justification for military classification of uranium enrichment technology. It should be declassified and given the same normal protection offered to any other technology of commercial value. Similar considerations should be given to other nuclear technology if it is held under a military classification. Prompt action on the part of the nuclear-weapon states in this regard will demonstrate that the NPT was not written merely to satisfy their own national interests.

VIII. *Future disarmament*

SALT and MBFR may be the most far-reaching nuclear arms control negotiations possible in today's political and military situation but there is no reason why much more cannot be or should not have been achieved. Throughout the past quarter century nuclear disarmament talks have always been conducted from the points of view of nuclear-weapon states. However, there is no provision which says nuclear-weapon states' obligations under article VI stop there. From the points of view of non-nuclear-weapon states party to the NPT, there are a number of additional things which would further extend the value of the treaty.

A ban on all underground testing is one such item, and this requires no further explanation. It may be very inconvenient for nuclear-weapon states to lose the last means of testing their newly developed modern warheads but that is precisely the reason that all underground testing should be stopped. The lack of verification techniques for small-scale tests seems to have been mostly overcome.

If safeguards are concerned about the danger of yet unrealized nuclear weapons, there should be an assurance that existing weapons will not be diverted from tightly held command and control networks to unauthorized uses. This is particularly true in the case of small tactical weapons which may be placed in different areas around the world. Nuclear-weapon states should be required to present sufficiently convincing proof that the system they implement for this purpose, including physical protection of such weapons against theft, is feasible and safe in all conceivable situations. To require safeguards for the peaceful nuclear industries of nuclear-weapon states will ensure that the states retain a concern for the well-being of the IAEA system, as well as avoid an unfair competitive position in regard to their nuclear industry. This will certainly make acceptance of safeguards under article III easier for the non-nuclear-weapon states. On the other hand, article III itself is an expression of distrust toward sovereign undertakings to abide by article II prohibitions. Why, then, should non-nuclear-weapon states be required to trust the intentions as well as capabilities of the nuclear-weapon states to observe article I without any mechanism such as safeguards? In fact, it is not inconceivable that the NPT will be greatly improved if a new article is added that ensures that the nuclear weapons in the possession or under the control of the nuclear-weapon states will not be used except in case of national survival and that even in such cases all other measures will be exhausted before their use is contemplated. Means of protecting against the inadvertent or unauthorized use of weapons should be demonstrated through an appropriate international organization.

Regarding the implementation of article VI, one may propose the creation of an appropriate international organization which will inspect and report to the world that nuclear-weapon states are faithfully observing the disarmament or arms limitation undertakings that they have agreed to under this article. For example, article XII of the SALT I agreements deals with satellite observation and supervision against violation of the agreement. In other words, satellite-collected information on this subject is no longer a military secret as far as the two major contracting parties are concerned. The USA or USSR can jointly offer an arrangement for an internationally administered satellite system for such a purpose. Satellite observation may also influence nuclear-weapon states, non-party to the NPT, by exposing the extent of their nuclear build-up to the rest of the world.

IX. *Conclusions*

It is possible that arguments such as the above will be immediately met with the charge that they are not consistent in a purely legalistic sense. For example, it has been a firm position taken by some of the countries that if an agreement cannot be verified technically, it is not worth entering into. Good management of nuclear werapons in the nuclear-weapon states cannot be verified without revealing certain military secrets to an international body. Some states may contend that any disarmament agreement entered into between nuclear-weapon states is a matter for themselves and does not concern the non-nuclear-weapon states. Hopefully, nuclear-weapon states would not seriously resort to such arguments because it would be taken as an admission that their own national interests are more important than the principles of the NPT.

On the other hand, what has been discussed in this chapter is no longer the absolute pre-conditions for Japan's ratification of the treaty. Sufficient progress has been made in the area of safeguards to remove that major source of inequality in the treaty, while developments of the past three years have made Japan's evaluation of the significance of the treaty much easier. Moreover, items regarding procedural provisions of the treaty may be improved and clarified to make the NPT easier to accept. At least this is the position I have been taking in Japan, and it seems that more and more people are listening to this argument.

References

1. Holst, J. J., ed., *Security, Order and the Bomb* (Oslo, 1972).
2. Imai, R., *Nuclear Safeguards*, Adelphi papers No. 86 (London, International Institute for Strategic Studies, 1972).

6. Indian attitudes towards the NPT

K. SUBRAHMANYAM

Abstract

India objected to the Non-Proliferation Treaty on the grounds that it did not stop vertical proliferation, it was discriminatory in character and it did not create mutually balanced obligations for the nuclear and non-nuclear-weapon countries. The experience of the last five years has shown that the dangers of horizontal proliferation were greatly exaggerated while the implications of vertical proliferation to international security were generally underrated.

Some recent treaties between the USA and the USSR have lessened tension but not eliminated or even reduced substantially the incentive for vertical proliferation in the near future. The dangers to international peace and security arising from the stealing or unauthorized diversion of fissile material and weapons and their subsequent use by organized criminal gangs of the type already existing in advanced industrial countries have not been subjected to adequate discussion and scrutiny. There is also the grave danger that during mutinies and revolts in the armed forces of a nuclear-weapon state, these weapons could fall into the hands of dissident forces and the possibility of a government circumventing its own constitutional provisions to use the weapons secretly and without authorization.

There are major technological constraints on India going nuclear in the next 10 years. However, in the light of the foregoing considerations, India feels justified in continuing to abstain from the NPT.

The Indian objections to the Non-Proliferation Treaty were listed in a statement made by Ambassador Mohammed Azim Hussain of India at the 57th meeting of the First Committee of the United Nations on 14 May 1968. These objections were:

1. The treaty did not ensure the non-proliferation of nuclear weapons but only stopped the dissemination of weapons to non-nuclear-weapon states without imposing any curbs on the continued manufacture, stockpiling and sophistication of nuclear weapons by the existing nuclear-weapon states.

2. The treaty did not do away with the special status of superiority associated with power and prestige conferred on those powers which possessed nuclear weapons.

3. The treaty did not provide for a balance of obligations and responsibilities between the nuclear-weapon states and non-nuclear-weapon states. While all the obligations were imposed on non-nuclear-weapon states, the nuclear-weapon states had not accepted any.

4. The treaty did not constitute a step-by-step approach towards nuclear disarmament.

5. The treaty did not prohibit one nuclear-weapon state from assisting another nuclear-weapon state by providing technical aid.

6. The long period of a quarter of a century provided in article X of the treaty would appear to endorse and legitimize the present state of affairs and legalize, if not encourage, an unrestricted vertical proliferation by the present nuclear-weapon powers.

7. Article VI did not create a juridical obligation in regard to the cessation of nuclear-arms race at an early date.

8. The treaty imparted a false sense of security to the world.

9. The treaty was discriminatory in regard to the peaceful benefits of nuclear explosions.

10. The treaty was discriminatory in regard to the safeguards and controls which were all imposed on the non-nuclear-weapon states while none whatsoever were imposed on the nuclear-weapon states.

11. The security assurances to the non-nuclear-weapon states could not be a *quid pro quo* for the acceptance of the treaty. This must be obligatory for the nuclear-weapon states.

These objections to the NPT and the government's decision not to accede to the treaty received the near unanimous support of the people and the parliament of India.

It must be emphasized that the reservation of the option to manufacture nuclear weapons was not one of the official considerations. On 14 March 1968 as the Prime Minister explained India's difficulties in acceding to the treaty, she declared, "India has repeatedly announced that she is not making an atom bomb and that she is developing her atomic energy programme exclusively for peaceful purposes." On 24 April 1968 she reiterated this stand in the parliament.

In various subsequent pronouncements, the government spokesmen have taken the line that nuclear weapons are not militarily usable. Consequently, the government does not propose to begin the manufacture of nuclear weapons in the immediate future. In an interview given recently to Mr Hassenlin Heykal, Editor of *Al Ahram*, Cairo, the Prime Minister, while restating India's current decision not to make nuclear weapons, speculated on the possibility of it being compelled to go nuclear at a future date. [1] Once again, speaking at Toronto on 20 June 1973 the Prime Minister emphasized that India was not interested in becoming a power—major or minor—and certainly not a nuclear power. India has also supported the proposal for making the Indian Ocean a nuclear-free zone.

The stand of the Indian government on nuclear weapons flows logically from its decision to stay out of the NPT but at the same time not to manufacture nuclear weapons. The NPT itself, as Ambassador Hussain spelled out in his objections, gave a special status of superiority associated with power and prestige to those powers which possess nuclear weapons. To this extent, the NPT was, in fact, an incentive to proliferation. The Indian government's opposition to the use of nuclear weapons was therefore consistent with its objections to the NPT as constituting neither a contribution to the principle of non-proliferation, nor a step-by-step approach towards nuclear disarmament. Unfortunately, the logic of this stand has not been evident to most of the writers on non-proliferation who appear to be more interested in freezing the status-quo in regard to the current international power distribution than in nuclear disarmament. To them, the refusal of India to sign the NPT only indicated an advocacy of nuclear weapons. Hence, the large number of articles written about the likelihood of India exercising its nuclear option have all proved to be risky exercises in political astrology.

The majority of the people who welcomed India's abstention from the NPT, however, had the security aspect very much in mind. Almost all the political parties in India—with the exception of certain sections of *Swatantra* and the ruling Congress Party, the Communist Party of India, and sections of the Communist Party of India (Marxist)—have expressed themselves in favour of India manufacturing nuclear weapons. An interesting analysis of the élite view was made in an opinion survey [2] carried out in Bombay, Calcutta, Delhi and Madras, which elicited the following response: sixty-nine per cent answered in the affirmative to the question on whether they would like India to develop a nuclear capability for defence; 53 per cent stated that they were in favour of this even if it meant an increase in the tax burden but 54 per cent were against India developing nuclear weapons if it meant a drastic cut in development expenditure. It was found that the higher the level of education of the respondents, the more favourable was the response for India acquiring nuclear weapons.

The problem of horizontal nuclear proliferation does not appear to cause any great concern in the Indian mind. The publication of a joint study prepared by the United Nations Associations of the United States and the Soviet Union, *Safeguarding the Atom,* evoked very critical comments in the Indian press. The line taken by the two national dailies, the *Hindustan Times* and the *Statesman* in their editorials, and a third paper, the *Times of India,* in a report from its Washington correspondent, was that the dangers of proliferation were vastly exaggerated and the main issue today was for the major powers to reduce their nuclear armaments.

Editorial comments on the Strategic Arms Limitation Treaty were also not very enthusiastic but they did take note of the fact that the Moscow declaration on the principles governing the bilateral relations between the two countries was a contribution of the spirit of détente and lessened the probability of a nuclear war. Similarly, the US-Soviet agreement on prevention of the outbreak of nuclear war was considered to contribute to a reduction in tension although the implications of such an agreement for third world countries were not clear and there were anxious speculations about its likely adverse impact.

SALT, however, was not a fulfilment of the obligations undertaken by the nuclear powers in article VI of the NPT. In fact, the conclusion of SALT indicated that the USA and USSR had not reached a point where they were willing to initiate meaningful steps in this direction. In India the same objections were raised in regard to SALT as were done to the so-called non-proliferation treaty.

1. The treaty does not ensure the non-proliferation of nuclear warheads. On the contrary, there appears to be a significant race between the USA and the USSR to add to their stockpiles of nuclear warheads. It also does not impose any curbs on continued R&D to increase the sophistication of warheads.

2. The treaty confers very special status on the USA and the USSR. In fact, the negotiations conducted exclusively between them which highlight their special status as possessors of vast nuclear arsenals, would tend to show that while the NPT was an attempt to confer a special status on the five nuclear powers, SALT was trying to establish the extra special status of two of these powers.

3. SALT, which provided an opportunity for these two powers to enter into an agreement of "no first strike" and thereby accept obligations commensurate with their power, had not come out with any such declaration.

4. SALT did not appear to constitute an approach towards nuclear disarmament since there was no reversal of the direction of the arms race. It was, by and large, an agreement on the limitation of only certain categories of launcher.

5. While the NPT attempted to freeze the *status quo* by providing for a quarter of a century duration of the treaty, SALT is to last for a very limited time. This indicated that while the nuclear powers were keen to establish their own pre-eminence *vis-à-vis* non-nuclear-powers on a long-term basis, the USA and the USSR were not willing to trust each other in regard to limitation of launchers.

SALT has been accompanied by attempts to intensify the qualitative aspects of the arms race such as the Trident submarines and B-1 bomber programmes, and so on. The pronouncements of some US officials in regard to new weapon programmes as well as the caveat of the US Congress in regard to future arms control agreements, are indicative of the fact that there has been no willingness to change the direction of the arms race.

This behaviour pattern must also be linked up with the differentiated attitude of the USA towards China and Japan in recent times. In 1954, the US Assistant Secretary of State, Walter Robertson, declared that it was the policy of the US government to adopt such a posture in Asia as to break up the communist régime in China. Richard Nixon was the Vice President of that administration. The United States threatened China with nuclear weapons in 1953 and 1958, and Quemoy and Matsu were declared vital to US interests. But in 1972 Taiwan was quietly abandoned and President Nixon became solicitous about China's "legitimate interests" in South Asia. Herbert Klein, the presidential aide, pointed out that 800 million Chinese armed with nuclear weapons could not be ignored. That is quite correct; 800 million Chinese could be ignored, as they were all these years, but not after 15 nuclear blasts at Lopnor and two earth satellites.

This sensitiveness towards China may be contrasted with the "Nixon shocks" administered to Japan. As an economic power, Japan is third in the world rating. The implications of this differentiated behaviour have not been lost on the Japanese. Kiichi Miyazawa, a former Japanese Minister for International Trade, has referred to the possibility of Japan's future generation considering the nuclear-weapon option if his country were being pushed around as he thought it currently was. [3]

The role of the NPT will have to be examined afresh in the light of the developments in the last five years. Although some of the countries have either not subscribed to the treaty or after subscribing to it have not subsequently ratified it, there has been no further horizontal proliferation or even threat of it. In fact, after the decisions taken by France and China in the middle 1950s, no country appears to have taken a decision to exercise its option to acquire nuclear weapons. However, in the last five years, the five nuclear-weapon powers have conducted more tests, added significantly to their nuclear stockpiles and also stepped up their R&D outlays on more sophisticated weaponry. There is not much evidence to show that the threat of horizontal proliferation was ever more than a smoke screen to draw attention away from the real issue of vertical proliferation which is still going on. Not even a small fraction of the attention devoted to the non-issue of horizontal proliferation has been paid to the real dangers arising out of the nuclear arsenals of the big powers and the fissile materials produced in the unsafeguarded installations of the five nuclear-weapon powers. This peculiar situation lends credence to the hypothesis that most of the discussions in regard to horizontal proliferation are red herrings designed mainly to serve the interests of the nuclear powers of the world. The problem of threats to international security arising from the weapon stockpiles of the nuclear-weapon powers and the continued production of fissile material will have an important bearing on the future decisions of the non-nuclear-weapon countries to exercise their nuclear options.

From time to time officials in the United States have added to the fears of non-nuclear-weapon countries by taking ambiguous stands in regard to nuclear weapons. The most recent instance was the testimony of Deputy Defense Secretary, William Clements, at the time of his confirmation in January 1973 when he said that he would not rule out the possibility of the use of nuclear weapons in Viet-Nam. Commenting on the recent agreement on the prevention of outbreak of nuclear war, Dr Kissinger emphasized that it was not a "no first use" declaration. The agreement was meant to prevent the outbreak of nuclear war. If that failed there were no restrictions on the kind of weapons that would be resorted to, he clarified.

Such stands of US officials must be viewed against the pattern of the US behaviour evidenced by the readiness with which the administration has been resorting to violence on a magnitude unprecedented in history. The Viet-Nam war is a current instance where force was resorted to on a scale wholly disproportionate to the objectives to be obtained. Moreover, as is now widely known, certain constitutional processes were deliberately circumvented and a policy of misinformation was employed on a gigantic scale. In addition, chemicals and defoliants were used on a vast scale in defiance of international public opinion. While all these things happened over a period of eight years, the matter was not even brought up before the Security Council of the UN. The use of atomic weapons would constitute a use of force wholly disproportionate to the objectives but there is nothing to suggest that the US Administration would not do so if a decision is reached that such a course would yield benefits of policy. Neither the Security Council nor the General Assembly is likely to exhibit a greater degree of political courage than they have done during the eight years of the Viet-Nam war.

During the course of this war, one US commander, Lieutenant General Lavelle, resorted to bombing on his own in violation of the prescribed procedures of his country. The commander got away with it very lightly. Even as the war was coming to a close and a draft agreement had already been concluded, an unprecedented bombing campaign was unleashed by the USA to extract further concessions from the North Viet-Namese. It has been revealed that the US Air Force conducted more than 3600 sorties and dropped more than 110000 tons of bombs on neutral Cambodia during 1969 and 1970 by deliberately misleading Congress and falsifying records. This was done with the consent of the highest civilian authority in that country. There are no studies on the risks to the world community arising from a value system and a behaviour pattern of this type. No nation can be sure that assurances given about the constitutional procedures in regard to authorizing the use of nuclear weapons would be treated as more sacred than the constitutional procedures that were circumvened through the Tonkin Gulf resolution or in the clandestine bombing and subsequent intervention in Cambodia or in the continued bombing of that country. It is difficult for anyone to be certain that there is a failsafe system which effectively prevents subordinate commanders from using nuclear weapons on their own just as General Lavelle resorted to his own private bombing or those involved in authorizing the Cambodian bombing falsified records and information. Very rarely does one come across pleas for international safeguards against such real dangers instead of against dangers which are non-existent.

The United States will have 123 reactors producing 98 520 MW of power by 1978. In addition, it will have 130 research reactors. The diversion by pilferage of just .01 per cent of the fissile material produced in these reactors would be enough to produce many bombs. There are criminal organizations with adequate resources to imploy scientific personnel to do this. This is not an imaginary scenario; at the Pugwash meeting in 1972 the American scientists were reported to have discussed seriously the ways in which Mafia-type organizations could develop their own atomic weapons. [4] Professor Mason Willrich is reported to have pointed out that in the United States, nuclear materials are checked by a watchman only every four hours and when shipped by a truck, no guard is sent along with the material. [5–6] Mr Timothy Ingram drew attention to the dangers involved when an aircraft carrying fissile material was hijacked to Cuba. [7] The Soviet representative, Mr D. N. Kolesnikan, while telling the UN General Assembly's Legal Committee that future terrorists would be able to blackmail any government they chose, drew attention to hijackers of a US airliner who threatened to blow up a nuclear facility at Oak Ridge, Tennessee. [8] One may also visualize link-ups between organized crime in the USA and certain oil-rich countries interested in promoting terrorism. For the Lod airport massacre, Japanese terrorists were hired by Arab organizations.

Four of the nuclear-weapon powers are at present controlling 55 per cent of the world's research reactors and will be producing around 65 per cent of the world's nuclear power by 1978. Nevertheless, safeguards are not prescribed to these countries which already have the personnel with the necessary knowledge to assemble weapons but they are prescribed for others in the name of safeguarding the atom. Neither in terms of organized crime rate, political violence, nor executive abuse of power, can these nations claim to be any better than others. Still there are no attempts at safeguarding international peace and security from the dangers of the current weapon stockpiles of these nations or the fissile material produced by them.

Considerable literature has been produced speculating about the contingent risks arising out of nuclear weapons in the hands of Arabs and Israelis, Indians and Pakistanis, and so on, but there is no discussion regarding nuclear weapons in the hands of Black Panthers, Negro nationalists or the followers of a future Lin Piao. These and not the non-existent nuclear weapons of the underdeveloped countries are the real dangers to international peace and security.

Even as the declaration of basic principles of US-Soviet relations was being signed in Moscow in May 1972, the United States was intensifying its air war over Viet-Nam and mining North Viet-Namese ports in a new bid of escalation. It would, therefore, appear that this statement merely constituted a mutual reassurance between the USA and the USSR that they would not act against each other's interests; it did not involve the renunciation of use of force by big powers against small powers. It also implies that where the interest of one of them is directly, immediately and intimately involved, and the other has no direct stake in that area, the first power may decide to use force in whatever form or category, with the reasonable assurance that the other power will avoid situations capable of exacerbating their relations and will do its utmost to avoid military confrontations and to prevent the outbreak of nuclear war. Similar interpretation is possible in regard to the US-Soviet agreement on the prevention of the outbreak of nuclear war. As the two powers were concluding these agreements one of them was planning to introduce billions of dollars worth of arms and thousands of military advisers into one of the sensitive regions of the world.

The conduct of the United States in the Viet-Nam war and the agreements and the understandings reached between the United States and the Soviet Union and between the United States and China tend to indicate to the third world nations (who unlike the industrialized nations of Europe, North America and Japan do not constitute a high stake area for these powers) that they can no longer depend upon the general deterrence which operated under conditions of uncertainty in a world of two or three nuclear powers whose relationships were not mutually reassuring. In other words, the power which is more aggression-prone can always get away with the fruits of its aggression under the present situation. One does not of course look for such a perception in regard to the Moscow declaration or the Washington agreement in the industrialized parts of the world. Those countries, which are mostly preoccupied with their own problems, are not able to look at the problems of the third world countries dispassionately, but at the same time they are confident that they constitute a high enough stake to deter the USA and the USSR.

The successful nuclear threats—successful as perceived by the threatener as in the case of Eisenhower's threat to the Chinese in 1953 over the Korean negotiations and the American threat to China on Quemoy and Matsu in 1958—were conveyed in situations where a nuclear assymetry was involved and no deterrence could be exercised by the threatened power. Khruschev's threat over Berlin did not work since it was a threat to a power which could deter the USSR. The nuclear weapons were threatened only in a situation of assymetry. The history of poison gas and large-scale use of chemicals has shown that the use of these weapons occurred only when there was no fear of retaliation. The United States stopped talking in terms of rolling back communism once the Soviet Union had acquired an appropriate equation of nuclear weaponry. Similarly, the 800 million Chinese could be ignored only so long as they did not have nuclear weapons.

Therefore, the main threat today to international peace and security is that of the use of nuclear weapons by those powers which possess them. The Security Council resolution of 19 June 1968 is likely to be no more effective in deterring nuclear powers from employing nuclear weapons or threatening to use such weapons than the UN charter (which itself set up the Security Council) has been in bringing the United States to account for the war in Viet-Nam. If the resolution were meant seriously by the US administration, Mr William Clements could not have made the kind of statement he made before the US Senate, nor could Dr Kissinger clarify that the agreement to prevent outbreak of nuclear war does not necessarily imply a no-first-use declaration. In these circumstances, it is reasonable to take the view that the last five years have seen threats to international peace and security increasing, mostly due to the actions of the nuclear weapon powers—especially their interventionist proclivities.

The continued nuclear tests of the USA and the USSR in pursuance of their policies of vertical proliferation has led to atmospheric testing by France and China. The French do not have a vast, sparsely populated area, and have not so far conducted underground tests. Presumably, they and the Chinese continue with their atmospheric testing mainly for cost considerations. It is not going to be easy to persuade France and China to change their policies as long as the larger powers are engaged in sustained vertical proliferation. Even the British are thinking of making their own contribution to vertical proliferation through MIRV-ing their submarine-borne missiles.

As already pointed out, the nuclear-weapon powers keep nearly 65 per cent of the world fissile material output outside the safeguards. It should give some food for thought to the framers of the NPT to ask how they expect the nations producing 35 per cent of nuclear power to submit themselves continuously to safeguards when 65 per cent of the fissile material produced is exempt from inspection. It was obvious from the very beginning that this exemption from inspection was, in fact, a political concession extracted by the nuclear-weapon powers and was not necessary to safeguard the secrets of weapon fabrication. The weapon fabrication process could easily have been separated from the process of fissile material production and, in regard to the latter, all the nations of the world could have been treated alike. That this was not done in spite of demands for it, would tend to show that the nuclear-weapon powers were trying to derive unfair commercial advantages by exempting themselves from the operation of inspection and safeguards procedures. The offer by some of them to place some reactors under international control was only a public relations ploy.

It is clear from the above account that all the fears expressed by the Indian delegation in regard to the NPT have, unfortunately, materialized. In India today there is hardly any worthwhile opinion in favour of signing the treaty. This does not, however, mean that India is likely to exercise its weapon option in the near future. In recent times, in the case of the Biological Weapons Convention, Sweden, while making a declaration that it did not propose to manufacture such weapons, refused to accede to the convention as it felt it would be subject to a veto by the big powers because the procedures for verification and inspection had been brought under the jurisdiction of the Security Council. In other words, Sweden, like India in the case of the NPT, was staying out of the treaty to exert moral pressure on the big powers. India has however participated in the development of safeguards procedures. The Indian objection was mainly against the unequal nature of the treaty and the misuse of international public opinion to subserve a policy of vertical proliferation by a few powers and obfuscation of the dangers of nuclear first use. In India's view this was not a non-proliferation treaty but a measure designed to disarm the unarmed.

Though in terms of both production and research reactor capabilities India ranked fairly low, the attempts to mislead persist. India is still in need of foreign technical assistance for its Rana Pratap Sagar stage-II reactor. Much more than in any other country, in India there has been repeated emphasis on the military non-usability of nuclear weapons (the latest view is that of Field Marshal Manekshaw). [9] The technological infrastructure necessary for undertaking a sustained nuclear weapon programme is yet to be developed in communication technology, radars, computers and delivery systems. When China began development of a nuclear weapon programme these technologies were immediately given very high priority and an allocation of appropriate resources. There are no signs of any such efforts in India. The 10-year Sarabhai programme put forward in 1970, if it had been carried through according to schedule, might have given India the necessary capability at the end of the period but it is now believed to be about three to four years behind schedule in nuclear power development, R&D and space technology. In fact, the budget allocations for the Atomic Energy Department (AED) for 1973–74 have been reduced from the previous year. The rate of induction of scientific personnel into the department is hardly 100 per year on an average. Under these circumstances, it is obvious that the chances of India exercising its nuclear option before the midldle of the 1980s, if at all, are not very high.

Often there are references in India to the option of conducting peaceful nuclear explosions. The pronouncements of the official spokesmen, while reiterating the option, have not committed the government to any firm course of action. Already there are reports of Canadian unhappiness about India remaining outside the NPT and its consequential impact on future Canadian technical assistance to the Indian nuclear programme. There appears to be little probability of India resorting to peaceful underground nuclear explosions before it makes significant headway with the fast breeder programme for which it depends on foreign assistance. Given the delayed schedule in the AED's Sarahbai plan of 1970 and its continued reliance on foreign collaboration, it is unlikely there will be pressure from the AEC itself for an underground nuclear explosion.

The Indian government's stand is to a large extent governed by the objective considerations of technological constraints in developing a balanced programme at the current stage of the country's development. The government has repeatedly pointed out that a nuclear explosion or two would not make for credible weapon capability. Hence it appears to have adopted the following strategy: at this stage it would discount the military usability of the weapons as the Soviet Union and China did during their periods of weakness. It would campaign vigorously for general disarmament and in particular for genuine nuclear disarmament and at the same time oppose such measures of doubtful validity as the so-called non-proliferation treaty. Meanwhile it would develop its technology, both nuclear and conventional, and ensure its security through various other measures. If over the next decade or so there is no real progres in disarmament, India may be compelled to exercise the weapon option. Prime Minister Indira Gandhi's remarks to Haykal have to be understood against this background. In fact, by continuing to stay out of the NPT, India continues to generate pressure for a real non-proliferation treaty which can be achieved only when the five nuclear-weapon powers agree to reverse the vertical proliferation and submit to international safeguards and supervision. This is only a hypothesis in that the Indian government has not spelled out its policy, but no other hypothesis fits in with all the government's pronouncements and actions.

The analyses of this problem carried out in the western world, including some of the prestigious international organizations, are extremely superficial. For if the existence of nuclear reactors alone is indicative of a weapon capability, and non-accession to the treaty indicates intentions to manufacture nuclear weapons, then on a logical extrapolation one must argue that a vertical proliferation is proof enough of the intentions of the USA and USSR to conquer the whole world or to destroy it. This superficiality of analysis was equally evident in the exaggeration of the threat from the Soviet Union in the early 1950s, the inflated accounts of the extent and magnitude of the Chinese weapon programme in the middle and late 1960s, and prophesies of runaway proliferation put out in the 1960s. Some of these institutions are extremely realistic and even overly critical when it comes to an analysis of India's performance in the production of conventional weaponry. But for reasons which can only be guessed, they become extremely optimistic and superficial when India's nuclear development plans are involved.

To adapt a statement of Mrs Alva Myrdal, the last 25 years constitute a history of wilfully squandered opportunities to carry out disarmament. In the case of the NPT, according to her, the major powers accepted not one iota of sacrifice of present or future nuclear weapon capabilities. She questions the value of the NPT as an instrument to bring about nuclear disarmament and feels that a number of so-called international disarmament treaties such as the Outer Space treaty and the Sea-bed treaty, are being used to turn away criticism of these big powers in the United Nations. She has pointed out that over a period of time the arms race has resulted in an incredible widening of the gap between the big powers and the rest of the world. This split into two discontinuous categories—big powers and other nations—has not only become more apparent in the disarmament negotiations, it has been made even more bluntly manifest by a conscious design on the part of the USA and the USSR. The best example of this is the NPT. This is the verdict of a person who has struggled hard over many years to bring this treaty about. [10]

It is time for all of us to clearly recognize how cleverly world opinion has been manipulated to bring about this treaty and how this manipulation continues. By turning away from the real problem of the dangers of nuclear proliferation in the five nuclear-weapon countries and misdirecting the attention to relatively less important issues, the world has been deliberately lulled into a sense of false security in regard to threats arising from nuclear weapons. Today the problems facing mankind are to find effective ways and means of reducing the existing stockpiles of nuclear weapons and to avoid searching for solutions to non-existent problems.

References

1. *The Patriot*, New Delhi, 31 March 1973.
2. *Indian Express*, Delhi, 14 August 1970.
3. *Newsweek*, 1 January 1973.
4. Zorza, Victor, "Hijackers and Nuclear Terrorism", *Statesman*, Vol. CVVXII-2526, 23 November 1972.
5. *International Herald Tribune*, Paris, 16 November 1972.
6. Anderson, Jack, "Dangers of Possible Nuclear Thefts", *Statesman*, Vol. CVVXIII-2363, 4 August 1973.
7. *Mainichi Daily News*, Tokyo, 3 January 1973.
8. *Times of India*, Bombay, 19 November 1972.
9. *The Guardian*, London, 10 February 1973.
10. Myrdal, Alva, "The Game of Disarmament", *Impact of Science on Society*, Vol. XXII, No. 3, July–September 1972, pp. 218–30.

7. Israel's attitude towards the NPT

S. FLAPAN

Abstract

Israel is the focus of concern for interested parties in the NPT because it is developing nuclear power in a troubled area of the world. Lack of concern and the taciturnity of the Israeli government make outside estimates of the country's nuclear capability rather speculative; however, evidence points to spectacular growth due to French assistance.

During the 1950s, an Israeli movement developed in favour of a peace option and neutralization but, until 1966, a deterrence doctrine similar to that of France was officially accepted. Under pressure, the Israeli government then shifted control of the nuclear programme away from the military.

In their distaste for a nuclear Israel, US presidents Kennedy and Johnson sought to bolster its security by conventional means conditional upon Israel's renunciation of a nuclear arsenal. Peaceful uses of atomic power were to be developed if Israel agreed to the restraining influence of US participation in its nuclear programme.

The June 1967 war heightened the explosiveness of the situation, pointing up Israel's overall advantages which, contrary to expectations, have continued to increase. Terrorism and the arms race have worsened, while Israel's occupation of Arab territories and psychological warfare have sown deep fear and distrust in the Arab world.

Granting an Arab desire for a peaceful settlement and certain great power reassurances, it seems that Israel's accession to the NPT offers a constructive way out of the present impasse. Were the great powers to restrain from global competitive strategies in this sensitive area, it would greatly improve prospects for a just, permanent settlement.

I. Introduction

Although international interest in Israel's attitude towards the NPT is out of proportion to Israel's demographic and economic dimensions and to the size of its small, 24-megawatt reactor, it has some justification. Israel is a party to one of the most dangerous conflicts of our time which threatens international stability and peace in an area of particular importance to all the major states. In the absence of a solution to the Israeli-Arab conflict, the Middle East remains a powder keg. If this conflict were to reach nuclear dimensions there would be not only disaster for the peoples in the region but also grave consequences on a global scale.

Israeli public opinion, however, is not interested in the subject; the press does not deal with it, the political parties do not try to take a stand, the parliament does not debate it and the government tries to evade the issue and avoid a clear decision by using the argument that the problem is "under consideration".

Non-accession, which seems to increase Israel's bargaining power, has more advantages than precipitous signature. There are, undoubtedly, many important things to bargain for: US assistance, renewed Soviet recognition and guarantees against a renewed Arab war effort or against atomic blackmail by nuclear or near-nuclear powers supporting the Arabs.

The problem of nuclear energy was discussed in the 1960s when plans for desalting sea water on a large scale were seriously considered. At that time, however, the project emanated not from needs inherent in economic development, but as a by-product of a nuclear effort initiated because of defence and security problems. This gave rise to a sharp and prolonged controversy between the proponents and opponents of a nuclear option.

Today the problem of using nuclear energy in the Israeli economy is real. A project for the construction of four or five nuclear plants, of 400–600 megawatts each, for the production of electricity was submitted to the government two years ago by the Israeli Atomic Energy Commission (IAEC) and still awaits a decision. Such a decision cannot be made on economic grounds alone. All other aspects of the problem, the technological-military, as well as the regional and international implications, will have to be reviewed and considered.

It is impossible to predict the attitudes and the outcome of the debate when it reopens but it is possible to have a glimpse into the future by shedding some light on the past. The people who make decisions today are the same people who shaped the course of events in the past. Of course, circumstances have changed but attitudes die hard; therefore, the following analysis, based on a reconstruction of circumstances that produced the nuclear effort in Israel in the 1960s, is relevant to the present.

II. *Israel's nuclear capability*

Israel's nuclear effort has been the subject of numerous reports and comments in the international press, serious studies by atomic experts and research institutes, and much conjecture and speculation. There are, however, no official statements or reports by the Israeli government or the Israeli Atomic Energy Commission on the nuclear programme, its budget, stages or targets. The Israeli government has also persistently refrained from commenting on the evaluation of Israeli nuclear capability by foreign experts who, on the whole, have a very high opinion of Israeli achievements.

According to George H. Quester, assistant professor of government at Harvard University:

After some years of French assistance . . . the Israeli program includes a reactor at Dimona which can produce five to seven megawatts of electrical power, or five to seven kilograms of plutonium (about enough for one bomb) a year . . . Israel is now approaching self-sufficiency in nuclear technology, perhaps capable of undertaking the construction of larger power reactors and of separation plants for reprocessing plutonium as well as more advanced projects. The assembly of fissionable materials into weapons is not beyond Israeli competence either, allowing a relatively small period to complete the basic research. It is only in the supply of uranium that Israel might remain for some time dependent on outside sources, although enough such material might yet be extracted from phosphates to support the Dimona reactor. [1]

Nearly all foreign experts have the same estimate of Israel's nuclear development. No one suggests that Israel has built a plant for the separation of plutonium or for the manufacturing of weapons. One expert, however, does not exclude the *possibility* of some separation capability at the laboratory level, [2] and another, of some clandestine separation facility. [3] This is, however, pure speculation not based on any evidence.

Professor Shimon Yiftach, a member of the Israeli Atomic Energy Commission and teacher at Haifa Technion, stated in a lecture entitled "Maariv" of 15 March 1973, that Israel is on the threshold of a revolution in the production of electrical power. Natural uranium will increasingly be replacing oil. As a result of this revolution, Israel is about to start a nuclear industry. The Israeli government is closer today than it has been in the last 10 years to a decision to order a nuclear reactor of 400–600 megawatts to generate electricity.

Since the planning and construction of a nuclear power reactor requires seven to eight years, nuclear power will make its entry into Israeli industry only at the end of this decade.

According to Professor Yiftach, Israel will have 10 nuclear reactors by the end of this century, of which four or five will be built in the next decade. Future reactors will use natural uranium extracted from phosphates. In his opinion, the reserves of phosphates in Israel amount to 220 million tons but they are poor in uranium. The maximum amount of extractable uranium is estimated to be 25 000 tons.

Professor Yiftach estimates the amount of extractable uranium as being 50–60 tons a year. "This quantity can serve to fuel three nuclear reactors, if the uranium is stored from now on."

He also made known the plan that the nuclear reactor in Nahal Sorek, which uses enriched uranium and natural water, will be increased from five to 10 megawatts.

There are at present in Israel 12 nuclear medical centres using radio-active material and six more are to be built in the future. Eighty per cent of the radioactive materials presently used in Israel are produced in the two nuclear reactors in Dimona and Nahal Sorek.

III. *The origins of the nuclear programme*

Background

The decision to build the 24-megawatt reactor in Dimona was made in 1957 after the war of Suez in October 1956, in which Israel, despite its military success in overrunning the whole of the Sinai and the Gaza Strip, was forced by United Nations, US and Soviet pressure to withdraw from all the territories conquered during the war without any political settlement or guarantees, except an assurance by the US state department and the stationing of a UN emergency force in Sharm-el-Sheikh and the Gaza Strip to guarantee Israeli shipping and prevent fedayeen border crossings.

Israel saw itself in a situation of political isolation and faced with a US embargo on arms supplies at a time when its Arab neighbours were rearming and building up a military potential at an accelerated rate with the help of the Soviet Union.

The only source of supply of military material and major weapons was France. A certain community of interests existed between Israel and France which brought the two countries into close political and military cooperation. France was facing a revolt in Algeria supported, morally and materially, by the United Arab Republic. Nasser was, in Israeli eyes, the archenemy trying to mobilize the Arab world for a total war against the Jewish state. The conception of a common enemy was predominant in Israeli and French policies. The close collaboration spilled over to scientific cooperation. The high level of Israeli scientists in physics and nuclear energy was an asset which the French, bent on developing their *force de frappe,* would not jeopardize. The Israelis, too, were not ready to forego the advantages offered by this cooperation. These circumstances gave birth to the Dimona reactor, conceived, planned and executed together with the French. The clauses, commitments and objectives of this cooperation have not been made known until this very day.

Israeli defence doctrines

It is necessary, in this context, to mention the strategic concepts of the Israeli policy makers and their perception of future developments in the Middle East. In the 1948 War of Independence, Israel achieved a costly victory over five Arab states which tried to prevent its establishment. Israel's casualties were 6000 killed and 15000 wounded, out of a population of 600000. This is comparable to a loss of 2000000 people killed and wounded in a nation the size of France or Britain.

Israeli leaders kept in mind that their victory was achieved, not only due to the heroism of a people determined to defend their sovereignty at whatever price, but also due to the lack of unity, common political objectives and military cooperation among the five Arab states which invaded Palestine.

Israel's political and military leaders were convinced, as were the Arabs, that in the course of time, the Arabs' quantitative superiority in manpower and economic resources would increase while Israel's qualitative superiority in education and technology would decrease. The spectre of an Arab world united by a charismatic leader speeding up the modernization of its economic, social and military potential haunted Israeli leaders from the very beginning. Their fears became intensified with the Nasser revolution in Egypt in 1954 and the failure of the Israeli-Anglo-French military intervention in Suez in 1956 which increased Nasser's stature as an undisputed leader of the Arab world.

In this context there have developed in Israel two schools of thought. The first was best characterized by Moshe Sharett, former foreign minister and prime minister of Israel:

. . . The *one approach* says that the only language the Arabs understand is force. The State of Israel is so tiny and so isolated . . . that if it does not increase its actual strength by a very high coefficient of demonstrated action, it will run into trouble. From time to time, the State of Israel must give unmistakable proof of its strength and show that it is able and ready to use force in a crushing and highly effective manner. If it does not give such proof, it will be engulfed and may even disappear from the face of the earth.

As far as peace is concerned—says this school of thought—it is doubtful in any event; whatever happens, it is very remote.

The second approach claimed that the question of peace must not be lost sight of and that retaliation against acts of sabotage and infiltration should be curbed so as not to allow an escalation of the conflict.

In the struggle for supremacy between these two doctrines, the proponents of the first, who fatalistically accepted· the continuation of the conflict, got the upper hand and determined Israel's policies until as late as 1963.

Within this school of thought there developed a strategic concept of military deterrent and interceptive war and as the only answers to Israel's defence problem. The length of borders disproportionate to the country's size and their proximity to population centres, created the danger that a sudden Arab attack could destroy Israel's industrial and communications centres, airfields and military bases; dismember the country, and demolish the cities. The strategy of deterrent and interceptive war was formulated by Yigal Alon (commander-in-chief of the Palmach and later many times minister of the Israeli government and its deputy prime minister today) in his book *Curtain of Sand*. [4]

Yigal Alon, however, did not conceive of the nuclear deterrent, and he insisted on keeping intact a peace option, to be accomplished by the neutralization of the Middle East and a pact of nonaggression between Israel and the Arab states to eliminate the danger of a suprise attack.

The strategy of deterrent and interceptive war was differently interpreted by Shimon Peres, Moshe Dayan and David Ben Gurion, the major architects of the Israeli-French alliance before, during and after the Suez crisis in 1956. The concept of a military alliance with France led to the adoption of the French strategic doctrine that a nuclear deterrent is the only solution to offset an inferiority in manpower and conventional weapons.

The decision

In 1957 the Israeli cabinet approved a proposal by Ben Gurion, then prime minister and minister of defence, to build a 24-megawatt nuclear reactor in Dimona. [5] The general public was kept in total ignorance of the decision until Ben Gurion disclosed it in the Knesset (Parliament) on 21 December 1960 in response to a request by US Secretary of State Christian Herter to clarify the rumours that Israel was building a plutonium producing reactor that would enable it to produce atomic weapons. Ben Gurion categorically denied the rumours that Israel was producing an atomic bomb; he stated that the Dimona reactor would serve the needs of industry, agriculture and health, and would train scientists and technicians for the future construction of nuclear power stations. This statement did not dispel the rumours in the West, nor calm the anxieties concerning the repercussions of the Israeli atomic enterprise on Arab countries. [6]

Neither did they dispel certain doubts and anxieties in Israel, which intensified when the news leaked to the public that six of the seven members of the IAEC, nominated by the minister of defence in 1952, had resigned because of their disagreement with the work of the commission, leaving only its chairman, Professor E. D. Bergmann, in charge of the nuclear programme. [7]

The doubts led to the formation, at the end of 1961, of the Committee for the Denuclearization of the Israeli-Arab Conflict. The committee was formed by prominent scholars and scientists who were well informed on Israel's political and security problems, having maintained close contacts with cabinet ministers and leaders of major political parties. Two members of the committee were scientists who had resigned from the IAEC. [7] The committee believed the search for a nuclear option to be a fundamen-

276

tal mistake from every point of view. It demanded that Israel announce a plan for the denuclearization of the Israeli-Arab region.

The committee's efforts were met with a great deal of sympathy. Some of the leading members of the major political parties, both the government coalition and the opposition, expressed their support for the idea; one coalition party, Mapam, adopted as its official position the programme for denuclearization of the Middle East with international guarantees.

In April 1962 the committee published the following demands:

1. That the Middle East countries refrain from military nuclear production, if possible by mutual agreement.
2. That the UN be requested to supervise the region in order to prevent military nuclear production.
3. That the countries of the Middle East avoid obtaining nuclear arms from other countries.

The call was signed by 17 prominent scholars and scientists, among them two former members of the IAEC (Professor P. Olendorf of the Haifa Technion and Professor S. Sambursky of the Hebrew University).

MK (Member of Knesset) Zalman S. Abramaov of the Gahal Party leadership, took issue with the Israeli government rejection of the proposal by Swedish Prime Minister Tage Erlander that the non-nuclear countries abstain from producing nuclear weapons. [8]

In a Knesset debate, MK Hazan, leader of the Mapam, called for an Israeli initiative to prevent the introduction of nuclear weapons into the Middle East. The government rejected all plans for a nuclear-free zone as irrelevant to the real threat originating from the conventional arms race.

There are no nuclear weapons in the Middle East and Israel will never be the first to introduce them. But Israel can be destroyed by conventional weapons and therefore the stress should be laid on conventional disarmament in the world and in the region.

This official position was reiterated again and again.

Ben Gurion's nuclear option policy caused growing strain in Israeli-US relations. On the other hand, the tendency for closer cooperation with France and Germany, both interested in the promotion of Israeli nuclear research for reasons of their own, met with growing dissent within the Labour Party (Mapai), the Government, the Knesset, and from the public who violently opposed closer diplomatic, economic and military relations with Germany.[1]

In June 1963, Ben Gurion finally resigned from the government which he had headed as prime minister and minister of defence since 1948 (with only a small break in 1954).

His successor, the late Levi Eshkol, also did not accept the plan for a "nuclear-free Israeli-Arab region". However, under growing US pressure

[1] Relations with Germany caused two cabinet crises (1957 and 1959) in Israel.

and intensified criticism from within, Eshkol's position increasingly shifted away from a nuclear option policy. This was facilitated by a US agreement to direct sales of conventional arms to Israel, needed to counterbalance Soviet supplies to Egypt. Assured of the prospect of building a conventional deterrent, Eshkol agreed to freeze operations at the Dimona reactor at a certain level. He reserved, however, the right to continue research and training activities at the Dimona reactor and to re-examine the situation and the possibility of exercising the nuclear option if and when conventional arms supplies would fall below the quantity and quality required to successfully confront Egypt in the arms race or in an eventual military confrontation. [5]

The change in Israel's nuclear policy reached its climax in April 1966 when Professor E. D. Bergmann was ousted as chairman of the IAEC (from which all other members had *previously* resigned, following the controversy over the type of reactor to be created in Dimona). The IAEC was entirely reformed and transferred from the ministry of defence to the prime minister's office, with the prime minister himself taking over the chairmanship. The composition of the new IAEC clearly indicated the shift from military to civilian priorities. The new IAEC included, in addition to nuclear scientists, researchers and managers from all fields in which nuclear energy could be applied: the National Water Authority, the Israeli Electric Company, the petroleum industry, medical research, and agricultural sciences as well as representatives of the financial sector and of the treasury.

That a far-reaching decision—to freeze for the time being activities aimed at the production of nuclear weapons—had been taken by the Eshkol administration can be deduced also from the severe criticisms on the part of RAFI, the party of Ben Gurion, Peres and Dayan (of which Professor Bergmann was also a prominent member) and the right-wing opposition party, Gahal, which favoured the policy of obtaining a nuclear option.

IV. *The critical years*

The debate in Israel

The debate which started rather timidly, by the end of 1962 was gaining momentum as the Dimona reactor was reaching the point where a decision had to be made as to what to do with the fissionable material. Two camps had emerged, cutting across parties and loyalties: those in favour of and those against a nuclear deterrent. The arguments for a nuclear deterrent that were put forward could be summarized as follows:

1. The danger to Israel's existence does not stem from nuclear weapons, which the Arabs do not possess and are not likely to possess in the near future, but from a massive buildup of destructive weapons.

2. Israel cannot assure its security in a conventional arms race with the Arabs who outnumber Israelis in manpower and in economic resources and who have the benefit of massive support by the USSR.

3. In a conventinonal arms race Israel cannot utilize its qualitative advantage—that of a higher level of science and technology. The Arabs have access to the same sophisticated weapons available in the arsenals of the great powers.

4. A nuclear option allows Israel to fully exploit its qualitative advantage and to create an absolute deterrent which will abolish the threat emanating from an Arab conventional buildup and will ultimately lead the Arabs to renounce all plans of a military confrontation, and to agree to a peace settlement.

5. Even in the eventuality of the Arabs developing a nuclear option of their own or obtaining nuclear weapons from a great power, a balance of terror will be established in the Middle East, making a new conventional war impossible.

6. In any case, the spread of nuclear technology is inevitable, as is the spread of nuclear weapons—despite man's yearning for peace and disarmament. The sooner Israel absorbs the new technology, the better the needs of its security and economic development will be served.

7. Until the Arabs reach the nuclear level, Israel's nuclear deterrent will prevent a new war, strengthen Israel beyond danger and perhaps even coerce the Arabs into peace.

The last argument was not stressed and not often resorted to—as it was too cynical to a people who, having experienced the Nazi holocaust, felt a moral abhorrence for weapons of mass extermination. These could be justified only if the very survival of the Jewish people were at stake. The possibility of such a contingency was made credible by the Arabs themselves, whose propaganda for the "destruction of the Jewish State" led the Israelis to overestimate external threats and over-react to alleged dangers.

Arab reactions to the Israeli nuclear effort facilitated its justification. In an attempt to reassure domestic opinion, the Arab press gave exaggerated publicity to their own nuclear designs, without distinguishing between blueprints and their execution, wishful thinking and reality. Thus, proponents of the Israeli nuclear deterrent could point to an Arab nuclear threat which no Israeli, unable to know if it was imaginary or real, could ignore.

The Israeli press gave much publicity to the two-megawatt reactor in Inchass built by the Soviet Union, the nuclear cooperation of Egypt with India and Yugoslavia, the numerous foreign scientists working in Egypt and a 150-megawatt reactor ordered by the Egyptian government from a British firm in 1963, to be built west of Alexandria.

MK Moshe Carmel, former minister of transport, stated that Egypt operates "two reactors certainly not for peaceful purposes". [9] He was not aware of the fact that the second Egyptian reactor had never been built.

Extensive coverage was given to Nasser's efforts to obtain nuclear facilities from the USSR and to build, with the help of India, warheads filled with radioactive debris which, even carried by missiles without a guidance system, could contaminate densely populated areas. [10]

When in May 1965, it became known that with the exit of German scientists, Egypt had been left with a costly but half-finished supersonic aircraft engine and that the cooperation with India had brought little progress, there were reports of forthcoming collaboration with China. "It seems possible", wrote the *Jerusalem Post,* "that the UAR would turn to China . . . for aid and advice in developing nuclear capacity". [11]

The arguments advanced by the opponents of the nuclear option not only dealt with strategic and defence problems, but also embraced the moral, political and economic aspects as well. Their starting point was that the Jewish people, a victim of mass annihilation, had a primordial interest in preventing the drift of humanity into an atomic holocaust and the degeneration of the Israeli-Arab conflict into a war of mutual destruction.

They neither ignored nor underestimated the dangers stemming from a conventional arms race but they believed that as long as a war was limited to conventional weapons, the emergence of trends towards moderation and realism in the Arab world would still be possible. Moreover, the qualitative advantages of Israel—social cohesion and organization, and education and technical skills—could be brought to play only in a conventional war fought by men.

The Arabs are gradually recognizing their inability to defeat Israel in a conventional war. Atomic weapons bought or built with the help of foreign technicians, might revive Arab hopes of destroying Israel in a pushbutton missile war. The possession of an atomic bomb by Israel (or by an Arab country) would produce only a short-lived advantage. Instead of acting as a deterrent, it would stimulate the adversary into an effort not only to equalize but also to obtain or produce more destructive weapons.

The balance of terror is valid least of all in the Middle East. The short distances make delivery a simple matter and warning systems inefficient. The margin of time left for preparations or interception or retaliation measures is minimal, almost nothing. Moreover, both in Egypt and Israel, the major part of the population, the centres of industry and national life are concentrated in very small areas easily destructible by a first strike.

In the absence of a hot-line to clear up misleading incidents or wrong intelligence, in an atmosphere of deep suspicion and fear, the probability is that nuclear weapons would not deter and stabilize but would tempt their possessors to strike. The danger of the USSR and China supplying nuclear weapons to the Arabs can be met by doing everything possible so that these two powers, or others, would have no reason, excuse, nor interest in doing so. This requires a policy of nonparticipation in the great power rivalry and of neutralization of the Middle East. Israel and the Arabs will lose nothing by delaying the introduction of nuclear technology until a later time when it could be done under auspicious political circumstances and when it could become a lever for peaceful development rather than a means of destruction.

The controversy with the USA

From the very beginning the USA took a serious veiw of Israel's nuclear initiative, expressed grave concern about the introduction of nuclear weapons into the Middle East and exerted heavy pressure on Israel to renounce any such intent.

The reiterated statements by Israeli spokesmen that the reactor would only serve peaceful purposes did not in the least alleviate US suspicions. The demand for verification through inspection by US experts grew stronger, in particular after John F. Kennedy became president in January 1961.

In a meeting with President Kennedy, arranged in May 1961 in New York, during Ben Gurion's private visit to the USA, the Israeli prime minister had to accede to the demand that US scientists be allowed to visit the reactor. Two such visits took place before Ben Gurion resigned in 1963. President Johnson, who took office the same year, continued the pressure of his predecessor. The first step towards an agreement was made in a meeting between Johnson and the new prime minister, Levi Eshkol, who was officially received in Washington in May 1964.

Johnson was reassured that Israel did not plan the separation of plutonium and the manufacture of weapons. A system of regular visits by US experts was agreed upon. Another outcome of this meeting was the sale of Hawk missiles to Israel—the first official and direct sale of US arms to Israel. This was later to become the pattern for a compromise on a problem which divides Israel and the USA until this very day.

In June 1965 the so-called Kennedy bomb exploded. Seemingly alerted by the report of Roswell I. Gilpatrick, chairman of a special committee to study the spread of nuclear weapons in the Middle East and Asia, Senator Robert Kennedy rose in the Senate to declare: "The need to halt the spread of nuclear weapons must be the central priority of American policy." He cited Israel and India as having supplies of "weapon-grade fissionable material and [able to] fabricate an atomic device within a few months''. He proposed an immediate joint initiative with the Soviet Union to obtain a pledge from Israel and other nations that they would neither acquire nor develop nuclear weapons, in return for which the USA and the USSR would provide guarantees against nuclear aggression and black-mail. [12]

Israeli reaction was summarized in an editorial in the London *Jewish Observer:*

... the limited attempt to restrict proliferation in the Middle East may increase rather than lessen the danger of war . . . The threat comes from the acknowledged aim of Nasser . . . to destroy Israel . . . The halting of such nuclear development as exists would not change this situation for the better. It might, on the contrary, encourage aggression by conventional weapons. [12]

The unrelenting US pressure and Israeli resistance resulted in hard bar-gaining. Israel claimed that it would not introduce nuclear weapons but needed nuclear power for urgent development projects such as desalting sea water. [13]

Israel was asking for real assurances of its security as the price of non-nuclear status. US experts seemed, however, more worried. On 7 January 1966, the *New York Times* reported that Israel entered into a secret contract to purchase a large number of medium-range ballistic missiles developed in France. The purchase of these missiles, able to reach Egyptian targets from Israeli launching pads, was seen as indicative of an Israeli intention to develop atomic warheads. [14] This might explain Nasser's ef-fort to obtain nuclear facilities from the USSR. The Soviets refused but agreed to a guarantee of Soviet nuclear protection if Israel developed or obtained access to nuclear arms. [15] In February 1966, US government circles made it known that it was considering a plan to build atomic reac-tors for desalting sea water as a means of heading off a nuclear arms race in the Middle East. Aside from the economic benefits, the major strategic purpose would be to cut through the present atmosphere of suspicion and distrust on the nuclear issue and to establish an international inspection system for nuclear facilities in the Middle East. [16]

The US desalination project caused a sharp controversy in Israel. Econo-mic experts doubted the competitiveness of nuclear power desalting and claimed that other methods are cheaper. The supporters of a nuclear de-terrent rallied to oppose the plan on the grounds that the submission of the Israeli reactor to US supervision (which was understood to be a condi-tion for US aid) was an infringement on Israeli sovereignty.

On 7 March 1966, the US Department of the Interior published a report confirming the feasibility of a 1 250 thermal megawatt reactor in Israel which would generate 200 megawatts of saleable electricity and power for a desalting plant producing 100 000 000 gallons of water a day. Such a plant could be in operation by 1972 at a cost of $200 million. Shimon

Peres, former deputy defence minister, declared that he was opposed to seeking financial aid from the USA and that Israel should turn to France or raise the money itself. It seems that the whole issue was resolved with the announcement of Prime Minister Eshkol that he was about to start negotiations with the US president on the ways and means to implement the project. [17] There can be no doubt that the plan for a joint Israeli-US nuclear undertaking was based on a tacit agreement about Israeli nuclear policy in the near future, because two weeks later came news about the "resignation" of Professor E. D. Bergmann, Chairman of the IAEC, and the formation of a new committee headed by the prime minister himself.

Replying to a debate in the Knesset in May 1966, Eshkol rejected, as before, the idea of a nuclear-free zone in the Middle East but he nevertheless hinted that: "While regional disarmament seemed out of the question now some 'understanding' must be reached lest nuclear weapons be introduced in the area". [18] He referred to recent threats by Nasser that Egypt would launch a nuclear programme if Israel did not renounce its plan to produce atomic weapons.

In July 1966, US and Israeli officials signed an agreement to increase the supply of enriched uranium to the US-built research reactor in Nahal Rubin and to transfer the authority for inspection to the IAEA. The growing opposition to a nuclear dimension in the Israeli-Arab conflict was evidenced in a symposium, published by the Mapai theoretical organ "OT" in September 1966. Foreign Minister Abba Eban and Minister without Portfolio, I. Galili (Ahdut Avoda) favoured the idea of denuclearization of the Israeli-Arab territory. Minister of Health I. Brazilai (Mapam) supported the plan for a nuclear-free Middle East.

V. *The future*

Prognostications and realities

The June 1967 war put an end to the prospects of a détente and created a new explosive situation in the Middle East.

The Arab states, unable to regain their lost territories, either by force or by diplomacy, are suffering from deep frustration that could lead to military adventurism with all its grave consequences. The Palestinians, unable to pose a serious threat to Israel's existence, are managing to create, by means of terrorism, worldwide tensions which the international community finds increasingly difficult to bear. The Middle East is again the scene of a monstrous arms race.

In the search for a way out of this impasse it is worthwhile to examine the doctrines and policies which have determined the course of events. The basic assumption shared by both Israelis and Arabs, that time is working in favour of the Arabs, has been proven wrong. The quantitative Arab superiority has *not* increased in terms of population and economic development. On the contrary, Israel, due to large-scale immigration and rapid economic development stimulated by the fear of the growing gap, has managed to *decrease* its quantitative inferiority.

Even more important, the *qualitative gap* in technology, science, sophisticated industries, communication-media, qualified manpower, education and so on, has *not* been reduced, in spite of considerable achievements in the Arab states. The gap has increased on an amazing scale in favour of Israel. The situation is not likely to change in the near future even if the Arabs decide to devote all their natural, economic and human resources to development and modernization.

Israel's military capability, as compared with that of the Arab states, has also undergone a drastic change. To use military expenditure as a general indicator: in 1954 the ratio of military expenditure of the five Arab countries to that of Israel was 3.85 to 1 ($250 million as compared to $65 million spent by Israel). Ten years later, in 1963, this ratio was reduced to 2.78 to 1 ($750 million to $270 million). In 1969 the ratio was further reduced to 1.68 to 1 ($1 675 million to $1 000 million). In 1972 Israel's military expenditure exceeded for the first time that of its major adversary, Egypt.

The above figures do not represent the real relationship of capabilities, because Israel's military effort has been built up with the sole aim of confronting the Arab military potential, while a considerable portion of the Arab effort is tied up and concerned with inter-Arab conflicts or problems of internal security; for instance, the war in Yemen, the revolt of the Kurds in Iraq, the clashes between Syria and Jordan, the tensions between Jordan and the Palestinian guerillas and so on. In addition, the "total Arab military potential" has never been more than a statistical definition, because the disunity and the political conflicts and rivalries among the Arab states have not allowed any coordinated military strategy, despite the common hostility towards Israel and incessant efforts to concert the struggles against it.

The transition to peace requires the solution of many problems—the Palestinians, the refugees, the restitution of the occupied territories, security guarantees, Israeli shipping and so on. Even if all these problems are resolved to mutual satisfaction, there remains the problem of the arms race and the danger of its escalation to nuclear weapons which will make any peace treaty extremely weak.

We shall try in this connection to analyse the role that the nuclear factor has played in the past and its possible role in the future.

When dealing with the past, the starting point is the *psychological* impact of the problem, because what mattered was not Israel's real activities and intentions in the nuclear field, but what the Arabs believed them to be, and what the Israelis wanted them to believe. The policy pursued by the Israeli government was that of a psychological deterrent, of letting the Arabs be influenced by exaggerated news and speculation intensifying their fears and suspicions. It is worthwhile, therefore, to examine its efficacy.

We find that the proponents of the nuclear deterrant were wrong in their prognostications.

1. The nuclear ingredient added to the conflict a psychological dimension of deep distrust, fear and distorted images that reduced the prospect of reconciliation to a minimum and made peace efforts extremely difficult. It exacerbated relations to a degree in which all attempts to find a way out of the impasse were doomed to failure.

2. The nuclear deterrent did not deter, but instead stimulated and intensified the *conventional* arms race and its quantitative and qualitative escalation. Neither did it deter—if it did not precipitate—the outbreak of a new war. There is not a single piece of evidence to prove that Arab political and military behaviour before, during or after the war of 1967 was influenced to any degree by a consideration of an Israeli nuclear capability which the Arabs believe does exist.

3. The Arabs have not responded to Dimona by launching a crash nuclear programme of their own; nor have they obtained nuclear facilities from the USSR and China. A number of factors combined to impede the development of an Arab nuclear option: the inadequacy of Egypt's technological and scientific base; the shortage of financial resources; the reluctance of the USSR to engage in and to encourage a nuclear race in the Middle East; the inability or the unpreparedness of China, still in its infancy as a nuclear power, to play a major role in the Middle East; and what is perhaps most important, Egypt may have received a Soviet protection guarantee, to be put into effect if Israel were to use nuclear weapons, or a US reassurance that Israel would not do so. A Soviet guarantee and a US reassurance—however qualified—may have proved to be enough to *offset any deterrent-impact of a nuclear option that Israel might have developed.*

Eshkol's new nuclear policy enabled Israel to strengthen its *conventional military* potential with substantial quantities of sophisticated arms from the USA and opened the door to close collaboration with the White House. Thus, the *non-exercise* of a nuclear option created a *conventional deterrent.*

Nuclear deterrent scenarios

A nuclear deterrent is useless as regards the concrete security problems confronting Israel today and those that they are likely to confront in the future. It cannot deter the Palestinians from executing terrorist activities around the world. It would be ineffective against a guerilla or resistance movement in the occupied territories if they were to arise. It cannot be employed against border incidents and small-scale warfare should the Egyptians or the Syrians revert to the tactics of the war of attrition.

It cannot deter the Arabs from launching a large-scale nuclear programme for peaceful purposes under the auspices of the IAEA or a great power. The only possible scenario for the deployment of a nuclear deterrent would be in the case of heavy strategic bombing of Israeli cities and/or a massive invasion by Arab armies overpowering Israeli defence forces and threatening to crush the whole state structure and to annihilate its population. Such a contingency, however, is unlikely to arise in the foreseeable future.

Two analysts point to other scenarios in which the use of a nuclear deterrent seems plausible and logical. They, therefore, conclude that Israel has or will develop an option for this purpose.

Professor Fuad Jabber in his book *Israel and Nuclear Weapons,* [19] remarkable for its painstaking accuracy and full documentation, suggests that Israel needs a nuclear deterrent to coerce the Arabs into acceptance of the post-June 1967 *status quo.* His is the kind of analysis where all the details are correct and the overall picture wrong. The facts are selected and organized so as to prove an *a priori* assumption, namely, that Israel's fundamental aim is territorial expansion to provide *Lebensraum* for a large-scale immigration [20] and the stabilization of the territorial gains by imposing a peace settlement.

Israel is impelled to resort to a nuclear strategy because the Arab states are restoring their military capabilities qualitatively and quantitatively, and the Soviet presence deprives Israel of gaining a decisive advantage by means of conventional weapons. [21]

Unable to sustain the cost of the war of attrition in terms of lives and expenditure, and faced with the prospect that the war "will stretch on . . . indefinitely into the future with the ever present danger of a sudden escalation of uncertain outcome", Israel will have to adopt the strategy of nuclear deterrent to stabilize "the status quo which has become her pre-eminent objective". [21]

Jabber, despite his scientific mind and method, seems to have fallen prey to a demonological attitude in regard to Israel's aims. He attributes to Israel expansionist aims, disregarding entirely the passionate debates and struggles between hawks and doves that divide Israeli society, political parties and the government itself. A recent debate inside the ruling Labour Party has demonstrated that a 70 per cent majority favours the return of most of the occupied territories, precisely in order to *safeguard* the essential aim of Zionism to develop Israel as a Jewish and *democratic* state that does not rule and oppress another people. The events have not borne out Jabber's prediction that the war of attrition would inevitably force

286

Israel to use a nuclear ultimatum. The war of attrition was also too much for Egypt which had to agree to a ceasefire. Meanwhile the Soviets departed, the military balance changed in Israel's favour and nothing compelled Israel to take its nuclear option.

J. Bowyer-Ball, writing on "Israel's Nuclear Option", [22] offers a different theory, according to which, Israel should by now have a nuclear deterrent. He suggests that the real threat to Israel's security comes not from Arabs but from the Arab-Soviet alliance. The Soviet Union, not the Arab countries, has the capacity to enforce a solution based on territorial concessions which Israel is not ready to accept. Therefore, "an atomic capacity and the ability to deliver a punitive strike on Russia would consequently narrowly limit the extent to which Russia might be willing to threaten Israeli security". [23] "Southern Russia rather than Cairo is by far more likely a target in any ultimate crunch." [23]

To compel the USSR to show restraint in their pro-Arab engagement, writes Bell, "requires that Moscow accept the credibility of an Israeli nuclear weapons system, the capacity to deliver and the willingness if sufficiently threatened to do so". [23] Mr Bell's "theory" is an example of pseudo-strategic speculation based on a passing situation.

The short-lived Soviet military presence occurred in consequence of Israeli bombing deep in Egypt; the missiles and other installations set up during this period had a pronounced defensive character. The USSR consistently refrained from supplying Egypt with offensive weapons and becoming directly engaged in the conflict. Their pressure on Israel to accept UN Security Council resolution 242 was exercised by political, not military, means. Not only is it unlikely that a great power like the USSR with an impressive system of interception would be deterred by an Israeli nuclear threat but it is even less likely that Israel, who sees itself responsible for the future of three million Jews in Russia, would try to pose such a threat. Israeli policy, whatever its mistakes and fallacies, aims at the survival of the state and of the Jewish people, not at a new Masada.

Dangers, difficulties and prospects

The *status quo,* based not only on Israeli military superiority, but also on the occupation of Egyptian, Syrian and Jordanian territories and on the nonsolution of the Palestinian problem, is untenable for a long time. The danger of a new war lies precisely in attempting to perpetuate the *status quo.* Egypt and Syria may take recourse to military action not because they believe in its success but because they believe it would force the great powers to intervene and impose a settlement.

The Arab countries, unlike Israel, are not in urgent need of nuclear power. They possess nearly inexhaustible resources of oil, natural gas and hydroelectric power. They are still very far from exploiting all available

287

water reserves and, if desalting is necessary in certain areas, it can be done with cheap conventional fuel. In conditions of peace, a different timing in introducing nuclear energy into Israel and the Arab states respectively would not be a problem. In conditions of warfare, hate and suspicion, it is inconceivable that the Arab world would stand aloof while Israel rapidly developed nuclear power. The Arab world can afford nuclear power even if only for prestige. The events in the 1960s have demonstrated the impossibility of a balance of terror. Both peoples have shown themselves liable to fall prey to fears, war scares and obsessions, and unable to act rationally according to the rules of the game. Israel, though advanced in science, technology and political organization, has a people with traumatic experiences who are obsessed by a survival complex. It is enough to recall the affair of the German scientists in Egypt to see what can happen when this complex is revived.

Similarly the Arabs have a complex of historical grandeur which cannot bear an overdose of humiliation. The introduction of nuclear energy would cause great anxiety if an agreement to ban nuclear weapons and submit nuclear facilities to agreed international and, perhaps mutual, inspection were carried out without a peaceful settlement of the Israeli-Arab dispute. On the other hand, a nuclear agreement could largely facilitate the achievement of peace.

Israel's accession to the NPT could *open the way* to negotiations on an issue which is antagonizing Israeli-Arab relations to an unprecedented degree.

Israeli apprehensions and objections are justified; the hostility of one of the depositary governments, which broke off diplomatic relations with Israel, and of the majority of IAEC governors and officials; the danger of industrial and military espionage by officials friendly to the Arab cause; the absence of guarantees against the violation of NPT obligations by the Arabs aided by a nuclear power outside the NPT membership; the clandestine diversion of fissionable material from an NPT-inspected reactor to the production of weapons and so on. All these difficulties seem insurmountable in the context of the unresolved Israeli-Arab conflict. They can be removed with the advance to peace. The problems of the NPT and peace must be tackled simultaneously, because any step forward in the solution of one facilitates progress in a solution of the other. The interdependence of the two problems presents a major difficulty also within Israel. Israel's reluctance to sign the NPT originates in the past. The two strategic doctrines which fought for supremacy in the past are represented today in the government. The June 1967 war brought back RAFI into the Labour Party and into the government. The NPT problem has become a delicate subject also from the point of view of unity and cohesion in the largest political party in Israel.

The ouctome of the debate on peace, now taking place in the Israeli government within the political parties that form the government coalition, will have a decisive influence on Israel's attitude towards the NPT. On the other hand, Israel's decision concerning the terms and conditions for a peaceful settlement will depend to a very large extent on whether the USA and USSR reach an agreement on the Middle East. It is not enough that they have agreed on the non-proliferation of nuclear weapons in the Middle East. The USA and the USSR have avoided being dragged over the brink by their clients but they are engaged in a clash over the future conditions in the Middle East. Their differences have very little to do with the solution of the Israeli-Arab conflict; in fact US and Soviet peace proposals are very close to each other. The USSR does not support the Arab thesis regarding Israel's future and recognizes Israel's right to existence, security and sovereignty. The USA does not underwrite Israel's plans for annexation of occupied territories and aims at preserving US influence and interests in the Arab world. Both the USA and USSR envisage a settlement based on Security Council resolution 242. What divides them are their conceptions of the status and role of the Middle East in the solution of their global strategy problems. President Nixon has declared that the prevention of Soviet predominance in the Middle East is a "vital national interest of the USA". US politicians and strategists are haunted by the fear that Soviet expansion in the Middle East will result in the disintegration of NATO, the withdrawal of the USA from Europe, and Soviet control over Western Europe and the Persian Gulf. [24]

The Middle East and the Mediterranean basin represent zones vital to the security of the USSR. These global strategy differences explain a good deal of US and Soviet policies in the Middle East, both exploiting the Israeli-Arab conflict to further their aims. Unless these differences are resolved, there is not much chance for peace.

Israelis and Arabs alike were victims of the massive involvement of the great powers in the Middle East. The conflict would not have acquired such frightening dimensions without the arms race which, with the help of the great powers, has reached the threshold of nuclear weapons.

The wars of 1956 and 1967 would have been impossible without the direct participation of the two great powers in one and of the brinkmanship of the two others in the second. The peoples of the Middle East have nothing to lose and much to gain by extricating their problems from the great power conflict. All the great powers have changed partners in the Middle East more than once and adopted alternately all possible attitudes —pro-Israeli, pro-Arab and neutral—to further their own interests.

A neutralized, demilitarized and denuclearized Middle East will not harm the great powers and will only help them to advance the cause of peace and disarmament which they claim to be their aim, and which is an essential condition for the achievement of justice and security for both Arabs and Israelis.

References

1. Quester, G. H., "Israel and the Nuclear Non-Proliferation Treaty", *Bulletin of the Atomic Scientists*, June 1969, p. 7.
2. Beaton, L., *New Middle East*, April 1969, p. 9.
3. Bell, J. B., *The Middle East Journal*, Autumn 1972, p. 382.
4. Alon, Y., *Curtain of Sand* (Tel Aviv, Hakibutz Hameuhad, 1959).
5. Hodes, A., "The Implications of Israel's Nuclear Capability", *The Wiener Library Bulletin*, Vol. XXII, Autumn 1968.
6. *The Times*, London, 12 December 1960.
7. *Israel-Arab States, Atom-Armed or Atom-Free* (Tel Aviv, Amikam, 1963) [in Hebrew].
8. *New Outlook*, Vol. 5, No. 9, November–December 1962.
9. *Lamerhav*, Tel Aviv, 17 July 1962.
10. Salzburger, C. L., *New York Times*, quoted in *Ha'Aretz*, Tel Aviv, 24 November 1963.
11. *Jerusalem Post*, 6 June 1965.
12. *Jewish Observer*, London, 2 July 1965.
13. Alon, Y., *Jewish Observer*, London, 24 December 1965.
14. *New York Times*, 7 January 1966.
15. *New York Times*, 13 February, 1966.
16. *New York Times*, 28 February 1966.
17. *Yediot Ahronot*, Tel Aviv, 4 April 1966.
18. *New York Times*, 19 May 1966.
19. Jabber, F., *Israel and Nuclear Weapons* (London, Chattog Windus, 1971).
20. *Ibid.*, p. 109.
21. *Ibid.*, p. 120–21.
22. Bowyer-Ball, J., "Israel's Nuclear Option", *Middle East Journal*, Autumn 1972.
23. *Ibid.*, p. 386–87.
24. Rostow, E. V., *Peace in the Balance: the Future of American Foreign Policy* (New York, Simon and Schuster, 1972).

8. European security and the non-proliferation treaty

J. K. MIETTINEN

Abstract

The effects on the NPT of recent global and European political events and of possible military measures in Europe are reviewed.

The SALT negotiations meet to some extent the NPT obligations ". . . to pursue negotiations for . . . the cessation of nuclear arms race . . . and for nuclear disarmament . . .", but qualitative improvements and modernizations, especially the introduction of miniweapons, violate the spirit of the treaty.

The NPT's survival presupposes the halting of the vertical arms race, especially restraint from improving tactical nuclear weapons which are a more likely threat against small powers than strategic weapons are. It also presupposes reinforcement of the treaty by better guarantees to the non-nuclear-weapon parties regarding the non-use of these weapons against them.

I. *The non-proliferation treaty*

The Treaty on the Non-Proliferation of Nuclear Weapons (NPT) was adopted by the General Assembly of the United Nations on 12 June 1968, 10 years after its initial proposal. The primary purpose of the treaty is to prevent the spread of possession or "horizontal proliferation" of nuclear weapons, although it also provides for progress in preventing the nuclear arms race or "vertical proliferation". The treaty obligates those nations possessing nuclear weapons not to transfer them to any recipients whatsoever and it forbids non-nuclear-weapon states to acquire or manufacture nuclear weapons.

The final vote in the General Assembly was 95 in favour of adoption and 4 against, with 21 absentions. None of the four countries that voted negatively (Albania, Cuba, Tanzania, Zambia) and only two of those which abstained (Brazil and India) were "threshold powers". Of the remaining threshold powers, several had indicated during the debate that they would be in no hurry to ratify the treaty. Thus, support for the treaty was even less general than the vote would suggest and, for the first time in United Nations history, a resolution concerning disarmament sponsored by both the USA and the USSR failed to get unanimous support.

The treaty came into force on 5 March 1970, after 47 ratifications (40, including the depository governments—the UK, USA and USSR, were required). On 1 June 1973, there were 78 parties to the treaty and the five non-nuclear-weapon Euratom countries (Belgium, FR Germany, Italy, Luxembourg, and the Netherlands) were undertaking measures to ratify it after having signed the safeguards agreement with the IAEA on 5 April, 1973.

A number of militarily important and near-nuclear states, however, have not joined the treaty, and 28 which signed prior to 5 March 1970 have not as yet ratified it. Many of the latter are "threshold powers".

When the treaty came into force some speakers hailed it as "the most important arms control measure since the beginning of the nuclear age". However, such rhetoric must be considered both premature and overly optimistic since the NPT was considered by many of the non-nuclear-weapon states to be more of an early, temporary freeze to allow the nuclear powers more time for nuclear disarmament, than as a final state of affairs. These nations considered the NPT to be highly inequitable, since it "binds the hands of the powerless and licences those whose stockpiles threaten the very existence of the powerless to further accumulate armaments". In order to reduce this polarity, statements were included in the preamble of the treaty in which the parties:

declare their intention to achieve at the earliest possible date the cessation of the nuclear-arms race and to undertake effective measures in the direction of nuclear disarmament

and

desire to further the easing of international tension and the strengthening of trust between states in order to facilitate the cessation of the manufacture of nuclear weapons . . .

In addition, an article VI was included in the treaty which requires the parties "to pursue negotiations in good faith on effective measures relating to the cessation of the nuclear arms race at an early date and nuclear disarmament . . ." Related to this article is paragraph 3 of an article VIII, which provides for a review conference in Geneva five years after the treaty's entry into force, "with a view to assuring that the purposes of the Preamble and the provisions of the Treaty are being realized".

Since the five-year period will have lapsed on 5 March 1975, the decision concerning the reivew conference must be made by the General Assembly this autumn (1973). Therefore, it is timely to review now the extent to which the provisions of article VI have been realized. An attempt is therefore made to analyse:

292

(*a*) the significance of these disarmament and security provisions to the durability of the treaty;

(*b*) those aspects of possible military security arrangements in Europe which might have significance to the treaty;

(*c*) the presumed significance of nuclear weapons to the security of small- and medium-sized states;

(*d*) the technological and economic possibilities of these states acquiring nuclear weapons in the 1980s should the arms-control and security provisions of the treaty be unfulfilled by the nuclear-weapon states or should the treaty fail otherwise.

II. *Arms control and security provisions of the treaty and their realization*

How have the obligations of article VI "to pursue negotiations . . . to the cessation of the nuclear arms race . . ." been filled since the treaty came into force?

Although SALT I, signed in May 1972, defined only the upper limits t the numbers of offensive and defensive strategic nuclear weapons, and set these limits quite high (possibly higher than either side had intended) the conclusion of SALT I and the continuation of discussions for SALT II may at least be considered to meet the obligation "to pursue negotiations in good faith . . ." as cited above. Thus far, no qualitative restrictions have been achieved by SALT negotiations which have served to catalyze rather than inhibit the vertical arms race by licensing the qualitative improvements.

Both the USA and the USSR have been developing ABM and MIRV systems unheeded since the conclusion of the NPT in 1968. Unlimited underground nuclear testing also continues although "negotiations are pursued in good faith on its cessation" at the Conference of the Committee for Disarmament in Geneva (CCD). Thus, it may be said that the letter of the treaty (to negotiate) has been met in at least some respects. The strategic arms race continues, however, to violate the spirit of the treaty.

The progress of SALT has probably met the expectations of most realists. Few expected the NPT to halt the strategic arms race "at an early date". The question of strategic nuclear weapons is rather over the heads of the small powers since the development of such weapons would certainly be too great a task to be met by their own nuclear capability. Therefore, strategic nuclear developments that have occurred during the past three years probably do not jeopardize the treaty.

The main purpose of the premature conclusion of the treaty was to gain time. The conclusion was actually premature from the point of view of the non-nuclear-weapon states which would have liked more concrete provisions for the cessation of the nuclear arms race than article VI. However, the loss of time which necessarily would have resulted from such negotiations, might have jeopardized the chance to have a treaty, since this was the advent of the era of plutonium-producing power reactors. As was discussed later, the "peaceful" plutonium produced by such reactors is suitable only for the manufacture of small nuclear weapons, of the order of one kiloton or less. This fact was doubtlessly well-known to the nuclear powers, although it was not generally recognized by the non-nuclear powers at the time the treaty was signed. This is why the time factor was critical.

Whether the time gained by the premature conclusion of the treaty has or has not been abused by the nuclear states in terms of the further development and modernization of their tactical nuclear weapons may be decisive to the durability of the treaty. It is just this tactical nuclear threat that has caused anxiety among most small powers and it is just this threat that they might be able to meet, to some extent, through the development of their own nuclear weapons based upon the plutonium produced by power reactors. Modernization by the USA and USSR of their "tacknukes" would thus be in sharp contrast to the purpose and spirit of the NPT, if not actually against the letter of the treaty, which is practically ineffective regarding vertical proliferation by the nuclear powers.

In other considerations as well, the treaty has weaknesses. It has no definitions (for example, "control" and "jurisdiction" have not been defined), it contains no adequate security guarantees for non-nuclear-weapon states and it lacks a dispute clause. The NPT has been justly characterized as hardly more than a "framework for future negotiations". Therefore, the durability of the treaty will depend primarily upon the success of efforts to control the arms race of the nuclear-weapon states. Many of the non-nuclear states wished to include in the treaty certain specific measures controlling vertical proliferation, such as a comprehensive test ban and a freeze on the production of fissionable materials destined for use in weapons and on delivery systems. In fact, these were quite modest proposals since the USA and the USSR have already tested a very large number of warhead types (probably enough for almost any conceivable purpose) and since their stock of fissionable materials is already considerable due to the fact that many of the military reactors producing plutonium have either been shut down or run at a reduced rate during recent years. The USA vigorously opposed any such specific measures and maintained that their inclusion might cause too much delay.

An additional item requested by the non-nuclear-weapon states was a specific guarantee that would protect them from nuclear attack or blackmail by any nuclear-weapon state. However, no such guarantee was included in the treaty, primarily due to the opposition of the USA, which considered such specific guarantees as being "too difficult and complicated to be reduced to a treaty provision". Such guarantees, the USA asserted, "should be dealt with in the context of the UN". Even a straightforward statement, suggested by Premier Kosygin of the USSR in February 1966, in the form of a no-use guarantee by the nuclear states to the non-nuclear parties of the treaty was rejected. Outside the treaty, but related to it, the UN Security Council adopted security assurances sponsored by the three nuclear-weapon states party to the treaty. These were intended to provide a "new basis for responding to threats of aggression with nuclear weapons against non-nuclear parties to the treaty . . ." However, these assurances have very little practical significance since any such assurance must depend upon the definition of "aggression". As is well known, attempts to define "aggression" have been made for many years at the UN, but without result. To define the "threat of aggression" would be even more difficult. Such questions should be resolved by a vote of the Security Council. Such a vote would, of course, be subject to veto by any of the five permanent members. Since "aggression" or "threat of aggression" can presently be caused only by one of the five nuclear-weapon states, which now (since 1972) are the same as the five permanent members of the Council, it is clear that the threatening nation would not vote against itself, but would veto. The action of the Security Council would thus be automatically barred. Consequently, it is perfectly clear that such security assurances by the Security Council have no practical value. In this regard, the Council is little else than a forum for debate. The USA played a curious role in this matter. While its representative at the UN solemnly declared that these assurances "form a new basis", Secretary of State Dean Rusk assured the US Senate that the Security Council's resolution did *not* create any responsibility for the USA, "both as a matter of law and as a matter of policy", over and above that which the UN Charter already requests. Most expressly, the significance of the NPT to the USA was played down by President Nixon who, at a press conference on 8 December 1969 [1] was quoted as stating that the NPT is "basically peripheral" and that what really mattered was SALT since "here you have the basic security of the United States of America and the Soviet Union involved". To the basic security of the non-nuclear powers, however, the NPT is *not* "basically peripheral", since it renounces their legitimate right to acquire nuclear weapons for their defence without granting any realistic security guarantees in return.

III. *Effect of other provisions upon the durability of the treaty*

Article IV which guarantees to all parties the right to employ nuclear energy for peaceful purposes, and article V, the Plowshare provision, which guarantees to non-nuclear-weapon states the benefits resulting from peaceful nuclear explosions, are probably of little significance to the durability of the treaty, at least in the short run. Article IV is self-evident. Article V is intended to whet the appetite of the non-nuclear-weapon states, but any benefits to be derived from peaceful nuclear explosions appear to lie in the distant future.

One provision which may play a part in the durability of the treaty is the concept of "widest possible adherence". This remains to be seen, however, since two of the five nuclear powers have abstained and a large number of the signatories (28) have still not ratified the treaty three years after its coming into force. Perhaps 10 of the so-called threshold powers may be purposefully "keeping the nuclear option open". The fate of the treaty will depend greatly upon their behaviour during the next few years.

France, though not bound by the treaty, has promised to behave as if it were party to it. The strong protests against its nuclear tests in May 1973 and the conveyance of the matter to the International Court in The Hague are indications of an increasing intolerance on the part of some non-nuclear-weapon states to the continuation of the arms race.

China has solemnly promised never to be the first to utilize nuclear weapons. Nevertheless, some Asian states may consider themselves threatened by China's growing nuclear capability. The USA has repeatedly justified the deployment of its ABM system for precisely this reason. Such a justification is not very credible since the USA was able to withstand the much more formidable Soviet threat during the 1960s without ABM.

The following points will probably be decisive to the durability of the treaty:

(a) cessation of vertical proliferation, especially on the tactical nuclear level,

(b) further easing of international tension, and

(c) provisions of better security guarantees to the non-nuclear states.

On the other hand, the nuclear-weapon states could exert the strongest *negative* effect upon the durability of the treaty by modernizing their tactical nuclear weapons and, especially, by developing a new generation of them, the so-called miniweapons. This would be a direct abuse of the time-gain provided by the treaty which is aimed primarily at barring the non-nuclear parties from similar evolvement.

IV. *European security arrangements*

The year 1973 promises to become the year of European security arrangements. After many years of laborious preliminaries the first phase of the European Security Conference (ESC) is just beginning in Helsinki, while preparations are underway in Vienna for a conference on reduction of forces and armaments (RFA) or, as originally proposed by NATO, mutual and balanced force reductions (MBFR). For the East, the principal goal of the ESC will be the confirmation by agreement of the political *status quo* in Europe and the increase of East-West trade and technical collaboration. One of the main goals of the West is democratization and liberalization of the Eastern European peoples by "freer movement of men and ideas". Simultaneously, as this collaboration aids the technological progress of the Soviet Union and the Western European countries, it will detach the EEC from the USA. It is of the utmost importance to the USSR that the EEC not develop into a military block which would provide FR Germany with nuclear weapons. In any case, Anglo-French nuclear weapon sharing is not a likely occurrance since France has developed such weapons independently and is not going to submit itself to US nuclear hegemony. Britain has had access to US information and nuclear equipment under the McMahon Act which prevents it from sharing such aid with other nations without US consent. Some rationalized collaboration regarding the production of such non-nuclear parts of the nuclear-weapon systems as the hulls of nuclear submarines is possible, however, as is a joint programme of patrolling and perhaps even targeting. Although the Soviet Union would naturally oppose all this, such opposition would probably not be very vigorous. West German nuclear sharing, however, would be a very alarming development and would immediately alter the entire military balance in Central Europe. Such an event, however, appears impossible, at least under Brandt's foreign policy.

Regarding military matters, only the so-called confidence-building measures, such as notification of troop manoeuvres and exchange of military observers, are likely to be discussed at the ESC. Although it will not be directly concerned with military matters, the outcome of the ESC will exert an important influence upon the future of the NPT. A successful outcome will "further the easing of international tension and the strengthening of trust between states . . .", as expressed in the preamble of the NPT.

Military security in Europe may be considered to consist of the following three intimately interwoven factors:

(a) strategic nuclear deterrence,
(b) nuclear deterrence on the tactical (theatre) nuclear level, and
(c) conventional military forces and armaments.

Strategic nuclear deterrence is discussed at SALT and was briefly mentioned above, while the two remaining factors are matters for the RFA negotiations. Since the three factors affect each other, the RFA talks are likely to be very difficult. The outcome may be decisive for the future of the nuclear arms race and possibly for the NPT as well.

However "European" these conferences are, the confrontation of the

USA and the USSR is global and the European situation cannot be separated from the global strategic situation, especially the one in Asia. Therefore, it is useful to review briefly the global strategic condition, especially the relations of the Soviet Union and the USA with China. Without such background, it is impossible to understand the aims of these powers on the European scene.

V. *Implications of the global strategic situation for the European theatre*

The Soviet Union has been consistently promoting détente in Europe since the mid-1960s. The desire for peace is as authentic in the socialist states as it is in the other nations of Europe. The constantly worsening relations between the Soviet Union and China, however, as well as China's growing nuclear potential have no doubt also promoted this development. The Soviet Union does not want to be involved in a cold war in Europe should a hot one break out in the Far East. Nixon's recent China Policy has been positive and extremely skilful. A kind of entente is emerging with stunning speed. This is very advantageous to the global strategy of the USA.

China's expansion is now directed to the north rather than to the south. A campaign for the peaceful reunification of Taiwan to the motherland as an autonomous province has begun and is being followed on the island with astonishing interest.

China is in dire need of economic and technological aid from the USA, France and Japan. Japan requires raw materials from China and considers itself to be in a privileged position regarding China's vast potential market. Chinese-Japanese relations are therefore also rapidly developing.

Although China is negative to the ESC, it has a positive attitude towards the EEC which it would like to see develop into an important military power.

For internal reasons, primarily of an economic nature, the USA is compelled to reduce its present European troop strength of 300 000 by at least one-third. Military leaders maintained that greater reductions are not possible since NATO's strategy is essentially based upon the US tactical nuclear deterrence backed by its strategic deterrence and they feel that the credibility of these would be lost by more sizeable reductions. The USA binds over one-half million Soviet troops to Eastern Europe by retaining the European "bridge-head" along with its European allies who contribute one million troops and whose collective economic power rivals that of the USA. This has been rather advantageous not only to the defence of Western Europe but also to the global military hegemony of the USA.

Economically, however, the USA has been losing its dominance. The USA considers the rigorous economic competition of the EEC improper since it was rendered possible by the relatively light military budgets of its Western European allies. The EEC countries do not consider it their duty to save the sinking dollar since there are other reasons for the US dollar crisis, especially the Viet-Nam war. The Western European countries consider that their present contribution to allied defence corresponds to their capabilities and to the realistic requirements of détente in Europe. British Prime Minister Edward Heath remarked in an NBC press interview of 4 February 1973 [2] that Western Europe maintains over 90 per cent of the ground forces, 80 per cent of the naval forces and 75 per cent of the NATO air forces in Europe, a not inconsiderable share.

Kissinger's new proposal for an Atlantic declaration combines economic, political and military matters into one parcel, the main purpose of which seems to be maintaining US dominance in the western world. Western Europe, however, desires to remain economically independent. Its lower defence budget has encouraged strong economic growth at the same time as the economy of the USA has been deteriorating. The USA and the USSR have utilized the ESC to compel each other to negotiate on matters concerning the RFA. An intense tug-of-war is occurring. Neither country wants to discuss military matters at the ESC, nor is the ESC allowed to set the goals for the RFA. Again, this is exactly what the smaller powers want. They would like to increase European security by reducing the all-important roles which the USA and the USSR have acquired through their development of nuclear weapons. The situation is thus rather delicate. In any case, it is evident that, should the goals for the RFA (MBFR) be set low and reductions are small and slow, it may begin later this year following completion of the first round of the ESC.

This, then is the background against which the European security arrangements and their influence upon the NPT must be examined.

VI. Recommended goals for new security arrangements in Europe

There is little doubt that most European countries, especially the neutral ones, and the smaller members of the two military blocks, as well as most individual Europeans, wish something more substantial than the above-mentioned small and slow reductions which may be compensated by qualitative improvements and modernization. The most important aspect of any future security arrangement for Europe would be the replacement of deterrence doctrines, at least on the tactical level, by more reasonable policies better adopted to the current political situation in Europe. Such policies might culminate in a non-aggression pact which could include:

(a) reduced levels of troops and conventional armaments,
(b) regional denuclearization or even demilitarization,

(c) regional agreement on no-first-use of nuclear weapons,

(d) a security guarantee on the non-use of nuclear weapons against non-nuclear-weapon countries, and

(e) a system of control and verification for denuclearization and prevention of surprise attack.

The NATO doctrine of "flexible response" is basically destructive as a defence policy and not fully credible as a deterrent to land warfare. This doctrine is based on the idea, that lack of conventional strength can be compensated by early use of tactical nuclear weapons (trip-wire policy). NATO explains that only a few of these small weapons will be used initially against purely military targets in the battlefield area. This doctrine has two faults. First, it assumes that NATO alone can regulate the number and size of nuclear weapons to be used after the onset of nuclear war. Second, it presupposes that the West (the defender) would have some advantage over the East from the use of tactical nuclear weapons. Neither fits the realities. All studies have demonstrated that even tactical nuclear war would be extremely destructive to both sides since neither would have any special advantage over the other. Such an ambiguous policy as that of flexible response cannot form a proper basis for the future security of Europe. Instead, the Western European states ought to reorganize their conventional defence for the purpose of a swift tank war. The West ought to realize that with Soviet parity, if not superiority regarding tactical nuclear warfare, these nuclear weapons are no longer militarily viable in Europe. It is necessary to agree about their withdrawal to a place where they may play a more distant deterrent role. The US trend to increase the usefulness of these weapons by miniaturization is a bad solution. It is true that it decreases the collateral effect of the West's own weapons, but it does not do that for the opponent's weapons. Any new proposals for military security in Central Europe should de-emphasize the role of nuclear weapons. Only such a policy will provide acceptable security to all Europeans and encourage the non-proliferation of these weapons in the future. Lofty resolutions at the United Nations and even well-intentioned treaties such as the NPT, with optimistic outlooks towards the future fulfilment of their provisions, are important as guidelines for recommended development but they alone, without proper guarantees and without nuclear disarmament, cannot long satisfy the non-nuclear-weapon countries.

VII. *Military role of nuclear weapons*

As mentioned above, the durability of the NPT may depend decisively upon the future military significance of nuclear weapons. European security arrangements, and especially the *future role of tactical nuclear weapons in*

300

the European military balance, will be of prime interest to most near-nuclear-weapon countries.

What, then, is the military significance of nuclear weapons to different countries? This is an immensely complicated question which can only be discussed cursorily in the present chapter. The example of the second level nuclear nations, Great Britain, France and China, may serve as a model for the more advanced threshold countries. The question is also difficult to resolve since the military use of nuclear weapons has occurred only once and under conditions unlikely to be repeated.

The value of strategic nuclear weapons as a *political instrument* during peacetime is great. Their military value is, however, dubious since they may never be used in a war; thus, only a deterrent role is left to them. Since the Cuban crisis, the USA and the USSR have been extremely cautious in avoiding nuclear confrontation. Nuclear weapons may, however, be utilized in limited nuclear war not directly involving these countries. The most notable nuclear strategists holding to the possibility of limited nuclear war are Henry Kissinger and André Beaufre. Although presented some years ago their views are still frequently cited. Kissinger assumes that the primary military use of tactical nuclear weapons will be to destroy an invading force and to augment the fire power of the defender. [2] Beaufre introduces the concept of "sublimited" nuclear war in which the use of nuclear weapons is possible but very restricted. He considers deterrence, however, to be the main role of tactical nuclear weapons.

There are others who attribute to these weapons a normal role for use in tactical battle, the only difference being their possession of considerably greater fire power than conventional shells or warheads. This is the view usually presented in the military handbooks of both NATO and the Warsaw Pact.

Nuclear war, even of a tactical or limited nature, has, however, one characteristic which differentiates it from conventional war—it is very much more destructive. While an ordinary shell contains a maximum of 0.1 ton TNT, the old type nuclear shells have the equivalent of 500–2000 tons; light and medium missiles 2000–200000 tons, and heavy missiles and free-fall bombs an equivalent energy of up to 5000000 tons of TNT. This enormous destructive power—one thousand to one million times that of a conventional weapon—is concentrated within a circle having a radius of a few kilometres. For military purposes, the use of many nuclear weapons as part of a complete operation would be necessary. In fact, most strategists visualize the nuclear war as being chaotic and short, due to the existence of several intrinsic escalation mechanisms. For example, when target acquisition and communication systems are destroyed, higher yields must be used to compensate for reduced accuracy. Moreover, these weapons are vulnerable to the adversary's own nuclear weapons. As soon as the nuclear threshold has been crossed, both sides are under tremendous pressure to employ their nuclear weapons quickly, before their destruction. Thornton Read writes that,

tactical nuclear war, by the very nature of the weapons, has a built-in escalation mechanism. It is hardly consistent to argue that nuclear weapons will inevitably be introduced because they are more efficient than conventional weapons and then assume that, once nuclear combat begins, both sides will be content to employ only the least efficient nuclear weapons. [3]

Few countries can compete with the USA and the USSR regarding strategic nuclear weapons. Even the three lesser nuclear powers do not really participate in the strategic arms race but instead have set themselves more limited goals.

VIII. *Strategic nuclear forces of Great Britain, France and the People's Republic of China and their justification*

Great Britain was able to acquire a small strategic nuclear weapon system consisting of a V-bomber force and five Polaris submarines built very economically with US aid. National security, independent deterrence, influence in NATO and prestige were some of the motives involved in the establishment of this system. The British Polaris force is subject to the command of SACEUR and its targets have been allocated by the American Targeting Committee located in Omaha, Nebraska. Britain's nuclear forces are thus closely bound to NATO. There may exist an alternative British targeting plan in case Britain is involved in a conflict in which the United States does not participate but this is not known publicly.

France began with a tactical nuclear weapon deliverable by Mirage IV bombers. De Gaulle's justification for the *force de frappe* was based upon military autonomy, questioning of the credibility of the US nuclear guarantee and the concept of an economically and politically independent Western Europe under French leadership. De Gaulle's *force de frappe* was primarily a political instrument for "returning the glory of France". France later amplified its nuclear programme to include a small strategic capability, the *force de dissuasion* equipped with 36 Mirage IV bombers, 18 land-based IRBMs (located on the Plateau d'Albion) and five missile-firing submarines (one of which has been launched). This year's nuclear tests concern fusion warheads for these missiles. France is also deploying its short-range tactical nuclear missile, Pluton SSM, next year, to six regiments of its *Force de Manœuvre* in eastern France but not to its Second Corps in Germany since this would involve an agreement with the Bonn government which France doesn't want to make.

The French nuclear programme, which is about four times more expensive than the British, has run into great technical difficulties. It is so far behind schedule that the systems may become obsolete before they are ready. As an example, the four submarines which will be ready sometime during the 1980s should really be provided with Undersea Long Range Missile Systems (ULMS) in order to form a modern deterrent at that time, but this would be too expensive for France without US help. The strategic arms race is an almost unbearable economic burden to France; its nuclear programmes cause constant dilemmas. In addition to technological head-aches there are the political troubles in the South Pacific, in France, at the CCD and at the UN.

China has a full-scale nuclear programme, but the number of its deployed ICBMs and IRBMs will remain rather small throughout the 1970s. US estimates in 1971 (refer to Melvin Laird's statement on the US 1972 programme) stated that China could have 10–15 liquid-fuelled ICBMs each with a range of approximately 10000 km and 80–100 solid-fuelled IRBMs in hardened silos by 1975. According to the latest estimates [4], China possesses 50 operational IRBMs and MRBMs having ranges of 1000–6000 km near the Korean border, south of Peking and west and east of Outer Mongolia. It may also have a small number of liquid-fuelled MRBMs with a range of about 1500 km deployed in Tibet, and some of its 30 submarines may be provided with short-range guided missiles having nuclear warheads. Although China's first hydrogen bomb test in June 1967 was held sooner than most experts had estimated, the testing of delivery vehicles appears to be behind shedule. According to the more recent US information [4], tests of an ICBM (liquid-fuelled; range: 8000–10000 km; approximately 20 per cent larger than the Soviet SS9) will be beginning soon west of Peking. The first 10–30 of these missiles will be operational by 1975–76. Evidently, access to Japanese knowledge in the field of electronics will be quite welcome to China. China's nuclear weapon programme has two goals: the military improvement of national security and the political re-gaining of China's greatness. Militarily, China's nuclear force is primarily deterrent, but it also constitutes a direct threat, especially to the Soviet Union, and this will increase after 1975. The number of Chinese missiles is not great but some are already sufficiently well-protected to withstand a Soviet first strike and their quantity is adequate enough to inflict enor-mous destruction upon Soviet society should a nuclear war break out. Compared with the Soviet Union and the USA, China is almost invulner-able. Its entire society has been oriented in only 10 years to withstand nuclear war. Urban populations can be evacuated almost overnight to agri-cultural communes which are fully independent and just as invulnerable to strategic bombardment as are the farms and villages of Viet-Nam. The largest cities have extensive underground civil defence shelter systems with a capacity sufficient to absorb that portion of the population which re-mains unevacuated. Chairman Mao is firmly convinced that China can withstand a nuclear war. In this respect, China is far superior to the technologically more advanced western nations.

IX. *Near-nuclear countries*

An up-to-date review of the nuclear preparedness of 15 near-nuclear nations (seven who have not signed and eight who have signed but not ratified the NPT) has recently been published by SIPRI. [5] Therefore, they are not treated here. Of the 15 countries listed, at least four (Japan, India, Brazil, FR Germany) could probably bear the cost of even a strategic nuclear weapon programme but at present they do not appear to have reason or plans to do so.

X. *Justification for the possession of modest tactical nuclear weapons by a small country*

Should the nuclear-weapon powers continue to develop and modernize their tactical nuclear weapons and should the international situation worsen, many small- and medium-sized near-nuclear countries may have to consider or reconsider going nuclear. They would probably justify such action by assigning the dual role of deterrent and defensive weapon to their potential tactical nuclear system. Such a system would not only deter an invasion of conventional forces by making the enemy wary, but it would also deter the enemy from utilizing its own nuclear weapons. Should the invasion nevertheless occur, the nuclear weapons of the defender would prevent the invader from concentrating his troops. When the defender does not possess these weapons but the attacker does, the defence must be spread out regardless of whether nuclear weapons are used or not, while the invader may concentrate his troops as spearheads. If conventional defence fails, the defender could employ his nuclear weapons as the last resort.

This was approximately the argument of Swedish military leaders when their country contemplated acquiring tactical nuclear weapons in the mid-1960s. After several years of discussion, the Social Democratic Swedish government rejected the plan against the advice of the military and the conservative party. The main reasoning behind this rejection was probably that the possession of a small tactical nuclear weapon would not constitute a sufficiently credible deterrent to prevent a country which had vastly superior nuclear capability from attacking. The attacker would merely scale up his nuclear firepower and thus cause much heavier losses and tremendous destruction which would not otherwise have been necessary. The military countered by stating that, according to such a principle, any resistance would be undesirable. With no resistance, occupation would occur without loss to either side. It appears likely, however, that politics and the desire to improve the international atmosphere also influenced the decision. Sweden has, after all, played an important role on the international disarmament forum and no doubt wants to set a good example.

Thus, the *status quo* might be maintained so long as there exists a clear-cut firebreak between conventional and tactical nuclear arms, and the role of tactical nuclear weapons does not increase. Should either of these provisions change and the international situation worsen, the small non-nuclear-weapon countries may be forced to review their positions.

XI. *Durability of the NPT*

As seen above, the NPT may be considered to be a kind of tentative treaty which presupposes a certain viable stance on part of the nuclear-weapon powers. What, then, can be done to reinforce the treaty?

In an excellent review of the NPT, John P. de Gara lists six suggestions "that might substantially increase the chances of success in achieving the aims of the NPT": [6]

1. Improvement of UN machinery for the maintenance of international peace and security.
2. The entrance of China into the international community. (This occurred in 1972).
3. Greater sensitivity on the part of the USA and the USSR to the needs and aspirations of the remainder of the world community.
4. Formulation of effective and realistic policy proposals by the non-nuclear powers.
5. Progress in halting vertical proliferation.
6. Re-examination of the problems of international security.

The last two requirements are probably decisive. Regarding vertical proliferation, the introduction of miniweapons on the level of conventional warfare by the nuclear-weapon powers is particularly damaging since the NPT has been especially designed to prevent such development by the non-nuclear-weapon powers. Should this politically dubious modernization not be cancelled, the non-nuclear signatories of NPT will justly feel themselves deceived. The prime injunction to the nuclear-weapon states is, therefore, that they restrain themselves from modernizing their tactical nuclear weapons. Perhaps the most significant reasons why nuclear weapons have not been utilized during the 28 years since their introduction are the effects of such use upon world opinion and the high threshold of escalation. The most discouraging effect of nuclear miniweapons might well be the lowering or abolition of this threshold. The advent of the miniweapon signifies that nuclear weapons are being taken for granted. Introduced in large number to front-line units, developed for every conceivable battlefield use, they would be extremely difficult to control and would constitute a tremendous risk of real use. Advocates assert that miniweapons are so small they would not cause risk of escalation. If 5-ton miniweapons are to be constructed, then why not 10-, 20-, 50-, and 100-ton models? Why not all sizes up to the beginning of the present scale, 0.5 kilotons? Such would certainly occur, and the built-in escalation mechanism described above would insure their employment. The introduction of nuclear miniweapons would be a catastrophic political error. It would mean the removal of old taboos and the beginning of an inflationary spiral of nuclear weapons and it would certainly render the NPT inoperative.

The greatest weakness of the NPT is its essential one-sidedness which deprives the non-nuclear countries of the right to produce basically defensive low-yield weapons even though they may soon face such weapons in quasi-conventional battles. No significant guarantees are granted in return. The number two injunction is therefore to provide such guarantees to the non-nuclear-weapon parties.

Highly desirable, but probably less significant to the life expectancy of the NPT, is the limitation of the strategic arms race. The adoption of new European security arrangements will be highly significant—all non-nuclear countries will be observing with great interest the role that tactical nuclear weapons will have on the European scene in the future. Should they be required in Europe despite the strategic capabilities of the USA and the USSR, it will be difficult to convince the underdeveloped countries that they do not need them. Important general requirements are a lessening of international tension and progress towards nuclear disarmament.

The use of nuclear weapons is a crime against mankind and civilization according to resolution No. 1653 (XVI/1961) of the UN General Assembly. Even the threat of such use is morally damnable and, especially when exerted against civilian populations, clearly contrary to international law. The prime goal of the UN disarmament programme during this Decade of Disarmament should therefore be international agreement upon the prohibition of nuclear weapons. Should this be achieved, the NPT would have a genuine chance of survival.

References

1. *New York Times,* 9 December 1969.
2. "Prime Minister Heath on American Television", *NATO Review,* Vol. 21, No. 2, 1973, pp. 34–35.
3. Kissinger, Henry, *Nuclear Weapons and Foreign Policy* (New York, Norton and Company, 1969) p. 145.
4. Knorr, Klaus and Read, Thornton, *Limited Strategic War* (New York, Praeger, 1962) p. 77.
5. *New York Times,* 5 March 1973.
6. *The Near-Nuclear Countries and the NPT* (Stockholm, Almqvist & Wiksell, 1972, Stockholm International Peace Research Institute).
7. de Gara, John P., "Nuclear Proliferation and Security", *International Conciliation,* No. 578, May 1970.

Appendix

Text of the Treaty on the Non-Proliferation of Nuclear Weapons[1]

1. *The States concluding this Treaty,* hereinafter referred to as the "Parties to the Treaty",

2. *Considering* the devastation that would be visited upon all mankind by a nuclear war and the consequent need to make every effort to avert the danger of such a war and to take measures to safeguard the security of peoples,

3. *Believing* that the proliferation of nuclear weapons would seriously enhance the danger of nuclear war,

4. *In conformity with* resolutions of the United Nations General Assembly calling for the conclusion of an agreement on the prevention of wider dissemination of nuclear weapons,

5. *Undertaking* to co-operate in facilitating the application of International Atomic Energy Agency safeguards on peaceful nuclear activities,

6. *Expressing* their support for research, development and other efforts to further the application, within the framework of the International Atomic Energy Agency safeguards system, of the principle of safeguarding effectively the flow of source and special fissionable materials by use of instruments and other techniques at certain strategic points,

7. *Affirming* the principle that the benefits of peaceful applications of nuclear technology, including any technological by-products which may be derived by nuclear-weapon States from the development of nuclear explosive devices, should be available for peaceful purposes to all Parties to the Treaty, whether nuclear-weapon or non-nuclear-weapon States,

8. *Convinced* that, in furtherance of this principle, all Parties to the Treaty are entitled to participate in the fullest possible exchange of scientific information for, and to contribute alone or in co-operation with other States to, the further development of the applications of atomic energy for peaceful purposes,

9. *Declaring* their intention to achieve at the earliest possible date the cessation of the nuclear arms race and to undertake effective measures in the direction of nuclear disarmament,

10. *Urging* the co-operation of all States in the attainment of this objective,

[1] The text is taken from UN document A/RES/2373 (XXII). A list of the states which have signed or ratified the Treaty is given in appendix 5, page 113.

11. *Recalling* the determination expressed by the Parties to the 1963 Treaty banning nuclear weapon tests in the atmosphere, in outer space and under water in its Preamble to seek to achieve the discontinuance of all test explosions of nuclear weapons for all time and to continue negotiations to this end,

12. *Desiring* to further the easing of international tension and the strengthening of trust between States in order to facilitate the cessation of the manufacture of nuclear weapons, the liquidation of all thieir existing stockpiles, and the elimination from national arsenals of nuclear weapons and the means of their delivery pursuant to a treaty on general and complete disarmament under strict and effective international control,

13. *Recalling* that, in accordance with the Charter of the United Nations, States must refrain in their international relations from the threat or use of force against the territorial integrity or political independence of any State, or in any other manner inconsistent with the Purposes of the United Nations, and that the establishment and maintenance of international peace and security are to be promoted with the least diversion for armaments of the world's human and economic resources,

Have agreed as follows:

Article I

Each nuclear-weapon State Party to the Treaty undertakes not to transfer to any recipient whatsoever nuclear weapons or other nuclear explosive devices or control over such weapons or explosive devices directly, or indirectly; and not in any way to assist, encourage, or induce any non-nuclear-weapon State to manufacture or otherwise acquire nuclear weapons or other nuclear explosive devices, or control over such weapons or explosive devices.

Article II

Each non-nuclear-weapon State Party to the Treaty undertakes not to receive the transfer from any transferor whatsoever of nuclear weapons or other nuclear explosive devices or of control over such weapons or explosive devices directly or indirectly; not to manufacture or otherwise acquire nuclear weapons or other nuclear explosive devices; and not to seek or receive any assistance in the manufacture of nuclear weapons or other nuclear explosive devices.

Article III

1. Each non-nuclear-weapon State Party to the Treaty undertakes to accept safeguards, as set forth in an agreement to be negotiated and concluded with the International Atomic Energy Agency in accordance with the Statute of the International Atomic Energy Agency and the Agency's safeguards system, for the exclusive purpose of verification of the fulfillment

of its obligations assumed under this Treaty with a view to preventing diversion of nuclear energy from peaceful uses to nuclear weapons or other nuclear explosive devices. Procedures for the safeguards required by this article shall be followed with respect to source or special fissionable material whether it is being produced, processed or used in any principal nuclear facility or is outside any such facility. The safeguards required by this article shall be applied on all source or special fissionable material in all peaceful nuclear activities within the territory of such State, under its jurisdiction, or carried out under its control anywhere.

2. Each State Party to the Treaty undertakes not to provide: (a) source or special fissionable material, or (b) equipment or material especially designed or prepared for the processing, use or production of special fissionable material, to any non-nuclear-weapon State for peaceful purposes, unless the source or special fissionable material shall be subject to the safeguards required by this article.

3. The safeguards required by this article shall be implemented in a manner designed to comply with article IV of this Treaty, and to avoid hampering the economic or technological development of the Parties or international co-operation in the field of peaceful nuclear activities, including the international exchange of nuclear material and equipment for the processing, use or production of nuclear material for peaceful purposes in accordance with the provisions of this article and the principle of safeguarding set forth in the Preamble of the Treaty.

4. Non-nuclear-weapon States Party to the Treaty shall conclude agreements with the International Atomic Energy Agency to meet the requirements of this article either individually or together with other States in accordance with the Statute of the International Atomic Energy Agency. Negotiation of such agreements shall commence within 180 days from the original entry into force of this Treaty. For States depositing their instruments of ratification or accession after the 180-day period, negotiation of such agreements shall commence not later than the date of such deposit. Such agreements shall enter into force not later than eighteen months after the date of initiation of negotiations.

Article IV

1. Nothing in this Treaty shall be interpreted as affecting the inalienable right of all the Parties to the Treaty to develop research, production and use of nuclear energy for peaceful purposes without discrimination and in conformity with articles I and II of this Treaty.

2. All the Parties to the Treaty undertake to facilitate, and have the right to participate in, the fullest possible exchange of equipment, materials and scientific and technological information for the peaceful uses of nuclear energy. Parties to the Treaty in a position to do so shall also co-operate in contributing alone or together with other States or international organi-

zations to the further development of the applications of nuclear energy for peaceful purposes, especially in the territories of non-nuclear-weapon States Party to the Treaty, with due consideration for the needs of the developning areas of the world.

Article V

Each Party to the Treaty undertakes to take appropriate measures to ensure that, in accordance with this Treaty, under appropriate international observation and through appropriate international procedures, potential benefits from any peaceful applications of nuclear explosions will be made available to non-nuclear-weapon States Party to the Treaty on a non-discriminatory basis and that the charge to such Parties for the explosive devices used will be as low as possible and exclude any charge for research and development. Non-nuclear-weapon States Party to the Treaty shall be able to obtain such benefits, pursuant to a special international agreement or agreements, through an appropriate international body with adequate representation of non-nuclear-weapon States. Negotiations on this subject shall commence as soon as possible after the Treaty enters into force. Non-nuclear-weapon States Party to the Treaty so desiring may also obtain such benefits pursuant to bilateral agreements.

Article VI

Each of the Parties to the Treaty undertakes to pursue negotiations in good faith on effective measures relating to cessation of the nuclear arms race at an early date and to nuclear disarmament, and on a treaty on general and complete disarmament under strict and effective international control.

Article VII

Nothing in this Treaty affects the right of any group of States to conclude regional treaties in order to assure the total absence of nuclear weapons in their respective territories.

Article VIII

1. Any Party to the Treaty may propose amendments to this Treaty. The text of any proposed amendment shall be submitted to the Depositary Governments which shall circulate it to all Parties to the Treaty. Thereupon, if requested to do so by one third or more of the Parties to the Treaty, the Depositary Governments shall convene a conference, to which they shall invite all the Parties to the Treaty, to consider such an amendment.

2. Any amendment to this Treaty must be approved by a majority of the votes of all the Parties to the Treaty, including the votes of all nuclear-weapon States Party to the Treaty and all other Parties which, on the date

the amendment is circulated, are members of the Board of Governors of the International Atomic Energy Agency. The amendment shall enter into force for each Party that deposits its instrument of ratification of the amendment upon the deposit of such instruments of ratification by a majority of all the Parties, including the instruments of ratification of all nuclear-weapon States Party to the Treaty and all other Parties which, on the date the amendment is circulated, are members of the Board of Governors of the International Atomic Energy Agency. Thereafter, it shall enter into force for any other Party upon the deposit of its instrument of ratification of the amendment.

3. Five years after the entry into force of this Treaty, a conference of Parties to the Treaty shall be held in Geneva, Switzerland, in order to review the operation of this Treaty with a view to assuring that the purposes of the Preamble and the provisions of the Treaty are being realized. At intervals of five years thereafter, a majority of the Parties to the Treaty may obtain, by submitting a proposal to this effect to the Depositary Governments, the convening of further conferences with the same objective of reviewing the operation of the Treaty.

Article IX

1. This Treaty shall be open to all States for signature. Any State which does not sign the Treaty before its entry into force in accordance with paragraph 3 of this article may accede to it at any time.

2. This Treaty shall be subject to ratification by signatory States. Instruments of ratification and instruments of accession shall be deposited with the Governments of the Union of Soviet Socialist Republics, the United Kingdom of Great Britain and Northern Ireland and the United States of America, which are hereby designated the Depositary Governments.

3. This Treaty shall enter into force after its ratification by the States, the Governments of which are designated Depositaries of the Treaty, and forty other States signatory to this Treaty and the deposit of their instruments of ratification. For the purposes of this Treaty, a nuclear-weapon State is one which has manufactured and exploded a nuclear weapon or other nuclear explosive device prior to 1 January 1967.

4. For States whose instruments of ratification or accession are deposited subsequent to the entry into force of this Treaty, it shall enter into force on the date of the deposit of their instruments of ratification or accession.

5. The Depositary Governments shall promptly inform all signatory and acceding States of the date of each signature, the date of deposit of each instrument of ratification or of accession, the date of the entry into force of this Treaty, and the date of receipt of any requests for convening a conference or other notices.

6. This Treaty shall be registered by the Depositary Governments pursuant to article 102 of the Charter of the United Nations.

Article X

1. Each Party shall in exercising its national sovereignty have the right to withdraw from the Treaty if it decides that extraordinary events, related to the subject matter of this Treaty, have jeopardized the supreme interests of its country. It shall give notice of such withdrawal to all other Parties to the Treaty and to the United Nations Security Council three months in advance. Such notice shall include a statement of the extraordinary events it regards as having jeopardized its supreme interests.

2. Twenty-five years after the entry into force of the Treaty, a conference shall be convened to decide whether the Treaty shall continue in force indefinitely, or shall be extended for an additional fixed period or periods. This decision shall be taken by a majority of the Parties to the Treaty.

Article XI

This Treaty, the Chinese, English, French, Russian and Spanish texts of which are equally authentic, shall be deposited in the archives of the Depositary Governments. Duly certified copies of this Treaty shall be transmitted by the Depositary Governments to the Governments of the signatory and acceding States.

In witness whereof the undersigned, duly authorized, have signed this Treaty.

Signed at London, Moscow and Washington on 1 July 1968.

Entered into force on 5 March 1970.